The
FOURTH
HORSEMAN

The

FOURTH
HORSEMAN

One Man's Secret Mission to Wage
the Great War in America

ROBERT L. KOENIG

PublicAffairs • *New York*
A Member of the Perseus Books Group

Published in the United States by PublicAffairs™, a member of the Perseus Books Group.

Library of Congress Cataloging-in-Publication Data
Koenig, Robert L.
    The fourth horseman : one man's secret mission to wage the Great War in America / Robert L. Koenig.
        p.cm.
    Includes bibliographical references and index.
    ISBN-13: 978-1-58648-372-2 (hardcover : alk. paper)
    ISBN-10: 1-58648-372-2 (hardcover : alk. paper)
    1. World War, 1914–1918—Biological warfare—Germany. 2. Dilger, Anton.
3. Spies—Germany—Biography. 4. World War, 1914–1918—Biological warfare—
United States. 5. War horses—United States. I. Title.

UG447.8.K66 2006
940.4'85—DC22

[B]

2006032954

10 9 8 7 6 5 4 3 2 1

For Mary Ellen, Laura, Mark, Chris, and Claire

CONTENTS

When he broke the fourth seal ... another horse appeared,
deathly pale, and its rider was called Plague, and Hades
followed at its heels.

— THE NEW JERUSALEM BIBLE, REVELATION 6: 7–8

PROLOGUE

Germany, November 1918. Two million of the nation's sons had perished in a lost cause. An empire had collapsed, causing social, political and economic upheaval. And a deadly plague, in the form of the Spanish Flu, had struck like a diabolical retribution.

When the knock came at the door of Eda Koehler's house in Mannheim, she stood there for a moment, frozen in the entryway, afraid to confront yet more terrible news. The war had been a disaster for her family, but all was not yet lost. Her despondent husband's business had been ruined, but they still had their house. And their son had survived, miraculously, four years as a cavalryman.

Steeling herself for a new disaster, she slowly opened the door and peered through the crack. It was a military courier carrying a package. He asked to be admitted and, once in the hallway, explained that the box contained possessions that had been found in her brother's apartment in Madrid. Germany's military attaché there had listed her as the next of kin.

She paid the courier a small tip—she had little to offer—and carried the package to the dining room table, where she unwrapped it. Anton had been her favorite brother and, in a sense, her son. She had taken him from the family's farm in Virginia and reared him in Mannheim since he was ten years old. She and her husband had paid his way through Germany's best medical school. They had been proud when he became a surgeon and served his adopted country. But then her little brother, her "son" and confidante, had disappeared into the half-light of rumored subversion and espionage.

Inside the box was a battered suitcase; she undid the clasps and removed its contents. Tears came to her eyes when Eda saw a bloodied white shirt inside. The cut was stylish, the sort of shirt that Anton would have worn. It had been carefully folded, even though no one could ever use it again. Why, she wondered, would the front of his shirt have been covered with blood? They told her that Anton had died of pneumonia.

She unfolded the shirt and examined the parts of the fabric that had not been stained with blood. In a rare moment of candor, Anton had once told her that he would use invisible ink to write secret messages on shirts. If customs officers searched his suitcase at borders, he had boasted, they would sometimes examine papers and books—but would never look at the dirty laundry.

The next object in the suitcase was a set of golden cufflinks bearing the seal of the King of Bulgaria. These Eda recognized as her brother's, for she had seen him wear the cufflinks at dinner parties in Mannheim when he bragged about how the King, who had a predilection for handsome young men, had given him the golden keepsakes.

Wedged into the corner of the suitcase was a book, written in English, that she had never seen before: *My Four Years in Germany*. The author was the former American ambassador, James Gerard, who had harshly criticized Imperial Germany. Her brother, an American who had become a German, would have despised the book. It was incongruous with the small collection of otherwise personal items.

When she looked closer, Eda saw that there was a secret pouch in the front cover of the book, a place where someone could hide a message or a photographic negative. Written in Spanish was an inscription to Anton, signed "Roberto Wilson." "Dedicated to my dear friend on his birthday, with the hope that this book will change his Germanophile outlook." Wilson, she learned much later, was the false name of a German spy.

There were more wrapped objects in the suitcase, but Eda did not want to explore them all at once. Her brother had meant too much to her; she wanted some time to think about what he had left behind. She boiled some water and made herself a cup of what passed for tea those days in rationed Germany, walked up the stairs to her bedroom and searched for the letter that her sister, Elizabeth, had sent to her the previous month, after hearing of Anton's sudden and mysterious death.

"I was devastated when I heard the terrible news last night," Elizabeth had written. She had been startled because a friend had sent a recent message from Madrid, saying that Anton—a civilian doctor, after all, and not a military man—had been in good health. "For those of us who remain behind, it is a constant hurt, a bitter wound—one wonders if one can continue to bear the burden of the cross."

Eda realized that her sister had only one cross in mind—that of the crucified Christ—but the letter made her curious about something else among her brother's possessions. Returning to the suitcase, she pulled out a few more articles of clothing and then saw a small black case—about the size of a cigarette case—hidden underneath. She knew what she would find inside as she opened the case because her son the cavalryman had been awarded the same decoration: the Iron Cross.

The simple ribbon was black with two white stripes. The medal itself was a stylized cross of black with a silver border. Stamped on the black surface was the image of the crown and a *W* for Kaiser Wilhelm II—the emperor who just weeks earlier had abdicated and fled to a safe haven in Holland. At the foot of the cross was stamped that year, 1918. Confused but intrigued, Eda rubbed her thumb over that date.

Years before, when she was a young woman still living in western Virginia, her father had been so proud to show off his Medal of Honor—America's highest military award. He had been born a German but had become a loyal American.

Under what circumstances had the Medal of Honor winner's son received a military honor—not from America, the land of his birth, but from its implacable enemy? What tragic chain of events, wondered Eda, had ended with the bloody shirt and determined the fate of the man whose meager personal possessions she now owned, her brother Anton Dilger?

part one

Virginia

Chapter 1

WARHORSES

*Take the [Germans] out of the Union Army
and we could whip the Yankees easily.*
—Attributed to ROBERT E. LEE, 1863

A NIMALS WERE FLEEING THE FOREST. Frightened rabbits, deer, and foxes snapped branches and rustled through the dry brush as they ran across the clearing in front of Captain Hubert Dilger's mount. Spooked by the wild-eyed terror in the animals' eyes, the horse moved nervously under the captain's tight rein. *Something* was moving through the woods; Dilger suspected an enemy assault.

Riding closer to the forest's edge, he heard a gunshot and then the sudden, terrifying sound of a hundred Rebel yells. The surprise attack on the Union Army had begun. Dilger's horse artillery battery moved into action, firing double-shotted canister—a lethal spray of shrapnel— at the Confederate soldiers who rushed toward his guns from deep within the woods. His men fought to delay the advance enough for their division commander, General Carl Schurz, to swing his troops around and confront the attack.

"Within little more than rifleshot of our right flank there stood 'Stonewall' Jackson with more than 25,000 men, the most dashing general of the Confederacy with its best soldiers, forming his line of battle which at the given word was to fold its wings around our feeble flank,"

Schurz wrote later. Lined up against the Rebels were the 9,000 Union troops of the 11th Corps, most of them stunned by the surprise assault.

"Stonewall" Jackson, riding his sure-footed horse Little Sorrel, had driven his men all night through the forest near Chancellorsville, Virginia, to attack the Union Army's exposed right flank. With fierce yells and frightening volleys of musket fire, the Confederate soldiers charged from the woods near the Wilderness Church, where Schurz had positioned the German-speaking regiments that now bore the brunt of the Gray onslaught. Wrote one chronicler of the battle: "So rapid was the advance, so utterly unexpected the attack, that the pickets were at once over-run; and ... the broad front of the mighty torrent bore down" upon the Germans.

Hubert Dilger—known to his troops as "Leatherbreeches" because of his doeskin pants—and his gunners were soon outflanked and attacked by an overwhelming force. With the Rebels firing at ever-closer range from the thickets, Dilger ordered his unit to continue firing canister to cover the withdrawal. They had to fall back, but Confederate sharpshooters began to pick off the horses that pulled one of the guns.

Suddenly a sniper's shot rang out and Dilger felt his own horse shudder beneath him. The wounded animal wheezed in pain as it fell, hitting the ground and pinning the celebrated Leatherbreeches under its dead weight. Blood oozed from the wounds as Dilger struggled to extricate himself. The Rebels were moving closer, firing at him and his men, and calling for Dilger to surrender.

Just as it seemed that the captain might be consumed by the carnage around him, a local boy named Ackley attempted a heroic rescue. He had seen the gallant captain lead his battery toward the front and then the boy realized that the captain was missing during the unit's retreat. "Seizing a horse, [the boy] rode directly into the front of the enemy in search of him," according to one account. Through the haze of gun smoke, Dilger spotted the stallion led by the boy. The captain freed himself from the dead horse, mounted the fresh one with the boy, and dodged Rebel bullets as they galloped back towards the Union lines.

As dusk fell, the Rebels reorganized and struck again at the Union rear guard—now down to Dilger and his cannon—withdrawing slowly toward Chancellorsville. Because the road was so narrow, Leatherbreeches could use only one gun. He had sent the others back to join a different artillery unit but then stubbornly held his ground. "Dilger himself stayed with his one gun, firing it like a pocket pistol—a couple of shots down the road, limber up and go back a hundred yards, unlimber again and fire some more; one man and one gun, standing off the advance of Stonewall Jackson."

One brave man's heroism did not sway the Battle of Chancellorsville. In the end, the Rebels claimed the victory, won by the brilliant strategy of General Robert E. Lee and the surprise tactics of Stonewall Jackson. It was May 1863, and the Confederates were nearing the apogee of their territorial strength. The Rebel cavalry still ranged through the Shenandoah Valley and across large swaths of Maryland. Meanwhile, the Union Army had suffered a string of defeats, and its soldiers—many of them Irish or German immigrants—were demoralized.

The night of his rear-guard heroism, an exhausted Dilger watched an artillery barrage so intense that it set the woods afire; he could hear the screams of wounded soldiers being consumed by the flames. Years later, in *The Red Badge of Courage*, Stephen Crane would attempt to convey the deadly artillery barrages at Chancellorsville:

> On a slope to the left there was a long row of guns, gruff and maddened, denouncing the enemy, who, down through the woods, were forming for another attack in the pitiless monotony of conflicts. The round red discharges from the guns made a crimson flare and a high, thick smoke ... A congregation of horses, tied to a long railing, were tugging frenziedly at their bridles.

That night, Stonewall Jackson rode his warhorse to the battlefield's fringe to scout ways of cutting off the retreating Union soldiers. As dusk fell, Jackson and his entourage of staff officers returned, but a Rebel unit mistook them for the enemy in the dark woods and fired a volley. Little Sorrel turned away from the gunfire, but too late to prevent three bullets from striking Jackson in the right hand and left arm.

When Jackson's stricken hand dropped the reins, his terrified horse ran into the woods toward the Union lines. A tree bough struck Jackson's head, but the general managed to hold on to the horse, grab the bridle with his bleeding hand and turn Little Sorrel toward the road, where a Rebel captain caught the reins. When the horse finally stopped, the mortally wounded Jackson slid forward into the captain's arms.

Stunned soldiers carried the general away on a stretcher as Little Sorrel watched, riderless. It was the last time the horse—which had been Jackson's trusted mount on nearly every campaign since Bull Run—would see his master. Doctors amputated Jackson's arm later that day; the fever-stricken general died within a week. Little Sorrel would live for another two decades, idolized throughout the South as a surrogate for its late master.

With Jackson gravely wounded, General Lee had precious little time to savor the victory at Chancellorsville. A few weeks later, the tide would begin to turn with Union victories at Gettysburg and elsewhere. The Union cavalry, which had performed poorly during the war's first two years, had begun its resurgence at Chancellorsville, and Lee's own forces already were feeling the pinch of tight supplies.

The day after the battle ended at Chancellorsville, General Lee rode his iron-gray horse, Traveler, across the abandoned battlefields. An old-school horseman, Lee personified the chivalry and gallantry that the brutal war lacked. Traveler, the mount Lee praised for its "sagacity and affection and his invariable response to every wish of the rider," would become perhaps the most famous warhorse in American history.

The victory may have seemed hollow to Lee. The battlefield was scarred by cannonball-shattered tree trunks and wide sections of woods and scrub that had been blackened by fire. Thousands of soldiers' corpses had been hauled away for burial. The bodies of dead horses—bloated, bloody, with flies buzzing around them—still littered the war zone.

What had been won, in the end? More dead men, more dead horses, a few square miles of territory destroyed and conquered. This could not go on forever.

With a pull on the reins, Lee urged Traveler onward, away from Chancellorsville and toward the next battlefield. Always faithful, the warhorse obliged.

"LET YOUR HEADQUARTERS be in the saddle," General Ulysses S. Grant had advised one of his Union commanders in 1864. Indeed, horses played a crucial role in the Civil War.

Less than a month before the Chancellorsville battle, President Abraham Lincoln had traveled to northern Virginia to review the Union cavalry, riding a steamer down the Potomac River to Aquia Creek, then riding horses or carriages to inspect the troops.

The tall and gangly Lincoln rode a short bay horse while Union Army Commander General Joseph Hooker rode a stunning white stallion to the reviewing stand. They were joined by General Schurz, a German-born political ally of the President, in reviewing the newly reorganized Union cavalry. It took an hour and a half for the columns of cavalry and artillery, including Hubert Dilger's unit, to march past the reviewing stand.

The long line of warhorses that Lincoln had inspected in 1863 represented a major reason why the Union would emerge victorious. Both sides were losing horses and mules by the hundreds of thousands, through battlefield injuries as well as exposure, starvation, and disease.

The North had begun the war with an advantage in horsepower, about 3.4 million horses and 100,000 mules, compared to 1.7 million horses and 800,000 mules in the South. But Union Army leaders had been slow to recognize the need for a mounted force, while Confederate generals moved quickly to organize their mounted units.

By the time of the Chancellorsville battle, however, the Union cavalry was maturing and the Confederate cavalry declining, hurt by shortages of both horses and mounted soldiers. General Hooker had ordered that a Cavalry Corps be formed from various mounted units that had been scattered through different Army commands. He also set up a Cavalry Bureau, charged with organizing and equipping the cavalry forces with horses, weapons, saddles, and other essential supplies.

Later, Union General Philip H. Sheridan began using his cavalry units independently against Confederate cavalry and infantry, rather than limiting them to guarding wagon trains or serving as advance guards for infantry columns. In the end, the North's new tactics and its advantage in horse resources proved decisive.

But the losses on both sides were devastating: in 1863, the Union Army needed about 500 new horses per day to replenish its losses; 1.5 million horses perished by the war's end. Many died from exhaustion or were killed outright by enemy fire, the targets of enemy sharpshooters on both sides. Aside from bullets and shrapnel, the worst enemy of horses was disease and exposure to horrible conditions. A horse disease called glanders struck with a vengeance during the war, when tens of thousands of horses—some have estimated 200,000—perished from the dreaded and incurable disease in Union and Confederate stables. It was the worst glanders outbreak in American history.

Some officers suspected that one side or another had deliberately left behind horses with glanders in an effort to infect the enemy's horses. After the Battle of Bull Run, Union Colonel Samuel Ringwald told the commanding general that when the Confederates abandoned the Virginia battlefield they had "carefully left behind . . . a number of horses infected with that horrible and contagious disease, the glanders."

Farther south, in the Rebel stronghold of Lynchburg, Virginia, glanders spread like wildfire at stables where the Confederates quartered thousands of horses and mules. The disease killed an estimated 3,000 animals in the depot over 15 months in 1863–64. The animal epidemic was so bad that two Virginia physicians were asked to investigate the "baneful scourge" of glanders in the horse depot. Their research, published in an 1864 pamphlet, is regarded as the first important American contribution to veterinary medicine.

After the war, when the horses and mules that were left in Union military depots were put up for sale, some buyers accused the government of selling glandered animals and spreading the outbreak. The *American Agriculturalist* magazine opined: "The Government might better have shot every horse, than to have them spread contagion and death (for the disease is utterly incurable) among the stables of the country, far and near." A half century later, that editorial seemed prophetic.

THE GIRL'S DELICATE HANDS trembled when she first made contact. In the darkened Philadelphia parlor, she sensed the presence of a sad-eyed man, a leader who had been struck down by an assassin's bullet at the time of his greatest glory.

Her pen, which she insisted was guided by a force that moved her pliant fingers, slowly wrote out the leader's "spirit messages" on a sheet of paper. The girl's older sister, Elise Tiedemann, read the first words aloud to the guests around the séance table:

I am present

The dinner guests—some enthralled, others merely feigning interest—murmured to one another in German amid the parlor's old-world furnishings. The spirit the girl claimed to be present was that of the President who had been murdered at Ford's Theater in Washington a few months earlier: Abraham Lincoln.

The guest of honor at that evening's séance was Carl Schurz, who was a political supporter of the late President, a Civil War general, and perhaps the most influential German American of his time. Half-jokingly, the bearded Schurz suggested to the girl: "Ask him if he knows why President Johnson has called me to Washington."

A few of the guests laughed or cleared their throats; others leaned forward to hear the supposed spirit's response. The girl—Charlotte, a fourteen-year-old with an angelic face—trembled as she slowly wrote out a message that Elise, sixteen, read aloud:

He would like you to make an important journey for him.

Amused but intrigued, Schurz—an intense man who wore wire-rimmed spectacles on a cord that clipped to the lapel of his long black dinner jacket—asked, again half-jokingly, if Lincoln's spirit had any more to tell him. After a long pause, Charlotte wrote:

Yes, you will become a U.S. senator.

Some at the séance table smiled. "This seemed to me so fantastic that I could scarcely restrain my laughter," Schurz recalled later. "I asked further, 'From what state?'" The spirit's response: *Missouri*. Schurz laughed aloud this time. "Nothing . . . was more unlikely than my becoming a senator from Missouri," he remembered. "My legal residence was Wisconsin and it was my earnest intention to return there."

Séance pronouncements that don't materialize tend to be forgotten. But those two predictions made by the young spirit-writers eventually came true. When Schurz met with the president at the White House later that week in 1866, Johnson sent him on a fact-finding mission to the South. Two years later, Schurz became a U.S. senator from Missouri, the first German American in the Senate. In his memoirs, written forty years later, Schurz—a rationalist who normally had little patience for the occult—praised the Tiedemann family's "circle of spiritualists."

Some in society regarded the spirit-writers Elise and Charlotte as more flatterers than occultists. They were daughters of Dr. Heinrich Tiedemann, a prominent physician, and his well-connected wife, Charlotte (née Hecker). In the years after the Civil War, the family hosted a parade of prominent German Americans at their home in the aptly named Germantown district of Philadelphia. They were among about six thousand German political refugees, known as "'48ers," who had fled the Old World after the failed democratic revolution of 1848–49 to form the core of a new German American intellectual and political elite. During the '48er insurrection, southwestern German reformers had taken up the banner of French revolutionaries to seek social and political changes, including the establishment of republics in what had long been kingdoms.

The Tiedemanns' revolutionary credentials were impeccable. Mrs. Tiedmann's brother, Frederich Hecker, was a lawyer whose fiery rhetoric had helped spark the Social Democrat uprising. Hecker was also widely rumored to have been an illegitimate son of Bavaria's King Maximilian I. Arguing for a new, democratic state that would distribute wealth and offer equal opportunities, Hecker had traveled widely through Baden, where years of poor harvests, unusually cold winters, and devastating floods had spread hunger and unrest. When the '48er revolution failed, Hecker had fled Germany and settled as a "Latin Farmer"—a highly educated agriculturalist—in southern Illinois.

Another famous revolutionary was Dr. Tiedemann's brother, Gustav, who had been executed by the Prussians for treason after serving as revolutionary governor of Fortress Rastatt, where a soldiers' mutiny had sparked the 1848 uprising. Schurz, then a twenty-year-old lieutenant, was one of Gustav Tiedemann's aides. Schurz became a '48er hero when he escaped from Rastatt, liberated revolutionary leader Gottfried Kinkel from a Berlin prison, and fled to America.

The network of revolutionary connections eventually extended into the next generation of German Americans, which brought the late-comer Hubert Dilger into the fold. At the time of the sèance at the Tiedemann home in Germantown late in 1865, Elise Tiedemann was engaged to Dilger, who had fought heroically under Schurz's command at Chancellorsville.

Like many of the '48ers, Dilger had grown up in Baden, a dukedom in southwestern Germany near the Rhine River and the borders with France and Switzerland that included the Black Forest, Karlsruhe, as well as Fortress Rastatt. He had served as a horse artilleryman in the Grand Duke of Baden's army, and had—by some reports—carried on an affair with one of the Duke's daughters, a relationship that got the young lieutenant into trouble with the Duke. Hot-blooded and unpredictable, Dilger—a handsome but brash fellow with a dueling scar across his left cheek—began looking around for alternatives and saw that a civil war was raging in the United States and that Union Army recruiters were looking for European soldiers to help fight it. In fact, they were willing to sign up just about any male who could walk a straight line.

Dilger took a leave of absence from the Duke's army in August 1861 and sailed to New York, where he met two uncles who had emigrated from Germany a decade earlier. Knowing that several prominent '48ers from Baden already were Union Army leaders—including Schurz, Hecker, and Franz Sigel, who had attended the same military school as Dilger in Karlsruhe—the eager immigrant volunteered to serve under them. He joined Siegel's command without pay for a while and then was recruited into the largely German-speaking unit led by Schurz. It was hardly lonely being a German; one out of every eight Union soldiers had been born in Germany.

Dilger did not speak much English, but he knew how to fight. In addition to his bravery and brilliant artillery tactics—some regarded him as the best horse artilleryman in the Army of the Potomac—Dilger was known for his outspokenness, which at times bordered on insolence. He was an advocate of mobility, accuracy of fire, and close support of the infantry—worthy tactics that did not always reflect the views of his commanding officers. In 1863, General Oliver O. Howard threatened to court-martial Leatherbreeches for disobeying an order to remove his men from a church in which they had been billeted. But with the help of the Army's commander, General Joseph Hooker—who described the German as "too valuable a soldier to be lost over such a minor incident"—Dilger managed to extricate himself from the insubordination charge.

A Confederate artillery expert later described Dilger's rear-guard actions at Chancellorsville as "an example of almost superhuman courage and energy." The 750,000 German American troops fighting for the North helped wear down the Confederates. Confederate commander Lee complained: "Take the [Germans] out of the Union Army and we could whip the Yankees easily."

Indeed, the Civil War marked the beginning of the golden age of German American influence in America, which lasted for a half century. When the war broke out in 1861, German Americans in the North and in border states were among the earliest and most enthusiastic volunteers for the Union Army, mobilizing rapidly with many German rifle organizations, *Turnvereins* (gymnastic clubs), and Wide Awake Clubs. In St. Louis, *Turners* from a medical school founded by a prominent '48er helped protect the city's arsenal from a takeover attempt by Confederate sympathizers. In Washington, D.C., *Turners* helped set up the capital's defenses, and in New York the United Turner Rifles regiment marched quickly to Union camps. As thousands of German American soldiers volunteered, local communities staged elaborate farewell ceremonies to show their patriotism. Rewarded for their Civil War bravery, eighty-two German American soldiers, including Hubert Dilger, would earn the nation's highest military award, the Medal of Honor.

Schurz and others contended that German American votes had played a crucial role in putting Lincoln in the White House and that their rifles had been crucial to the Union victory in the Civil War. Both claims may have been exaggerations, but historians tend to agree that the growing political, military, and economic involvement of German Americans during the 1860s helped the ethnic group integrate into American society. By the beginning of the twentieth century, Germans and Irish were the two most numerous and influential immigrant groups in the United States.

Lincoln, a savvy politician, had realized long before his 1860 presidential campaign that the ethnic German vote could help him win the election—if, indeed, there proved to be a solid German American political bloc. He cultivated Schurz and other prominent '48ers; during the campaign, Schurz alone traveled 21,000 miles—by rail, coach, and horseback—speaking on behalf of Lincoln, for whom he promised to deliver 300,000 German votes. Another '48er, Dr. Heinrich Canisius, even sold his German-language newspaper, the *Illinois Staats-Anzeiger*, to Lincoln in 1859. Under the secret contract, Lincoln kept Canisius as editor under the condition that the paper—the most widely read German publication in southern Illinois—would support the Republicans. After winning the election, Lincoln returned the newspaper's ownership to Canisius and later named him U.S. Consul in Vienna. Of the 265 German-language newspapers in America in 1860, only three—all weeklies based in the South—had favored secession.

By 1888, there were about eight hundred German-language publications in America, about half the nation's foreign-language press. A million and a half Germans left their newly unified homeland during the 1880s, the decade in which Anton Dilger was born. It was the greatest flow of Germans across the Atlantic in any decade. In all, about 5.5 million Germans settled in the United States during the ten decades before World War I.

The list of German customs and concepts that eventually were adopted as typically American is extensive: Christmas trees, Santa Claus, hamburgers, frankfurters, the Easter Bunny. From kindergartens to graduate schools, the German educational system exerted a profound influence on its American counterpart. Toward the end of the nineteenth century, thousands of German musicians, teachers, and well-trained amateurs helped transform the U.S. music scene from marching bands to choral groups and classical orchestras.

Carl Schurz was the most prominent German American of the post–Civil War era. In addition to becoming a U.S. senator, he was U.S. ambassador to Spain, a newspaper publisher in St. Louis, Secretary of the Interior, and later editor of *Harper's Weekly* and the *New York Evening Post*. A persistent advocate of civil service reform and a spokesman for German Americans, Schurz transformed his '48er revolutionary zeal into intellectual achievement and leadership in the New World. It was not altogether surprising that Schurz would have known both Hubert

Dilger and Elise Tiedemann—as they had been closely associated with the '48er crowd of ethnic Germans.

By the turn of the century, Schurz was the gray eminence of his generation of German American intellectuals. As the old man lay dying in 1906, visitors to his home in New York included luminaries such as authors Mark Twain and William Dean Howells, and philanthropist Andrew Carnegie. While Schurz's political influence had waned in his final decade, the former revolutionary had continued writing essays and making speeches harshly critical of imperialism, both American and German.

During his last decades of life, Schurz had sought to keep cordial relations between America and Germany, a relationship that had begun to strain in the aftermath of the Spanish-American War (regarded by Berlin as imperialist) and with the rise of German militarism during the twentieth century's first decade.

"Hier wird Deutsch gesprochen"—*Here German is Spoken*—proclaimed a sign on Schurz's front door; he always spoke German with his family and exchanged letters in German with those friends and relatives who spoke the language. In his speeches, he often stressed the importance of German Americans maintaining their native language and culture while also contributing to American culture and politics.

"I have always been in favor of sensible Americanization, but this does not mean complete abandonment of all that is German," he said in one late speech. "It means that we should adopt the best traits of the American character and join them to the best traits of German character."

Schurz had moved to the New World with a commitment to social democracy and skepticism about Prussian militarism and other disagreeable aspects of his Old Country. Otto von Bismarck, the power behind the Kaiser, had engineered German unification, creating an empire led by Berlin that stretched from Alsace to East Prussia. After defeating the French armies in the Franco-Prussian War of 1870–71, Germany had become a major power, with colonial as well as regional ambitions. Schurz, a Social Democrat who had fled likely arrest and execution by the Prussians in 1849, recognized the New Order in 1868 when he met for an hour and a half with Bismarck to discuss U.S.-German relations. But later, in 1877, Bismarck opposed the rumored appointment of

Schurz as U.S. Minister to Germany. In turn, Schurz worried aloud that his native land had become "too Prussian and too little German."

That concern intensified with the change in Kaisers that led to the saber rattling of Kaiser Wilhelm II. Germans in America watched the news anxiously in 1888, a year in which the Second Reich had three Kaisers: After Wilhelm I died in March, he was briefly succeeded by his cancer-stricken son Frederick III, who died after a three-month coma, leaving the empire in the inexperienced hands of his son, twenty-nine-year-old Wilhelm II.

While imperial Germany boomed as an industrial and economic power at the turn of the century, far fewer Germans left for the United States, and a growing number of Americans—including several of Hubert Dilger's children—abandoned America for the Old Country. Germany's industrial development had created jobs and prosperity. And as Germany rose to become a major industrial and military power, the newest generation of German Americans—unlike the '48ers who had criticized the Prussians—focused more on the achievements of the *Vaterland* (fatherland).

By the turn of the century, millions of Americans had a strong affinity with the German language and culture, often through membership in a club or a church where German was spoken. The hundreds of German American newspapers and magazines, which formerly had been controlled by political liberals of Schurz's generation, had begun to be edited by younger immigrants, many of whom had more sympathy for resurgent and newly confident imperial Germany. The massive tide of immigration in the late nineteenth century had made German Americans a powerful political force, and they tended to vote as a bloc on issues such as prohibition and Sunday closing laws—which they opposed.

Schurz had personified the thoughtful class of German Americans, a recognized intellectual leader and a conscience who always fought for social democratic ideals. When he died in 1906, there was no one of his stature to assume that critical role.

Chapter 2

GREENFIELD FARM

Oh! That summer breeze, how warm and sweet it was!
Blossoms everywhere—a visit in the brightest sunshine.
That was life eternal, where happiness and joy knew no sorrow
And we all stood under your spell, dear good little mother.
—ANTON DILGER, Greenfield poem, 1905

I N THE DEAD OF WINTER IN 1884, the tenth child of the spiritualist Elise and the horseman Hubert Dilger was born.

The boy's first two names—Anton Casimir—were relics of distant German relatives, middle names that his father never used. But the child inherited far more than names from Germany. The Virginia mansion of Greenfield Stock Farm, where he spent his first ten years, had as much in common with the Black Forest as it did with the Blue Ridge Mountains.

At home, Anton Dilger spoke more German than English. On the wall hung a portrait of the boy's father as a lieutenant in the Duke of Baden's horse artillery. When Anton was three, his oldest sister, Elizabeth, married a German soldier, Hubert Lamey, who served with the Baden Grenadier regiment "Kaiser Wilhelm." Describing the wedding ceremony, a local newspaper's society columnist enthused: "The happy bridegroom wore the handsome uniform of an infantry lieutenant in the German Army. A close fitting, dark blue suit faced with scarlet, the dress sword bound to his thigh with a silver sash, and the polished helmet with its snowy plume carried in his hand."

The wedding and the glorious German uniform were among Anton Dilger's earliest memories. Over the next fifteen years, three other Dilger girls would follow Elizabeth's example and move back to the Old Country with a new German husband. Those sisters and their families later would give Anton Dilger a sense of belonging when he became the only one of the six Dilger boys to follow his sisters back to Germany.

Anton idolized his father and loved his family and Greenfield farm. His siblings called him "An." He spent much of his early life around horses. At Greenfield, the Dilger boys were taught to ride horses, to hunt, and to fish. Anton would sometimes help his older brother Edward, the family's best horseman and a sometime jockey in local races, care for the horses on the farm.

Greenfield was divided into three parts—the main farm, Valley Retreat, and Mountain View (also known as Mountain Farm)—which Leatherbreeches had bought in parcels starting in 1881 using his inheritance from an uncle in New York. When the last section of the farm was purchased in 1888, the property in the foothills of the Blue Ridge Mountains amounted to 1,800 acres. Greenfield lies in a lovely hollow of the Shenandoah Valley between the village of Linden, to the east, and the city of Front Royal to the west.

When the Union Army hero bought the land, some of his neighbors were not pleased. After all, the Shenandoah Valley had been Confederate country and locals still had bitter memories of "The Burning"—an 1864 campaign led by the arrogant General George A. Custer to punish local families for lending support to Mosby's Raiders, a Rebel cavalry unit that had used the valley as a staging point to raid Union forces in Virginia. Some in the North had called the valley "Mosby's Confederacy."

The Union Army's commander, General Grant, had ordered General Sheridan to "eat out Virginia clear and clean as far as they [soldiers] go, so that crows flying over it for the balance of the season will have to carry their provender with them." Sheridan's cavalry had proceeded with the help of the blonde-haired Custer, a descendant of a Hessian soldier named Kuesters. After laying waste to hundreds of farms and hanging members of Mosby's Raiders in Front Royal, Custer became a hated man, derided as "Atilla the Hun." When the Civil War ended in 1865, it left behind scars in the Shenandoah that lasted for decades.

When he rode his horse through the region during the war, Leather-breeches had been impressed by the Shenandoah Valley's lush beauty and its resemblance to parts of the Rhine River valley. One reason he was attracted to the Greenfield property was that Union Army regiments had once retreated through the "Valley Retreat" area.

By the time Anton was born, the family patriarch had grown a beard to hide the dueling scar on his cheek and had sought to make peace with neighbors and townsfolk who had sympathized with the Rebels. But a notice he published in a local newspaper in 1888 showed his fierce loyalty to his family land against poachers, rustlers, or fence smashers:

TRESPASS NOTICE

Public notice is hereby given that in order to stop the annoyance
To which I am daily subjected, I forbid all persons from entering
Any portion of the 1800 acres of land I own in Warren County,
Hunting over or on the same felling timber, throwing down fences
Or opening gates or drawbars, or committing any other manner of
Trespass, for I am resolved to enforce the remedies provided by law
Against trespassers, regardless of persons. —*H. Dilger*

More than two decades after he had left Germany to fight in the Civil War, Leatherbreeches still spoke imperfect English and bristled when he was reminded of that flaw. A soldier by nature, he had never quite found himself after quitting the Army.

He had settled on a Virginia stock farm only after he had tried his hand at running a business in Pennsylvania and serving as Adjutant General of Illinois. Relatives described a man whose "moods swung from depression and high cynicism to high humor, who could laugh at his own foibles and who was at the same time both tenderhearted and strict, a no-nonsense disciplinarian."

As an expert horseman with "a lifelong love affair with horses," Hubert Dilger taught his sons and daughters to ride as soon as they could hold the reins, showing the boys how to ride like soldiers and the girls how to ride side-saddle, drive buggies, or even handle horse teams for the coach. "The youngsters groomed, fed and watered their animals and were adept at saddling up and harnessing horses to the carriages and wagons," a grandson wrote. "Together, father and sons hunted Greenfield's woods, fished in streams, rode its hills and pathways, and, with the help of hired hands, worked the farm." The old man's horses, especially Lynwood and Valley Boy, were his "personal pride and joy." Carl Dilger's daughter recalled, "They were wild boys. Each of them had a horse and a gun."

WHILE HIS OLDER BROTHERS were riding horses and baling hay, young Anton Dilger was fascinated by a bronze bust, dusty citations from kings and princes, and old leather-bound books that graced the shelves of the Greenfield mansion's library.

The bust depicted the intelligent, perceptive face of his great-grandfather, Dr. Friedrich Tiedemann, known as "the great physiologist of Heidelberg." In the fertile mind of his granddaughter Elise, the famous professor's spirit was present in the mansion and would influence the life of her son Anton.

Elise Dilger had wanted a high-quality education for all her children, but family finances had limited their opportunities. She "tried to convince [Hubert Dilger] of the importance of giving the boys an education, more important than horses," a granddaughter recalled. "She went on and on and Granddaddy said, *'Bist du noch nicht fertig?'* [Are you finished yet?] and walked out." In 1898, Anton's older sister Emmeline (Em) would complain bitterly that the old man had neglected the education of the other brothers.

The determined mother wanted at least one of her children to follow in the footsteps of her famous grandfather—as well as her father, Dr. Heinrich Tiedemann—and study medicine in Germany. Anton was the logical choice. He was playful, mischievous, adventurous, and—above all—intelligent.

No record survives of Elise Dilger's early predictions for her fifth boy's future. As a spirit writer, her specialty was receiving messages from the dead, not the living. But Anton, the only boy with a passionate interest in schooling, would become her great hope to rekindle the glory of her Tiedemann ancestors. On top of his intelligence, Anton was fascinated by German culture. "The whole Dilger family at Greenfield was German-feeling," wrote a relative from the Old Country who had visited them.

In September 1894, Anton's sister Eda married a wealthy Mannheim businessman, Martin Koehler, at Greenfield. A month later, the couple took ten-year-old Anton with them to Germany. Living at the Koehler home, Anton would learn German and prepare for a university education that the Koehlers would finance. The tradeoff was that Anton would, in effect, become a German.

Anton's interest in things German had been stimulated since the arrival at Greenfield in 1892 of his German-born grandfather, Dr. Heinrich Tiedemann. There, the old doctor and his grandson spent many hours together in the echoing mansion, surrounded by the trappings of the Old World—furniture from Germany, Hubert Dilger's commission from the Grand Duke of Baden, dusty old books in the library, and, above all, the bust of the great Heidelberg scholar. Heinrich Tiedemann shared with Anton his tales of the '48 revolution in Germany and how his family had been divided as a result.

Heinrich's father—the Heidelberg professor, Friedrich Tiedemann—had been devastated by the exile of his son Heinrich and the execution of his eldest son Gustav as a result of the '48 revolution. In an impassioned letter written to Gustav at the besieged Fortress Rastatt, the professor had pleaded with his son to forsake the revolution and surrender Rastatt to the Prussian soldiers who surrounded the fortress city. "Should you be deaf to the prayer of your old father ... then I can only regret that the bullet which wounded you did not rob you of life," the professor wrote. He begged Gustav to flee Germany and join his brother in the New World: "Leave then Germany and Europe and go to America as quickly as possible, to thy youngest brother [Heinrich] who was misled by Hecker. The means for thy voyage across I will forward to thee by thy uncle in Bremen; maintain thyself there by hard work on the land."

Heinrich Tiedemann was the only one of the three sons to follow his famous father's path into medicine. But he had disappointed the professor by marrying into a revolutionary family, leaving Germany, and then settling for a medical practice in America rather than becoming a university don.

Elise Dilger shared few traits with her professorial ancestors, but she was tenacious in pursuing her spirit writings, which documented the contacts she claimed to have made with the dead. For most of his life, her highly rational father had resisted the notion of contacting spirits. But, as the old man weakened with disease, Elise finally convinced him that she could contact the one person he wanted to reach: his father, the great physiologist. Both of them may have been heartened by one of the professor's lines in an old family letter: "Beware of burdening the conscience. There is a Beyond."

Late at night, when the children were asleep and velvety darkness shrouded the Greenfield mansion, Elise sat with Heinrich in séance after séance, trying to contact the famous professor. "My heart and soul was bent upon fulfilling my mission to convince my Father of the existence of a better world," she wrote. "Then followed many a lonely séance, in which he would enter into serious topics with his own father … putting such questions as would have baffled me had they been addressed to me.…"

Young Anton Dilger had witnessed his desperate mother's efforts to reconcile her dying father with their ancestor. To the ten-year-old, it must have been a mystical experience to see his mother and grandfather huddled together, trying to commune with a spirit from old Germany. There was, therefore, a sense of unfulfilled destiny in Heinrich Tiedemann, which he conveyed to his grandson Anton. Perhaps he would be the one destined for greatness. Anton soon became the chosen one, the heir apparent to the family medical tradition. And soon after the boy's departure for Germany, Dr. Tiedemann's condition worsened—he was so sick that he survived for weeks on a meager formula of "six teaspoons of milk with a little brandy," and he became "a living skeleton" before his death a few months later. In several ways, the soul of the family had returned across the Atlantic. Greenfield would never be quite the same for the Dilgers again.

"Continue to be a good little man," Elise Dilger wrote to Anton a year after he had moved to Germany. "Be obedient, loving, and try hard to please those dear ones who are trying to make a good useful man out of you. Do not make any noise about the house and disturb little baby.…"

For both Elise and Hubert Dilger, the separation from Anton and Eda was painful. In her letters, Elise constantly admonished the boy to work hard at his studies and behave himself at his older sister's house in Mannheim. Not to be outdone, old Leatherbreeches—who seldom wrote to his children—also sent a letter to "My dear good German boy!" Describing life on the farm, the old soldier told of "how much I miss my little helpers"—Anton in Germany, and his older brothers in a Virginia boarding school.

"Edward thinks he could do better if he could ride home every night," the old man wrote. "When the weather is nice, I always send the horses down for the boys." But the weather had been nasty that winter in western Virginia, covering streams with ice and blowing bitter winds through the snowy Blue Ridge Mountains. As an aside in one letter—in a reference to the weather that might also have applied to the family's financial straits—Leatherbreeches told his son: "... you are really better off, old doctor..." in Germany.

The contrast was stark between the diminishing fortunes at Greenfield and Anton's comfortable new life in Germany. Eda lived in a lovely home in Mannheim, and the boy and his nieces and nephews enjoyed life to the fullest. During the Christmas season, the children sang carols like "Silent Night" under the *Tannenbaum* lit with candles and decorated with glass icicle ornaments and silvery tinsel, candy angels and ginger-bread men. There were festive meals of roast goose, sausages, dumplings, and cheese, with the best wines and liqueurs from the Rhine and Mosel river valleys. On New Year's Eve, there would be yet another feast, followed by family games, including "fortune-telling climaxed at midnight when the children read the future from the odd shapes that formed from spoonfuls of molten metal dropped into a cup of water."

After a few years, Anton's letters home showed that he had started to lose some of his fluency in written English and was starting to lapse into German phraseology, sprinkling his prose with German quotations. He excelled as a student and enjoyed the life of a wealthy merchant's "son" in Germany. He also had begun fancying German girls, and he accused his older brother Edward of breaking the hearts of some old-world maidens during a visit there. "The Karcher girl always makes eyes at me, as if she wanted to say, 'Will you take dear Teddy's place?'" Anton wrote.

"But I can only call back over the street, 'No, I regret very much, but you look too much like a seahorse—but a dried-up one.'"

In Virginia, a drought had parched the Shenandoah Valley in the spring of 1900. The old soldier decided it was time to clear brush, so he and the remaining boys and hired hands started scything and hacking at weeds on April 1. It had been a calm day when they first set ablaze the brush piles, but the wind picked up and the fire started to spread toward the mansion. All hands rushed to try to contain the flames, but sparks flew up into the gutter of the family homestead. Smoldering for a few minutes, the fire got into the wood and suddenly the first floor of the house burst into flame.

Equipped with only a few buckets and little well water, the family watched helplessly as the fire raged. When the fire reached Leatherbreeches' store of ammunition, explosions shook what was left of the house and sent people fleeing from the site. Within an hour, the wooden mansion—the family's pride and storehouse, their only home for two decades—had burned to the ground, leaving only the stone chimney still standing.

The heat was so intense that Leatherbreeches' decorative swords had melted, as did his prized Medal of Honor and the priceless awards, citations, and books of Elise's famous grandfather. All of Leatherbreeches's illustrated war diaries and Elise's spirit writings, painstakingly saved over four decades, went up in smoke. Mounted deer and moose heads, expensive German furniture, knicknacks from a quarter decade of family life—all were destroyed.

There were no casualties from the fire, but Hubert and Elise Dilger would never be quite the same afterward. With their finances in shambles and the house destroyed, the family's Virginia branch was now desperate for help from the country they had left behind.

In the few moments before the heat inside the house became unbearable, Leatherbreeches—wincing at the exploding ammunition that reminded him of Civil War battles and later weeping at all he had lost—was able to save only a few belongings. Tellingly, the most precious to him was also the most German: the lavishly-illustrated family Bible, printed in 1561, that he had hand-carried to America. The book was printed "by grant of the Holy Roman Emperor." The most precious family heirloom, at least, was safe.

In the Old Country, Anton was working hard as a student. After earning his *Abitur* (secondary school degree) from a *Gymnasium* in Bensheim, he scored high enough on his exams to be accepted to study medicine at the University of Heidelberg in 1903. Dilgers, Koehlers, and other relatives on both sides of the Atlantic were extremely proud of the young scholar—the family's greatest hope.

That spring, Anton joined the Koehler family and his nephew, Carl-Erik, in a voyage on the S.S. *Bremen* to New York, followed by train trips to Washington and then Front Royal. It was Anton's first visit home in eight years, and he found a markedly different landscape in Greenfield. His parents had aged considerably, and life in rural America seemed primitive in contrast to the old-world cities he had grown accustomed to in Germany. Also, two of his brothers, Carl and Louis, had left Greenfield for work outside of Virginia.

Disheartened and in financial straits, Leatherbreeches and his family had moved into a neighbor's house after the fire and later would occupy the ramshackle farmhouse in the Valley Retreat section of the Greenfield estate while they built a new home on the foundations of the old one. Neighbors said the old soldier was in tears when he talked about all he had lost. But he perked up during Anton's visit. With the eighteen-year-old medical student came not only his grandson Carl-Erik but also Eda and her husband.

Martin Koehler, whose business in Mannheim was prospering in parallel with Germany's rise as an economic and trading power, was greeted with special warmth at Greenfield. He had promised to help finance the reconstruction of the mansion and already had footed the entire bill for Anton's education, extended a letter of credit in 1898 to help bail the Virginia farm out of financial troubles, and paid for dozens of transatlantic voyages for various members of the Dilger family.

Carl-Erik recalled that his visit had been a happy one, a brief reunion of the family and a chance to share in the bucolic pleasures of the Virginia farm. In a letter written decades later, he recounted how happy he had been to play with his war-hero grandfather Hubert and to ride horses with his uncles over the foothills of the Blue Ridge Mountains. "We ... had such a wonderful time with granddaddy. During the same visit, I shocked the whole family by cutting off the mane and tail of good Edward's horse."

Elise Dilger doted on Carl-Erik, but her deepest affection was devoted to her son Anton, who in the eight years since she had last seen him had grown into a handsome and bright young man with a decidedly European demeanor. That caused some concerns, for—even though she wanted her son to succeed in Germany—Elise did not want him to become a German. The most outspokenly American in the family's older generation, Elise Dilger told her Germanified daughters during old country visits that she missed Virginia so much that she would kiss the ground of Greenfield when she returned home.

As Anton Dilger's grammar and penmanship became unmistakably old world, his mother could tell that he was gradually becoming more and more of a German. In December 1901, while Anton was still in secondary school, she listed the Christmas presents she had bought for each of her children. For Anton, the gift was a copy of *Roget's Thesaurus*—a reminder that his native language was English. To one of her daughters, perhaps more in hope than expectation, she wrote: "[Anton] can use it to advantage, since he declared he was an American and would remain an American. Good for him!"

A MAGNIFICENT CASTLE LOOMS over Heidelberg, an ancient and picturesque city on the Neckar River. When Anton Dilger first arrived at the university there in 1903, he was awed by the scene. And when the young American began taking anatomy classes, he soon learned to appreciate the achievements of his great-grandfather Tiedemann, whose memory was still revered at the university four decades after his death.

While his mother in Virginia sought to communicate with the spirits of her ancestors, Dilger in Germany tried to follow in the footsteps of the most famous of them. Already in his early postcards from Heidelberg—showing stunning perspectives of the castle and the city—Dilger referred to himself as "the absent-minded Professor" and the "celebrated sawbones of Heidelberg."

Tiedemann had been a professor of anatomy and physiology at Heidelberg from 1816 until the middle of the century, directing the university's anatomy institute and writing a number of significant books and scientific treatises about comparative anatomy and human anatomy, with special emphasis on the human brain.

He had earned his medical degree at the University of Marburg in 1804, but he left medicine to pursue natural science in Paris, where he studied under the famous French naturalist Georges Cuvier. He became a professor of anatomy and zoology at the university in Landshut in 1806 and—creating what would prove to be an important precedent for his great-grandson Anton a century later—he served during the Napoleonic Wars as a field surgeon, caring for the war-wounded in the Landshut military hospital.

A dedicated and conscientious scientist, Tiedemann had distinguished himself by advocating anatomical research based on observation rather than speculation. His three-volume textbook on zoology broke new ground because it presented his conclusions from extensive studies of animal anatomy. In a brilliant scientific treatise in 1816, Tiedemann showed that the stages of the brain's development in the human embryo roughly correlate with the adult brains of lower vertebrates (fish, reptiles, birds, and mammals) in the order of their complexity. That remarkable observation proved to be one of the most important and most-cited findings of early nineteenth-century zoology.

Tiedemann's studies of the development of the human brain correlate somewhat with his philosopher father's studies on the development of intelligence. But he took a far more scientific approach to his work. His most significant scientific treatise was an 1836 paper about the Negro brain, published in the *Philosophical Transactions of the Royal Society of London*. In that essay, Tiedemann argued that the brains of blacks and whites were not significantly different, indicating that the races had similar capacity for intelligence—an enlightened position for his era. The German professor wrote that "neither anatomy nor physiology can justify our placing [of blacks] beneath the Europeans in a moral or intellectual point of view." After analyzing numerous skulls of Africans and Europeans, Tiedemann concluded "there are no well-marked and essential differences between the brain of the Negro and the European."

In an appreciation written a century and a half after Tiedemann's death, Harvard University biologist Stephen Gould described the "great physiologist of Heidelberg" as "a most admirable man whom history has forgotten but who did his portion of good with the tools that his values, his intellectual gifts, and his sense of purpose had provided." Tiedemann, who had been a close friend of England's chief surgeon, had received awards from both King George IV and Queen Victoria.

Anton Dilger's postcards to Greenfield show a pride in his Tiedemann ancestry as well as a nagging homesickness for his family in Virginia. In his studies of zoology and anatomy at Heidelberg, Dilger learned the importance of his ancestor's careful observations and dispassionate approach to science, and his postcards are replete with images of birds and flowers. Showing hints of homesickness in a postcard written to his sister Em in November 1903, Anton offered condolences on the death of her pet bird, writing that "it was lonesome since I am gone, because nobody played 'Home Sweet Home' for him." The young medical student got his wish to visit Greenfield less than two years later, when he traveled to Virginia to spend a pleasant summer on the farm. When he returned to Germany, he sailed with his nineteen-year-old sister, Pauline (Honeybee), on the *Grozer Kurfürst*. She, like her older sisters before her, had met a German in Virginia and was planning to marry him.

The following year, in the summer and fall of 1906, Anton's aging parents visited their five children in Germany, spending weeks at the homes of daughters Eda, Lalla, and Janie. The travel and rich food taxed Elise's strength, and she was stricken with a liver ailment. Anton, despite his medical training, was at a loss to help. Back at Greenfield, a worried Em Dilger appealed to her brother, who had interrupted his medical studies to spend more time with his ailing parent. "Anton, please write me with all the particulars and the exact state of her condition," Em wrote. "What causes this swelling and enlargement of the liver? Why did it come so suddenly? Was the ocean trip the cause of this trouble developing?"

Elise was diagnosed with an inoperable liver ailment, and her health faded over the autumn and winter; the holiday season was subdued. It was soon clear that she would never return to her beloved Greenfield. Jaundiced and feeble, Elise died quietly at age fifty-nine at the house in Mannheim in January 1907. She was buried in Germany, with Anton and Hubert Dilger and other family members present at the funeral.

A few days later, the heartbroken old soldier embarked on the long journey back to the New World. His son Anton, like four of his daughters, remained in Germany, by now firmly anchored in the intellectual and social life of the fatherland.

Chapter 3

TISSUES AND CYANIDE

The cultures were put away in the incubator, under a guard—relieved every eight hours—of half a dozen warriors.
—JULIAN HUXLEY, "The Tissue-Culture King," 1926

MILITARY RANK AND SCIENTIFIC STATUS were on Anton Dilger's mind when he wrote a short personal history, or *Lebenslauf*, as a postscript to the proudest achievement of his academic career: the publication of his medical thesis.

Clearly anxious to impress, the young doctor exaggerated his father's military rank—the elder Dilger had served briefly as the Adjutant General of Illinois but was never an active-duty general—and emphasized his maternal link to the famous Heidelberg professor, Tiedemann:

I, Anton Dilger, was born on 13 February 1884 in Front Royal, Virginia, USA. My father, Hubert Dilger, was an artillery captain from Baden who later became an American General. My mother, Elizabeth, was born a Tiedemann.

After my graduation in the spring of 1903 from the Humanische Gymnasium zu Bensheim a.d.B., I registered at the medical faculty of Heidelberg for the summer semester of that same year, registered for the summer semester in Munich in 1905/06, and returned in the summer of 1906 to Heidelberg, where I passed

the medical exam in the summer of 1908. Since October 1909 I
have been assistant at the surgical clinic in Heidelberg.

Dilger attended medical school during a period of transition, when
the time-tested techniques of medical education—the mind-numbing
tedium of memorization, the intensive study of human organs—were
being supplemented by exciting new fields of research.

The University of Heidelberg had been founded in 1386, with its
initial growth curtailed by an outbreak of bubonic plague that struck the
city two years later. By 1425, an early doctor had established a canon of
Heidelberg medical studies, using study of the treatises of Hippocrates,
Galen, and other great classical physicians. The medical faculty
expanded gradually until the nineteenth century, when it grew rapidly as
medicine became a more scientific study.

From his early days at Heidelberg, Dilger seemed determined to
become a surgeon and perhaps a professor of surgery. In October 1907,
he mailed a humorous postcard to his sister Em at Greenfield showing a
whip-snapping German horseman driving a two-horse carriage—with
the passenger next to him completely flattened under the weight of a
huge trunk. Dilger wrote to Em: "If I become a professor some day, we
will have experiences like this. Have patience!"

Six months later, Dilger announced in another card that "tomorrow
I will finish up with the women's hospital. Have passed Pathology,
Anatomy and Eyes with a No. 1. This time, I don't count [on] more than
a No. 2." Using very German grammar, he added that medical school
involved a great deal of stress: "I am kept very busy and am commencing
to feel the work."

That summer, Dilger passed his medical examinations. Before he
started his thesis and the next phase of his training at Heidelberg's surgical clinic, he took a year to visit family in Mannheim and his father and
siblings at Greenfield. He then attended a spring and summer graduate
course for doctors in 1909 at one of America's most innovative institutions of higher education: the Johns Hopkins University Medical School
in Baltimore. At the time, Johns Hopkins—an innovative research university with a curriculum based in part on the German university

research system—was thought by many to be the leading American medical school.

Medical education was in turmoil and transition in the United States in the decade before the Great War. In the mid-1800s, a student could earn an M.D. degree at many American medical schools after less than six months of college instruction plus an apprenticeship; by the early 1900s, a four-year course was required for the degree. Johns Hopkins Hospital pioneered the first formal one-year internship for young doctors in 1889. A 1905 report by the American Medical Association found that half of the nation's 160 medical colleges were unsatisfactory; an independent analysis in 1910, the Flexner Report, sharply criticized the quality of U.S. medical education. But Johns Hopkins and Harvard were among the best medical schools of the time.

At Johns Hopkins, Dilger took the "Medicine" summer course, which included training in microbiology, diagnostics, and other subjects in the realm of internal medicine. The graduate courses were popular among up-and-coming M.D.s; the list of physicians who took the course along with Dilger that year includes doctors from the Netherlands and Canada as well as cities such as Philadelphia and Boston.

In a postcard sent from Baltimore in March 1909 to Em at Greenfield, Dilger said he was "OK" but that "it did me good to get out of Baltimore" to visit his sister Josephine (Jo) in Washington, D.C. "I often wonder how I am going to stand the summer here" in Baltimore, Dilger wrote. "I have plenty of work to do, but I think I'll only keep up the present kind of work until end of May and then take it easier. Em, I really don't know why I left those white shirts at home!" In a cryptic note at the end of the postcard, he encourages Em to "take good care of patient in the stable" at Greenfield—likely meaning a sick horse. "Particulars in every direction will follow in letter."

In June, Dilger sent another Baltimore postcard, this one picturing the city's Wildey Monument column, making it clear he was studying at the Johns Hopkins hospital. "Em, please mail that letter from Tubingen. It is from the publishers of my 'Arbeit' [work] and probably important," which was likely a reference to Dilger's doctoral thesis research. To stress the importance of that letter, Dilger scrawled on the color front of the postcard: "Mail letter from Tubingen to the hospital." Judging by his letters, he was then an ambitious, dedicated young doctor—a model professional keen to benefit from the best teaching hospitals in the United States and Germany.

Later that fall, according to family letters and postcards, Dilger also spent a few weeks at Harvard University's medical school and its teaching hospital, Massachusetts General Hospital in Boston. Harvard has no record of his taking any courses there, but it is possible that Dilger met with scientists who were experimenting with tissue cultures, the field in which he was pursuing his thesis.

On November 5, 1909, after his stints at Johns Hopkins and at Harvard were over, Dilger sent his sister Em a postcard from New York as he was about to board a ship to Germany. "Only an hour's time for letters cannot write more ... The scarves are beautiful. Your farewell greetings moved me to tears. Good by good by. An." The postcard from the Hamburg-America Line showed a color drawing of a *Kinderzimmer* (the playroom for children) on one of the line's transatlantic passenger ships.

He returned to Heidelberg to take an assistant surgeon position in the university's renowned surgical clinic. The clinic, which opened in 1818, claimed a series of surgical firsts, including the successful removal of a human kidney (1869), extraction of a cancerous uterus (1878), removal of a cancerous prostate gland (1887), and successful operation on a brain tumor (1890). The surgical clinic where Dilger worked had been modernized in 1898. In 1906, one of the clinic's surgical teams introduced a new anesthetic consisting of alcohol, chloroform, and ether.

At Heidelberg, Dilger was taught the techniques of modern surgery. He also learned how to assemble a laboratory for his tissue-culture research. In medical school, Dilger had studied microbiology and germ culture to understand the microbial origins of wound infections and the techniques to avoid them. In the wake of the discoveries made by Frenchman Louis Pasteur, German Robert Koch, and other great microbiologists of the late nineteenth century, the germ theory of disease had been widely accepted and bacteriology was à la mode in the first decade of the twentieth century. Tissue culture—finding ways to keep alive and grow living tissues in the laboratory, outside of the animal itself—was an even more pioneering field of study, one of the earliest examples of biological engineering.

German-born scientist Leo Loeb, working mainly with guinea pigs at the University of Chicago, had conducted research into the conditions under which animal tumor cells could be cultivated outside the body and transplanted into other animals as early as 1901. Six years later, Ross Harrison of Yale University—widely regarded as the founder of the technique of tissue culture—adapted the "hanging drop" method previously used by bacteriologists to culture bacteria, using it to grow a nerve cell from embryonic frog tissue. During the same decade, future Nobel Prize winner Alexis Carrel and his assistant Montrose Burrows—conducting their research at the Rockefeller Institute in New York—modified Harrison's technique and used it to grow adult mammalian tissue and cancer-tumor tissue in vitro.

Dilger's medical thesis, *"Concerning* In Vitro *Tissue Cultures: With Special Consideration of the Tissues of Adult Animals,"* made a modest contribution to the emerging field of tissue propagation. As part of his thesis research, conducted mainly in 1910–11, Dilger examined recent experiments in propagating live tissues in the United States and other leading centers of medical research during the first dozen years of the twentieth century. Working about a year after the early Carrel and Burrows experiments, Dilger mainly followed their techniques in working with tissues extracted under aseptic conditions from dogs, rabbits, and rats.

Citing the work of those predecessors, Dilger said that tissue-culture success "opens wonderful perspectives for all fields of medical research." He and his Heidelberg medical colleague Arthur Meyer—who would later travel and work alongside Dilger as a wartime surgeon—established a tissue studies laboratory at the Heidelberg surgical clinic to experiment with the tissues of adult animals rather than with embryos. Their goal was to repeat various earlier experiments and determine whether scientists would observe true growth of the tissues and whether all elements of the animal tissues—that is, epithelial cells as well as connective tissues—were reproducing in the in vitro cultures.

In his thesis, Dilger describes how he and Meyer built their tissue-culture laboratory at the Heidelberg surgical clinic. "In order to conduct the experiments, a well-equipped laboratory was necessary and for the success of the experiments the first challenge was fast work with good assistants and under strongly aseptic" conditions. Dilger describes how he prepared the mediums in which to grow the animal tissues, how a fast centrifuge was required to prepare the tissue cultures, and the careful monitoring of temperatures in which the cultures were grown. Dilger knew how to use incubators, microscopes, centrifuges, and other specialized equipment, along with the usual laboratory glassware—pipettes, petri dishes, test tubes—and cages for laboratory animals.

During the Heidelberg experiments, Dilger used guinea pigs in the lab for the first time—an experience that would come in handy years later. One of Dilger's challenges in his doctoral experiments was to avoid bacterial infections of the animal tissues. Later, in Washington, he would apply his laboratory expertise and discipline to exactly the opposite purpose.

The perfection of tissue-culture techniques in that decade had real-world implications for organ and tissue transplantation in humans, as well as for cancer research. For centuries, surgeons had been unable to replace diseased organs because they did not have a reliable technique for reestablishing circulation in the transplanted organ without the danger of bleeding or clotting. Alexis Carrel had discovered ways to revolutionize blood-vessel surgery, laying the groundwork for later organ transplants.

Tissue-culture research in that era also created a "tissue cult" of scientists who cultivated in vitro tissues. Carrel, for example, was able to cultivate a section of heart muscle from a chicken embryo in a nutrient medium inside a glass flask. For more than two decades, Carrel or an assistant transferred and trimmed the growing tissue every forty-eight hours. In a macabre celebration, doctors and nurses at the Rockefeller Institute would sing "Happy Birthday" to the chicken tissue on the anniversary of the initial tissue transfer.

"Tissue culture developed almost into a tissue cult, a mystery the secret rites of which were revealed only to a narrow circle of inaugurates with Carrel as their high priest," observed a Nobel Prize–winning scientist many years later. In 1926, British biologist Julian Huxley wrote a parable he called "The Tissue-Culture King" about a fictional British scientist who produced cell cultures that were misused by an African tribe to develop human and animal monsters. "Every now and then some new monstrosity in the shape of a dwarf or an incredibly fat woman or a two-headed animal would be visible," wrote Huxley. When the British scientist shows off his "Institute of Religious Tissue Culture," the narrator writes:

> My mind went back to a day in 1918 when I had been taken by a biological friend in New York to see the famous Rockefeller Institute; and at the word[s] tissue culture I saw again before me Dr. Alexis Carrel and troops of white-garbed American girls making cultures, sterilizing, microscopizing, incubating and the rest of it.

Huxley's cautionary tale, implying that some developments in modern biological engineering could do great harm, hardly constituted a warning. By 1926, it was too late for that, for certain bridges already had been crossed during the Great War. And central to the propagation of those biological threats was a German-trained doctor.

BY THE LATE NINETEENTH CENTURY, the *Totenkopf*, or skull and crossbones, had become the standard symbol for poison or extreme danger. When Anton Dilger drew the symbol on a postcard to his brother Edward in June 1904, he meant it as a joke. Three years later, the joke would seem prophetic.

Anton had sketched the *Totenkopf*, punctuated by four upright daggers, on a card he addressed to "Mr. Edward Dilger, brother of the most celebrated sawbones in Heidelberg." At the time, Edward was visiting relatives in Germany. At a family gathering in Mannheim, Anton had paid Edward to make a drawing. Threatening punishment if Edward failed to deliver on time, Anton closed the postcard: "Written by the Company for fining dirty American cheaters in the German Empire."

Edward was the most dedicated and talented horseman among the five Dilger brothers. He was as obsessed with horses as his father, whether riding, grooming, or breeding the noble animals. As a boy, Edward had ridden to school every day on spirited steeds. By the time he was a teenager, he would ride his horses through the Blue Ridge foothills and along the lush Shenandoah Valley. He would spend hours grooming the horses at Greenfield. And occasionally he would ride fifty miles with his father to the site of the Chancellorsville battlefield, where the old man would relive the glory of the battle and tell the story of how he was saved by a boy with a new horse.

Short and small boned, Edward had wanted to be a jockey ever since he had first sat upon a horse. For awhile, he wore the colors of a wealthy neighbor, Kingston Salisbury, in various Virginia races. Edward raised foals, among them a favorite named Sweetheart, but he could never quite make a career as a jockey. In fact, he never managed to make a career of anything other than working on his father's farm.

The fire that destroyed his family's mansion almost crushed Edward. He was so depressed that his mother fretted in a letter that "he won't talk to any of us; he will not sit with us, but seems to be always desirous of sleeping. I fear he will make himself sick—brooding over bygones." But when in 1904 Edward sailed to Europe, at the expense of brother-in-law Martin Koehler, to visit Anton and his older sisters he was in high spirits. The would-be jockey from Virginia and the aspiring doctor from Mannheim had seemed a mismatch, especially after being separated for eight years. But they shared a quirky sense of humor and soon became fast friends—exchanging comic cartoons for months.

One of Edward's hand-drawn postcards shows his sketch of goose-stepping soldiers who saluted his brother-in-law Hubert Lamey, a German Army officer. Edward wrote on the card: "The first time I saw them do this for Hubert I got so darn scared that I almost crawled into Hubert's pants. I thought they were going for me." Edward was joking, but the rising German militarism was not particularly funny.

The bond formed during Edward's year in Germany was sufficient to make Anton complain in a note, written after his older brother returned to Greenfield in the fall of 1904, that Edward "had to pull out right before Christmas and make my heart feel dreary." But it was Edward's heart, back in Virginia, that suffered more. He led a life of highs and lows, with periods of exhilaration followed by weeks or months of despondency. His mother's death in 1907 sent him into another tailspin, during which he convinced himself that he had fallen in love with a beautiful widow in Front Royal, a close family friend he had known for most of his life. But she felt that Edward was unstable and rejected his talk of courtship. After that, he seemed to be unable to control his roiling emotions.

One day in October 1908, Edward rode a horse to the widow's family home, telling her that he had come to town to buy cyanide to kill sheep. He took a nap on the sofa and morosely meandered around the house as family members went about their business. When the widow walked into the parlor she saw that Edward was eating a white powder. She asked what it was, whereupon Edward shouted "Cyanide!" and lunged at her and tried to force the poison into her mouth as well, so that she would share his death even if she would not share his life. Hearing his daughter's screams, her father ran into the room and pushed Edward to the floor, where he went into convulsions. Within a few minutes, he was dead.

Edward's restless thoroughbred waited—tied to a post outside the house—as the doctor, neighbors, and his older brother Butz gathered at the house. His dutiful brother led Edward's horse back to Greenfield, where Butz broke the news to his elderly father, who heard it in dead silence, saying not a word. Within a few days of Edward's burial, the old man wrote a will, beginning: "Being afraid that I might not long survive the terrible shock received by the untimely sad end of our dear Edward ... "

Edward Dilger's suicide broke the heart of the man who had taught the boy all he knew about horses. Hubert survived another three years, but only as a shadow of his former self. When Anton finished medical school and sailed to America to visit Leatherbreeches for the last time, in 1910, it was like talking with a ghost. The white-bearded man had buried his wife and son within two years, and now was clearly preparing for his own death. A photo from that last visit shows the old man gripping the attentive Anton's left arm as they walk through the garden. No one knows what he was trying to impress on Anton, but certain facts would have been unmistakable to him in 1910. The family farm no longer contained a family and was scarcely financially viable as a farm. For all Hubert's patriotism and courage, the Dilger venture in America was on the threshold of economic failure. "Anton could only stay for a short time, and the parting was more difficult than usual for he realized that it would be the last time he would see his 'Daddy,'" a relative wrote later. Despite his father's poor health, Anton had to return to his medical work in Germany.

As he neared the end of his life, Hubert Dilger worried about the fate of Greenfield, the farm he loved so much. He had ridden up and down that land for more than three decades. He had ploughed its fields, gaining an intimate knowledge of every rise and fall of its terrain. He had built one mansion for his family, faced turmoil when it burned to the ground, and then stoically built another house in its place. He had spent his inheritance and borrowed from anyone he could to keep the farm going.

He was clear about his wishes in his will: "It has always been my wish, as it had been your mother's, to retain the possession of our lands, which we loved so much, which we retained with great sacrifices within the family, as a home for all, in luck or adversity." Now he was dying, and he wanted to keep Greenfield whole. He wanted to make sure some-one took care of his favorite horses, Lynwood and Valley Boy, and the fields he and another Virginia landowner's former slave, Abraham Lewis, had worked. And he wanted to preserve Greenfield as a gathering place for his family, even though five of his children lived in Germany.

Hubert Dilger died peacefully at home on May 14, 1911, and was buried in Washington, D.C. His will left Greenfield farm in a family trust headed by his eldest son, Butz Dilger, who had faithfully worked the money-losing operation as a farmer. The old man urged his other children in the will to contribute to the farm's operating costs, so that the family would not lose the homestead.

But Greenfield had been losing money for decades, and the family had only been able to keep it by mortgaging the property and through the generosity of Martin Koehler. Wrote one relative: "In effect, the family has been consuming capital in blissful, unworldly innocence, and was about to be confronted by the unpleasant consequences."

In September 1911, a few months after Hubert Dilger's death, the family began the process of selling about a third of Greenfield's acreage (522 acres) to the U.S. government for $15,680. That included the sta-ble and other structures in Anton's favorite part of Greenfield, which the

Dilgers called Mountain View or Mountain Farm. When he was a boy, Anton used to clamber over the rock walls, explore the rickety old stable, and ride horses through those hilly fields. It was where the boys went to escape farm chores and have fun.

"You don't know how happy you made me by sending me that card from the Mountain Farm," Anton had written his siblings from Germany in 1904. "It called back to me that fine time we spent over there last year—it cost me a lot of laughter to think back."

In the years leading up to World War I, that same tract would become known as "Dilger Field" at the new U.S. Army Remount Depot at Front Royal, assembled from segments of several farms. The Front Royal depot had been one of several established by the Army after the U.S. Congress, in May 1908, had approved a new Army remount service to gather, evaluate, and train horses and mules of military quality.

The first depot was established at Fort Reno, Oklahoma, in 1908; the second at Fort Keogh, Montana, in 1910; and the third in Front Royal in 1911. The Virginia depot, which handled horses for military units east of the Mississippi River, would become an important horse center during World War I.

Over the next few years, thousands of horses and mules—with the U.S. brand burned into their left shoulders—would be led up the hill to the Army depot to be bred to produce a new generation of warhorses. When American troops joined the Great War, many of those warhorses were led down the hill and herded onto boxcars at the Front Royal train station.

Few, if any, of those horses would ever return.

WHEN THE BRITISH FOUGHT THE BOERS in South Africa at the turn of the twentieth century, tens of thousands of horses and mules that had been foaled in faraway Virginia, Kentucky, and Missouri became victims of the ruthless and relentless war.

The carnage on the veld was awful, for horses as well as for soldiers, with the British plagued by severe problems in buying, shipping, and caring for the astounding number of horses the Royal Army used in South Africa from 1899 to 1901.

So many of the animals perished during the Anglo-Boer War—probably close to a half million when both sides are taken into account—that the *Spectator* in London cited the horse casualty rate in its scathing attack on the British conduct of the war. The British War Office calculated later that more than 400,000 horses, mules, and donkeys were "expended" in the war. Boer horse losses probably exceeded 150,000.

That high rate of equine casualties resulted from a number of factors, including poor transport conditions in ships and trains as well as inadequate veterinary treatment and exposure to African horse diseases. Once the tired and often sick animals arrived at Cape Town, they were loaded quickly onto trains that took them to battlefields rather than given adequate time to adjust to the food and climate in South Africa.

The war's demands completely overwhelmed the British Army's remount department. In years of peace, that section easily supplied about 2,500 fresh horses a year. Suddenly, with so many horses dying or sick in South Africa, the Army demanded a huge influx of horseflesh: a quarter million horses and nearly 100,000 mules over two years. The Army's horse reserves had begun at less than 15,000 horses, so the remount department was forced to search for remounts in North America, Australia, Argentina, Spain, and even the Austro-Hungarian Empire.

Supplying those horses, and keeping them healthy, turned out to be a chaotic, sometimes nightmarish task that the British Army had trouble fulfilling. An Army remount director near Cape Town was so distraught by the problems that he shot himself. Lord Kitchener, a prominent general in the South African campaign, faulted the War Office "for the tens of thousands of sub-standard horses sent out to South Africa."

A court of inquiry that later criticized the remount service investigated numerous complaints of payoffs, gross incompetence, and fraud, in addition to charges that the shipping conditions had been awful. One British captain was accused of taking bribes from mule dealers in New Orleans. Remount officers in Spain fell victim to the gypsy practice of "bishoping" mules—filing down their teeth to make them appear younger—and often paid ridiculous prices for substandard animals.

British purchases during the Anglo-Boer War represented the first massive export of American warhorses, amounting to at least 100,000 horses and 85,000 mules bought from American stockyards. The British forces "swallowed horses as a modern army swallows petrol." The cavalry depended on horses, and the infantry and artillery units needed mules and pack horses to pull guns and wagons.

The horses and mules fell by the thousands not only to bullets and disease, but to the butcher's knife. During the siege of Kimberly, starving townspeople turned to horsemeat. The chief medical officer, Dr. E. Oliver Ashe, wrote later that the diamond town's British residents had to overcome their aversion to butchering horses after the Boer siege cut off food and medical supplies. Eventually, the people of Kimberly consumed more than 164,000 pounds of horsemeat—more than a third of the available meat supplies. "I brought my chunk of horse home and that night we had it for dinner," wrote Ashe. "It took some pushing down. I guess I am not hungry enough yet."

Cavalry horses were so important that when their forage ran out the British would at times feed them "mealies"—food supplies intended for troops. But as provisions dwindled during the siege of Ladysmith, British General Sir George White decided to stop the issue of mealies to horses. "White's new policy had two immediate and dramatic effects on the garrison's own food supply. The remaining stock of mealies ... could be used for men's rations. And most of the horses themselves could be turned into men's rations."

There was one silver lining: the scandalous miscues involved in Anglo-Boer War horse shipment and veterinary care spurred investigations in London, leading to reforms. Concluding that the conditions for horses and mules during the Anglo-Boer War had been "utterly inadequate," British veterinarians drew up elaborate plans to implement the lessons learned in South Africa before the Great War began in 1914. They expanded remount purchasing operations, deployed the latest veterinary techniques to control diseases at horse depots, improved transport ships, and required breaks for pasturing so that the horses arrived on the battlefields in better shape.

While the British at that time had no hints that the Germans would target horses, the new veterinary and shipping rules would later play a crucial role in minimizing the impact of the germ sabotage.

As the Great War approached, the British geared up for huge purchases of North American horses and mules in 1914. The French and

Germans also sent buyers before the war. "Our home resources are ...
exhausted," reported Britain's remount director shortly after the war
broke out. He estimated that the Royal Army could buy another 68,000
horses in the U.K. itself, but would have to import about three times
that many animals.

That turned out to be a gross underestimation, since the British
eventually bought nearly three quarters of a million horses and mules
from North America. During the four war years, transport ships full of
horses and mules left U.S. ports for Europe an average of every one and
a half days. Each of those ships carried between five hundred and one
thousand animals. The Royal Army spent an astounding £36.5 million
on its remount purchasing and related operations in North America—
the equivalent of more than $10 billion in 2006 dollars.

Royal Army officials worried at first that the U.S. policy of neutrality
would cause problems with the massive horse-buying program. But by
the fall of 1914, there were British remount offices in St. Louis, Kansas
City, Chicago, Denver, and Fort Worth. Bought through dealers or
businesses like the Guyton & Harrington Horse and Mule Company,
animals were collected at large inland depots and then sent by train to
ports, such as Newport News, for shipment.

There was no shortage of horses in the United States: a 1910 census
found about 21 million horses on American farms. But the military
required special breeds and colors, and not all private horses were for
sale. Light-colored horses were not considered appropriate for cavalry
because they were too visible from a distance. Slight horses or mules
were no good for pulling artillery pieces across fields of mud.

A Missouri-born cavalry general of German extraction would play
one of the most important roles in the Army effort to bolster its war
horses: General John J. Pershing. His ancestor, Frederick Pfoerschin,
had immigrated in 1724 to the United States from his home near the
Rhine River in the Alsace region, an oft-disputed territory on the border
between Germany and France. The family name later became Pershin,
then Pershing.

A graduate of West Point, Pershing had served as a cavalry officer
with both the 6th and 10th Cavalry regiments against the Plains Indians,
but he learned the vital importance of logistics the hard way in the

chaotic Spanish-American War campaign in Cuba in 1898. As he rode the transport ship back home from Cuba, Pershing wrote that one of the most important lessons he learned from the little war was the crucial importance of transport and logistics to supply the troops. After the debacle of the stranded soldiers and horses, he suggested that in the next war the U.S. Army must focus on its supply lines. He took a special interest in assuring adequate supplies of horses.

Starting in 1913, stallions owned by the Army and the Department of Agriculture were made available for stud service to privately owned mares. Many of those stallions had been donated or sold below market value for patriotic reasons by prominent horse breeders such as August Belmont II, who donated five racing stallions in 1912–13, including the great Thoroughbred Henry of Navarre. Most of those stallions were stabled at the Front Royal depot, and mares were shipped to them. The half-bred geldings—in most cases the offspring of Thoroughbred, saddlebred, Morgan, or Arabian stallions out of ranch-bred mares—were then bought by the Army as mounts for the cavalry or artillery.

The stallions and their offspring at Front Royal and other depots were given the best of care. Remount Service officers consulted the leading private horse breeders for the best techniques to feed, breed, and keep up the health of the valuable stallions. Veterinarians conducted research into equine diseases and undertook great efforts to make sure that glanders and other horse diseases were not introduced into the depots.

Belmont, one of the nation's leading horse breeders at his Nursery Stud Farm in Kentucky, where Man o' War would be foaled in 1917, called the warhorse breeding plan "a splendid idea. It is practical and workable." As the Great War commenced in Europe, the new U.S. warhorse program began in earnest, and the Front Royal depot began what would turn out to be a thirty-year relationship with General Pershing.

The depot sent a half-breed mare, Number 1083, to Pershing's camp in El Paso, Texas. The Front Royal horse depot's commander wrote to the general: "At times, especially after periods of idleness, I think you will find your mare somewhat ambitious, but with daily work I believe she will prove very attractive and quiet."

Pershing was a connoisseur of horses, and Number 1083 was one of hundreds that he would ride during his career. After the Great War, Pershing, the commanding general of the American Expeditionary Force, advised a young boy who asked how to treat a horse: "If given proper care and treatment, a horse proves himself a valuable friend to mankind in many ways by using his strength and fine instincts. You see, I spent many years in the Cavalry and am very fond of horses."

"MURDER NEAR GREENFIELD." That jarring headline topped a story in the *Warren County Sentinel* about "a horrible murder" at Greenfield Farm in May 1912. A drunken intruder wielding a single-barreled shotgun had shot one of the farmhands in the chest, "making a hole as large as a hen's egg." A week later, Em and Louis Dilger—who had been visiting Anton, the Koehlers, and other family members in Germany—arrived to find Greenfield in turmoil.

"The affair is so disgusting, and was done in such a cold way, it makes one's blood curdle," wrote Louis in a letter to the Koehlers, enclosing newspaper clippings about the slaying. But the murder was not the only piece of bad news that spring; in the same letter, Louis alleged that the U.S. government had tried "to bluff Butzie in the sale of" the Mountain View property. "All I can say is that I am ashamed that a government can be so outrageously common."

Even though the patriarch Leatherbreeches had died the previous year and his children were scattered on both sides of the Atlantic in 1912, family members kept an avid interest in the Virginia farm—and not only the two-thirds of the Greenfield property that was now in a family trust. The family, in Germany as well as in America, also watched closely what was happening at the Army remount depot that would soon include the Mountain View acreage. Letters show that Martin Koehler, in particular, took a persistent interest in the remount depot besides wanting to know about Greenfield's own stable of horses, one of which had been named for Eda.

On July 10, 1912, Louis sent to Martin "a survey of the entire tract of land consisting of 1,500 acres or thereabouts. This includes Greenfield, Mountain [View], and Valley Retreat. The heavy dotted line running from one boundary line to another, shows that portion of the farm which is under consideration for purchase by the Government." Louis added: "I am sending you this sketch because I believe it will interest all you dear ones on the other side."

Three days later, Louis wrote in a letter to Eda and Martin that two of Greenfield's "young draft colts" were still stabled at the Mountain View area but that those young horses would be moved elsewhere "anytime that the government orders it." In an apparent reference to the remount depot's recent loss of some valuable breeding stallions, Louis wrote: "Those Government devils have lost within about two years over $10,000 worth of horses. Did Anton show you my letter? In it I wrote about the Remount Station."

That particular letter to Anton Dilger has been lost, but its significance is clear. The Dilgers, like the British Army suppliers and the German High Command, were very interested in what was going on at the remount stations. Louis, then living at Greenfield, made a habit of clipping local news items about the Remount Depot and sending them to the Koehlers and other German relatives with commentary in his letters. Some of those articles discussed the qualities of an ideal military horse, others described horse and cattle diseases, and still others detailed the news from the rapidly expanding remount depot.

In 1912, the *Sentinel* printed a regular column, "Remount News," recounting recent developments at the Army depot, with plenty of news reports about August Belmont's donations of retired race horses to be used for stud service with local mares. Louis included several of those newspaper clippings in his letters to Germany, including one column that said: "The government is practically giving everything to the farmer in the hopes that horses of the proper kind for military purposes will be bred." Army officials hoped that local farmers would "lead in [more] mares to be bred to remount stallions." The remount depot, after inspecting and registering the mares to ensure that they were appropriate, would pay local farmers $25 per colt sired by one of its Thoroughbred stallions. Those colts would later become warhorses.

That fall, however, the prime topics of Louis's letters to the Koehlers suddenly shifted away from the remount depot to more pressing concerns about politics and the future of his brother Anton. In a letter dated the day after the U.S. election, November 5, Louis predicted that Woodrow Wilson's election as the next U.S. president "means hard times for four more years." In the same missive, he expressed surprise and concern that Martin had given Anton permission to suspend his Heidelberg medical career that fall to put himself in harm's way as a war surgeon in the First Balkan War, which had just broken out.

Referring to his brother as "Tony," Louis wrote: "I am surprised that you, M.K., sanctioned Tony's venture" to the dangerous war, which was making headlines even in faraway Virginia. Despite his worries, Louis said he prayed that "everything turns out well for An[ton]."

Chapter 4

DISQUIET ON
THE WESTERN FRONT

I have never heard a horse scream and I can hardly believe it.
There is a whole world of pain in that sound, creation itself
under torture, a wild and horrifying agony.
—ERICH MARIA REMARQUE,
All Quiet on the Western Front, 1929

WHILE THE U.S. ARMY was staking out its section of Greenfield Farm, the first sparks of the impending war that would consume many of Europe and America's warhorses suddenly became visible in the Balkans. The First Balkan War, which began in 1912, quickly stressed Bulgaria's medical care system almost to the breaking point, with wounded soldiers inadequately treated and cholera striking in the countryside.

The country's unlikely heroine proved to be Queen Eleonore—technically, the Bulgarian tsaritsa—who devoted herself to the war-wounded. Ignored by her husband, King Ferdinand, she had avoided the boring royal court in Sofia and traveled to see the countryside, where she was stunned by the sickness and suffering she witnessed.

The queen set up hospitals, established nursing schools, and recruited excellent doctors from Germany to help with the wartime public health crisis, which extended far beyond battlefield wounds. Among the young women she sent to the Red Cross for training to become nurses was her stepdaughter, Princess Nadejda. And one of the young physicians she enlisted was Dr. Anton Dilger.

It was no accident that the queen recruited Dilger. The young doctor had an impressive résumé, displaying a medical degree with highest honors from Heidelberg and graduate studies at Johns Hopkins. By 1912, when a representative of the Bulgarian queen was searching for German surgeons to improve her field hospitals, Dilger was working in a surgical clinic at Heidelberg.

How could the young doctor ignore a queen's request? Dilger, with youthful wanderlust and an inherited interest in war, seized the Balkan opportunity. Over the objections of his surrogate parents, Dilger volunteered to practice medicine in the war zone. He later explained to his sister Eda: "When I made up my mind last July [1912] to leave you, I did not make the decision based on my heart, but rather my mind." He added: "If I have in any way grieved you by staying away too long and not being nearby to help you, I ask your pardon, and I can only assure you again and again that I never did it intentionally."

In October 1912, Dilger and his friend and fellow Heidelberg surgical assistant Arthur W. Meyer, traveled by rail to Sofia, where they were taken to the Clementine Hospital. The queen had recruited a German surgery professor from her home city of Coburg to run that hospital, which was under her jurisdiction. During that fall and early winter, Dilger and Meyer reported having an "exhausting, exciting and interesting time" at the hospital. When the Coburg professor returned to Germany at the end of January, Dilger became surgical director of the queen's Sofia hospital while Meyer joined another German colleague in running a field hospital in the outlying town of Philippopel.

Bulgaria's king and queen—native Germans, denigrated by some as "the Prussians of the Balkans"—were worlds apart on many issues, but they seemed to agree on the importance of Dilger's medical mission. King Ferdinand took a liking to the young doctors and sent his personal physician to help Dilger and Meyer with the hospitals. The queen, meanwhile, sent trained nurses and had her staff make sure there were ample supplies of bandages and medications.

Eleonore was said to have "a special gift for relieving suffering." That may be because she suffered greatly herself, being the second wife of a known bisexual. King Ferdinand, who had a preference for handsome young men, neglected her throughout their marriage, and Eleonore devoted her considerable energy to medical care during the Balkan Wars and the Great War.

Henry Morgenthau, then the U.S. Ambassador to Turkey, wrote later that "Queen Eleonore was a high-minded woman, who had led a sad and lonely existence, and who was spending most of her time attempting to improve the condition of the poor in Bulgaria. She knew all about social work in American cities, and, a few years before, she had made all her plans to visit the United States in order to study our settlements at first hand." At one point, the queen recruited two American nurses from New York's Henry Street Settlement to teach American Red Cross nursing techniques to a group of Bulgarian women. One observer described her as a "plain but practical ... capable and kind-hearted woman." While Ferdinand was blamed for the bad outcome of the Second Balkan War, Queen Eleonore was regarded by many Bulgarians as a woman of the people.

The First Balkan War ended in May 1913 with a victory over the Ottoman Empire, soon followed by a struggle among the erstwhile allies—Bulgaria, Serbia, Greece, and Montenegro—over how to carve up the Macedonian territory that the Turks had controlled. That cessation of hostilities allowed an exhausted Anton Dilger to take a vacation in Germany. He visited his family and friends in Mannheim and apparently rekindled a romance with Margarethe Katz, a charming and intelligent woman from a wealthy Jewish family. Her father traveled in the same business circles as Martin Koehler, who seemed to encourage the match. Anton had first met Margarethe during his years at the surgical clinic in Heidelberg. Surprising his sisters in America, the lothario Anton would become engaged to her in the spring of 1915. But he would break off the relationship a year later after an acrimonious dispute with her father.

Margarethe Katz was hardly the only woman Dilger saw during those years. Dashing and cosmopolitan, and with a generous streak, Dilger enjoyed the company of women. One of the letters in the family archives is from a married woman in Washington who was aflutter about her relationship with the handsome doctor while he was there. Later,

Dilger would carry on a sporadic affair with an opera star. His brother
Louis once joked that Anton had dated so many German girls that his
brothers were impatient for him to choose one and get on with it. "I am
anxious to see what our Tony's selection will be like," he wrote in July
1912. "We boys are waiting with a great deal of impatience for a nice
sweet sister-in-law. Tell him not to wait until we are dead."

During that brief break between the two Balkan Wars, Dilger also
spent time with the Koehlers trying to smooth over his sister's concern
that he had dropped everything in Mannheim to work in the Balkans.
Martin was formal and conservative; Anton—mischievous, charming,
and with a streak of daring—was fond of practical jokes and, in the
words of his brother Louis, of "stirring things up a bit." Consequently,
Anton's relationship with the Koehlers had had its ups and downs, but
he remained loyal to his sister and brother-in-law, who had sponsored
him so generously.

Both Anton and Eda had at times chafed under Martin's stern edicts
in Mannheim. He "was very jealous and did not allow outsiders to enter
his house," a relative said later. "I am sure that it was Anton who
brought nice and interesting people just to please his sister. Anton
brought all his friends to their home ... and made his sister so happy."

Dilger's experience as a field surgeon had given him new confidence
in himself and determination to make a difference in the war that now
seemed inevitable in Europe. His confidence in his own future was bol-
stered by his intense pride in the accomplishments of his ancestors, most
importantly his father's military record.

The young surgeon even had the arrogance to confront one of Germany's most famous men, Count Ferdinand von Zeppelin, the inventor
of the rigid airships, or dirigibles, that came to be known as zeppelins. A
former cavalryman, Zeppelin had fought in the Prussian wars against
Austria and France and then turned to airship design. When the Great
War began, Berlin had high hopes that the zeppelins would revolutionize warfare by carrying out bombing and reconnaissance missions.

But Dilger's complaint had nothing to do with the airships. Instead,
he was outraged by what Zeppelin had written in his memoirs about
Leatherbreeches's conduct in the Civil War a half century earlier. Rather

than simply swallow his family pride and ignore the insult, Dilger took up a pen and wrote a letter. Zeppelin, to his credit, replied.

As a German observer to the Civil War, Zeppelin had commented on Hubert Dilger's outspoken criticism of senior officers. He also wrote that Dilger's German service had amounted to no more than being a "commissioned flag-bearer" in Baden, when in reality Dilger had been a first lieutenant in the Grand Duke's horse artillery.

Anton Dilger defended his father as a hero and a brilliant tactician. After all, he reasoned, Leatherbreeches has been widely regarded as one of the Union Army's most effective artillerymen. And, of course, he had won the Medal of Honor for heroism.

Zeppelin's reply is a unique example of the strange confluences of the Great War era and German sensitivity to a casual slur on someone's honor. Zeppelin, one of the founders of air warfare, found himself apologizing to a cocky young doctor. In his letter, Zeppelin offered to "make any factual corrections that you would wish" about Hubert Dilger and promised to correct the misimpression in any future publications in which he would discuss the Civil War.

"I don't believe that anyone who reads this single critical anecdote of the prevailing discipline in the American Army at that time will form a negative picture of the especially gallant, loyal and—in terms of military training—the exceptional Capt. Dilger," Zeppelin wrote defensively. "I myself had nothing but admiration and respect for him after our short meeting together."

DILGER'S STAY IN GERMANY in the late spring of 1913 proved to be short, for another war was brewing back in the Balkans. King Ferdinand, a staunch German ally, began to exchange harsh words with the leaders of his former Balkan League allies Serbia and Greece over how to divide their joint conquest of Macedonia. On the night of June 29, the king ordered Bulgarian troops to attack Serbian and Greek forces.

When he heard the news, Dilger rushed back to Bulgaria and was sent to the outlying city of Kustendil, near the disputed border with Macedonia. There, he ran a hospital sponsored by Queen Eleonore that had taken over a former high-school building. The severely wounded from the front lines about seventeen kilometers away were transported and treated at Dilger's new hospital. A lovely resort town in the mountains, Kustendil became a brutal battle zone because it was the headquarters of Bulgaria's 5th Army.

When the war went awry for the Bulgarians, Kustendil and Dilger's hospital were under direct threat. An American observer, U.S. Army Medical Corps Major Clyde S. Ford, visited the hospital in 1913 and met Dilger. In a report, Ford wrote that the Kustendil hospital, which Dilger directed as chief surgeon, "was the personal possession and under the direction of the Bulgarian queen, who had quarters adjacent thereto, which she frequently occupied ... The queen's hospital was most complete in its personnel, materiel, organization, and administration, and was quite well prepared to do scientific surgery."

The hospital was in constant turmoil, at one point taken over by the American Red Cross when Serb forces neared the city center. Ford reported that, "it was so feared that Kustendil would fall into the enemy's hands that the queen's hospital was evacuated and the personnel ordered to Sofia. The materiel, however, could not have been removed, and I presumed to arrange to purchase it in the name of the American Red Cross ... in order to save the hospital and patients from the enemy."

During his time in Kustendil, Dilger learned about infectious diseases as well as battlefield surgery. More than 1,000 of the 60,000 men in Bulgaria's 5th Army came down with cholera; at least 150 of those soldiers perished from the disease. The director of the Royal Hygienic Institute in Sofia took numerous measures to fight the spread of cholera, which had killed thousands of Turkish troops during the first Balkan War. Dilger and other physicians near the front also had to deal with the disease as well as other microbial pathogens that infected wounds.

Dilger and his colleague Meyer worked with a bacteriologist from Sofia to analyze the germs discovered in various wounds, including streptococcus and staphylococcus bacteria as well as tetanus infections. Asserting that the prevention of such infections was "a key issue of battlefield surgery," Dilger described how soldiers who had been given tetanus antitoxin injections before being wounded could avoid the disease, commonly known as lockjaw. Later, in the United States and Germany, Dilger would administer antitoxin injections to himself and others who handled germ cultures.

Treating an astounding variety of wounds during his Balkan service, Dilger had gained an arcane knowledge of the wounds caused by various types of bullets. He learned to distinguish among injuries caused by Bulgarian, Serb, Greek, and Turkish bullets. In a paper written after the war, he described bizarre wounds, including the holes left by a bullet that entered a man's forehead and exited from the back of his skull. The Bulgarian patient survived, albeit with some brain damage.

Dilger and Meyer examined bullet-shattered bones and collected various types of shrapnel and ammunition casings they found near battlefields. They also studied the impacts of near- and long-distance shot and analyzed the experiences of the first-responders and the transport of the wounded to the field hospitals. "In Sofia and Philippopel we saw wounded who had been injured months before, weeks before, or only a few days earlier," the two surgeons wrote. "In Dedeagatch and Kustendil we saw soldiers who had been freshly wounded, only one or two days after the battles; and at the front we could study wounds that had been received only a few hours or minutes earlier."

In the 153-page report, "Battlefield Surgical Experiences from the Two Balkan Wars," which was published in the *German Journal of Surgery* in 1914, Dilger took a step to bolster his academic credentials as an expert on war surgery. He and Meyer contended that experience is essential to train battlefield physicians and that the existing literature in the field was woefully inadequate for preparing new field surgeons. Having arrived in the Balkans with "no idea" of the challenges facing war surgeons, Dilger reported that he "became convinced of the complexities of this discipline and . . . continued to learn more new things up until the end."

The goal of the lengthy paper, the two young physicians wrote, was to help battlefield surgeons in future wars: "We are doing this in the hope that our observations will bring some clarity to a series of disputed questions related to war surgery." They would not have to wait long. World War I erupted just a few months after their paper was published.

In the end, Bulgaria lost the Second Balkan War, signing a peace treaty in August 1913 under which Greece and Serbia divided most of

Macedonia between themselves. That short war had been a bust, but the king and queen were grateful to Dilger, who was awarded a Bulgarian medal as well as a pair of golden royal cufflinks for his medical service He would proudly display those medals for years afterwards, carrying them with him and telling Balkan war stories. Aside from the medals, the battlefield service burnished Dilger's credentials as a war surgeon and, perhaps more importantly, whetted his interest in the military.

Dilger moved to Vienna after the war to conduct research and to write the article with Meyer about their experiences at the front. In a letter sent to his sister in Mannheim shortly before Christmas 1913, Dilger hinted at the hardships of his year in the war zone: "I shall feel very lonesome here tomorrow [Christmas Eve] and the following days, indeed maybe lonelier than last year when I was in such surroundings that one could hardly realize or even think that anything in the world was going on like Xmas. Just about this time of night I arrived in [a border town]. The weather was very cold and I remember how glad I was when I finished preparing a plate of pea soup and a cup of tea . . . The old Turk in whose house I was kept grumbling every time I would ask him for any little favor. I don't blame him if he took me to be a Bulgarian."

In what may have been an oblique reference to his initial exposure to German military intelligence, which some family members associated with his service in the Balkans, Dilger added in the letter: "Only a year has passed since I was down there and how many curious things have happened since. Such is life!"

THE NEXT EUROPEAN CONFLICT, the Great War that broke out barely a year after the Balkan Wars' end, would put to the ultimate test all theories and practices of war surgery. The casualties would number in the millions, and the challenges at battlefield hospitals would be devastating, even to experienced war surgeons.

For Anton Dilger, who would witness the horrific consequences that the Great War would unleash, the most personally painful injury resulted from a single round fired in one of the earliest encounters of the war, long before the lines of trenches had settled deep into the Flanders mud. The Great War was just two weeks old when a single gunshot shattered the summer morning as a platoon of the German Crown Prince's 5th Army, in a boisterous mood as they headed for France to engage the enemy, marched down a road in Luxembourg. The bullet, fired by a French sniper on August 20, 1914, killed a twenty-year-old lieutenant who, like so many, had been eager to win glory for his family.

At that moment, Anton Dilger—having completed his exhausting year as a field surgeon in the Balkan Wars and interning at a Vienna hospital—was back at the surgical clinic in Heidelberg. The dead lieutenant was his friend and nephew, Peter August Lamey, who was also Hubert Dilger's first grandson. Word of the death struck the young surgeon as hard as any news since the death of his own father three years earlier.

"Peter passed his last happy hours with Anton in Heidelberg," the young soldier's father, Hubert Lamey, wrote later. "Anton wrote so charmingly about [his final meeting with Peter] that it touched my heart." Dilger was "devastated" by Peter's death and feared that his other nephews "might be lost" in the war. Anton Dilger, hardened by his first-hand experience of the consequences of war, was approaching a momentous choice. He could return to America and neutrality or become drawn into the conflict. His dilemma was the same as that faced by America itself. But the Dilgers were a Mannheim family as well as a Virginian one. Once the family blood began to be shed, it was just a matter of time before Anton Dilger joined the combat. "More and more," one relative wrote, "he wanted to contribute to the defeat of the Allies...."

With the death of Peter Lamey, the grim reality of the war—a conflict that had been welcomed by many Germans who had celebrated in the streets when it was declared three weeks earlier—was brought home for the extended Dilger family, both in Germany and across the Atlantic.

As a military family, the Lameys had supported the war as an opportunity for Germany to win a quick campaign with overwhelming military strength. It was Peter's father, Hubert Lamey, who had been married to Anton's sister Elizabeth at Greenfield Farm proudly wearing the Baden Grenadiers uniform, complete with a silver sword in an ornate German scabbard and a polished helmet. A career soldier, Colonel Lamey had been fighting with his unit in France at the time of his eldest son's death.

Three of Dilger's other sisters who had married Germans also had sons of military age when the Great War began. Within weeks of Peter's death, two of Dilger's eighteen-year-old nephews—Albrecht Lamey and Carl-Erik Koehler, almost a younger brother to Anton, with whom he had lived for more than a decade—volunteered for service in the German Army. The wave of patriotic enlistments had left Anton, the son of a highly decorated soldier, feeling useless. As an American citizen, he was excluded from German military service, but he was a doctor. Just two months after Peter Lamey's death, Dilger volunteered for service as a "noncombatant surgeon" at the Military Reserve Hospital in Rastatt. He began his medical work there in early November 1914.

Rastatt, a fortress city near the confluence of the Rhine and Murg rivers, was not far from the Western Front. More importantly for Dilger, Rastatt was in Baden, the epicenter of the Dilger family heritage. The province's northernmost city is Mannheim, where Anton had lived with his sister Eda's family. Heidelberg is about 20 miles away and Karlsruhe and Rastatt are further south.

From the stories told by his father, Anton Dilger knew the family's military history in Baden by heart: Leatherbreeches had served in the Grand Duke of Baden's horse artillery at camps in both Rastatt and Karlsruhe. Anton's uncle Gustav Tiedemann had been executed by the Prussian Army for his defiance as revolutionary governor of Rastatt. And it was from Rastatt that the family's friend Carl Schurz, one of Tiedemann's aides during the 1848–49 revolution, had managed to escape and emigrate to the United States.

Badly damaged during battles in 1329, 1424, and 1689, the ancient city of Rastatt was accustomed to war. It had a long military tradition, having been rebuilt as a fortress to help protect the upper Rhine Valley. During World War I, it was the site of an army garrison, a prisoner of war camp, and a reserve hospital that played a secondary role to the main center in Karlsruhe. Dilger worked long hours as a civilian surgeon there. While he spent most of his time treating wounded soldiers, he also made connections—both through his medical work and through his family—with officers who served with the Army's powerful General Staff.

Relatives said that Dilger "could not conceal his pride" in his German nephews who had volunteered for military service in the Great War. Albrecht Lamey had joined an infantry unit and soon would be sent to France, where he would win the Iron Cross and the Knight's Cross for bravery and be commissioned as an infantry lieutenant. His younger brother, Hubert, would enlist a year later, as soon as he became eligible for service, and would serve as an officer on the Eastern Front.

The family's most successful military man, though, would be Dilger's surrogate younger brother, Carl-Erik Koehler, nicknamed "Bubs." Young Carl-Erik had idolized Leatherbreeches. Like his grandfather the Civil War hero, Carl-Erik was an avid horseman, so it was a natural decision for him to join one of the elite Uhlan cavalry units in 1914. He took pride in the Uhlan uniform and proved to be a brave and talented soldier. He would win two Iron Crosses for heroism near the Western Front and later would rise through the postwar ranks to become one of Germany's highest-ranking cavalry officers.

The Uhlans—crack Prussian cavalrymen who still carried lances when the Great War began—would become obsolete by the conflict's end, but for the moment, Carl-Erik rode with his fellow Uhlans into the French battlefields, anticipating the glory of cavalry charges and knowing little of the barrage of machine-guns and shrapnel they were about to encounter.

THE BELGIANS CALLED IT the "Battle of the Silver Helmets," a clash of rapidly advancing German cavalry with stubborn Belgian units at a river crossing in Haelen. It was not one of the Great War's major battles and it had little strategic significance. But Haelen was among the war's first big cavalry actions and also one of the first slaughters in which tradition-bound mounted soldiers faced the hot steel of machine guns.

That day, August 12, 1914, units of German cavalry and horse artillery—colorfully uniformed Uhlans, Dragoons, Hussars, and Kurassiers—rode down a main road into a barrage of shrapnel and shell fire. With their second charge, the mounted Germans reached the Belgian barricades but were held back by sustained rifle fire. Regrouping, the German cavalry then charged the Belgians, spurring a counter-charge by Belgian Lancers and Chasseurs that ended in hand-to-hand combat.

Finally, the Germans gathered again for a final charge against what seemed to be the weak point in the Belgian defenses. It was a terrible decision, for the cavalry rode toward Belgian machine gunners and massed formations of riflemen who proceeded to mow down the attackers, causing "a pitiful carnage of horses and men and was as courageous as it was disastrous." One German cavalry officer wrote later that the retreat was "paralyzed by the number of riderless horses roaming about, and by the stragglers of the 2nd Kurassiers and 9th Uhlans who had been cut up by machine-guns."

In the end, at least 150 German cavalrymen and more than 400 horses lost their lives; another 600 soldiers were wounded and several hundred were captured. The Haelen slaughter did not halt the German advance through Belgium, but it showed that machine gunners were capable of decimating cavalry units on the attack. The success of the Belgian machine gunners was interpreted as "an early demonstration of the modern-day irrelevance of the cavalry in offensive situations."

An official from the American Legation in Brussels, Hugh Gibson, described the scene at Haelen after the battle:

> The Prussians had charged across the field and had come upon a sunken road into which they fell helter-skelter without having time to draw rein. We could see where the horses had fallen, how they had scrambled to their feet and tried with might and main to paw their way up on the other side. The whole bank was pawed down, and the marks of hoofs were everywhere. The road was filled with lances and saddles, etc. All through the field were new-made graves. There was, of course, no time for careful burial. A shallow trench was dug every little way—a trench about thirty feet long and ten feet wide. Into this were dumped indiscriminately Germans and Belgians and horses, and the earth hastily thrown over them—just enough to cover them before the summer sun got in its work.

That mass grave of Prussian cavalrymen and their horses at the Belgian town of Haelen also marked the beginning of the end of mounted warfare in the Great War.

In 1914, horsemen accounted for about a third of the total strength of most of Europe's armies. Those mounted troops were regarded as a key element—in some cases, the major component—of traditional offensive battles. Typically, European cavalrymen carried swords, rifles, and sometimes lances—as in the case of the Uhlans. Cavalry officers in the German, French, and British armies still had great influence over battle planning and tactics; in fact, nearly all the highest-ranking officers in the British Army were former cavalry officers.

Kaiser Wilhelm II loved to ride spectacular horses. Some days he would stay in the saddle for five or six hours, especially when he inspected troops. He basked in the trappings of the military and he made up for his lack of physical presence—his fragile health and withered left arm—by donning elaborate uniforms. During one public function, he was said to have changed uniforms five times.

Like the Kaiser, and like their counterparts in the British and French armies, the German mounted units began the Great War with high hopes, grand traditions, and flamboyant style. Until late 1914, all German cavalry regiments were armed with ten-foot-long tubular steel lances that had been designed in 1890. The ten Kurassier regiments had only recently abandoned the heavy metal breastplates. The German Army also included thirteen *Jager zu Pferd* (Mounted Rifle) regiments as well as twenty-eight Dragoon, twenty-one Hussar, and twenty-four Uhlan regiments.

The Kaiser's Army began the Great War with more than 58,000 mounted troops in 110 regiments, adding many more cavalry regiments when the Reserve Cavalry was mobilized. In all, 550 German squadrons would fight in the Great War, giving its cavalry a stunningly wide range of mounted troops. The Germans also began the war with nearly 4.5 million horses—the second-highest number in Europe, after Russia.

The German cavalry took its highest profile on the Western Front in the war's initial month, when the mounted forces spearheaded the initial thrust into Belgium. In the late summer and early fall of 1914, it seemed

as if the Kaiser's cavalry might be a major force in the war, with numerous small cavalry engagements, sweeping mounted actions, and massed
cavalry charges taking place before and after the debacle at Haelen. Forward squadrons of cavalry scouts and reconnaissance patrols thundered
across the countryside around recently captured villages and towns. The
Uhlans, in particular, were instantly recognizable to villagers and enemies because they were the mounted lancers, wearing square-topped
caps and uniforms with stiff plastron fronts.

But cavalry was largely ineffective in the offensive standoff that soon
developed. The Uhlans, Dragoons, Kurassiers, Hussars, and Chasseurs—riding bold steeds, wearing colorful uniforms, and carrying out-
moded weapons—soon proved to be splendid anachronisms. The initial
fluidity of the Western Front had deteriorated into trench warfare by
the end of 1914, dooming the cavalry to secondary roles in the war's
final four years.

Three weeks after the war began, a young German cavalry lieutenant
named Manfred von Richthoven—a soldier who would later abandon
the cavalry and become the "Red Baron" ace pilot—was startled by how
easily French sharpshooters picked off his regiment during a skirmish
near Etalle, Belgium. "In spite of my orders, all the other [Uhlans] had
bunched together and offered the Frenchmen a good target," von
Richthoven wrote. "I brought only four men back. . . . That evening
some of the others came back, although they had to come by foot, as
their horses were dead. It was really a miracle that nothing happened to
me or my horse."

While French sharpshooters had a field day, it was the machine guns
that massacred many cavalry regiments. The Germans had not expected
such heavy casualties from automatic fire. The French had first used a
primitive version of the machine gun, the *mitrailleuse*, against Germans
during the Franco-Prussian War. A quarter century later, the British
infantry had deployed a bulky but more reliable automatic gun called the
Vickers-Maxim in the Anglo-Boer War. But the machine guns of World
War I, especially the Royal Army's Lewis guns, which could be fired
either from the shoulder or from a tripod on the ground, were used with
devastating results in the war's initial weeks.

The disaster at Haelen was echoed a few weeks later in France, during the battle for the city of Nancy. On September 8, the Kaiser himself ordered a "grand assault" on the entrenched French "Iron" Division. There, the Kaiser learned that even his crack cavalry units could not overcome machine-gun fire and shrapnel from a protected foe. When Bavarian battalions failed to advance, the Kaiser ordered a full cavalry assault to be made by one of his best units, the White Kurassiers of the Prussian Guard. Riding stirrup to stirrup and wearing full cuirass (metal breastplates) in their charge across an open plain, the cavalrymen became easy targets for French artillery gunners, who made quick work of the Germans and their horses.

Within an hour, the dead and dying horses and men covered the battlefield. The next wave of cavalry was forced to ride or jump over the piles of bodies, which at some points were six feet high.

AT THE FORTRESS CITY OF RASTATT, the dual family traditions, medicine and soldiering, converged for Anton Dilger during a period of momentous transition in his life.

He was a restless man, seldom in one place for more than a few months. Intensely proud of his heritage, Dilger was a brilliant conversationalist, a charmer at dinner parties, a practical jokester to his siblings, and he was extremely ambitious about succeeding in the tasks he undertook.

Louis Dilger's mother-in-law, who had known Anton well in Mannheim, later described him as "the most charming, fascinating, and likeable man she had ever met." But she often had misgivings about his personal conduct, especially "the way he broke hearts, left and right, even if unintentionally." Also she always had the suspicion that, despite his tremendous charm, "he was up to no good in some way."

For Anton Dilger, however, the definition of "no good" was relative. He came to believe that the greater good was intertwined with the dominance of Imperial Germany, and he did not hesitate to employ every means—including deceiving and in some cases endangering his own siblings—to make his contribution toward that goal.

When he talked with Army acquaintances in Rastatt and Mannheim in 1915, Dilger would hear complaints about the "neutral" stance of his native country, which allowed for major shipments of munitions, food, and horses to the Allied armies. "There are 10 million Germans in America," they would say. "How can they allow their country to tilt toward the Allies?" Washington professed a willingness to sell the same supplies to Germany, but of course it was a hollow offer. The British Navy controlled the seas. The Royal Navy's blockade effectively shut off German trade with the United States.

Clearly, Anton Dilger was eager to do his bit for Germany in the war, and, with his nephews joining the military, being a surgeon did not satisfy his patriotic yearnings. He was a potentially valuable asset, a U.S. citizen trained as a physician who was fully bilingual and a German patriot. A family member wrote later: "Someone recognized that with his American background and unrenounced citizenship, he might perform useful services for the Fatherland in America."

No official recruitment records survive, but there were many opportunities for German military intelligence officers to approach Anton: as early as the Balkan Wars; during his year of service in Rastatt, which was an important army base as well as a prisoner of war camp; or through his two closest German uncles, Martin Koehler and Hubert Lamey, each of whom had many connections with the military and the government. One family friend was Rudolf Giessler, who worked for the intelligence department of the Army's General Staff. Documents show that Giessler knew Captain Franz von Papen, the Army's military attaché in Washington at the time and a key figure in coordinating parts of the fledgling German sabotage campaign in America.

One of Dilger's confidantes in Baltimore later told investigators that Giessler was a lieutenant colonel in the General Staff and described him as "a personal friend" of Dilger. A cable sent early in 1918 from the General Staff to Madrid, where Dilger was then staying, indicated that the Giesslers and Koehlers knew one another well. The message for Dilger read: "Greetings from the Giessler and Koehler families." According to a U.S. investigator, "Giessler and Dilger were on very friendly terms...." The German Foreign Office preserved a separate file that included "information from ... Giessler about his acquaintance with Dilger."

Some of Dilger's German relatives suspected that it was Martin Koehler himself who introduced the young surgeon to Army intelligence contacts. Eda Koehler had an address book with a listing for Rudolf Giessler. And one of Koehler's granddaughters recalled being told that Anton "was fascinated by Nuxe Giessler"—the colonel's vivacious wife. The granddaughter added: "Perhaps another love affair."

Louis Dilger's mother-in-law once said that "Martin Koehler had a great influence on [Anton] getting into those circles that were involved and instrumental in the whole business. [Anton] was an ideal person for their work [but] he was much too refined and sensitive to be mixed up in such doings. ... Although he seemed full of fun and ready for every kind of nonsense, this seemed like a coverup for a deep anxiety and seriousness ... and the crazy recklessness. ... "

Dilger's brother-in-law, the professional German soldier Hubert Lamey—a colonel in 1918, a general by the end of World War II—also may have played an important role in introducing Anton to Army officers in the General Staff. In 1918, Lamey told Anton's sister Eda that he was aware of the nature of Anton's "business ... and the goal of his commission and endeavors." Lamey also described Anton as being on "a special mission" for "his newly adopted Fatherland."

And Carl-Erik Koehler's wife, Lisa, recalled later that Anton had established important military contacts in Rastaat that may well have influenced his later decisions. "In his time at Rastatt, he made the connection [with the] family of a [future] German general," she wrote.

What is clear is that Anton Dilger had exemplary references through his German family—and a record of service in the Balkan Wars. He had put himself in harm's way as a surgeon. He was daring and accomplished in his profession. And, perhaps most importantly, he had become a German patriot while possessing an American passport.

A FEW DAYS AFTER the Great War broke out, Dilger's older brother Carl wrote from Montana to his sister Jo about "this terrible, murderous, uncivilized war," and expressed deep concerns about his sisters' families in Germany. They may have opposed the war itself, but the Dilgers and most other German Americans hoped that Washington eventually would join Berlin's side or would, at the least, remain neutral in the war.

While Anton Dilger continued his surgical work in Rastatt, a German U-boat sunk the British liner *Lusitania* in May 1915, drowning 1,200 innocent people, including 128 Americans. In the end, sabers were rattled and harsh words were flung between Washington and Berlin, but no declaration of war was forthcoming, in part because of the strenuous opposition of the more than 10 million German Americans.

"I am anxiously waiting to see what will come out of the sinking of the *Lusitania*," wrote Dilger's sister Jo in Washington to Eda in Mannheim shortly afterward. Indeed, the whole world wondered whether the United States might be incited to declare war on Germany. She added: "Those Americans [aboard the *Lusitania*] invited this trouble and so they received all that was coming to them. I only feel sorry for the little children. [The] United States will never go to war over it, for we know we would get a good thrashing from Germany.... "

Her views on the *Lusitania* were common to many ethnic Germans, including journalist H. L. Mencken, one of the most outspoken and prominent Germanophiles of the twentieth century's first decade. In his column in the Baltimore *Evening Sun*, Mencken called Britain "the bully" who "has at last met an antagonist who knows how to strike boldly and terribly." Two weeks after the sinking, Mencken wrote: "Without the help of the United States, England faces an almost absolute certainty of defeat and destruction in this war." He accused Britain of "unrivaled casuistry and dishonesty" for enticing innocent American civilians to travel on a passenger liner that secretly contained ammunition and explosives the Allies would use against the German Army in Europe.

Mencken, who had been born into a family of German American cigar makers in 1880, once described himself as "a larva of the comfortable and complacent bourgeoisie." Joining a newspaper staff at age nineteen, he quickly rose to become one of America's best-known newspapermen, critics, and magazine editors. A member of the German Society of Maryland, Mencken displayed in his home a photo of Kaiser

Wilhelm that the emperor had autographed in appreciation of one of the scribe's magazine articles.

Known as the "Sage of Baltimore," Mencken was proud to defend Germany in what he regarded as an Anglicized profession, a feeling he shared with Theodore Dreiser, with whom he developed a lively friendship. Dreiser, also a German American, was a Midwestern newspaperman who became a celebrated novelist, author of *An American Tragedy*, *The Genius*, and *Sister Carrie*. In their letters, Mencken and Dreiser poked fun at the New England literary establishment. As World War I approached, both writers continued to defend the Kaiser and criticize the British king. The two men often differed on literary questions, but they shared a disdain for the British intelligentsia and a fervid enthusiasm for imperial Germany before the U.S. declared war.

Shortly after the Great War erupted in 1914, Mencken had written to Dreiser: "How do you stand on this war? As for me, I am for the hellish *Deutsche* until hell freezes over." Dreiser's response: "Personally, I think it would be an excellent thing for Europe and the world—tonic—if the despicable British aristocracy—the snobbery of English intellectuality were smashed and a German Vice-Roy sat in London." Mencken agreed: "My one hope is to see them in London. English pecksniffery must be crushed."

In November 1915, Mencken wrote to Dreiser that critics' attacks on *The Genius* demonstrated that "the grand crime, in these days, is to bear a German name ... There can never be any compromise in the future between men of German blood and the common run of 'good,' 'right-thinking' Americans. We must stand against them forever, and do what damage we can do to them, and to their tin-pot democracy."

A month later, Mencken complained of the "maniacal fear of the German." In February Mencken warned Dreiser, tongue-in-cheek, to take care during his upcoming visit to Savannah, Georgia: "Be careful. The presence of barbarian Germans in any American seaport provokes grave suspicion and you may find yourself in jail on the charge of trying to mine the forts in the harbor." Their public praise of Germany would stop abruptly when America entered the war in 1917.

In the meantime, America's English-language press tended to support the Allies in the war, and events in 1915 and 1916 began to turn the tide of American public opinion against the Kaiser. Those events included the *Lusitania* sinking and the attempt by a fanatic ethnic German to assassinate financier J. P. Morgan on July 4, 1915.

But the nation's German American press, which in the old days had been controlled mainly by political liberals, tended to be strident in its defense of the Kaiser during the war's early years. By the time of World War I, many of those ethnic newspapers were edited or owned by younger immigrants whose attitudes more closely paralleled those of imperial Germany. They were also highly susceptible to German propaganda efforts. In August 1915, the *New York World* published a series of articles documenting the German government's considerable financial backing for pro-German propaganda in America. What was left unsaid was that the practice was legal and that other governments—notably, the British—had operated their own propaganda campaigns.

One of Berlin's propaganda arms was a pressure group called the German-American Alliance, founded in 1901 mainly to influence politicians. The Alliance's pro-Kaiser propaganda became increasingly virulent as the Great War progressed. Many of the German-language newspapers went so far as to suggest that America stop selling munitions to the Allied armies.

Germany's submarine warfare might subside, the editorialists suggested, if they stopped carrying ammunition that British and French soldiers would deploy against the Kaiser's Army.

By 1916, the Great War had become a war of attrition. As the battles on the Western Front began to show signs of a stalemate, the German Army's General Staff worried about the consequences of the British sea blockade and the U.S. shipments of supplies and materiel to the Allies. As German soldier and novelist Ernst Juenger wrote in *Storm of Steel*: "What we had ... been through had been the attempt to win a war by old-fashioned pitched battles, and the stalemating of the attempt in static warfare. What confronted us now was a war of materiel of the most gigantic proportions."

The German Army faced two related problems. It was blockaded by sea, so supplies of conventional munitions were difficult to sustain, and the Allies had almost unchecked access to shipping from America. With the sea blockade strangling transatlantic shipments, the Germans could not import horses and mules, which were then badly needed mainly as pack animals to haul artillery pieces, supplies, and soldiers. Unable to buy and transport such animals from the Americas, the Germans could obtain large numbers of horses only by seizing them in conquered territories. The German Army commandeered an estimated 375,000 horses, mules, and asses in French districts it occupied during the war, and at least another 140,000 fresh remounts came from the Ukraine. But it did not take long for those horse supplies to be exhausted.

The Army's General Staff—which, as the war progressed and the Kaiser weakened, increasingly ran Germany as an unofficial military dictatorship—knew that something had to be done. The Navy's U-boats could go after British ships, but they could not stop American exports to the Allies or open up the sea lanes for German trade with North America. As the war began to atrophy for Germany, the General Staff decided to deploy two dangerous new weapons—chemical warfare on the battlefields and germ sabotage behind the scenes.

During the Second Battle of Ypres in April 1915, German soldiers released 168 tons of chlorine gas from 5,730 cylinders along Hill 60 near the Belgian village of Langemarck. The gas moved in a gray-green cloud across positions held by French troops who fled on foot or on horses, opening a temporary gap in the Allied line that was soon filled by reinforcements. British infantryman Anthony Hossack of the Queen Victoria Rifles described the mass confusion as Algerian and French soldiers fled the first successful German gas attack.

"Suddenly down the road from the Yser Canal came a galloping team of horses, the riders goading on their mounts in a frenzied way; then another and another, till the road became a seething mass with a pall of dust over all ... In the northerly breeze there came a pungent nauseating smell that tickled the throat and made our eyes smart. The horses and men were still pouring down the road. Two or three men on a horse, I saw, while over the fields streamed mobs of infantry...."

Chlorine was an effective weapon of terror, but hardly an ideal chemical weapon. It was easy to detect because of its visible cloud and its smell. Because the gas dissolved in water, soldiers could simply breathe through a damp cloth to lessen its impact. And, at typical battlefield concentrations, it tended to scare troops more than kill them.

The British and French had both been experimenting with tear gas, but they cried foul at Germany's use of chlorine gas at Ypres. Over the next three years, the German gas effort, led by future Nobel Prize–winning chemist Fritz Haber, kept a step ahead of the enemy, but the British Army ended up launching more gas attacks than any other combatant. In gas attacks, the Allies had an advantage because the prevailing breezes on the Western Front normally blew toward the Germans.

The British Army's first deployment of chlorine gas, at the Battle of Loos in September 1915, failed because the wind shifted, blowing some of the poison back toward the British trenches. In December, the Germans first used phosgene, a less detectable and more potent killing agent that had the disadvantage of taking as long as twenty-four hours to debilitate its victims. But it was mustard gas, introduced by the Germans in July 1917, that would prove to be the most feared chemical agent. Delivered in artillery shells, mustard gas was heavier than air; it settled to the ground as an oily liquid that evaporated slowly and polluted the battlefield with a potent irritant.

The first wave of gas attacks did not have an immediate impact on horses, which were kept behind the trenches. But once both sides widened the reach of poisonous gas behind the front lines the animals become vulnerable. Mustard gas was extremely hard on horses and mules because it hurt their hooves and forelegs as they walked or trotted across fields covered with the oily material. "It's the animals that suffer the most, the horses, mules, cattle, dogs, cats, and rats, they having no helmets to save them," wrote British soldier Arthur Empey, who said the gas-masked German soldiers looked "like some horrible nightmare." Even the warnings of gas attacks were eerie. At some trenches, soldiers would ring a bell made from a spent artillery shell to warn that poison clouds were coming. Near artillery batteries, gas warnings shrieked out of compressed-air loudspeakers that could project the shrill noise as far as nine miles away.

By the war's end, about a quarter of the artillery shells fired on the Western Front contained gas. While chlorine and phosgene gases attacked the lungs, forcing their victims to struggle to breathe, mustard gas attacked the skin, especially areas like the eyes, armpits, and groin. It caused searing pain as it burned blisters into its victims.

When the German Army launched its last major gas attack on Verdun in June 1916, its artillery fired more than 110,000 chemical shells filled with phosgene. The concentrations of the gas were so high in parts of the battlefield that "men and horses were caught and killed by the terrible fumes," one witness said. In all, at least several thousand horses were killed and probably well over 10,000 injured by gas attacks. Between one and two horses died out of every ten animals exposed to gas; only three out of every one hundred exposed soldiers perished from the gas. Even so, the human death toll was far higher than the equine casualties; an estimated 85,000 soldiers died as a result of gas attacks on the Eastern and Western fronts.

The effect of the poison depended on the type of gas used, where it was deployed, and the weather. The "blister gases" affected the largest number of horses, but mainly maiming the animals—sometimes causing terrible damage to their forelegs and hooves—rather than killing them outright. The asphyxiating gases, such as chlorine and phosgene, hit fewer horses but killed a much higher percentage.

When the German Army first deployed gas, Haber was at the front lines, observing the attack. A few days after he returned to Berlin, his wife Clara—a brilliant fellow chemist—used his Army-issue pistol to commit suicide. Friends said she had been depressed by the war and repelled by Haber's work. One German general who had opposed the use of gas on the battlefield observed: "The higher civilization rises, the viler man becomes."

The same year that the German Army first deployed poison gas, a unit of the General Staff in Berlin began its separate and highly secret campaign to use germs as a weapon of sabotage. The target would be horses being supplied to the Allied Armies by neutral countries, led by the United States. That unit—known euphemistically as the Political Section, but in reality directing military sabotage and some covert operations—needed to recruit someone who knew how to propagate deadly bacteria, who could enter the United States without suspicion, and who was completely loyal to Germany.

Even though field hospitals near the Front badly needed war surgeons—with German casualty lists from the Second Battle of Ypres in

Belgium and Neuve Chapelle in northeastern France reporting tens of thousands of wounded soldiers—Anton Dilger's work as a surgeon in Rastatt was abruptly interrupted that summer.

His new mission had nothing to do with battlefield surgery. German records indicate that between September 29, 1915, and February 2, 1916, Dilger left Germany "in the service of the Imperial Prussian War Ministry in America."

Shortly before his departure, Dilger met with Margarethe Katz and wrote to his sister Eda in Mannheim that he and his fiancée "will not see each other for a long time." Carefully packing a suitcase, Anton took a train to Amsterdam, boarded the Dutch passenger liner *Noordam*, and sailed for New York City. His ultimate destination: Washington, D.C.

Chapter 5

DEADLY CULTURES

Patriotism is not enough.

—British nurse EDITH CAVELL, the night
before she faced a German firing squad, 1915

WITH A HAUGHTY LOOK OF FRENCH DEFIANCE, the copper lady rose
like a warrior from the harbor's choppy waters—her right arm
raised high, her spiked crown more martial than maternal. The *Noordam*
cut through the waves a few hundred yards away, sending a fine spray
onto a passenger who was leaning against the ship's railing.

A New Yorker encountering him for the first time would have found
a slim man, slightly over six feet tall, with intense green-brown eyes,
black hair, and decidedly continental manners. Dr. Anton Casimir Dilger, at age thirty-one, had an air of sophistication, even mystery—a
charming fellow who might catch the eye of an opera singer or an
heiress on a transatlantic voyage. He spoke English with a slight German accent but insisted to Americans that he was a proud Virginian. As
he wiped off the salty water of New York harbor, he gazed across the bay
at the massive statue.

"Give me your poor," proclaimed the statue's pedestal—in English,
of course—in a city made rich by war profiteers who wanted no part of
the blood of battle. Those poor were now working in dark factories to
make munitions for the Allies. America, he thought, was neutral in name
only. The giant's ornate torch had been fashioned in Paris; the signs on

the island around her appeared in English. He saw no traces of the German culture that had sent millions of immigrants through her portal to America, men like his father who had fought to preserve the Union.

Just two weeks earlier, he had admired the weathered copper skin of the four glorious stallions that pulled Victory's chariot atop Berlin's Brandenburg Gate. Those steeds lunged forever forward. In this time of war, he thought, Victory trumped Liberty.

As the liner passed the Statue of Liberty that evening in early October 1915, Dilger could see the harbor lights flicker through the smoke. Lower Manhattan's stolid brick and stone buildings loomed to the right; across the way, he could make out the dim outline of the Black Tom rail freight terminal and warehouse complex on the New Jersey side of the harbor.

The last time he had seen the great statue, five years earlier, just a few months before his father's death, Europe had been at peace, and he had admired the brash symbol of Liberty. But on this visit, Dilger found no inspiration in France's gift to America.

With a whistle shriek that startled its passengers, the *Noordam* began its slow turn toward the wharves, which streamed with dockhands, baggage carts, and horse-drawn cabs. The ship shuddered as its motors shifted gears and towboats eased the giant vessel into a dock. The sailors tossed down ropes, thick as a man's leg, to dockhands who wrapped them around bollards and slowly drew the ship to shore. Dilger was prepared for a visit that would last several months, and nearly all of his clothes and books and family presents from Germany had been packed into a thick black trunk. But he carried a small case which would not leave his sight now that he had arrived in New York. Without it, he might as well head back to Berlin.

As the steamer docked, motor taxis and horse-drawn carts approached the customs house, waiting for the baggage-laden travelers to emerge. With nothing to declare other than his black trunk and his handbag, Dilger walked quickly through the customs and immigration lines. A coach pulled up to him. The animal hauling it was old, its back sloped, its mane straggly. Coach horses were a dying breed, he observed. Soon they all would be replaced by motor taxis.

At the train station, Dilger stopped to buy a newspaper. To his disgust, the headlines screamed of Allied victories. A week earlier, the French and British had launched three major offensives along the Western Front, bombarding the German lines with artillery shells shipped from New Jersey. At a cost of tens of thousands of lives, the French had advanced by three thousand yards at the Second Battle of Champagne and made small but transitory gains at Artois. The British, unleashing a poison-gas attack for the first time at Loos, had advanced some four thousand yards, and might have gained more ground had they not found the gas blowing back into their faces.

One small news item in particular caught his eye: the German secret police had arrested a British-born nurse, Edith Cavell, and charged her with using her Red Cross cover in Belgium to help two hundred Allied prisoners of war escape to freedom. Within two weeks, the hapless nurse would be convicted and then executed by firing squad. Cavell had been betrayed by a German spy who had posed as an Allied prisoner. Before she was shot, Cavell had asked to be remembered as "a nurse who did her duty." Now she was a hero to the Allies.

Dilger tossed the newspaper into a trash can. He was, after all, a doctor who was doing his duty. Walking to the ticket window, he paid his train fare to Washington, D.C., from where the Anglophile president professed sham neutrality while his profiteers sold munitions and a half million horses to the Allied armies. His sister Jo had warned him that America's English-language press was, on the whole, firmly behind the Allies. The Kaiser was lampooned daily; the Germans were called "Huns," and false reports of German atrocities—cutting off children's hands, raping Russian women, rendering soldiers for oil—were widespread.

The last time Dilger had been home, he basked in the glory of being an educated German in America. Then, the Old Country's music, philosophy, literature, science, and universities were widely admired. He had been able to boast of his M.D. from the University of Heidelberg. But the sinking of the *Lusitania* had changed the national mood. The U.S. Ambassador in Berlin had decried the "wave of exultation" that spread across Germany "to celebrate the sinking of the *Lusitania*" just as reports were circulating of the German Army's initial poison-gas attack at Ypres. Barely six weeks later, a Secret Service agent had discovered documents in New York confirming reports that the Germans had spent $28 million to pay for extensive sabotage and propaganda activities within the United States.

Sabotage: such a strange word, a relative concept, Dilger thought. When two nations were at war, nothing was considered to be sabotage— every heinous act seemed fair game. But when the United States actively supported the Allies by selling them ammunition to kill German soldiers, and horses to pull the big guns and carry the shells, it was not considered sabotage against Berlin. It was simply good business. The United States pretended that its business was neutral. But weren't those busy munitions factories and ceaseless horse sales sabotaging German prospects in the war?

As the train to the nation's capital rumbled through rural New Jersey, Delaware, and Maryland, Dilger watched horses pulling carts in streets and plows on farms. America was a great horse-breeding country, from Kentucky's Thoroughbred stud farms to Missouri's mule factories to the Army horse depots of Virginia, Montana, and Oklahoma. When the train finally screeched to a halt at Washington's Union Station, Dilger gripped his bags, stepped onto the platform, and looked around. There, across the crowd, stood Jo. As soon as she saw him, Jo ran to embrace her younger brother.

Her husband, Adolf, was working, but she had hired a cab whose driver loaded the doctor's trunk into the storage area and drove them down North Capitol Street. Dilger held on to his handbag. He could see the white dome of the U.S. Capitol in the distance, the nearby office buildings—so new and small when compared to the glories of Berlin. The horse-drawn cart clopped down the cobblestones of the city's tree-lined streets, finally stopping in front of a stone house on Lanier Street in the Mount Pleasant neighborhood. The autumn air was brisk, the trees along the street ablaze with red and yellow leaves. It was the perfect season to be in Washington.

I need to find a house, he told his sister. They talked about trendy neighborhoods and rental prices. He explained that he wanted a place that was secluded, a place where he could hang his shingle as a physician and set up a small laboratory for his medical experiments. Dilger presented gifts to Jo and told her about their sisters and their families in Mannheim and about life in wartime Germany. He didn't conceal his pride in his nephews.

Later, Anton held court at the dinner table, every inch the cultivated and brilliant doctor back from the Old Country. Conversation touched on President Woodrow Wilson, American exports to the Allies and the president's plan to keep America out of the war. Between courses of Jo's sumptuous meal, they spoke of the growing pressures on German Americans to distance themselves from Berlin. And they discussed the U.S. Army horse farm that now occupied nearly a third of their late father's Virginia estate, Greenfield. The next morning, they visited Rock Creek Cemetery in Washington to view Leatherbreeches's grave—the first time that Dilger had seen it.

Lichen already had encrusted the gravestone's top, even though the white-bearded Hubert Dilger had died just four years earlier. Anton Dilger, hat held in his hand, stood in silence before the grave. He listened for a few minutes to the wind in the trees and, in the distance, the trickling of water in the distance. Then he turned and walked away.

GREENFIELD FARM EXERTED a powerful attraction for Anton Dilger, but something beyond pure nostalgia drew him to visit Front Royal and Greenfield for a few days that autumn.

Night frosts had begun to paint the oaks and maples of the Blue Ridge Mountains, adding stunning reds and yellows to the Shenandoah Valley's summer pallet of the deep green and brown. As he looked out the window of a train that was passing through Virginia, Anton could see why his German father had loved those hills.

From the Black Forest to the Blue Ridge, his journey over the past few days had replicated the life journey his father had taken more than a half century earlier, quitting the Grand Duke of Baden's horse artillery to make a name for himself in Abraham Lincoln's America.

The train passed the horse country of central Virginia, rivaled only by Kentucky as a grassy equine Eden for breeding the best horses. Then it began to rise slowly in the rich green foothills of the Blue Ridge, the ancient Appalachian range that had been worn down to knobs of stone, forested over so that only patches of rock were visible. Dilger was getting close to home. After crossing a bridge over the Shenandoah River, the train pulled into Front Royal station.

Waving from the back of the small train station was his older brother Butz, who stolidly ran Greenfield Farm. He wore dirty overalls but had pulled on a pair of good boots and run a comb through his thinning hair. Butz had thickened over the years, and he had the weathered tan of a man who had spent much of the summer outdoors, in the fields and pastures. They gave each other a hug, with Anton greeting "Butzie" *auf Deutsch* while his brother responded in English. A porter carried Anton's trunk to the horse-drawn cart, harnessed to one of Leatherbreeches's favorite steeds.

They rode down the dirt highway from Front Royal, across rolling hills, and then came to the tin "Dilger" mailbox and the simple wooden sign: *Greenfield*. The memories welled up in Anton: riding behind his father; digging up bullets and rusted shrapnel from the Civil War skirmishes in the woods; walking to the big wooden barn with his older brothers—Butz, Edward, Carl, and Louis—to feed the horses, shovel manure, and herd the prize cattle into their corrals. And, one by one, the departures of his older sisters—first Elizabeth, then Jo and Eda, and finally Honeybee—to marry wealthy German men after ceremonies at the Greenfield mansion, with its spacious parlor, dining room, and front porch.

Finally, the cart turned up the dirt road, past the marsh and around the bend, where he could see the rebuilt Greenfield mansion, a Southern-style house with cedar pillars supporting its big front porch. It was an idyllic setting, with the house up on a small hill above a rich green valley of marshy land. A black walnut tree, planted by the patriarch, grew to the left of the porch, and three hemlock trees loomed on the right. Oaks, lindens, walnuts, and princess trees also grew in the valley by the house.

On the porch stood his sister Em, still handsome at age forty-eight, her hair pinned back and a wide smile on her face. She untied her apron and let it fall to the wooden porch floor as she rushed to meet her favorite brother. They embraced for a long while, for they had always been close. When the war had broken out in Europe, Em, more than any of the others, had been afraid that her brother would enter the fray and be killed on the Front. Now, at last, he was home at Greenfield.

The farm wasn't as well kept as it had been in the old days. Some of the fields lay fallow; there were fewer cattle and horses in the giant barn; and weeds sprung from around the rock walls that crossed the property. The most remarkable change, however, was the presence of the U.S. Army in "Dilger Field."

Anton walked around the house and reminisced about the good times his family had on the farm. Before the fire, the grand old mansion had hosted piano recitals, fancy formal dinners, even Gilbert and Sullivan operettas, and family readings of books or plays by Johann Wolfgang von Goethe, Friedrich Schiller, and Charles Dickens.

Even the new house, financed by Martin Koehler's generosity, had its charms: formal living and dining rooms with plaster and lathe walls, a spacious kitchen, and a side entrance with a driveway for visitors' carriages to drop off passengers for special events. Anton's favorite spot was the whitewashed porch, full of chairs and lounges. Thick ropes of wisteria vines had wrapped themselves like Christmas garlands across the porch front and cedar posts. Opening onto the spacious porch was a wide door flanked by six shuttered windows.

As he walked past the porch and toward the barn, Anton heard the whinnying of hungry horses, waiting impatiently for their hay and oats. He spotted his father's favorite horse, Valley Boy, waiting at the barn door. The animal's back was bowed; his eyes looked tired as he strained to recognize the stranger who had left the farm so long ago. Dilger saddled up a younger horse and was riding across the fields when he saw a long procession of horses heading up the hill toward the high fields that his father had called Mountain View. The Army was breeding and training horses, brought to Front Royal by train from Kentucky and Tennessee and Virginia. A hundred or more of the animals wound their way up the hill toward the army stockade.

At the dinner table that evening, Anton told Butz and Em that their sister Jo had helped him find a house in the new Chevy Chase neighborhood in Washington where he could set up shop as a doctor. He suggested to Em that, if she were willing, she might keep house for him. And he invited their brother Carl, who was looking for work, to come along in two weeks and help with the lab.

The day before he left Greenfield, Anton saddled up Butz's best stallion and took one last ride. He galloped across the Valley Retreat area and then rode into Front Royal, past the house where Confederate spy Belle Boyd had lived when she fed Union secrets to Stonewall Jackson. Then his horse trotted past the house where his older brother Edward, the jockey, had committed suicide a decade earlier. He rode back through woods toward Mountain View. It was a journey through a land of wartime valor and passion, but often divided loyalties.

Dilger slowed his horse, dismounted, and sat in the shade near an old rock fence from the Civil War years. His father and Abraham Lewis had rebuilt some of the fences in the 1880s and '90s with rocks ploughed up from the fields. Near the bank of Posey Creek, Dilger spotted a rounded object in the dirt. He leaned over and picked it up: a minié ball, the mainstay of Union rifle ammunition. Red dirt flaked off the lead sphere as he rolled it gently between his fingers. He dropped the bullet into his pocket—a war relic, a good omen—as he walked back to the house.

Em had just finished brewing a pot of tea. She served him a piece of apple pie and they sat in the parlor, listening to the birds. In the distance, Butz was shouting at something—perhaps one of the old horses that pulled the plough. *You need to get away from here, Em*, he said. She gave him a long look. Devoting her life to her parents and, now, her older brother, she had passed up earlier opportunities to marry. Now she was trapped, with nowhere to go.

Come to Chevy Chase with me, he said. *It's a nice house. There will be plenty to do. And Jo's place is not far away. I expect Carl to come soon. It will be like old times.*

He had mentioned all this before, but Em had demurred. She had lived for so long at Greenfield that it seemed wrong ever to leave. This time, though, on the verge of Anton's departure, and perhaps sensing that he would not be coming back to the diminished farm again, she changed her mind. Butz would have to make a go of the place. She would spend her time with her two brothers who had been away for so many years.

I'll come, she said, picking up the empty tea cups and carrying them to the kitchen sink. Now that the decision had been made, Em felt exhilarated. She would have a new house, a new neighborhood. Perhaps she could find a new life outside of Greenfield.

Then that's settled, Anton said, bounding up the stairs. He badly needed a housekeeper whom he could trust in Washington, and he trusted no one more than Em.

At dawn the following day, as the first rays of the sun shot through the window, Anton opened the small case he had been guarding ever since he had left Berlin a month earlier. He unwrapped the velvet padding inside the case, revealing four glass tubes within. They had been carefully wiped clean of fingerprints. The sunlight caught the glass cylinders as he held them up and peered inside. One of them, marked "B," contained a brownish gelatin that he had hesitated to carry with him. *B* stood for *bos*, the Latin word for "ox" or "cattle." He had lived in fear that the vial would break—in Berlin, in Holland, aboard ship, in New York, or in Washington. But it was in pristine condition.

Another vial, marked "E," held a pale yellow gel that glowed softly in the reflected sunlight, giving the contents a surreal look. It seemed odd that this innocent-looking substance could hold something dangerous, even fatal. Carefully, Anton rewrapped the vials in their velvet and placed them gently in the case.

His luggage was ready, and Butz had brought the carriage to the side entrance of the house. Out the window, Anton could see the horse, pacing impatiently and biting at the bit as it waited for them to walk down the creaky wooden stairway and out the door.

The three Dilger siblings had a quick breakfast and dragged the luggage to the side door. Butz loaded Anton's trunk into the back of the carriage, but Anton held on to the smaller bag, patting the horse, Valley Boy, before he climbed into the seat next to Em.

As the carriage rattled down the driveway, Em looked back at Greenfield, watching it disappear behind a stand of oak trees. She hardly said a word on the way to the Front Royal train station. Anton was looking ahead, not behind. He pulled the old minié ball from his pocket and rolled it in his hand as Valley Boy took him over a rough Virginia road to the next stage of a journey that had begun in Berlin. For all his fondness for Greenfield Farm and the many pleasant memories of childhood, it was not his family, but *B* and *E* that had brought him back to America.

E stood for *equus*, Latin for "horse," and the code word chosen for a deadly germ that Anton Dilger would deploy in the sabotage campaign he was about to begin.

Chapter 6

"ABSOLUTE SECURITY" IN CHEVY CHASE

A morbid product, I am afraid ... How he gloated on those cultivations of disease germs!
—H. G. Wells, "The Stolen Bacillus," 1895

ECHOING DOWN THE EMPTY STREETS, the *clomp-clomp-clomp* of hooves striking pavement woke Anton Dilger in the middle of the night. He got out of bed, pulled on a robe, and walked downstairs in the darkness, careful to avoid knocking into the unfamiliar edges and corners of the new house. When he opened the front door, a strong wind pressed against his face. Tree limbs rustled; their fallen leaves scuttled across the street. Anton could hear the horse trotting off into the distance—perhaps a lone rider on a nearby street, the horse tired after a long night on the road.

The sound reminded him of his boyhood. Then, the night rider would have been his father, the white-bearded old soldier galloping his horse down the gravel road and dirt paths of Greenfield Farm. The aging war hero, often restless late at night, would saddle up his white stallion, Valley Boy, and ride through the darkness while his wife and children slept. Sometimes he would not return until dawn, showing up at the kitchen door with his face bloodied by scratches from tree branches that had whipped across his face as he rode.

Like his father, Anton Dilger was restless; like his mother, he some-times saw and heard things that no one else seemed to notice. Both of his parents were long dead, but Anton could feel their presence now as he stood in the autumn darkness, his first night in the house in Chevy Chase, and listened to the fading sounds from the street.

Dawn was fast approaching. The milkman, dressed in white, soon would be riding his horse-drawn cart down the street, placing cool bot-tles on the neighbors' doorsteps. Dilger quietly shut the front door and—careful not to wake Em, who was sleeping upstairs—walked down the wooden stairway into the cellar. The house was new and, thanks to the genius of Thomas Edison, the flip of a switch turned on an electric lightbulb. The sudden illumination painted the bare walls and cast shad-ows into the far corners.

This basement would be his work space; it was the reason why he had decided to rent this house. Over there, in the corner, he would place the incubator. On the walls near it, he would have a workman install wooden shelves to hold the dozens of glass bottles and vials and petri dishes he would need. Fortunately, there was an easy source of water—a small laundry sink with a faucet. In another corner, a hot-water boiler, connected to a network of pipes that crisscrossed the exposed ceiling, would keep the place warm.

He snapped open the latches of the case he had carried from Berlin and examined the glass vials inside.

This was Anton's armory. His father, an artilleryman, had carried a sword and pistol in the Civil War; his favorite nephew, a German caval-ryman, carried a lance and gun; his infantrymen nephews toted rifles on the Western Front. But Anton—doctor, spy, and soon-to-be saboteur—brought nothing but glass vials with him when he set up his headquar-ters, six miles from the White House.

THE NEW TENANTS ON 33RD STREET were the talk of the neighbor-hood. Em was a charming Virginia hostess, a beautiful lady of refined tastes. She chatted with her new neighbors and brought out cups and saucers of fine European china when she served coffee and biscuits to her sister Jo, who rode the Connecticut Avenue tram to Chevy Chase from time to time for pleasant afternoon visits. It's true that Em was a bit old-fashioned and had become accustomed to having servants at her home in Front Royal. But she had grown up on a farm, albeit a genteel Virginia estate, and she had no qualms about sweeping floors and washing dishes herself.

Eligible young women in the neighborhood could not help but take notice when Anton strolled about. After all, he was handsome and approachable, with sophisticated tastes in opera and theater. His manners were perhaps too refined for the comparatively provincial Washington scene, but he tried not to be a snob; he did not want to draw too much attention. A friend described him as "clean shaven, a good looking chap.... He was dark, tall ... and rather slender; had large eyes."

On top of all that, Anton Dilger was *fascinating*. In contrast to the white-coated dullards who normally manned Washington's medical clinics, he brimmed with stories about his harrowing wartime adventures as a surgeon in Germany and Bulgaria. At dinner parties, he would pull up his jacket sleeves to show off the golden cufflinks that had been presented to him by the grateful Bulgarian king for his exploits and expertise as a battlefield physician. His soulful eyes would hint of the terrors of war; his slightly accented words added panache to the finely polished tales.

The pleasant and impeccably dressed pair seemed to be perfect tenants for the two-story brick house that opened up for rent in the summer of 1915 on a quiet street not far from Connecticut Avenue and the Chevy Chase Circle tram turnaround. Chevy Chase, which had been named for a famous hunting ground in the Cheviot Hills of northern England, had remained a mostly rural area until an ambitious U.S. senator began buying up the land in the 1880s and lobbying successfully for a tram line to connect the fields with the District of Columbia's more established neighborhoods. "What fun we did have!" wrote a Chevy Chase schoolteacher about those early days. "The robins and bluebirds flew in and out of the windows, the chipmunks darted here and there in the halls, and the flying squirrels thoroughly enjoyed our unoccupied second floor." In the pasturelands around Chevy Chase Circle, she wrote, bloodroots grew "almost as large as water lilies." Farther to the west, "the banks of Broad Branch were carpeted with birdfoot violets, spring beauties and anemones grew in the woods east of Connecticut Avenue, while west of the avenue hepaticas were plentiful."

By 1915, Chevy Chase was a fast-growing neighborhood, made feasible and fashionable by the construction of the tram line across the Rock Creek valley, which separated the semirural area from downtown Washington. "CHEVY CHASE—In a Grove of Trees" proclaimed a real estate ad in the *Washington Post* boasting of "houses that are buttressed into absolute security.... Uncle Sam couldn't build better if erecting fortifications." With houses selling for as little as $7,000, real-estate agents claimed their deals made "outright purchase easier than the payment of rent."

But Anton Dilger, for his own special reasons, had opted to rent. It helped that Chevy Chase was a new neighborhood, with lots of house construction, plenty of fresh faces, and strangers coming and going. With all the distractions, no one had any reason to notice what the next-door neighbors were doing in their basement.

The house on 33rd Street was a pleasant place for Em to spend her days. It had oak floorboards, cherrywood window frames, a nice brick fireplace in the parlor, and a cherrywood sliding door that could be pulled shut to separate the entry parlor from the living room. The two bedrooms upstairs had doorways that opened onto a six-foot-wide roof terrace with wooden banisters. And the spacious and clean basement, with its secluded exit to the backyard, was a vast improvement from the damp cellar that used to scare the children at Greenfield Farm.

Anton told his sister that his basement laboratory would be necessary for his medical research. To bolster giving the impression of the young professional—even though he had no license to practice medicine in the United States and apparently no interest in seeing patients—Anton Dilger boldly listed his real name and his new address in the Washington, D.C., directories under the rubric "physician."

BEER BREWERS KNOW a thing or two about propagating yeast, and Carl Dilger was no slouch when it came to beer—brewing the stuff as well as drinking it. After all, the burly, mustachioed fellow had learned his trade around the vats of the Heurich Brewery in Washington, where every worker got free beer as well as a decent wage.

Carl, called "Jackie" or "Fat" by family members, moved into the Chevy Chase house just a few days after his brother and sister had arrived there from Front Royal. The rental cottage, a perfect fit for two people, was a bit crowded when Carl brought his bags, which were covered with stickers from faraway places like Chicago and Milwaukee and Miles City, Montana. But Anton didn't plan to stay at the Chevy Chase house for very long.

Anton loved his older brother—whom another relative described as "sentimental and loyal," devoted to Anton and his other siblings—and always forgave Carl's failings. As the second son of a large family, Carl had not inherited any part of the ancestral Virginia farmland, and, in contrast to Anton, had not distinguished himself in school. Carl had fallen in love with a woman in the District of Columbia who bore him a son out of wedlock, but then his stern father had forbade him to marry her. Unhappy and restless, Carl had embarked on a series of jobs and unsuccessful business ventures that took him from Washington to the Midwest and then to Montana. But then, in the early fall of 1915, Anton had offered Carl a paying job in Chevy Chase that would involve some travel and the use of his brewing talents. Carl, who at age thirty-six tended to be morose and emotional, was primed for a new adventure, and he needed the money. His Montana brewery may have failed for financial reasons, but the beer itself had been tasty, a rich German-style lager. Carl's knowledge of the brewer's ancient art—using yeast and other ingredients to ferment beer in vats—was a quality that could prove useful to Anton.

Dilger did not waste time getting down to business in Chevy Chase, for he was anxious to get back to Germany. He had not left Germany to escape the war but rather to participate in it, in a way that made use of his unique skills. In Chevy Chase, the only way he could help his nephews in the German army was to try to slow supplies to the Allied forces in Europe. Other saboteurs aimed at ammunition; his target was horses.

The doctor decided to tell Em nothing, to protect her if things went wrong. Invoking the mysteries of his profession, he told Em that he needed to set up a laboratory in that basement to pursue his medical research. He and Carl started making the rounds of supply shops to find laboratory equipment and small wire cages for the guinea pigs they bought. By the time they were done, the formerly empty cellar had been transformed. The incubation oven, the sterilizing machine, and the rows of glass vials and Petri dishes on shelves gave the place a scientific look.

Later, Anton's associates would call the Chevy Chase cellar "Tony's Lab." The basement, about twenty-five feet square, was a far cry from the bacteriology laboratories at the Heidelberg or Johns Hopkins medical schools. But it was new and clean, and daylight streamed in from the windows, which were set in casements just a couple of feet from the ceiling. Best of all, the house featured a secluded rear entrance at the basement level, under the kitchen, through which Anton and his collaborators could enter and exit discreetly, out of view. The most important piece of apparatus was the incubator, which one less-educated saboteur called the "germ-hatching oven."

By the time Dilger set up that basement lab, most of the bacteria that caused major ailments had been identified and isolated in pure cultures, a technique that allowed researchers to conduct detailed studies of each pathogen, including the conditions in which they would thrive or perish. In Berlin, scientists at the institute founded by bacteriologist Robert Koch—a medical doctor who had won the Nobel Prize for pioneering many techniques used to identify and study bacteria—had discovered many connections between germs and diseases, attracting microbiologists from leading American medical schools who wanted to learn the techniques of the German masters.

Dilger was no Koch, but he had learned in medical school and during his thesis research how to set up a proper laboratory and to isolate and propagate pure cultures of bacteria. Now that he had assembled the necessary equipment in Chevy Chase, he was ready to start producing germ cultures. He waited for an evening when Em was out, spending time with Jo's family, and the house on 33rd Street was quiet. He donned surgical gloves and unstoppered the first vial, labeled "B," which emitted a stale odor. This was the most dangerous bug, so he took pains to avoid breathing too close to the gelatinous culture. Holding a thin wire loop over a flame to kill any contamination, Dilger let it cool for a moment and then plunged the wire into the glycerin-like substance in the vial. With germs now covering the wire, he carefully traced it across the dark growth medium—a mixture of beef broth and blood—inside a glass petri dish marked "1." At the proper temperatures, the microbes would grow along the path traced by the wire. He dipped the wire loop into the original culture again, and then drew it across the contents of a second dish.

Dilger had studied this bacterium in his microbiology courses. *Bacillus anthracis*: the anthrax microbe that had made Koch famous and, later, had sparked a Franco-Prussian war of words between the German physician and the nationalistic French chemist, Louis Pasteur. That scientific battle had occurred in the decade after the Franco-Prussian War of 1870–71, a humiliating French defeat that had led to the demise of Pasteur's chief patron, Emperor Napoleon III, and sparked the French scientist to write: "Each of my studies, to my dying day, will bear the epigraph: *Hatred to Prussia, vengeance! Vengeance!*"

In old Europe, as Dilger knew well, science and nationalism were intertwined. He did not deceive himself into thinking that what he was doing in the Chevy Chase basement was pioneering science. But he would at least be taking the theoretical issues into the real world. Once he had finished the initial propagation of the anthrax germs, Dilger carefully peeled off his rubber gloves and dropped them into the sink. Then he turned to the second set of stoppered vials, the ones marked "E" for *equus*. These contained cultures of the second germ, then called *Bacillus mallei*, which had first been isolated by one of Koch's assistants in Berlin. This microbe, essential to Dilger's purpose, caused glanders in horses and mules.

Anton the doctor and Carl the brewer propagated the glanders germs using a concoction called "Ragitagar-glycerine," a dried culture medium produced by a German chemical firm that provided a perfect meal for the microbes after it was mixed with boiled water and decanted into sterile tubes or dishes to gel. One trick was to keep the culture pure from outside bacteria—the garden-variety bugs that float in the air and flourish in floor dirt—which would otherwise contaminate the bacterial concentrations. Once a culture became contaminated with colonies of other bacteria, it lost its usefulness as a biosabotage agent.

Glanders bacteria grow well at human body temperature and need to be incubated for about two days. After a few days, the microbe's colonies look a bit like curdled milk on top of the glycerine. A few days later, the layer becomes tougher and more yellowish, later turning brown. At that point, colonies can survive at room temperature for about a month, and for longer periods if kept a bit warmer. But too much sunlight or temperatures of more than 130 degrees Fahrenheit (55 degrees Celsius) quickly kills the bacteria.

The germ cultures would be tested on guinea pigs, which were susceptible to both diseases. Testing was essential, for Anton's mission was to propagate viable cultures of bacterial pathogens that would *work*. The first German attempt at germ sabotage in America, earlier that same year, had been a fiasco. Anton Dilger, though, intended to be a different order of saboteur.

WALTER T. SCHEELE'S SPECIALTY was bombs rather than bacteria. But the German chemist knew enough about germs to be disturbed by the contents of a battered suitcase that a stranger brought to him in May 1915.

The intruder who knocked on the door of Scheele's laboratory in Hoboken, New Jersey, claimed to be a special agent sent from Berlin. The man said his name was Erich von Steinmetz and that he was a German naval captain. After Scheele reluctantly allowed the visitor inside the cluttered lab, the captain proceeded to spin a fabulous tale.

Steinmetz claimed to have hand-carried the suitcase all the way from Romania to Clinton Street in Hoboken. Rather than take the usual route through a neutral Scandinavian country to North America, the captain had adopted the false name Steinberg, bought several dresses, and headed eastward through Russia with his deadly baggage. Disguised as a woman at opportune moments, Steinmetz claimed to have crossed Siberia to the port of Vladivostok and then traveled by steamer across the Pacific Ocean to San Francisco. From there, he rode a train across the United States to New York.

Steinmetz opened the suitcase, in which he carried explosive devices and also what he called "cultures." Scheele later described these contents: "A case of these germ cultures containing tetanus, some form of glanders or foot-and-mouth disease, and possibly the germ which they term 'dust germ' occasioning infantile paralysis or meningitis. . . ." It is possible that Scheele confused tetanus with anthrax. However, there are no other mentions in documents of German agents deploying a "dust germ" or the virus that causes foot-and-mouth disease. Clearly, the captain was carrying potentially dangerous pathogens.

Scheele knew enough about pathogenic bacteria to keep his distance from the stoppered glass vials. He had studied chemistry at the University of Bonn and served as an artillery lieutenant in the German Army before moving to New York in 1893. Settling there, he became an agent and "confidential staff officer" for the German General Staff, on a secret cash retainer. Initially, his assignment was to keep track of the American chemical industry and its major factories. Later, after World War I broke out, the German Army attaché in Washington, a cavalry officer who would later become the German Chancellor and play a role in Adolf Hitler's rise to power—Franz von Papen—had asked Scheele to expand his portfolio to cover ammunition and explosives factories.

Earlier in the same month that Steinmetz showed up, the new German agent charged with overseeing the sabotage campaign, Captain Franz von Rintelen, also had asked Scheele to set up a "factory" to make explosives for German saboteurs. But von Rintelen—the self-styled "Dark Invader" whose avowed sabotage motto regarding American war supplies for the Allies was "I'll buy up what I can, and blow up what I can't"—had told Scheele nothing about germ sabotage.

When Steinmetz first showed up in New York, he traveled at once to the German representatives' office at 60 Broadway, where he was directed to take his suitcase to Scheele's lab in Hoboken. But now that Scheele had discovered what was inside the baggage, he told Steinmetz to get out. When the naval captain protested, "after a violent altercation, [I] struck Steinmetz in the face and knocked him down, and put him out of the office with his germs," reported Scheele. Later, he described Steinmetz as "a scoundrel of the lowest order."

Dr. Scheele, it seemed, had certain scruples. He didn't mind making explosive or incendiary devices to damage transport ships or knock out ammunition factories and depots in neutral America. Nor did he object to manufacturing capsules in his lab that would ruin shipments of American cornmeal by spattering it with methylene blue dye. But, as Scheele told U.S. investigators in 1918, he had drawn the line at propagating and using pathogenic bacteria for sabotage.

But killing American horses and mules had become a strategic priority. The first tactic employed was conventional sabotage: bombing or otherwise derailing trains packed with horses or mules bound for British remount depots that would ship the animals to Europe. In the middle of January 1915, a German army agent drew up elaborate plans to bomb transport trains on Canada's east coast that were the prime carriers of ammunition as well as warhorses being sold to the British and French. Already, the targeted Canadian Pacific line had carried an estimated 20,000 horses and mules intended for the Allies.

In the end, that saboteur had abandoned the bombing because he had trouble laying the explosives in the cold Canadian winter. Another saboteur did manage to blow up part of the Croix River rail bridge before he was arrested and tossed in jail. Meanwhile, a German agent in Chicago tried to recruit a young German American from Milwaukee early in 1915 to help kill horses and blow up ammunition plants in the East—a mission that was never fulfilled. That agent "told me he had men on hand to poison horses," the Milwaukee recruit testified later, adding that the agent wrote to another German operative in 1915 "about the poisoning of horses, and I was supposed to help him."

Out west, in San Francisco, a young Dutchman discovered yet another horse-poisoning scheme early in 1915. A high-living German baron and his wealthy California fiancée introduced the Dutchman, J. H. van Koolbergen, to a German agent in room 7076 at the posh Palace Hotel. The young Dutchman said the German agent, an adventurer named C. C. Crowley, later "talked to me about the tremendous amount of horses that were being sent to the Old Country, and asked me if I did not know means to destroy these horses. I answered him that I wasn't a veterinary surgeon." Later, however, Crowley told the Dutchman that germs, not bombs, were the ideal way to stop the American horses from getting to the Allies: "The best way to get rid of horses was to procure a culture of glanders [germs] and infect the hay to be loaded with the shipments of horses." The Dutchman said later that he did not know whether Crowley ever deployed such germs but was convinced that "there was a conspiracy to commit an outrage."

Asked about reports that the Germans had sent an agent to the Chicago stockyards to investigate horse shipments, the German consul general in San Francisco said he and an agent had discussed "the horse market in the neighborhood of Chicago, where the Allies used to buy their horses." The agent said the horse stockyard was "probably of interest to [von] Papen ... to find out how many horses the Allies got from the United States."

The surveillance eventually led to a plan to bomb horse shipments out of the Chicago stockyards. The two agents—Crowley and a partner— "went to Chicago, where they visited the stockyards, investigated the shipments of horses to the Allies and made plans to put bombs in the cars transporting them," according to later testimony. The focus on horses intensified as war planners in Berlin saw that resupply would be crucial if the war continued as a stalemate and the British sea blockade could not be broken. Yet another German agent said he had been sent on several missions in 1915 to investigate Allied supply shipments from East Coast ports—including "information from those cheap employment offices who advertise for Americans to take horses to England and France."

British intelligence operatives in New York were concerned enough about horse sabotage by Germans to send a former Scotland Yard Special Branch agent to Chicago "for the purpose of investigating a number of complaints which had come to the British Consulate in New York City respecting the poisoning of horses that were being collected in the United States for shipment to British forces abroad." But the agent was later diverted away from the horse-killing investigation and asked instead to find out if Germans were involved in blowing up a munitions depot. Meanwhile, a British journalist reported that German agents were paying saboteurs to poison feed and water troughs at holding corrals for horses in the Midwest.

So it should not have been a complete surprise to Scheele when Steinmetz turned up in May 1915 with a suitcase full of germ cultures. After Scheele booted him and his germ cultures out of his laboratory, Steinmetz tried to deploy the germs anyhow that spring, but nothing seemed to happen to the horses and mules he sought to infect. In one effort, Steinmetz gave cultures to a pier superintendent, who in turn asked an interned German seaman to "shove them up the nose of every third or fourth horse he would see in the stockades and along the ships on waterfronts." But the seaman, it seems, didn't like the idea of infecting horses, and tossed the germs into New York harbor.

Finally, after several tries that seemed to have no impact whatsoever, Steinmetz is said to have posed as a scientist and taken the remaining germ cultures to a microbiologist at the Rockefeller Institute in New York, "under the pretense that they were intended for experimental purposes." That microbiologist pronounced the germ cultures worthless, prompting Steinmetz to abandon germs and embrace explosives for sabotaging ships.

In Berlin, the General Staff apparently realized that the North American germ sabotage would be ineffective unless they sent an agent who knew how to propagate and deploy the deadly but vulnerable microbes. Steinmetz, Crowley, and the other German agents in America had known nothing about bacteriology. By the summer of 1915, the first wave of German sabotage in America was coming to an end; von Rintelen, who had gotten into disputes with the military attachés, was suddenly recalled to Germany. He sailed in August under an assumed name on a Holland-America liner, the S.S. *Noordam*, which stopped in England on its way to the continent. Tipped off that von Rintelen was aboard in disguise, British authorities arrested the Dark Invader on the ship and interned him as a prisoner of war. Shortly afterward, Steinmetz fled to Germany, and parts of the main German sabotage operation began to disintegrate.

But a sabotage group in Baltimore that had operated independently from the New York saboteurs was able to escape detection. That summer, plans were made to expand the group, led by merchant marine Captain Frederick Hinsch, so that its mission would include germ sabotage against horses and mules.

What Hinsch badly needed was someone who knew how to propagate germs. Six weeks after British agents had snatched von Rintelen from the *Noordam*, that same Dutch passenger liner carried a fresh and well-trained agent from Europe to New York to begin his mission. On the passenger manifest was his name: Anton Dilger.

⤳

When the knocking began, Dilger was downstairs in the foul-smelling basement, adjusting the incubator and checking on the cultures. The pounding on the front door grew louder—probably a visitor who knew the Chevy Chase house wasn't empty. Dilger pulled off his rubber gloves and quickly washed his hands before he bounded up the stairs, hurrying through the kitchen and parlor to the front door.

The big man who stood outside was a familiar sight in Baltimore's harbor, but not to Dilger. Tall and stout, with a chubby face and steely eyes, the fellow wore a gray suit, a jaunty fedora, and black boots that went halfway to his knees. Later, a journalist would describe him as "a huge, ruddy man, with blue eyes and yellow hair, agile and energetic and said to be a hard taskmaster." A fellow German seaman was less kind, assailing Hinsch's "vicious and ruthless disposition," which made him completely untrustworthy. On this day in Chevy Chase, Captain Hinsch had a specific task in mind.

So this is the Tony I've been hearing about, Hinsch said in German. He extended his right hand for a vigorous shake. *You have packages for me—yes?*

Hinsch had commanded the Norddeutsche Lloyd steamship company's passenger and cargo ship *Neckar*, which had just left the port of Havana when the Great War broke out. The *Neckar* managed to evade British warships for several weeks in the Atlantic but had put in to Baltimore harbor in the fall of 1914 when its engines had trouble. A year later, the ship was still there, tied up at pier 9 in the Locust Point docks.

Later, a fellow captain would describe Hinsch as being "fearless.... He knew how to handle the men on the docks and commanded their respect by his shrewd intelligence, his flow of seafaring language, and the ready use of his fists when necessary."

Dilger invited Hinsch inside and poured him a drink. The two men reminisced about port cities they both knew, talked about the progress of the war and the men they knew who were fighting for the Kaiser, on sea and on land. Hinsch knew plenty of merchant officers who were now in the navy, spread over the globe. Anton talked about his nephew Peter, who had been killed during the march into France during the war's first weeks, and the Dilger family's military history.

Your father was a German soldier? Hinsch asked, impressed. Anton raised his beer in a mock toast: *a German* and *American soldier ... the best artilleryman in the Union Army*. He told the story of how, as a young man, Hubert Dilger had joined the Grand Duke of Baden's horse artillery and seduced the Duke's daughter. *He would have done anything to fight in the Great War*, Dilger insisted. He would have moved back to Germany, lied about his age, and ridden the best warhorse in Europe to the Front. War offered the opportunity for glory, and the horse artillery and cavalrymen were the noblest warriors.

It's not the cavalry where the horses are needed now, Hinsch said. On the Western Front, they now pulled the big guns and hauled supply wagons. The Germans desperately needed more warhorses, but the American horses were all going to the wrong side in the war. He shook his head.

When they finished drinking their beer, Dilger led Hinsch down the basement steps and into the lab. There, on the shelves, were the vials of deadly cultures, marked "1" and "2." Later, Hinsch would ask Carl and Anton Dilger to "always keep 24 to 36 bottles on hand," so that Hinsch or one of his men could pick them up once or twice a week, as needed.

As for the virulence of the cultures, Hinsch had been quite anxious to avoid the Steinmetz problem of ineffective dead bacterial cultures; Dilger was eager to prove that his concoctions were deadly. He opened the doors to a cage of guinea pigs, each of which had been fed pellets laced with the bacterial cultures a few days earlier. The two animals were languid, sickly. "They will be dead soon," Dilger said.

Satisfied, Hinsch pulled out a thick wallet and counted out money to cover Dilger's expenses. There had been equipment and glassware purchases, the house rental, and salaries for Anton and Carl. A few thousand dollars were handed over, money that came from the Baltimore paymaster Paul Hilken, who in turn had withdrawn it from a German account in New York City.

Finally, it was time for Dilger to give Hinsch the packages. He had carefully stoppered several vials, sticking corks onto the steel needles to prevent an accidental infection. He showed Hinsch how the apparatus should be carried and how it should be used. He included a pair of rubber gloves in each package, and warned the captain that no one should touch the germs directly or they would risk infection themselves. Ideally, the liquid marked "2" should be rubbed directly onto the inside of the horses' nostrils or poured into their feed or water troughs. The cultures labeled "1" could be added to the feed or jabbed into the horses using syringes.

Dilger inserted the two-inch-long vials into the slots in round wooden containers, stuffing cotton into the gaps in the slots and between the vials to protect them. He carefully wrapped each container with brown paper and neatly tied them with string. Hinsch must be careful not to drop them, he warned. And, if the vials should fall and crack, Hinsch should find a way to dispose of the packages before their contents leaked out. Otherwise, Dilger said, the diseases might spread well beyond the corrals.

If a neighbor had seen the portly sea captain leaving the house that afternoon, she might have thought Hinsch was carrying shoe boxes to his Model T Ford parked on 33rd Street. But the big German was extremely careful with those packages, gingerly setting them on the floor near the passenger seat so they would not be toppled or thrown onto the road if the ride ahead proved to be bumpy.

From the doorway of the Chevy Chase house, Anton Dilger watched as the first glass-encased weapons of Tony's Lab were packed into the car. He watched as Hinsch's Ford disappeared around the corner of Livingston Street, and he listened until the sound of the sputtering motor faded into the distance. A threshold had been crossed, Dilger thought, as he stepped inside.

To be sure, there had been previous efforts to use germs as weapons—giving Native Americans the blankets of smallpox victims or catapulting diseased corpses into besieged cities in the Middle Ages. But the people who had collected the blankets or operated the catapults had known nothing about either bacteriology or the microbial causes of disease. This German sabotage campaign had the distinction of being the first systematic use of germs as a tool of modern warfare.

HINSCH DROVE HIS MODEL T along the paved but bumpy roads to Baltimore, a two-hour trip during which he passed more horse-drawn carriages than automobiles. He parked in front of the Hansa Haus, a half-timbered building at the corner of Charles and Redwood streets that had become the nerve center of German business in the thriving port city.

In 1915, Baltimore was a hectic and bawdy port city, with vast harbor quays filled with ships from all over the world. H. L. Mencken's city was also full of German Americans. Built in 1910 as a Teutonic center to house Germany's consulate, shipping lines, and other commercial offices, the Hansa Haus had been designed in the German Renaissance style. A Viking ship fashioned out of ceramic tiles decorated one gabled end of the two-and-a-half-story building; the second floor was lined with stucco panels displaying the shields of the Hanseatic League trading cities, including Hinsch's home town of Bremen.

On the first floor of the Hansa Haus were the offices of the Norddeutsche Lloyd steamship line, whose Baltimore agents were the Hilkens: Henry, a pillar of Baltimore's German American community, and his son Paul, a graduate of the Massachusetts Institute of Technology who was slowly taking over the reins of the business from his father. As prominent businessmen and members of the Germania Club, both Hilkens knew Mencken. With the benefit of hindsight, Mencken wrote later that he had always held the father in "high esteem," but had regarded Paul as "a suspicious character." That suspicion had not prevented Mencken from lunching with the younger Hilken during the war years.

Buoyed by Baltimore's friendly reception of Germans, Captain Hinsch reveled in his sabotage mission. He was a hard drinker and a womanizer. When he stayed overnight in New York City, Hinsch often spent time in Martha Held's hideaway at 123 West 15th Street in Manhattan, where he and other Germans would be entertained by the cherubic former German opera singer or by the attractive young women who also congregated in the jolly and raucous row house.

For all his faults, Hinsch had a reputation for getting things done and keeping quiet about it afterward. Another captain had recommended Hinsch to von Rintelen as being "made of good stuff; he has given ample proof of what a man can do ... once he is bent upon outdoing the enemy."

When the Great War broke out, several Norddeutsche Lloyd ships had taken refuge in U.S. ports, where they were interned and eventually seized when the United States entered the war against Germany in 1917. The chairman of Norddeutsche Lloyd seemed to have no objections to using one of its captains for sabotage missions. Von Rintelen wrote later that the chairman had made a blanket offer: "Take all our ships, take all our men, make use of everything you find in America, and go after those iniquitous munitions. What else are the ships for! The fatherland requires us to do our duty, and the British will have to pay the price anyhow."

Those were Hinsch's feelings, too. In May 1915, he had met with von Rintelen, who asked him to assemble dockhands, German sailors, and others for three main sabotage campaigns: planting explosive devices in U.S. ships carrying munitions to the Allies; distributing flyers urging dockworkers in key ports to strike; and poisoning or infecting horses and mules that were being shipped to the Allied armies.

The top floor of the Hansa Haus was an attic punctuated by six gables with windows that let light stream into the room. That's where Hinsch headed with his packages, which he carried up the stairs with the help of a black dockhand, Eddie Felton, who would help plan how to deploy the deadly products of Tony's Lab.

Felton, a stevedore foreman from a rough neighborhood in Baltimore, had earned Hinsch's trust earlier that year when he delivered printed circulars urging dockhands at two Virginia ports to go on strike. Then Hinsch had paid him to recruit dockhands who would be willing to plant egg-sized incendiary devices aboard transport ships that were carrying Allied supplies including munitions, wheat, and cotton. The circulars and the "dumpling" bombs had been von Rintelen's idea—part of a sabotage campaign to disrupt ship traffic between American harbors and the British and French forces in Europe.

Felton was paid between $150 and $200 a week, depending on how many stevedore helpers he paid to work. He would pay their travel expenses and maybe $10 a night. Whatever was left over, the foreman would pocket for himself.

This time around, Hinsch asked Felton to organize another group of trustworthy dockhands for a special mission, for which Hinsch would pay extra to make sure that no one talked about what they were doing. Hinsch explained what was in the brown-paper packages that he had

carried upstairs. He wanted Felton and his crew to take trains to East
Coast port cities where horses were corralled and loaded into British or
French transport ships.

The biggest British horse corral was at Newport News, but Hinsch
knew of other corrals in Norfolk, Baltimore, and even in New York City,
at an area near Van Cortlandt Park and Yonkers. Felton would either
pick up the germ packages in Baltimore, or Hinsch would deliver them
to him or to the other dockhands when they got to the ports. Later,
Hinsch would praise his foreman to the skies: "Ed Felton was a smart
fellow, always on the job from morning to night."

RESTLESS IN THEIR DOCKSIDE CORRALS, the horses and mules shifted
nervously when the stranger approached through the darkness. The man
had pulled up his collar against the nasty wind that rippled the James
River and whipped across the animal pens of Breeze Point wharf. The
dark hulks of transport ships loomed in the harbor waters, which shim-
mered with lights cast by welding torches at the Newport News shipyard.

The dockhand carried a brown-paper package in his right hand; the
fingers of a pair of rubber gloves hung out of the back pocket of his dirt-
caked pants. Crouching in the shadows, the longshoreman set down the
package, snapped on the gloves and carefully removed the paper to
reveal a round wooden container with a screw-on lid. Inside, protected
by layers of cotton, were two glass syringes, each about two inches long
and three-quarters of an inch in diameter, with a cork stopper at one
end. He pulled the cork from one of the syringes, exposing a steel needle
that extended into its liquid contents.

His foreman had given him the package with the warning that he
was not to touch the needle or to let the yellow liquid come in contact
with his skin. If he did, the boss had warned, he could get as sick as the
horses would.

Pacing the perimeter of the corral, the intruder—a black Baltimore
stevedore named John Grant—looked over the horses and mules in the
British remount depot. There were hundreds of the big animals,
crowded into pens and restless for a run. A few of the corrals were shel-

tered, but most were out in the open, within sight of the dark transport steamers that would take them soon to the battlefields of Europe.

Grant figured that his biggest problem would be avoiding the night watchmen who made rounds across the giant depot, which included wire pens, wooden corrals, and old cotton warehouses that had been converted into stables. His boss, Eddie Felton, had paid off one of the watchmen and the other guard was known to drink cheap whiskey in his station when times were slow. During the day, the place crawled with British remount officers, but they left after dark for their homes or local taverns.

Carefully, Grant drew closer to the first mule corral. This wasn't a job he wanted to do, but he'd been well paid and Felton had said he'd top it the next time if this job was done right. Besides, these were animals, not people. Grant had worked for a few months at a slaughterhouse, and this night duty was nothing compared to the rivers of cattle blood, the gore-splattered tile walls, and the awful stench of death.

At the first pen, where the reddish-brown haunch of an animal pressed against a wooden slat, he took a deep breath before jabbing the needle into the thick hide. The animal flinched and brayed, and before Grant could pull out the steel point the mule turned its neck and came within an inch of biting his rubber-gloved hand. Grant pulled out the needle and ducked out of the way as the animal turned and kicked at the wood slats of the corral.

The sudden action in the pen roused the other mules. They began shuffling around, snorting and brushing into one another. The corral's fence shook with all the movement, which began to disturb animals in the neighboring pen. Surely even a drunken watchman would hear the ruckus. Grabbing the syringe package, Grant crossed the dock to hide in the shadow of a wooden storage shed, his heart racing. He was not a religious man, but he prayed silently that no watchman was close enough to hear the animals' cries of alarm, the whinnies and neighs signaling that danger was near. His first instinct had been to toss the syringes into the river and then lie to his foreman about having finished the job.

But Grant, knowing that the boss would be watching, waited until the night guard had passed; then he came out of the shadows to try again. This time, he would first try to soothe the nervous beasts. Then, when they had dropped their guard, he would strike the nearest animal—jabbing it and immediately pulling out the needle. The second pen was crowded with high-spirited and nervous horses, whinnying and ramming into their neighbors. Grant whispered soothingly to the nearest animals, but then jabbed mercilessly at nine or ten of them. When there was no longer enough fluid in the first vial to refill the needle, he poured the remaining liquid into the animals' water basins and food troughs, which had been set up near the fence.

The stevedore kept in the shadows, wary of any sign of a watchman or British guard. The Brits, he had been told, knew about the sabotage and would shoot at intruders. Grant had a family on Haw Street in Baltimore, and he wasn't willing to die for $10 plus travel expenses. He had gone to work for Norddeutsche Lloyd three years earlier, in 1912, and had worked under Felton the whole time. After war broke out, stranding all of the German line's ships, the regular paychecks had stopped. Then, Felton had offered him "some other work that he was handling." At first, it had been easy: handing out circulars urging dockworkers to strike. Then he had been asked to plant incendiary devices that would start fires aboard ships. And now something that turned his stomach: "sticking needles into horses to make them sick."

Later, Grant explained his easy access to the wharves. "I had visited both Newport News and Norfolk from time to time before starting in this work for Felton and I knew the situation pretty well around the waterfronts. In view of this and the fact that I was a stevedore, I found no difficulty in getting access to the wharves and to the place where the horses were. I did a good bit of the work myself and also occasionally found two or three men whom I thought I could trust and got them to help me."

That cold December night in Newport News, Grant was working alone. He walked over to a third corral, this one full of mules. He knew a little about mules because his father had worked cotton fields as a slave with "cotton mules." There were all sorts of mules in this pen—sorrels, grays, big and small, pack mules, and cotton mules. They all had the broad-arrow British Army brand. And they all looked tired and frightened.

The dockhand wanted to finish the job and get out of there. The wind was getting colder; he'd head someplace nice and warm. Grant pulled out the second vial, exposed the needle, and quickly pierced the hides of wide-eyed mules that shuddered when they felt the needle's bite. They whinnied and moved back and forth, bumping against one another. The jabbing took another hour, and then he was done for that night. He dumped the remaining germs into the feed bins and watched the animals sniff at the poisoned bran and oats. When they got hungry enough, they would eat just about anything.

For the money, this had been easy duty—much less work than hauling and loading crates into ship holds. As the dockhand walked along the wharf, he looked over the remount depot and the animal pens. He wondered how far these mules and horses had come, and how much farther they had to go. They were headed to the war, he knew. Some might die here in the corral, some would sicken in the stinking holds of transport ships, and some would perish on the battlefields.

For a moment, he felt sorry for the horses. How many of them would ever return to their home soil, to the green pastures where they had been foaled? But his second thoughts didn't last long. They were animals, after all, and no better than the thousands of cattle that are herded into slaughterhouses every day.

Grant pulled off the rubber gloves and tossed them and the empty syringes into the river. The vials quickly filled with water and sank, the translucent glass disappearing into the depths. But the germ-tainted gloves floated, the plastic fingers moving in the current like ghostly hands.

ONE OF THE FIRST ANIMALS to be jabbed that night at Newport News had been shipped across the country from a barn dubbed the "mule palace" in a Missouri town called Lathrop that billed itself as the mule capital of the world.

Lathrop was the home of the Guyton & Harrington Mule Company (G&H), the prime exporter of mules and horses to the British Royal Army beginning with the Boer War and continuing through the Great War. At its peak during World War I, G&H housed forty thousand horses and mules at a time.

On the company's six thousand acres of pastureland were the world's largest horse barns, stretching a city block long and half a block wide. G&H had convinced the British Remount Service to locate one of its main animal depots in the town and—making money hand over fist from the Allied army sales—the company built an artificial lake to water the animals, hired four hundred workers, and got three railroads—the Santa Fe, Rock Island, and Burlington lines—to lay track into the small town to transport animals.

The first sorrel jack that Grant jabbed had been a Missouri mule with all the attributes of that famous pedigree—tough, headstrong, and tireless. The term "Missouri Mule" was first used in the late nineteenth century to describe a stout, strong animal that is more easily managed and more agile than his draft horse cousins. At the turn of the twentieth century, nearly half of Missouri farmers either used mules, bred them, or both.

A mule—also known as a "half ass"—is a male offspring of the breeding of a donkey and a horse; the female offspring is called a "hinny." There are two variations on the breeding: a "jack" (male donkey) can breed a horse mare, or a "jinny" (female donkey) can be bred to a stud horse (stallion). The resulting offspring are sterile.

Because they are sturdier and less nervous than horses, mules were considered preferable to their more aristocratic cousins for some battlefield and supply duties. Buyers bought mules from all over the country and shipped them by rail—with as many as nine hundred mules and horses packed side by side in boxcars for two days—to the G&H depot in Lathrop. When mule trains arrived, muleteer boys whooped and snapped their whips to move the animals into the corrals.

Then the mules and horses were driven in herds by "chigger gangs," groups of two dozen or more cowboys who loaded and unloaded the animals from boxcars and drove them to and from the depot corrals to the G&H pastures. "They'd just take down through Main Street or any other street, with four or five horses and riders in front of 'em and three or four at the side of 'em and three or four behind 'em and whoopin' and hollerin' and crackin' their blacksnake whips." A local newspaperwoman described the Lathrop herds using Faulknerian prose:

A murmuring rumble, comes a subdued and lengthened roar, comes at last over the low ridge, a burst of dark and shapeless thing, massive and quivering. . . . Led by a single horseman, a rider driven and swept by crowding beasts behind him, an oncoming surge of flanks and weathers, a hall of hammering hooves and a shriek of wheezing breath and doubling, leaping, gathering, plunging with frightened eyes and quivering nostrils, with thumping flanks and pulsing necks, choked with dust and seared with foam, two thousand bays, blacks and roans. Montanans, Texans, and Missourians jammed, crushed, blurred, dizzy, turbulent and convulsed, choke the road from side to side, sweep on in noise and dust to the measuring tremor of pounded earth.

Mules in Lathrop had been shipped from as far away as Texas and Wyoming, and they faced threats ranging from sabotage poisoning to a pneumonia-like disease called "shipping fever." Others were cut by barbed wire, lamed by kicks from frightened animals in crowded pens, or trampled to death during stampedes. According to one report, German agents sometimes scattered small metal spikes—barbed like fishhooks at the ends—into feed bins full of oats. The spikes could puncture an animal's stomach or bowel. One gang of chigger boys spotted a stranger pouring a yellowish liquid into the water tank in a mule pen one night. When they caught the man and roughed him up, he said he'd been paid by a man with a foreign accent to poison the mules.

When British remount officials found out, they suspected German sabotage. They notified the horsemen and muleteers, put extra guards on duty at corrals and livestock depots, and authorized the local vigilantes to "take justice into their own hands" when someone was caught trying to kill horses. Wrote one British journalist: "Any unauthorized person found near the horses or their pasture was well-nigh lynched. That was rough justice, but it served well."

Dying or lame animals were put down and sent to one of Lathrop's two rendering plants, which the locals called "glue factories." Veterinarians ran a mule hospital in one old barn that sometimes housed seven hundred sick animals, an overwhelming number for a handful of vets. A

Lathrop farmer described "quite a loss" of animals, which died from "anything, everything ... I think the buyers bought about anything they could buy and shipped it because he was getting so much a head."

Most dead mules were skinned so their hides could be sold. One old mule skinner, a former worker recalled, "used to bring his dinner out with him and he'd skin a hide back, maybe the horse had been dead two or three days, and spread his dinner out on that dead animal and set there" to eat his meal.

Over the years, thousands of horse and mule carcasses were either rendered for fat or buried in trenchlike mass graves. One worker described plowing burial trenches that were two hundred feet long, nine feet wide and six feet deep. "They'd fill that trench full of [dead] horses and mules," he said. A local woman said "that was one thing that they never talked a lot about ... because they didn't want 'em to know how many horses they lost."

For the British Army's North American Remount Commission, Missouri was a horse and mule mecca. In Lathrop, the British officers and their wives lived well. There were "real formal ... big dinners and things" to entertain the British and French army buyers, one woman recalled. There were even English-style fox hunts through the Missouri countryside—using some of the eighty-five fox hounds owned by the company's founders—which saw the huntsmen decked out in "snazzy outfits." A local newspaper reported that "officers of the British Remount Department with their leggings and khaki breeches give an atmosphere of color and form to the streets of the town."

After the mules and horses had been rested from their train trips to Lathrop, they were inspected for diseases or physical faults. Then came the big test: whether cowboys could ride them through the huge barn where the British remount inspectors decided whether or not to buy individual animals. The vets and inspectors would stand at one end and watch chigger boys saddle up the horses and try to ride them the length of the barn. "No matter how much [the horse] bucked or how much he raised Cain or what he done, if the man stayed on him 'til he got up to where the buyer was, that horse was qualified." If the horse threw the rider, it was rejected.

The horses that passed muster were taken to a section of the giant barn that smelled of charred horse flesh. Each animal would be held down while a red-hot iron burned into its flesh the broad arrow, the British Army insignia it would carry for the rest of its life. Next, the animals were led to the "hogging" room, where their manes were trimmed and tails "squared" in military style. The most fortunate horses and mules would be rested in pastures for a month or so before they were herded back into the depot corrals and onto train cars by the whip-snapping chigger gangs. Then came the awful train rides, often switching to another locomotive at the stinking stockyard rail junction at East St. Louis before the three-day torture of another train ride to the East Coast.

The North American animals bought by the Allies were not white stallions bred to carry triumphant generals in parades or lead the thundering charges of old-style cavalry brigades. They were equine foot soldiers, the working-class draft animals assigned to haul supplies, pull ambulances, and slog two-ton artillery guns across miles of mud on the bloody battlefields of France.

Their manes trimmed and tails squared, the mules were packed onto a train crammed with two dozen animals in each boxcar, rattling over tracks across the Midwest and the Appalachians. The freight train was headed for the British Remount Service's largest American depot for animals, from which 457,000 horses and mules were shipped to Allied armies abroad during the Great War: Newport News.

THE MAN HAD DISGUSTING SORES all over his body as well as red nodules the size of hickory nuts on his legs and feet. When he was first admitted to a New York City hospital in serious condition in 1915, doctors had trouble agreeing on a diagnosis.

But there was one important clue to the disease: the man's job was to clean out stalls and feed horses during voyages of horse transport ships to Europe. He had come down with the illness after his third such voyage and was rushed to the hospital as soon as that ship returned to America.

The nodules continued to swell, bursting with yellow pus, as the man's condition worsened. He became feverish, delirious, then comatose, dying at age 47 about three weeks after he had entered the hospital. He was a victim of glanders.

When doctors injected some of the patient's blood and pus into guinea pigs, they confirmed that he had been infected with the glanders microbe—the same pathogen that Anton Dilger was culturing in his basement in Chevy Chase. Most likely, the doctors said, the man had a cut or sore that was exposed to the germs when he touched an infected horse or changed its water or cleaned its stall. An autopsy revealed a "glanders invasion of the liver and lungs" leading to degeneration and swelling of the tissues.

Exposure to the germs Dilger had handled for months could be fatal. Before embarking on his mission to America, he had scanned the medical journals for descriptions of cases of human glanders and anthrax. Both diseases were rare in humans, but both were severe—often fatal. Nearly every person who contracted glanders either worked with infected horses or directly with the microbe.

As for anthrax, Dilger did not need to read the medical literature about the danger of that disease to humans who are exposed to the bacteria. When inhaled, anthrax spores cause an awful, pneumonia-like disease that nearly always led to a feverish death. If the bugs get into sores or cuts, they can cause disgusting cases of skin anthrax, with large areas around the wound swelling and turning black. If eaten with food, anthrax spores can infect the gut and kill quickly.

Dilger was extremely cautious when he handled the pathogen cultures, checking his rubber gloves carefully for any tears or defects. And he never tired of warning Carl and the others who came close to the germs—Hinsch, the messengers, and the dockhands—that they could not be too careful in handling them.

After ten weeks, Dilger's main mission in Washington had been accomplished: the "germ factory" was operating smoothly. The shelves in the basement were now lined with gleaming glass vials marked "1" and "2." Dilger did not dirty himself with the actual work at the wharves; in fact, he shuddered at the idea of jabbing a horse.

Once Tony's Lab was in production, Dilger spent more and more time traveling back and forth to Baltimore and other East Coast cities to meet with his paymaster, Hilken, and with other German agents. He enjoyed the smoky back rooms of the Hansa Haus in Baltimore, where the shipping agents and stranded German captains congregated to grumble about the British sea embargo and the American war profiteers who were making huge sums of money selling supplies to the Allied armies.

Dilger especially liked Paul Hilken, a well-educated fellow who enjoyed plays and opera and had quite an eye for pretty ladies. Anton had met quite a few of them himself. Hilken—who at times used the fake name Hildesheimer—knew what was going on at Tony's Lab. He set up a special sabotage account at the Corn Bank and kept meticulous notes about each payment, as if he were doing ship-cargo accounting for imports and exports. One of the recipients was Dilger, referred to as "Dr. D." in Hilken's notebooks.

In November 1915, when Hilken was recuperating from a lung ailment at a beach cottage in New Jersey, Dilger and Captain Hinsch drove up the coast to spend an afternoon and evening with him. The next day they met with Hilken and another German sabotage paymaster, the banker Federico Stallforth, at a New York restaurant. The subject was money: the sabotage account at the Transatlantic Trust Company. Working through Stallforth, Hilken arranged for at least $5,000 in cash to be paid to Hinsch and the dockhands for distributing "the anthrax germs at Norfolk." Dilger was paid separately.

Shortly after those sessions with his paymasters, Dilger began making plans to leave the germ factory in the care of his brother Carl and head back to Germany. If he could get a U.S. passport allowing him to return there, Dilger planned to meet up with Hilken in Berlin early in 1916. Near the end of November, Hilken and Hinsch drove to Washington, probably to visit the germ factory and to pay Dilger. In early December, the entire group met again with the banker in New York.

By the Christmas season, Em was getting a bit concerned about her younger brother, who was clearly not conducting a medical practice in Chevy Chase. No patients came in or out of the house, and he spent less and less time in his basement medical lab—instead, leaving the day-to-day work, whatever it was, to Carl. Later, Em confided to her sister Jo that "she found many of [Anton's] activities and behavior strange and puzzling."

Em hated the pungent smell of the beef broth that the Dilger men brewed and mixed with glycerin for their basement research. Another nuisance was the glassware that Anton kept carrying in and out of the basement, often with markings on them. Most disturbing was the squealing of the guinea pigs, which Anton insisted were part of his medical work. Kind-hearted Em felt sorry for the creatures, especially when Anton would carry out one of their corpses and bury it in the backyard.

Anton wasn't the only problem. Carl was drinking too much beer again and hanging out with unsavory characters, some of whom would show up late at night in Chevy Chase. And then there was the fat captain, Hinsch, whom Em avoided whenever he came to the house to collect the brown-paper packages from Anton or Carl. Despite all the signs that something in the basement was amiss, family members say Em always claimed to be in the dark about the germ sabotage. "I'm absolutely convinced, beyond a shadow of a doubt," wrote Louis Dilger's daughter, that Em did not know what Anton "was doing behind the scenes."

While British remount officers were on the lookout for sabotage at the horse depots, no one suspected the Chevy Chase basement as the origin of the infectious agents. As Christmas approached, with family dinners in Washington and at Greenfield Farm, Anton and Carl kept the germ factory running while Anton waited for permission to travel back to Germany.

He got help from an unlikely source: the U.S. Army's medical corps. He had met a couple of Army physicians when they visited the hospital that he had directed during the Balkan Wars, and he had gotten in touch with them in Washington. One contact was a Medical Corps major, Dr. Robert U. Patterson—who would later become U.S. Surgeon General, the highest-ranking military physician. On the last day of 1915, Patterson wrote a letter of support for Anton Dilger's State Department application to return to Germany.

The letter, typed on the stationary of the American Red Cross Bureau of Medical Service, First Aid Department, gave Dilger the endorsement he needed:

> This is to state that Dr. Anton Dilger, a native born American citizen, is known to me. He has recently returned from Germany where he acted as Consulting Surgeon to a German Red Cross Hospital in Heidelberg. From documents in his possession, and particularly one from the German Red Cross Delegate in the United States . . . I am satisfied that Dr. Dilger will be reinstated in his former position as soon as he arrives in Germany. It is recommended that he be issued a passport in order to enable him to return to Germany to continue his humane work.

WITH A SHRIEK, the steam whistle of the passenger liner *Kristianafjord* announced its departure from the port of New York for the voyage across the cold Atlantic, infested with icebergs in the north and U-boats in the south. The Norwegian ship was one of the few that offered a relatively safe route for Germans trying to return home from the neutral United States in wartime.

Anton Dilger had easily crossed through customs, flashing the freshly granted U.S. passport announcing that the State Department approved his return to Germany for "relief work." On the ship, Anton tried out a new false name that he and Hilken had cooked up that fall: Delmar, an amalgam of Delaware and Maryland. Always up for a new prank, Anton introduced himself to fellow passengers as "Dr. Albert Delmar," an American doctor of German ancestry who would be visiting his parents' homeland.

Also walking up the gangplank to board the *Kristianafjord* that day—January 29, 1916—was a younger, blonde German American named Frederick Laurent "Fritz" Herrmann. He was not well educated, but he was smart and good looking, with the boyish features of a young Charles A. Lindbergh. Herrmann had been born in Brooklyn, grown up in New Jersey, and recruited to be a spy for the German Admiralty, counting ships at British ports. Now he was headed for a bigger game in Germany.

At the time they settled aboard the steamship, neither man knew that the other was a German agent. "Dr. Delmar" and Fred Herrmann settled into their first-class berths, unpacked their suitcases, and prepared for the voyage aboard the Norwegian America Line vessel to Bergen, Norway. Their fellow passengers were the European and American elite—business executives, opera singers, diplomats, writers—and the first-class accommodations were luxurious, with outward portholes and outstanding meals in the best section of the ornate dining room.

Dilger would light his pipe and sit out in a deck chair reading the most recent German newspapers or magazines he could find. He would chat with his fellow passengers and the pleasant Norwegian crew. And he would block out any thoughts about Tony's Lab, Carl and Em, and whatever Hinsch was doing with those germs.

Hinsch's dutiful dockhands had been busy that fall and winter. Up and down the Atlantic coast—at animal pens in Baltimore harbor, near Van Cortlandt Park in New York City, and the corrals at the naval port of Norfolk, Virginia—they jabbed horses and dumped germs into feed and water bins. So long as the German captain doled out the cash and Carl the brewer kept growing new cultures, the germ sabotage would continue.

On board the luxury liner steaming toward Norway, Dilger tried to forget the grisly details and focus his attention on fine wines and sparkling conversation. Chevy Chase seemed so far away now, as the newly christened Dr. Delmar stretched out on his deck chair and gazed across the rough Atlantic swells.

Across that cold ocean, Europe was burning; the patriotic doctor longed to be closer to the fire.

FOUR HUNDRED MILES to the south, an overworked British transport vessel was preparing to load its equine cargo at Newport News. It was shipping day for the seven hundred mules and horses at the dusty British remount depot.

During the Great War, the British Army's Remount Department was the leading player in the intercontinental horse trade. Newport townsfolk were favorably disposed toward the British because the depot was a good customer for local feed and supply firms. At the same time, anti-German sentiment ran high there because the president of the port's single biggest employer, the Newport News Shipbuilding Company, had been one of the Americans to go down with the *Lusitania* when the steamer was torpedoed.

No one liked to think about torpedoes on shipping days in Newport News. After weeks of preparation, the remount horses were setting off for Europe. With a steam whistle, the giant British transport ship edged along the wharf and was tied tightly to the bollards. The horse transport ships had been converted for carrying animals, for horses took up nearly seven times as much room per ton as did the average wartime cargo. The problem was the acute shipping shortage during the war, which led to crowding. The horses and mules would need to stretch their legs and move about.

In the depot's pasture area, members of the remount commission chose the animals in the best condition to ship. They would point to a horse and the chigger boys would rope it and lead it into a special pen. Veterinarians and commission members scrutinized the horses and mules as they passed into the pens; any animal that looked sick was channeled into a "cut out station," where other vets would examine them and test them for glanders and other diseases. The vets took the temperature of every animal and examined their nostrils for discharges—a telltale sign of disease.

The healthy-looking animals were channeled into a wooden viaduct to the wharf, where another commissioner stood at the gate and clicked a hand-held mechanical counter for each horse and mule that passed through driveways into narrow pens where horsemen fitted each animal with a halter. With a man holding each halter, the nervous animals were led up the sloping wooden chutes to the steamer's main deck, which scurried with sailors, "horse boys," and muleteers.

The horses that John Grant had jabbed a few days earlier still looked healthy, for animals exposed to glanders germs take at least a week to show any signs of infection. They were haltered and led to the main deck. The mules, considered hardier than horses, were led into the bowels of the steamer, down two gangway ramps to small pens that were two levels below the deck. The mules were spooked by the dim light, which came only from small electric fixtures above the pens, into which a half dozen of them were locked. The animals were no more crowded than they had been in railroad boxcars, but they were unsettled because they could feel the ship sway.

Soon the mules heard the clomping of hooves on the deck above. These were the horses, which the army vets considered "more delicate and liable to lose condition at sea." The horses, too, were led to pens of five to six animals, with their heads facing a narrow alleyway. The hired horse handlers had to move down that alleyway, brushing against the heads as they rushed up and down with water or food or straw.

Mules are stubborn but tough. Their death rate on transport ships during the Great War, as well as in depots near the battlefields, was about half that of horses. Their other advantage was that they could survive on about three-quarters of the hay and oats rations that horses required. Of the different types of horses, the most disease prone were the heavy draft horses, which pulled heavy artillery and other large loads.

Before the animals boarded the transport ship, their pens and stalls had been "mucked out" and disinfected with lime wash. The foreman and his workers had checked to make sure that feed tins, pails, shovels, brooms, and hay forks were in place and that all water barrels had been filled. But that did little to reassure the nervous animals.

They heard the sharp calls of the deckhands far above, the rumble of the giant engines below, and the grating rattle of anchor chains. They could feel the surface beneath them start to vibrate and then sway slightly. Then the rumbling lessened and the horses and mules felt a strange sensation, a floating movement that surged into the unknown. The dim electric bulbs above each pen began to flicker and then the animals were plunged into darkness.

LATER THAT WINTER, German U-boat Captain Adolf von Spiegel described his encounter with another British transport ship on the same Atlantic crossing.

Peering through a battered periscope, he spotted the steamer cutting across the Atlantic swells toward his submarine. As the ship approached, von Spiegel saw "with surprise and a slight shudder, long rows of wooden partitions right along all decks, from which gleamed the shining black and brown backs of horses."

"Oh heavens, horses! What a pity, those lovely animals!" the German captain said to his officers. But it took no time at all for von Spiegel to resign himself to destroying the steeds. "War is war, and every horse the fewer on the Western front is a reduction of England's fighting power," he wrote in a 1919 memoir.

When the torpedo struck, smashing into the transport vessel and exploding, it spewed a column of water two hundred yards high and fifty yards wide,

> terrible in its beauty and power.... From all the hatchways a storming, despairing mass of men were fighting their way on deck, grimy stokers, officers, soldiers, grooms, cooks. They all rushed, ran, screamed for boats, tore and thrust one another from the ladders leading down to them, fought for the lifebelts and jostled one another on the sloping deck. All amongst them, rearing, slipping horses are wedged.

Then came a second deadly explosion, followed by the awful release of hot white steam that hissed out of the ship's scuttles and hatchways, sending the wild-eyed horses into frenzied but fruitless gallops across the nightmarish decks, which had begun to tilt as the ship's holds filled with water. The animals were doomed, as was most of the crew.

The Atlantic crossings of the Great War became a twentieth-century version of the old "horse latitudes"—the belts of latitude where horse losses were worst in the 1600s and 1700s, when the Spanish first shipped animals to their New World outposts. In those zones, ships sometimes were becalmed for weeks. If their water supply ran out, the horses would perish in the heat and be thrown overboard.

The animals on the British steamer that the U-202 sank in 1916 were among the 6,600 horses and mules that went down with torpedoed transport ships. Another sixty-three animals were reported killed at sea by German shell fire at the transports. A British journalist commented that "more than one good Army horse had his first taste of war and gun fire as he was crossing the sea from his native land."

part two

Germany

Chapter 7

CROSSINGS

Four things greater than all things are—
Women and Horses and Power and War.
—RUDYARD KIPLING, "The Ballad of the King's Jest," 1890

LOUNGING IN FIRST-CLASS BERTHS on the Norwegian liner *Kris-tianafjord*, two Americans—Anton Dilger and Fred Herrmann—were heading, unknown to one another, to the same destination in Berlin. Their ship had become popular for Atlantic crossings because it took the safest route between the icebergs and the U-boats. The same could not be said for these two passengers who, despite their U.S. passports, were heading toward the war.

The spies were a study in contrasts. Dilger, then age thirty-one, was a highly educated and well-connected European sophisticate. Herrmann, who had Lucky Lindy good looks, was a smart but uneducated twenty-two-year-old from New Jersey. Both men spoke German, but Dilger's was flawless; Herrmann spoke the language like a foreigner, with a thick American accent.

Dilger already had a profession and a reputation. Herrmann was an adventurous youth who had done nothing more than work as a sales clerk in New York and, later, report British ship sailings to German naval intelligence. Aboard the *Kristianafjord*, the two drank with abandon, enjoyed the sumptuous meals, and danced with pretty women. They became friends, neither knowing that the other's voyage had been paid for by a German espionage fund. During the war, the *Kristianafjord* was a ship brimming with spies, artists, and the wealthy elite of America and Europe—men and women consuming five-course dinners, quaffing champagne, and waltzing to the small hours in the grand ballroom.

Herrmann enjoyed intrigue and loved to tell stories. In a notebook he kept during his early travels, he boasted of his exploits in Britain and in Germany as an agent for the German Navy. He had been recruited a year earlier aboard a Dutch vessel, the *Ryndam*, by another German agent who had introduced himself as William Kottkamp but whose real name was Paul von Dalen.

Just eleven months before his voyage with Dilger, a wide-eyed Herrmann had traveled to Germany for the first time in February 1915 to visit his grandmother. "We would walk around the boat, play cards, that sort of thing. [Von Dalen] was supposed to be a traveling salesman for the European Textile Co., which made vestments used by Catholic priests," Herrmann recalled later.

It was not until they arrived in Rotterdam and were sharing a room that von Dalen told Herrmann that he was a German agent. He asked the young American: "Well, don't you want to get in on some of that after seeing your grandmother?" Without blinking an eye, Hermann responded: "Surely, why not?"

In Rotterdam, he and his friends from the ship danced with local girls at a music hall, skated at a roller rink, and then caught a morning train for Germany. At the border, Herrmann wrote, "I saw for the first time the famous olive-gray uniforms and spike helmets. They surely did look fine." He chatted in German with the army officers, who told him: "If they were all like you in America, we would be alright."

Herrmann spent a few days with his grandmother before von Dalen contacted him and asked the young prospect to meet him at the Fredrichstrasse train station in Berlin, where they had dinner at a hotel café. The next day they went downtown to talk with Captain F. Prieger of Naval Intelligence. "He asked me if I wanted to go to England ... I thought I would get a kick out of this thing," Herrmann said later. Within two weeks, Herrmann and von Dalen were in Britain.

The young American was given a "pass," stamped with the seal of the German Admiralty, identifying him as a second lieutenant in the

Navy and giving Herrmann permission to travel on any troop train to any point in the German Empire. His mission: "Watch out for the British fleet and report the movements for military intelligence." Herrmann and von Dalen—still posing as vestments salesmen—spent about three months in Britain before British detectives started to follow them. Von Dalen could not speak very good English—a problem for a salesman—so the German spies decided to leave.

Von Dalen wanted Herrmann to accompany him via Holland, but the American, sensing danger, insisted on leaving aboard an American ship from Liverpool to New York. He laid low in the New York area before getting in contact with the German naval attaché, Captain Karl Boy-Ed, on whose request he recrossed the Atlantic in the summer of 1915, this time as a courier carrying secret letters from Boy-Ed to a naval intelligence officer in Berlin.

After another voyage back to New York, Herrmann was asked to travel to Scotland to watch the movements of British ships as they headed in and out of Scapa Flow, the anchorage for Britain's Grand Fleet. In September, Herrmann enrolled as a forestry student at Edinburgh University as a cover so that he could spy on ships in the Forth River's estuary and along the Scottish coast. The previous fall, the German submarine U-18 had tried to get into Scapa to attack the British fleet but was spotted and rammed by a patrolling trawler. After that, the British laid defensive minefields and built gun batteries to support them. Despite the precautions, British Navy commanders lived in fear of the potential damage that an undetected U-boat could do to the ships in Scapa.

Herrmann's coastal surveillance raised suspicions in Scotland. "Things were getting rather warm up there," he said later. He was expelled from England and put on a ship bound for New York. Two close calls with Scotland Yard would be a signal for most amateurs to switch to a less risky career. But Herrmann, who reveled in the excitement, the expense accounts, and the high life of transatlantic cruises, did not hesitate to head back to Berlin. He wanted a new assignment and the Germans again paid for his ticket.

"It would seem to be [more than a] coincidence that Fred Herrmann, an admitted German saboteur, should have sailed for Germany on the same ship with Anton Dilger," an American investigator observed later. But Herrmann maintained that it was purely a matter of chance, and perhaps fate, that he and Dilger boarded the *Kristianafjord* in January 1916 as strangers—and ended the voyage as friends.

Seeking shelter from the cold North Atlantic winds, the two men spent long hours dining, drinking, and playing cards aboard the passenger ship. Once they got to the Norwegian port of Bergen, Dilger and Herrmann decided to share a train compartment to Copenhagen. "I . . . said goodbye to him there," Herrmann recalled.

The next day, the two spies were startled to meet again—this time at the office of Germany's naval intelligence agent in Copenhagen. "That was the first time that [Dilger] told me that he was connected with the German General Staff."

That meeting would have a profound effect on Tony's Lab, on Dilger's future missions, and—a decade afterward—on the investigations that finally shed light on the German biosabotage campaign.

A WEEK AND A HALF into the voyage of the British horse transport ship, a stallion that had been jabbed in the dockside corral at Newport News began to cough and shake its head to discharge the thick mucus that dripped from the sick animal's nostrils.

The horseman who took care of the stallion clambered up a ladder to the top deck and found the conductor, who grabbed a bag with a mallein testing kit. After examining the coughing horse, the conductor shaved a small patch on the animal's neck. He swabbed the exposed skin with alcohol-soaked cotton and then injected a syringe full of the mallein liquid under the skin.

The next day, the stallion's fever had spiked to 104 degrees Fahrenheit (40 degrees Celsius), and the patch of skin was swollen and red. The horse clearly had glanders. The conductor had no choice. He asked the horsemen to lead the sick stallion to a secluded spot on the main deck. Using a gun designed for killing large animals, he shot the horse in the head.

A few minutes later, a group of horsemen dragged the animal's body to the ship's edge and pushed it overboard into the roiling waters of the cold Atlantic.

If it had not been for the mallein tests, the reliable diagnosis for glanders that had been introduced a decade earlier, the germ sabotage campaign at U.S. ports might have wiped out many of the Allied horse shipments. But those tests, first developed by Germans, helped the Allies blunt the impact of the germ warfare.

Most of the seven hundred American horses and mules on the transport ship that had left Newport News in January 1916 would make it to the battlefields in France and Belgium. But they first had to survive the harsh journey. In their first few days at sea, the animals were disoriented by unsteady footing inside a ship. Jammed into pens and facing alleyways, upset by the flickering lights and the stench in the holds, the horses and mules suffered. While the most common health problems aboard the horse transports were "shipping fever" and equine influenza, the most dreaded disease was glanders.

The forty horsemen and muleteers who manned the horse transports filled the water troughs at 6:00 a.m., lightly groomed the animals, watered them again at noon, fed them bran and grain in the early afternoon, watered them again at 5:15 p.m., and gave them hay feed fifteen minutes later. By day's end, the stalls were mucked out and the muleteers and "horse boys" examined the animals for any signs of disease.

The animals finally settled down into the dull ship routine. But then, about two weeks into the sea voyage, the mood would suddenly lighten. Like the beat of distant drums, the noises of horses stamping their hooves soon rumbled through the British transport ship. As the animals tugged at the head ropes that held them in their cramped stalls, their nostrils flared to catch the distant smell of land. British journalist Basil Clarke, who traveled on a horse transport ship from America to England in 1917, described the animals' excitement as they sensed the new continent:

> The restlessness would increase, until at last the emotions of some horse found vent in a long-drawn whinny or neigh. Land! He had smelt the land. It might be a hundred miles away, but he had smelt it, and he gave vent to his joy in the only way he knew. He even tried to cut a little caper in his narrow stall.
>
> Soon the cry would be taken up by horses on both decks all round the ship, and from the lower deck mules would join in the

horse chorus of the upper deck. In every alleyway horses' heads would be tossed high, right to the beams overhead, and nostrils, widely dilated, taking in long sniffs of that new and welcome scent—the land. Even sick horses seemed to brighten up after that great shout from their comrades. From that moment onwards the horses would be all impatience till land was reached.

The horses would soon see England's green pastures and benefit from their brief respite there before they were shipped across the English Channel to the battlefields. Despite the often harsh conditions they endured, the great majority of the horses shipped across the Atlantic to the Allies during the Great War survived. Most of the credit for their high survival rate goes to British veterinary officers and transport experts who had learned the hard lessons of the Anglo-Boer War.

FROM COPENHAGEN, Dilger hurried directly to Berlin in a private railway compartment, with only Herrmann for company. During the journey, they discussed the possibility that Herrmann might transfer from his naval duties to army espionage so that he could directly assist the saboteurs in America.

In Berlin, they rode a hackney coach from the railway station. On the way to the hotel, they passed by the Brandenburg Gate, topped by four magnificent copper stallions that pulled the chariot of the goddess Victory. A harsh Prussian wind scattered snowflakes across the city's streets on that bitterly cold day. Dilger dropped Herrmann off and then headed to the Kaisershof Hotel, where he would share a room with Paul Hilken.

A few weeks earlier, Hilken had been called to Bremen by his Norddeutsche Lloyd masters to help plan a major event: arranging a trade mission of the new "commercial" U-boat, the *Deutschland*, to Baltimore and other East Coast ports. Hilken's role would extend beyond purely commercial transactions to arranging for local press coverage and German American receptions for the sub.

After Hilken talked with Berlin bankers to arrange financing for cargo shipments, he met separately with Franz von Papen, the former

German Army attaché in Washington who had been recalled a few months earlier for being linked to sabotage. At a meeting in Berlin on February 14, 1916, which Dilger also may have attended, the cavalryman Papen suggested that Hilken could play a larger role in sabotage operations in addition to his role in laundering the money paid to Captain Hinsch and other saboteurs.

Dilger introduced Paul Hilken to his new friend Fred Herrmann. The two men seemed to hit it off, although Paul was older and more serious than Fred. After the session with von Papen, Hilken and Dilger brought Herrmann with them to a much more important meeting on Wilhelmstrasse with the men who coordinated sabotage operations for the General Staff's Political Section: Count Rudolf August Nadolny and his chief assistant, military intelligence specialist Captain Hans Marguerre.

With his Prussian bearing and a dueling scar across his left cheek, Nadolny had the military presence to dominate virtually any meeting. But the formidable Nadolny was a diplomat first and a soldier second. A lawyer from East Prussia, Nadolny had mastered English, French, and Russian during a series of prewar postings that had taken him from the freezing boulevards of St. Petersburg to thrilling rides in four-horse coaches between Turkey and Tehran.

A captain in the army reserve, Nadolny had volunteered for a military assignment as soon as the Great War broke out. He had been dissatisfied with his first two military postings, but the third assignment, late in 1914, was more to his taste: helping to lead the Political Section of the General Staff's Department IIIb, which handled military intelligence and covert operations. His section coordinated Army sabotage in support of the Kaiser's war.

"I felt it was my duty to place myself at the service of the military," wrote Nadolny, boasting of his wide-ranging authority in the Section. The stint of army service also boosted his career, for he would later become chairman of Germany's delegation to the postwar disarmament conference in Geneva, the German ambassador to Turkey and the Soviet Union, and the director of the German Red Cross.

In his memoirs, Nadolny recalled being deeply impressed by "how many Germans volunteered to undertake the most dangerous missions."

Early in February 1916, Nadolny encountered three such paid volunteers when he walked into a meeting room at the Army's General Staff building in Berlin. Nadolny and Marguerre knew they had to be careful who they sent on the new missions. The tasks they would entrust to these three men and their associates were risky and volatile. The missions would backfire if the sabotage was exposed in neutral countries, which included the United States until April 1917. The adverse publicity would cause major diplomatic problems for Germany.

Earlier that cold morning, Dilger had accompanied Herrmann when he met with his naval intelligence contact, Captain Prieger, to discuss the young American's next mission. "I mentioned ... that Anton Dilger was with the General Staff, and that I would like to take a crack at that [sabotage] if he did not see any objections," Herrmann recalled later. The navy captain gave Herrmann permission to accompany Dilger and Hilken to the Army General Staff's Political Section the next day to discuss a possible new mission.

Sabotage was topic A of the meeting with Nadolny and Marguerre, but the main target discussed was American ammunition rather than remounts. The spymasters in Berlin had a technical shop—a gadget center that was a Great War version of James Bond's "Q-Branch" in London—where an "incendiary pencil" that could be concealed and easily used to set fires at ammunition plants or depots had just been designed.

"The pencils were packed in cartons," Marguerre recalled later in an affidavit, adding that "it is possible" that he gave Herrmann two cartons, each containing thirty of the incendiary devices. Within a few weeks, Herrmann also received a trunk with a double bottom to hold "glass tubes in a secret partition."

After the war, Marguerre testified that his mission was "to prepare and carry through actions against establishments essential for war and situated in countries at war with us, and to build up an intelligence service concerning the establishments essential for war and existing in those countries." While Marguerre was not technically authorized to carry out such missions in neutral countries, he said "the possibility was, of course, taken into consideration that countries then still neutral might join in the war against Germany...." In effect, Germany was targeting America.

Herrmann recalled later that Nadolny and Marguerre "brought up the thing about the destruction of munitions plants in the States," and "I told them it was a pretty hard job." But the German officers insisted it would be "very easy" and asked whether the Americans thought it would be feasible to recruit agents inside ammunition plants. In the end, Herrmann agreed to return to the United States to play a role in the germ-sabotage and munitions-targeting missions along with Captain Hinsch. Herrmann was paid "whatever [he] required," channeled through the paymaster Hilken.

Later, investigators said that the Berlin conspirators also discussed new plans "for the distribution ... of disease germs for the inoculation of horses and cattle intended for shipment to Germany's enemies abroad."

THEIR FUTURE MISSIONS SETTLED, Dilger and his fellow American agents were at liberty for a short while in Berlin to forget the agony of the war in France and the anxiety of espionage in America.

At the Ice Palace, an exclusive skating club under patronage of the Crown Prince, Prussian high society mingled on the bright ice with high-rank officers, diplomats, and industrialists—as well as intriguing foreigners. Dilger and Hilken sipped coffee as they sat at a rinkside table. Every afternoon, tea was served to the flushed guests during the intervals between skating sessions; high tea for the skating club's fashionable members was served once a week.

Muscular male instructors taught ladies how to skate their circles or how to waltz on the ice. Fit and sassy blonde women from East Prussia would instruct the men. Even the U.S. ambassador, James W. Gerard, "tried to improve [his] skating and spent many hours making painful circles under the efficient eyes of a little East Prussian instructress."

Gerard was an American attorney and judge who had gained President Wilson's trust as an emissary to Berlin. He feared that Germany had become a hostage to "Kaiserism," which was enforced by an authoritarian regime led by a military-dominated Prussian minority that he blamed for Berlin's lust for conquest and war. Gerard had called the *Lusitania* sinking "submarine murder" and described Germany as a

"Cloud-Cuckoo Land," a patchwork of disparate principalities dominated by Prussia. The Germans, he argued, were a neurotic people
obsessed with military uniforms, dullness, and meat-heavy meals.
"Meat-eating nations," he observed in a fit of gastronomic nationalism,
"have always ruled vegetarians."

The outspoken but opinionated ambassador—whom H. L. Mencken
once called "a blatant and very offensive ass"—likely met Dilger and
Hilken at the Ice Palace or at another Berlin haunt frequented by high
society in the winter of 1916, little suspecting that the two men who
seemed comfortably at home in Germany were in fact Americans.

Berlin's dance halls and theaters had closed in the first weeks after
the war's outbreak in August 1914, and the initial productions when they
reopened had tended to be insipidly patriotic plays. By the winter of
1915–16, however, Berlin's theaters had begun to open up, and opera
performances had resumed.

Dilger and Hilken, joined for awhile by Herrmann, spent nights at
the theater or opera followed by sumptuous dinners and rounds of
drinks. Herrmann was a favorite of the Berlin girls, many of whose
boyfriends were at the Front. They were lonely but lively, willing to
spend time with handsome men claiming to have mysterious missions.
One woman described Herrmann as "very military looking, blonde, with
ruddy cheeks" who wore his hair in a pompadour.

In early 1916, Berlin's wartime wildness had not yet been tempered
by famine and impending defeat. There was even excellent horse racing,
at least until severe horse shortages at the Front claimed too many of the
Thoroughbreds at the Hoppegarten track, owned by Berlin's Union
Club (the equivalent to New York's Jockey Club). At the popular
Grunewald track, there were steeplechases and "flat" races; at the Karl-
shorst track were hurdle races as well.

Sometimes, taking advantage of Hilken's business expense account,
Dilger and Hilken dined together at the fashionable Kempinski Hotel.
Many evenings they would show up late at the Cabaret Fledermaus,
where a table was reserved every night for Hilken's party, which often
included Dilger and executives of Norddeutsche Lloyd. In the space of a
week, the two friends attended a musical comedy called *Der Sterngucker*

("The Stargazer"), the operetta *Maria Theresa*, and a musical called *Jung Muss Man Sein* ("One Must Be Young").

Dilger had long admired German culture, spending his youth in Mannheim, which was renowned for its opera house and for great conductors such as Wilhelm Furtwängler. In Hilken's address book for 1916 is an entry for an internationally famous coloratura soprano, Frieda Hempel, who maintained one apartment in Berlin and another on Central Park West in Manhattan. Hempel, Dilger, and Hilken were friends, and—in Dilger's case—family members say the relationship went much further.

Hempel, who turned thirty in 1915, was one of the great sopranos of the early 1900s, renowned for her performances in Mozart and Verdi operas. She was not a great beauty, but she was a cosmopolitan and charming woman with a wide circle of influential and wealthy friends in both Germany and America. Hempel's recordings—among the earliest for a soprano—display a voice of clarity and beauty, performing the trills, staccatos, and florid passages required of coloratura sopranos. She sang opposite Enrico Caruso in several operas at New York's Metropolitan Opera and was popular in the roles of the Queen of the Night in *Die Zauberflöte* ("The Magic Flute"), the title role in *Lucia di Lammermoor*, and Marschallin in Richard Strauss's opera *Der Rosenkavalier*.

One of Hempel's admirers was the German-born Otto Kahn, a wealthy American railroad financier and art patron who was for years the most influential director on the Met's board. "Miss Hempel," he once told her backstage, "no matter how often I hear you in *Der Rosenkavalier*, I never fail to get chills down my spine when you sing." She was the most outstanding of the six German-born sopranos who sang at the Met during the war years, a group that included Margarete Ober, Emmy Destinn, Johanna Gadski, Melanie Kurt, and Margarete Matzenauer.

It is not clear if Dilger and the singer met in New York, Berlin, or on one of the transatlantic voyages. He claimed to have made friends during one voyage with Artur Bodanzky, the Met's Austrian conductor, who often cast Hempel in Met productions. An inveterate card player, Bodanzky would invite Dilger to the card games aboard ship and they and the other German speakers would talk long into the night.

On one of her wartime tours, Hempel arrived in Germany in August 1916 on the same Norwegian ship that Dilger had taken earlier that year, the *Kristianafjord*. Also on the ship was her Met benefactor, Otto Kahn, who had business in Germany. Hempel had come to Berlin to sing at a benefit concert for blinded soldiers at the Charité Hospital. "This was a very moving experience for me," she recalled later. "I had two brothers [German soldiers] on the Front, and although I was living and singing in America, I still felt very deeply the plight of the German soldier."

While in Berlin, Hempel stayed at her own apartment, which her father had maintained for her while she was away. She does not say in her memoirs what she did between August and October—when she sailed back to New York—but the Dilger family recalled that Anton and Freida spent part of one summer in a Swiss resort near St. Moritz that was still accessible to Germans during the war.

According to his family, Anton had an on-and-off affair with Hempel, despite his year-long engagement, which began in 1915, to his Heidelberg sweetheart, Margarethe Katz. His brother Louis, then living in Bern, reported seeing Anton and Frieda as they headed to St. Moritz during the war. Hempel loved Switzerland, and Louis's family used to have photos of her with Anton at Swiss resorts like Sils and Ober Engadin. Anton, Louis Dilger's daughter reported later, "was there during the war years." She added that Freida and Anton "moved in the same circles in Berlin. . . . I'm sure Uncle A. and Frieda saw a lot of each other, and both traveled about all over the place."

Hempel did not mention Anton Dilger in her autobiography, *My Golden Age of Singing*, which was not written until the 1950s, by which time it was well known that Dilger had been a German saboteur. However, it is clear that she spent time in Berlin that summer of 1916. In a rather strained attempt at optimism, Hempel recalled noticing that Berlin women were thinner and "more elegant" because they were being stressed by the war: "The wear and tear of anxiety and privation were removing the superfluous fat, and the women were reaping the reward of sleepless nights, bleak days, and awful suspense."

In October 1916, Hempel returned with Bodanzky to New York for the fall season at the Met. When the British Navy stopped the ship near the Orkney Islands of Scotland, British officers asked to meet with her privately in her stateroom because she held a German passport. She feared that the British might not allow her passage, mainly because "my prominent position in Berlin and my previous connections with the [German] royal family had made me suspect."

> The officer-in-charge went carefully through my trunks and checked my papers. One young officer who was looking through my suitcases gave up his search when he came across a photograph. He hesitated for a moment and then boldly asked me if he could have it. So I autographed it for him."

That night, Hempel sang for British officers at a concert on the ship, just as she had sung in Berlin for the German war-wounded. "As we sailed away, I thought to myself, 'How unbelievable! These wonderful English officers and my brothers are being asked to fight one another.'"

Chapter 8

BACILLI IN BERLIN

Martians—dead!—slain by the putrefactive and disease bacteria...
the humblest things that God, in his wisdom, has put upon this earth.
—H. G. WELLS, *The War of the Worlds*, 1898

THE CONCEPT OF BIOLOGICAL WARFARE and sabotage was hardly unknown at the beginning of the Great War. During the fourteenth century, a Tartar army catapulted the corpses of plague victims into the walled city of Kaffa to try to start an epidemic. In 1763, a conniving British captain sent blankets and a handkerchief used by smallpox victims to Native Americans during the French and Indian War. And during the U.S. Civil War, there were accusations that one side or another had intentionally led glanders-infected horses into the stables of the enemy.

Some early efforts to spread disease to weaken the enemy forces might have been effective, others were complete failures, and still others may have backfired. But they all had one thing in common: the perpetrators did not fully understand what caused the diseases and certainly had no way to isolate those infectious agents and deploy them in a scientific way.

It took the germ theory of disease, developed and accepted toward the end of the nineteenth century, and the laboratory techniques of modern microbiology to awaken armies, anarchists, and others to the possibilities of isolating, producing, and deploying specific stocks of infectious bacteria in a focused, planned, and deadly manner.

By the turn of the twentieth century, the concept of using bacteria as weapons had become a subject of fictional fantasies as well as a topic of international conventions and army manuals that condemned the practice while at the same time recognizing it as a possibility.

In the 1890s, the British writer H. G. Wells foreshadowed the concepts of modern biological warfare in two works of fiction. *War of the Worlds* ends with the tentacled aliens that had overpowered human weapons falling victim to the simplest creatures on the planet: germs. In a short story, "The Stolen Bacillus," Wells wrote about an anarchist who steals what he thinks is a cholera-causing culture from a bacteriologist and tries to spread the disease.

The disguised anarchist tells the scientist: "These anarchists—rascals ... are fools, blind fools—to use bombs when this kind of thing is attainable." In the end, however, the anarchist ends up with the wrong germ—a microbe that causes its host to turn blue, rather than die. The bacteriologist had lied to him.

The potential use of germs as tools of anarchists or military men was hardly limited to fiction. In 1902, for example, the German Army's land-war handbook had excluded biological warfare from its list of acceptable or legal practices. That handbook, still in force when the Great War began, said that "certain means of war which lead to unnecessary suffering are to be excluded. Those include: The use of poison both individually and collectively (such as poisoning of streams and food supplies) ... [and] the propagation of infectious diseases."

But the international conventions and treaties in force at the time were not specific on whether the military in wartime should be allowed to use "poisons" or germs against animals that were being shipped for use in the war. Article 23 of the Convention Respecting the Laws and Customs of War on Land (1899 and 1907) says that "it is especially prohibited ... to employ poison or poisoned arms." The Hague Convention of 1899 adopted similar language from the Brussels Declaration of 1874. (An earlier draft of that document had explicitly banned "the spreading, by any means whatsoever, of disease on enemy territory"; that wording did not appear in the final version.)

There were gaping loopholes, however, aside from the fact that the conventions had no enforcement provisions. Most notably, those international agreements could be interpreted as banning only biological warfare directed against humans. That interpretation, embraced by the German General Staff, left wide open the possibility of biowarfare against animals and crops.

That was a legal gap that the General Staff's Political Section exploited during the Great War. But even if there was no specific prohibition against intentionally infecting animals with disease, the concept was repugnant to most cultures. After the war's end, German officials steadfastly denied ever ordering, or even being aware of, a coordinated biosabotage campaign. In practice, however, it appears highly unlikely that a coordinated campaign such as the one Dilger and Herrmann participated in could have proceeded without knowledge of senior members of the General Staff. Crafty bureaucrats like Nadolny and Marguerre would not have allocated resources or given final approval completely on their own.

"It is just inconceivable that the work of the General Staff [in ordering the sabotage] . . . was done without authority from Marguerre's superior officers," wrote a U.S. investigator in a 1930 memo, adding that he had "no doubt" that the orders to initiate the germ warfare and other sabotage in the United States and other then-neutral countries had come from a high level in the Kaiser's imperial government.

Documents show that sabotage against horses began almost simultaneously in the United States and Romania in 1915, just a few months after Nadolny had joined the General Staff's Political Section. In his memoirs, Nadolny boasted of his "far-ranging authority" in the position: "Together with the Foreign Office, I led various difficult operations, was able for my purposes to requisition any officers or personnel that I needed, and reported directly to the chief of the Army General Staff." He claimed, however, in his memoirs and in testimony to investigators, to have had no role in "the sabotage actions in America."

Nearly all of the documents from the Political Section were intentionally destroyed by Marguerre and others shortly after the war's end. Even so, several surviving German cables—as well as the testimony of Herrmann and others—link Nadolny directly to decisions involving sabotage campaigns against both horses and munitions. While Nadol-ny's personal responsibility for sabotage operations may have differed from region to region, it is clear that the Political Section initiated a campaign of conventional and germ sabotage in 1915 that eventually extended from Baltimore to Bucharest.

Before Germany's biosabotage campaign of 1915–18, there had been many crude attempts to deploy germs in wartime. What distinguished the German effort was its scientific expertise. A limited number of labo-ratories in 1915 could have provided pure cultures of the germs used in the German sabotage, the bacteria that cause anthrax and glanders. But one of the few places in the world where there were plenty of sources for germ cultures was the city where Nadolny and Dilger met.

At the time of the Great War, Berlin was one of the world's great centers for the study of disease-causing bacteria. It was also a major cen-ter for the veterinary study of horses.

THE FIRST NOBEL PRIZE for medicine was awarded to a German doc-tor who used horses in his research into deadly bacteria. Emil von Behring was inspired by the example of Robert Koch, the great German bacteriologist who had, among many achievements, revealed the secrets of the anthrax bacterium and studied sleeping sickness in horses. Another of Koch's devoted associates, Fredrich Loeffler, discovered the germ that causes glanders in tissue samples from the liver and spleen of an infected horse.

During the years that Anton Dilger was studying medicine in Heidelberg, all three of those microbiologists were still making pioneer-ing discoveries. Behring's 1901 Nobel Prize was awarded for his serum work with horses on tetanus and diphtheria. He showed that injecting dead or weakened bacteria into horses causes their immune systems to produce an antitoxin in the blood that neutralizes diphtheria or tetanus toxin, providing immunity against the disease. Another of Koch's out-standing scientific collaborators, Paul Ehrlich, had shown Behring how to use the blood of live horses to prepare an effective antitoxin serum against diphtheria. Ehrlich would win his own Nobel Prize in 1908 for his pioneering work in immunology and "magic bullet" chemotherapy.

The master, Koch, received his Nobel Prize in 1905, mainly for his work on tuberculosis. The following year, the aging but tireless Koch headed to East Africa as the leader of a scientific mission to investigate sleeping sickness. Obsessive about his research, Koch woke his research assistant at 5:00 a.m. one day to help dissect an infected horse. When the young assistant declined—complaining that he was too tired and had dreamed of horses all night long—Koch demanded, "How can you hope to make any progress if you *don't* dream about horses?" Koch was so revered, as a patriot as well as a scientist, that the Kaiser created a research institute in his honor to study infectious diseases. In the 1880s and '90s, Koch and his assistants revolutionized microbiology by developing methods for simply and easily obtaining pathogenic bacteria in pure culture, free from other organisms, and for detecting and identifying them. Koch also formulated the conditions, known as "Koch's postulates," that must be satisfied before it can be accepted that a particular bacterium causes a specific disease.

"Almost daily, new miracles of bacteriology displayed themselves before our astonished eyes," recalled Loeffler. Although he did not win a Nobel Prize, Loeffler became the first scientist to identify the diphtheria microbe and was a pioneer in the field of virology, demonstrating that foot-and-mouth disease was caused by a virus. Barred from studying that highly contagious virus near Berlin, Loeffler established a research institute on the Baltic island of Reims in 1910. Three years later, he was called back to Berlin to head the Koch Institute of Infectious Diseases.

German scientists and doctors volunteered to help the fatherland and its soldiers during the Great War. Shortly after the war's outbreak, the aging Loeffler reenlisted at the rank of general in the Army Medical Corps. When deadly tetanus struck wounded German soldiers during the war's first months, the military turned to Behring for help. The Nobel Prize winner would be awarded the Iron Cross and hailed as "Savior of the German Soldier" for his work to stop infection among the war-wounded.

In that research, an expert remarked later, horses became "Behring's most important coworkers." The scientist helped standardize the dosage for tetanus antitoxin serum and mobilized a way to mass-produce the serum by taking blood from inoculated horses. A 1914 engraving shows one of those serum-producing centers in Germany: a large room in which white-coated assistants use intravenous needles to drain blood from "volunteer" horses that have been injected with weakened tetanus bacteria. Each of the animals—waiting patiently while bags of blood are removed from them—is standing in its own wooden half-stall, more of a polished church pew than a rough stable stall.

By April 1915, those inoculated horses had donated enough of their blood serum for Army medics to distribute it at field hospitals so that every wounded man could be inoculated. Within weeks, tetanus infections plummeted to virtually zero.

All of those great German bacteriologists devoted their careers to curing diseases and benefitting medical science. And all of them were gone by the end of the Great War. Koch was the first to die, in 1910. While his former research colleagues Loeffler, Ehrlich, and Behring lived to see the war, none of them survived it. For Loeffler, the strains of leading Koch's institute during the devastating war were too much. He died in April 1915. Ehrlich was "much distressed" by the war and suffered a stroke at Christmas 1914. A second stroke ended his life the following year. Behring, a former military man who spent some of his last years working on the tetanus serum, survived until March 1917.

The bacteriological research techniques developed by Koch and his circle were widely known by the time World War I began, but there were only a few likely sources for the anthrax and glanders germ cultures that the Germans used for their biosabotage campaign against pack animals. On the surface, Koch's Institute of Infectious Diseases would appear to be a possible source, mainly because the famous laboratory in Berlin still conducted research on the anthrax microbe, and the institute was headed in 1914 and early in 1915 by Loeffler, who had discovered the glanders microbe. But the Koch Institute's research plan for that period showed no experiments involving glanders, although its labs still worked with anthrax. It is possible, however, that Loeffler—then a general in the Army Medical Corps—might have provided some advice on isolating and culturing glanders bacteria before his death in April 1915.

Aside from Koch's former institute, there were several other possible sources of the germ cultures, including the Military Veterinary Academy, the Imperial Health Office, and—oddly enough—the Imperial Colonial Office. There is evidence in documents that the Colonial Office may have been used as cover by an intelligence agent in shipping pathogens. At about the time that Dilger was preparing to grow cultures in Chevy Chase, in September 1915, a German diplomatic official in Romania requested a shipment of glanders cultures through "Director Steinwachs" of the Colonial Office. Four days later, Steinwachs sent the cultures to a German agent in Romania.

"Director Steinwachs" was almost certainly Hans Steinwachs, an influential German military intelligence case officer who had maintained an office on the third floor of the Colonial Office building on Wilhelmstrasse. Before the Great War, he had surveyed mineral sites in Morocco and directed a mine for a German company. When war broke out, Steinwachs and two mining colleagues worked to procure and transport—as well as prevent the Allies from obtaining—war materials through the General Staff's Political Section. Among the "materials" Steinwachs arranged to transport were cultures of glanders and anthrax germs for sabotage in Romania and probably elsewhere.

Steinwachs, who had good contacts in Russia and Eastern Europe, also was the case officer for an agent named Alexander Keskula who provided reports from Vladimir Lenin (then living in exile in Switzerland) about political unrest in Russia. Later, Steinwachs and his agents helped arrange the secret train trip that took Lenin and fellow exiled Bolsheviks through Germany in April 1917 on their way to the Russian Revolution. Imperial Germany had no love for the communists, but its agents were willing to do just about anything that would foment unrest in Russia to end the war on the Eastern Front.

Aside from providing cover for Steinwachs, Germany's Colonial Office also played a role in the study of tropical diseases and pathogens because it was responsible for sanitation in Germany's far-flung colonies. Among the research centers supported by the Colonial Office was the Imperial Bacteriological Institute in a town near Windhoek in the German colony of South-West Africa (now Namibia).

Anthrax is endemic in southern Africa, and one of the institute's researchers was an expert in both anthrax and glanders. However, the complex logistics of sending cultures all the way from southern Africa to

Germany during wartime blockades make it seem unlikely that the Colonial Office was procuring samples from abroad. At most, it may have served mainly as a cover for Steinwachs and a conduit for shipping germs.

The real source for the germ cultures seems to have been in the German military's own veterinary ranks. To discretely secure a plentiful supply of glanders and anthrax germ cultures, it would have made sense for the General Staff to use a military research institute whose scientists were controlled by the Army: the Military Veterinary Academy. Founded in 1888, the academy's bacteriological lab had been moved in 1907 to the former stable buildings of the Army's old Cavalry Artillery Camp at 27 Hannoverische Strasse in Berlin.

When the Great War began, the academy was the only center for glanders research in Germany, and it also conducted anthrax tests and research. In the war's first year, it was small, with only two examination rooms, one cleaning room, and stalls for horses and other animals. But as horse diseases became a major issue in the conduct of the war, the academy was expanded in July 1915—at the time when glanders and anthrax cultures were being prepared in Berlin for sabotage agents—to include the former anatomy building of Berlin's Veterinary College. An ambitious construction project also started that year to expand and modernize the veterinary research center.

The Military Veterinary Academy's chief veterinarian, Professor Carl Troester, was a leading expert on glanders research. In 1915, the institute had tested 346,815 blood samples from horses, finding more than 1,700 horses that tested positive. Those samples of infected blood provided the potential for a wide variety of glanders germ cultures for research—and, quite possibly, for propagation. Troester was one of the highest-ranking veterinarians in the German Army during the war and had taught veterinary medicine in Japan for several years earlier in his career.

The extent of the veterinary academy's involvement in the sabotage campaign may never be known; most of its archival records were destroyed or lost after the war. However, scattered pieces of circumstantial evidence survive. In 1914, a German researcher told colleagues that the academy could provide cultures of the glanders microbe within the space of a few days.

There is yet another telling piece of evidence. Three researchers on the staff of the Military Veterinary Academy during the Great War later played roles in German biowarfare research during World War II.

WHILE ANTON DILGER was working in Germany in 1916, the *New York Times* splashed on the front page a detailed story about glanders and anthrax germs being used for German sabotage.

That September 22, 1916, lead article tells a story that is remarkably similar to what was going on a few miles from the White House. It is surprising that the Romanian revelations, in conjunction with anecdotal reports of "poisonings" at various horse depots in America, did not tip off the U.S. authorities.

DEADLY GERMS AND BOMBS WERE PLANTED BY GERMANS IN RUMANIAN LEGATION WHEN THEY LEFT IT IN AMERICAN HANDS

said the three-column headline. A subheading added: "Anthrax and Glanders Microbes Imported to Poison Cattle of Neutral Neighbor." Yet another read: "Explosives and Poison Sent from Berlin and Bore Official Seals and Directions."

Those three statements summarized the main thrust of the North American biosabotage campaign as well. But while the Romanian germs were front-page news in 1916, the American biosabotage was not revealed until more than a decade after the war's end. Very few documents detailing the American germ sabotage survived. But the story of what happened in Romania opens a window into a parallel program.

In May 1915, Count Rudolph August Nadolny asked the German military attaché in Romania to plan a campaign to destroy munitions factories and infect military horses. The attaché promised to assign someone to germ sabotage and asked for instructions on how to deploy the glanders cultures, which began arriving in Bucharest that summer.

The cable that most directly implicates Nadolny was sent on May 17—the same month that the mysterious Captain Erich von Steinmetz had shown up in New York with a case full of glanders germs. In that secret cable, Nadolny asked the German military attaché in Bucharest to lay the groundwork for "attacks against railroads, military facilities, especially munitions factories, and in addition the infecting of military horses, etc." That sabotage was planned "in the case of a Romanian attack against us," according to the cable, which added that "explosives and cultures of glanders [bacteria] can be provided by us."

Germany's envoy in Bucharest responded quickly with a cable saying that "we could immediately attempt to infect horses. Precise instructions on how to use cultures of glanders [bacteria] are necessary." While he endorsed such sabotage, Nadolny made it clear in another cable that the germs were to be deployed only against animals in Romania, and not against humans.

A month later, on June 10, the German envoy in Bucharest sent a cable confirming that an agent named "Berg" had received anthrax and glanders cultures. "If necessary we will request additional supplies of [bacterial] agent," the cable continued. Those new cultures were requested on behalf of Berg in early September, and the shipment was confirmed by a September 7 cable from Steinwachs to Berg in Bucharest: "Consignment of glanders cultures will leave tomorrow, under guard, by diplomatic courier. This time it should be sufficient to pour each vial into a water pail" as a method of infecting horses. The clear implication is that Berg or his agents used the bacterial cultures to try to kill Romanian horses being shipped to the Allies.

Documents show that the new glanders cultures were shipped by Steinwachs during September 1915, the same month that Anton Dilger—who knew Romania well from his days in Bulgaria during the Balkan Wars—first retrieved similar cultures in Berlin to hand-carry to America. Dilger and Steinwachs, who both conducted operations for the Political Section, may well have been involved in coordinating the shipments of bacterial cultures.

Over the following year, Berlin continued to use diplomatic couriers to ship more bacterial cultures, as well as explosives for sabotage, to the German consulate in Bucharest. The situation came to a head after Romania declared war against Austria-Hungary in August 1916, triggering imperial Germany's declaration of war against Romania the following day. At that point, the U.S. government (still neutral) assumed responsibility for German interests in Romania, as well as for property that was left by the German diplomats who had been forced to depart.

Romania's foreign minister had placed those German diplomats under surveillance after receiving reports of possible sabotage actions being coordinated from the legation. Romanian agents had observed suspicious "parcels and boxes" being carried into the German Consulate in mid-August. After the mutual declarations of war, the foreign office asked the prefect of police in Bucharest to find those boxes and examine their contents. In order to do so, the police contacted the ranking U.S. diplomat, who protested—but did not stop—the search for the boxes.

What the police found in mid-September 1916 warranted the three-column headline in the *New York Times*. Most of the cartons contained explosive charges, but inside one rectangular wooden box that had been hidden under firewood were four stoppered vials, each containing a yellowish liquid. The vials were covered by a layer of protective cotton upon which a typewritten note of instructions was found. In German, the note said:

> Enclosed 4 small bottles for horses and 4 for cattle. To be used as formerly stipulated.
>
> Each phial suffices for 200 heads. If possible to be administered directly into the animals' mouths, otherwise into their fodder. We ask for a small report about success obtained there and in case of good results the presence for one day of Mr. K. would be required.

Scientists at Romania's Institute of Pathology and Bacteriology determined later that the vials contained cultures of the microbes that cause anthrax and glanders. In a memo dated October 5, 1916, the director of that institute concluded that:

> 1) The phial wrapped in red paper contained cultivations of the ANTHRAX bacillus, which has been identified with the aid of cultivations and vaccinations carried out on guinea pigs.

2) The phial covered with white paper contained cultivations of the bacillus of glanders which has been identified by cultivations and by vaccinations made with it to animals.

While the identity of those pathogens came as a shock, Romanian officials were even more disturbed by the evidence pointing to the germs' source, mode of delivery, and ultimate destination. The box had been carefully wrapped in white paper scribbled with various inscriptions and bearing, in red wax, the seal of the Imperial German Consulate at Kronstadt—a city (now Brasov) situated in the disputed section of Transylvania that then belonged to the Austro-Hungarian Empire.

The inscriptions on the paper and envelopes outside the box—addressed to the Bulgarian and German military attachés—implicated both the Germans and their Bulgarian allies. The Romanians claimed that the germs had been sent to the German attaché, who intended to have the box delivered to Bulgaria's attaché. Then the Bulgarians would have their agents deploy the germs against Romanian horses and cattle.

Could Anton Dilger, who had been decorated by Bulgaria for his service during the Balkan Wars, have played any role in preparing the anthrax and glanders cultures for Bulgarian agents to deploy in Romania? While official records show that Dilger was assigned to hospitals in Baden—first in Rastatt, then in Karlsruhe—through most of 1916, his travels back and forth to Berlin in the winter and spring of that year make it clear that his work schedule was, at the very least, flexible, and perhaps simply a cover for other intelligence work. With his contacts and prior experience in the Balkans, Dilger undoubtedly paid close attention to the war in Romania. His nephew Hubert won the Iron Cross for bravery when his German army division occupied Bucharest in December 1916.

One scholar, microbiologist Mark Wheelis, contends that it is "quite possible that [Dilger] played a central role in the [germ sabotage] program from the outset." The circumstantial evidence includes the fact that he was the only person with medical and microbiological training who was known to be involved with the biosabotage program. Also, Dilger's association with the Political Section appeared to start in mid-1915 and he "could have been involved before that." Certainly, Wheelis argues, Dilger "was in Germany when microbes were produced ... and when new culture methods were developed." In addition, the fact that German agents used more than one method to deploy the germs (syringes, glass vials hidden in sugar cubes) suggested that there had been a research and development phase to test the methods of propagating and deploying germs.

While Dilger's exact role is not fully defined, one thing is clear: the General Staff's Political Section initiated in 1915 the first systematic effort at modern biological warfare, a sabotage campaign using glanders and anthrax germs that eventually spread in 1916–17 as far north as Scandinavia and as far south as Argentina.

At about the same time that the *New York Times* was reporting germ sabotage in Romania on its front page in September 1916, Fred Herrmann was starting a campaign to expand the North American germ sabotage campaign—which had been limited to the East Coast until then—to the Midwest. But despite numerous anecdotal reports of sabotage against horses at U.S. ports and rail depots, no one connected the Romanian reports to what was going on under their noses in America.

A few months later, in the winter of 1917, Norwegian police arrested another biological sabotage agent, a Swedish baron named Otto Karl Robert von Rosen who had been provided by the German General Staff with germ-laced sugar cubes as well as a bottle of "toxic bacteria bullion" that was labeled as mouthwash. There were two boxes of the sugar cubes, each cube containing a tiny glass ampule with a few drops of liquid medium containing anthrax cultures. Later that spring, Norwegian police also found such germ-laced sugar cubes when they searched a German diplomatic courier's bags.

The German General Staff had been willing to help von Rosen because his goal was to help Finnish "freedom fighters" overthrow Russian domination. He had been shipping explosives and germ cultures across the border to northern Finland for more than a year. As part of a wider campaign, the Finnish guerrillas were supposed to toss the deadly sugar cubes into the feed troughs of horses and cattle at Russian army garrisons.

The Norwegian and Romanian discoveries were among dozens of reports and clues that might have alerted U.S. investigators to the possibility of germ sabotage in America. In retrospect, there seems little excuse for U.S. investigators not to have discovered the domestic biological sabotage. The *New York Times* had given the Romanian germs a banner headline, and a British journalist reported in the spring of 1917 that "in several cases, disease germs were poured into depot [feed bins] or water supplies" at American horse depots by German agents.

Yet no one seems to have tipped off the Bureau of Investigation in Washington. Not until a dozen years after the Great War's end did the germ sabotage in America itself make headlines in U.S. newspapers.

TONY'S LAB WAS STILL propagating germ cultures in mid-1916, but neither Paul Hilken nor Captain Hinsch trusted its Chevy Chase custodian. It's not that Carl Dilger had trouble operating the germ factory; the problem was that he had trouble managing money and keeping his mouth shut about the sabotage.

Carl was known to knock down a beer every now and then at his old haunts in Washington. Word had gotten back to the Hansa Haus in Baltimore that Carl had been bragging about his mission, and Hilken had confronted Carl about how wisely he was spending the several thousand dollars in German funds that his brother Anton had set aside in January. Carl had to be handled delicately, however, because Anton was considered a valuable asset in Berlin.

In May 1916, Hilken and Hinsch came up with a plan to ease Carl out without upsetting his brother. Replacing the mercurial Carl would be the more dependable Fred Herrmann, who they considered to be useful and trustworthy—both at the germ lab and with the new incendiary pencils. Since his return to America, Herrmann had been staying at the Chevy Chase house, which he shared with Carl and his sister Em, who claimed later not to know what was going on in the basement. Herrmann had diversified the germ operation by setting up a separate table in the basement to work also on incendiary devices, filling tubes with sulfuric acid and other chemicals. He carried a supply of incendiary devices to Baltimore for Hinsch, and the two saboteurs then mapped out a plan to make use of them. One author reported later that "a number of factories were marked for destruction, and each of them chose the ones they would attend to."

Herrmann said he and Carl Dilger used to drive to the Hansa Haus in Baltimore or to the train station in Laurel, Maryland—a town halfway between Washington and Baltimore—to deliver germ cultures or incendiary pencils to Hinsch, Hilken, or their go-between, Carl Arendt.

The new focus on incendiary sabotage aimed at munitions factories made it even more important for the saboteurs to ease the talkative Dilger brother out of the way. Convincing Carl that they were sending him on an important mission, Hilken and Hinsch gave him a free ticket on a ship to Germany and a sealed letter—inserted into a packet of other sealed documents—that he was to deliver to the Political Section officers in Berlin. What they did not tell him was that the confidential letter asked the German spymasters in Berlin to find a way to keep him in Germany so he could not mess up the American sabotage operation.

"I was sent to Germany by Captain Hinsch," Carl testified later. "My brother, Anton Dilger, was in Germany at that time. I telegraphed him from Copenhagen to meet me at Warnemünde [a German port on the Baltic Sea], but he did not come. All my papers, money and personal belongings were taken from me at Warnemünde."

Spooked by the thorough search of his baggage at the German customs and immigration station, Carl said he destroyed the sealed packet at the port. "I never delivered the package that I had been given because I thought the package contained reports of fires and other things that Hinsch and his men had been doing, and I was afraid that I would be caught with them, so I destroyed the papers." Unknowingly, he may have saved himself from being detained in Germany.

Unable to find his brother at the port, Carl took the train to Berlin and spent two days at the Hotel Charles. After he finally heard from Anton, Carl took a train westward to meet him and their older sisters in Mannheim. Later, he visited Anton in nearby Karlsruhe.

On paper, at least, Anton Dilger had been in Baden since early February. His official service record indicates that he returned to the Rastatt hospital as a "civilian physician under contract" on February 11, 1916, even though other testimony placed him in Berlin later that month. Sometime after his Berlin meetings, Anton had traveled to Baden, where he had family, a fiancée, and—again, at least on paper—a job at the Rastatt hospital.

For the previous five months—during the time he had lived in Chevy Chase—that same record in Baden lists Dilger as being "in the service of the Imperial War Ministry in America." This is the only surviving official German record that confirms that Anton Dilger conducted missions for the German military. In early May of that year, he moved to Karlsruhe—just twenty miles from Rastatt—to begin service at a reserve military hospital that was operated by the German Red Cross.

The General Staff's Political Section, having never received Hinsch's letter detailing Carl's unreliability, still presumed that Anton Dilger's brother was an asset to be used in America. So when the two brothers traveled to Berlin in June 1916, they met with military intelligence officers, including the Mannheim family friend, Rudolf Giessler. The topic, as usual, was sabotage in America. Carl Dilger recalled that with Giessler were Nadolny and Marguerre. They talked about new sabotage projects and then later "met some officials out at a place near Spandau where they had an experimental station for guns and munitions. The German officials that I met in Berlin fixed up a trunk for me to take back to Captain Hinsch in Baltimore with some false sides, in which they placed a number of incendiary tubes for use by Captain Hinsch in his work of destroying factories and munitions supplies."

During the 1930s, German officials—testifying when the U.S. government sued for damages that German sabotage had inflicted while America was still neutral in the war—claimed that they had told the saboteurs not to conduct sabotage until the United States declared war. Carl Dilger later refuted that assertion. "Nothing was said to me in Berlin about not using them unless the U.S. got into the war. It was my understanding that they were to be used right away and I gave them to Hinsch for that purpose."

After six weeks in Germany, Carl Dilger sailed back to the U.S., departing from the Baltic port of Warnemünde on July 13. He brought along the trunk with its secret compartment of fire-starting weapons.

"I personally saw the incendiary tubes in the trunk," he said later, "and I know that they were delivered in Baltimore."

Chapter 9

"A DIFFICULT INNER STRUGGLE"

*During those terrifying hours, Black Tom and its vicinity might
well have been part of the Western Front during a gigantic battle.*
—CAPTAIN HENRY LANDAU, *The Enemy Within*, 1937

T HE FEAST OF CORPUS CHRISTI was celebrated by Roman Catholics
every June in the ancient German city of Karlsruhe. Priests carrying
the communion wafer that represented the body of Christ would lead
white-robed children and pious adults in the annual parade through the
city's cobblestone streets.

On the holiday afternoon of June 22, 1916, many of the city's children were looking forward to another festive event: a performance of the
Hagenbeck Circus, which brought its traveling show to town once a
year. Children and their parents lined up to see the fantastic creatures in
Germany's premiere animal show, a welcome distraction from events on
the Western Front just fifty miles away.

The Hagenbeck Circus featured animals and curiosities from all over
the world. The kids giggled at the oddly striped legs of the half-
horse–half-zebra that ran around the dusty ring. They marveled at the
huge Indian elephants that thundered back and forth. And the children
gasped when a trainer led out a hybrid tiger with a lionlike mane.

Hagenbeck seldom failed to please it audiences. That afternoon, the
circus tent was so full, and the children so loud, that no one heard the
distant buzzing sounds of the approaching planes. The snapping of

trainers' whips and the ringmaster's singsong announcements had captured everyone's attention. But then the air outside shook with the pounding of anti-aircraft guns. An ominous whistling noise sounded, high above the tent. Then came the first explosion, just a few meters away, which sent pieces of broken brick crashing through the canvas. That's when the screaming began, a screaming that would not end for hours.

The next bombs hit the tent itself, turning the circus into a bloody nightmare. Some of the explosions scored direct hits, sending pieces of jagged metal into the crowd. Dozens of children and adults were killed outright; scores more were badly injured. Fire soon engulfed the tent, which quickly filled with smoke as those who could still move ran out of the exit flaps.

The first warning of the French air attack had come from a military observer at 3:00 p.m., ten minutes before the first two bombs, which were "small but with unusually high explosive power," fell in the western part of Karlsruhe. Some bombs struck near the palace, where the Queen of Sweden and her children, who were staying there as guests of the Grand Duke, were rushed into the cellar. The church service that the Grand Duke and Duchess of Baden were attending was suspended because of the explosions. In the face of the French attack, the Duke and his wife led the congregation in singing Martin Luther's defiant hymn, *Ein feste Burg ist unser Gott* ("A Mighty Fortress Is Our God").

The church was spared, but firefighters and ambulances crowded around the circus tent, quenching the blaze and rushing the wounded to a nearby reserve military hospital housed in a former trade-school building on Krieg Strasse. The hospital scene was horrifying, with beleaguered doctors and nurses working feverishly, trying to save the youngsters with flesh wounds, mangled limbs, or shrapnel lodged in their skulls.

Anton Dilger was on duty that awful day, along with another staff physician named Roth, an eyewitness said later. As a surgeon, Dilger had dealt with grotesque battlefield injuries in soldiers during the Balkan Wars and the ongoing Great War. But he had never seen anything like the rows of dead and badly wounded children that lay on stretchers in the hospital operating room, in wards, and in cramped hallways. Some of the children had gone to the circus wearing their robes from the Corpus Christi procession, their once-pure white now stained a terrible red.

A local newspaper described "piles of bodies and body parts" in the streets, and "heart-rending scenes played out" as weeping parents identified the bodies of their dead children. The Grand Duchess, Louise, went into the old city to help with the wounded, while frantic search parties sought missing children. The children of two of Baden's most prominent aristocrats, Prince Max and Count Berthold, had gone missing for hours that day before searchers finally found them.

The Karlsruhe bombing killed 120 people, 71 of them children; another 169 German civilians, many of them children who had been at the circus, were badly injured. A large number of them were treated at Dilger's Red Cross reserve hospital. The French bombers had intended to strike Karlsruhe's main train station, but they had used an out-of-date map to guide them into the city center. They had bombed the wrong place.

Later, Dilger would tell family and close friends that that day in Karlsruhe changed his life. An American investigator wrote later:

> According to Hilken, at the time of this bombing Dilger was in the German Red Cross in charge of surgical operations at the Karlsruhe hospital. He had been on duty for 48 hours straight. Following the bomb raid many badly wounded little girls in their confirmation robes were brought in for attention. The sights were too much for Dilger, who had a complete nervous collapse from which he never recovered to an extent sufficient to operate again. He was then sent over to this country by the Germans, arriving in New York on July 4, 1917.

Some investigators thought later that Dilger had spread the story of a nervous breakdown as a cover for his sabotage work, and it is true that official records show him still assigned to Karlsruhe until February 1917. But there is also evidence—some of it hearsay—to corroborate Dilger's breakdown story. One German eyewitness reported that he saw Dilger at the Karlsruhe hospital that day. And Hilken testified under oath many years later, at a time when he had no reason to protect Dilger, that his friend was indeed at the Karlsruhe hospital when "about 50 or 60 children" were killed during the Corpus Christi bombing. He said Dilger told him that "he helped carry these wounded children into the hospital, and his nerves went to pieces."

Within the family, the Karlsruhe story also rang true. "Seeing the casualties in the Karlsruhe hospitals affected my uncle Anton and aroused his hostility toward the wicked, beastly French and British, just as in France and Britain their losses and return of their wounded generated passionate hatred of the wicked, beastly Huns [Germans]," his American nephew Carl Keyser wrote. Dilger was later awarded the Baden Red Cross medal and cited on the Grand Duke's "honors list" in recognition of his work on behalf of the wounded.

For German Catholics, an attack against civilians on a church holiday—the Holy Mass celebration of the consecrated wafer as the body of Christ—was an act of sacrilege. Wartime attacks on civilians, which had occurred at the edges of both Fronts, were still rare in Germany itself. The bombing of Karlsruhe was one of the bloodiest Allied attacks on German civilians during the war, and was later cited by some as one of the war's many atrocities. Condolences poured in, including messages from the Kaiser and Field Marshal Paul von Hindenburg, who would soon become the Army's Chief of Staff.

As Dilger was finding out, the brutal war was now threatening German civilians who lived in cities within range of French and British bombers. The previous month, seven British and six French aircraft—carrying out a reprisal for a German air raid—had struck the city of Freiburg. Attacking in two waves, the bombers killed numerous civilians and destroyed many historic buildings. Germans were appalled by the attack, even though zeppelins were being launched two or three times a month against London as well as other targets in Britain and France.

The zeppelins had opened the door to Germany's aerial bombardment of Allied civilians, which began early in 1915. Soon afterward, the British launched their own form of strategic bombing, mainly attacking the zeppelin production area and its hangars. But it was the French who conducted some of the most damaging bombing raids against German cities along the Rhine River.

The bombing of cities, the imprecise violence against civilians from an aerial adversary, may well have played a role in Anton Dilger's decision to become a saboteur for his adopted country. In June 1915, while Dilger was a surgeon at nearby Rastatt, two dozen French aircraft attacked Karlsruhe for the first time, dropping 285 bombs that killed 29 civilians, wounded another 58, and destroyed numerous buildings. It was one of the first bombing raids that caused terror in a German city. Dilger agreed to become a saboteur for Germany, leaving with germ cultures for the United States just three months later. The second, far more devastating, Karlsruhe bombing raid just a year later apparently hardened his resolve to work against the Allies and then against his native country.

If he had not been already, by the summer of 1916 Dilger became completely dedicated to thwarting the Allies. He abandoned any pretense to having a career as a surgeon; he broke off his engagement; and he slowly began to distance himself from his family. He would dedicate the rest of his life to being a spy and saboteur for Germany.

Dilger could not escape the reverberations of his breakup with Margarethe Katz, however much his other liaisons must already have put their relationship to the test. Her angry father, who knew Martin Koehler from Mannheim business circles, sent Koehler a scathing letter complaining that Dilger had seduced his daughter and ended the engagement in a disreputable manner. Before the abrupt breakup, Dilger's relationship with Katz's family had been strained by tensions resulting from his income, nationality, and religion. Margarethe was from a wealthy German Jewish family; Dilger was nominally Catholic, hardly rich, and an American.

Confronted by Koehler with the father's complaints, Dilger defended himself in a September 16 letter to his benefactor. Written in a tone that is at some points quite emotional but at other times distant and detached, the letter haughtily dismisses Mr. Katz's complaint. The phrasing reveals almost no real emotion for Margarethe.

In the interest of our family's reputation, I must challenge [Mr.] Katz's remonstrance blaming me for breaking off my engagement to Margarethe without justification. In my last letter to

Margarethe I told her that I would no longer enter the house of a man who told me that the quality of our relationship had degenerated into that of a pimp and prostitute and that he would speak to me only in the presence of witnesses.

Dilger blamed the Katz family for exacerbating the former couple's problems. His fiancée's letters to him, he explained, "were full of bitter complaints against her family for their handling of our engagement." At one point, her irate father had barred her from staying at her family's home. "When she was sent away from Mannheim, she wrote me from Gernsbach that she had been thrown out of her house because of her engagement to me."

I owe no explanation to [Mr.] K. regarding my relations with Margarethe in Heidelberg. He never acknowledged my engagement to Margarethe and as soon as I announced my intention to marry her he treated me with disdain. He spoke of irresponsibility and said that if one planned to take a wife one must be able to support her.

I thank you and Eda that you taught me from the very first to regard the truly difficult medical profession idealistically, monetary reward being only a secondary consideration. I believe the nature and extent of my efforts, until now devoted to the relief of humanity's suffering, should be enough to convince [Mr.] Katz that I have not acted irresponsibly. . . . It disgusted me when Margarethe told me that her family clearly stated that I wanted to marry her for money.

Dilger ended his letter with a dramatic flourish: "No one can blame me for this! Margarethe faces a continuous conflict between her love for me and her love for her parents. . . . I see no need to further justify my decision to break my engagement. You all know that I didn't reach this point without a difficult inner struggle."

Manifesting that inner struggle, he threatened to "insist on a Court of Honor for a decision" if Katz continued to accuse him in public of breaking off the engagement without just cause. Such courts, typically available only to the German military, would on occasion help solve disputes related to acts or omissions considered ungentlemanly or unworthy of an officer. As his supporters in such a proceeding, Dilger said he would "immediately name two gentlemen, a captain or first lieutenant of the High Command and a gentleman from the Ministry of the Interior."

Unless he was bluffing, is seems puzzling that Dilger, who carried U.S. documents and had no official status with the German military, thought he was entitled to a Court of Honor. But if Dilger had been given citizenship and a German officer's rank, as some relatives believed, the court would have been within his rights.

Its final page lost, what remains of Dilger's letter ends: "All I can say is that this is very painful to me." Photos taken after mid-1916 show a different Anton Dilger, one looking older and more sober, with a drawn face. He no longer had the look of youth; he had aged with the war and the stress.

While his active service as a surgeon in Karlsruhe may have ended sometime after the air attack the previous summer, the official record shows that his transfer to Berlin did not occur until February 10, 1917, when he was assigned to the Central Sanitation Depot. That transfer—coming just a week after the United States broke off diplomatic relations with Berlin—was most likely a cover assignment for espionage and perhaps for continued work on germ sabotage.

One particular phrase in Dilger's letter to Koehler—stating that his life's work "until now" had been devoted to relieving human suffering—may have alluded to his apparent decision to move away from surgery and deeper into the intrigues of military intelligence.

Even though he still liked to be called "Herr Doktor," the Virginia-born physician's medical career was over. Instead, he would help Germany take the battle to North America.

IN THE DARKNESS OF EARLY MORNING on March 9, 1916, fifteen hundred armed Mexicans rode across the border into the U.S. Cavalry camp in Columbus, New Mexico, terrorizing the sleepy American troops, seizing or killing one hundred horses and mules, and then setting fire to some of the town's buildings. The raid, which killed seventeen Americans, was the first and only military attack on the continental United States in the twentieth century.

The aggressors, led by Francisco "Pancho" Villa, came from Mexico, but the incursion may have had more complex origins related to the great power struggle in Europe. Villa crossed the border mainly to catch President Wilson's attention and spark a U.S. counterraid into Mexico, which he hoped might help his forces in the ongoing Mexican power struggle. But there may have been an ulterior motive: tying up American troops, munitions, and horses in Mexico, which would in turn slow the shipments of similar war supplies to the Allies. Clearly, Germany stood to gain from any American conflict with Mexico.

When Wilson ordered a punitive expedition on March 16 to find and punish Villa, German officials were thrilled. "As long as the Mexican question remains at this stage, we are, I believe, fairly safe from aggressive attack by the American government," wrote the German ambassador in Washington to the chancellor in Berlin, two weeks after the United States sent 6,600 troops into Mexico.

It was the last true cavalry action mounted by the U.S. Army and, in a sense, the end of an era for the military horsemen who rode the Old West. The search for the Villista raiders was led by General John J. "Black Jack" Pershing, who, even though he was a cavalryman, experimented for the first time with mechanized vehicles such as trucks, cars, and airplanes in northern Mexico.

The terrain was so rough that, at times, pack mules carried the vehicles' fuel. A cavalry officer, Captain F. L. Case, concluded from the Mexican experience that animals were still essential to such rough-terrain expeditions. "The horse and mule cannot be replaced by gasoline," he wrote in 1916, "although the latter can relieve the former of much of their burden."

Pancho Villa had been the ablest general of Venustiano Carranza, who became Mexico's president in 1915 after an armed struggle. Villa, backed temporarily by the United States, then launched an armed revolt against Carranza, whose forces defeated Villa and cost him the backing of Washington. That relegated Villa to the status of a populist bandit with a chip on his shoulder against America.

He had no shortage of foreign suitors, for the Germans and British each sought to take advantage of Villa's need for money and munitions to try to use him toward their own ends. The British wanted to use Villa to try to topple Carranza, whom they regarded as pro-German. The Germans wanted to use the bandit to harass the Americans.

There is evidence that the Villistas may have received munitions bought with money channeled through a German agent, Felix A. Sommerfeld. A con man, he was one among a "shadowy army of agents, double agents and lobbyists who swarmed like locusts over Mexico once the revolution had begun."

A few months before Villa's raid, Sommerfeld's bank account in St. Louis received $340,000 from a New York account associated with German agents. U.S. investigators found out that the money had gone to the Western Cartridge Company, which supplied ammunition and arms to Villa's forces.

Sommerfeld later denied channeling German money to the Villistas. He even wrote a letter condemning Villa for ordering his troops to execute seventeen American mining engineers they found riding a Mexican train near the town of Santa Ysabel, the first of some four hundred Americans who were killed on both sides of the border during the years of struggle with Villa's forces.

For their part, Villa's troops were also infuriated by an atrocity committed against Mexicans in Texas on March 7, when twenty Mexicans were burned alive in El Paso after being arrested by local police. Someone had splashed kerosene on the prisoners, in theory to kill lice, and the Mexicans caught fire and burned to death. That was the final outrage that sparked the Villa raid.

Pershing's expedition, which eventually expanded to involve twelve thousand troops, scoured the deserts, mountains, and valleys of northern Mexico searching for Villa and his soldiers. Mexico's president protested the incursion but did not move decisively to stop it, although Mexican troops killed a dozen U.S. soldiers near the town of Carrizal in June.

President Wilson ordered the National Guard to protect the U.S.-Mexico border and sent American warships to international waters along both of Mexico's coasts. By November, four-fifths of the regular U.S.

Army troops were either in Mexico or stationed along its northern border. The foreign office in Berlin was elated. German agents did everything they could behind the scenes to prolong the mission, including shipping weapons to Villa from a German-owned factory in Bridgeport, Connecticut. German agents in San Francisco devised a plan to smuggle weapons into Mexico using coffins and oil tankers.

In November 1916, the blunt and outspoken Arthur Zimmerman became Germany's Foreign Minister and stepped up secret discussions about a possible alliance with Mexico and Japan against the United States. At the end of that month, the massive Allied offensive along the Western Front came to a standstill, having moved the Front eastward by seven miles at a cost of about a million casualties. The stalemate continued.

On a different political front, the Political Section had been working secretly with an Irish nationalist, Sir Roger Casement, to plan a spring uprising in Dublin that, in theory, would divert British troops and resources away from Europe. On April 24, 1916, Easter Monday, the Irish rebels took over the Post Office and other key points in Dublin, and nationalists read a proclamation announcing the establishment of an Irish Republic.

It seemed to be a promising beginning. But Casement's recruitment of Irish prisoners of war in Germany had fallen far short of his goals, and a German shipment of arms never reached the Irish nationalists, who were crushed by British forces. Casement himself was imprisoned and later executed as a traitor.

Berlin's tactics may have failed in Ireland, but its operatives were more widespread in North America with its millions of German-speaking immigrants. So far, the nation's German-language newspapers remained solidly against the war. America's Irish tended to agree. But it remained to be seen how loyal those immigrants and the children of earlier immigrants would be to their adopted country in the event of war. Ethnic politics was one of numerous reasons why President Wilson had kept U.S. troops out of the Great War.

Germany's new foreign minister enjoyed making the argument to Americans that their internal politics should keep them neutral. The blustery Zimmerman, a former judge, had become friends earlier in the war with another former judge, U.S. Ambassador to Germany James W.

Gerard, a harsh critic of Germany but who had nevertheless cultivated Zimmerman, once describing him as "a very jolly sort of large German."

As early as 1916, Gerard had begun to advocate war against Germany "to have it decided that the United States of America is not to be run from Berlin." He argued that Germans believed that Americans "could be slapped, insulted and murdered with absolute impunity," in part because of the political clout of German Americans in the United States. "There is no question that there is a deep-seated hatred of America here, which must be reckoned with sooner or later."

The "jolly" German diplomat and the skeptical American ambassador would meet in Berlin, Gerard recalled later, in a spacious room in the Foreign Office, which was housed in a structure that had once been the home of a seductive Italian dancer who had counted Frederick the Great among her admirers.

Zimmerman—whose diplomats in Washington had consistently exaggerated the strength of pro-German sentiment in the United States—warned Gerard about the fragility of American democracy in the face of ethnic tensions. The foreign minister argued that America's much-vaunted melting pot might boil over if an unpopular war—a war against the fatherland of one of the nation's largest ethnic groups—were added to the mix: "In case of trouble," Zimmerman told Gerard, "there are half a million trained Germans in America who will join the Irish and start a revolution."

Startled that Zimmerman was serious, Gerard reportedly replied in kind. "In that case, there are half a million lamp-posts to hang them on."

IN THE MEANTIME, Germany scored a publicity coup in America. In July 1916, Captain Paul König piloted his U-boat, the *Deutschland*, across 4,250 nautical miles through the British sea blockade from Bremen to Baltimore. The *Deutschland* was history's first commercial submarine, built expressly to carry trading goods through—in this case, under—the blockade.

"The film companies were able to score a triumph," the leather-faced captain recalled later in his book, *The Voyage of the Deutschland*, describing his crew's pandering to movie cameramen as the U-boat sailed up the

Chesapeake Bay toward the port of Baltimore. "I fulfilled their desire to immortalize the entire crew upon their first treading American soil."

Entering a city with one of the nation's largest German American populations, Captain König described his trip from the docks to downtown Baltimore as "a triumphal procession. The auto was obliged to halt every moment, and I was congratulated upon all sides, and everybody wished to shake my hand.... The following days were to become one continual festival for us."

Germany needed a propaganda boost that summer; the *Deutschland* provided it.

GIANT GERMAN SUBMARINE ARRIVES IN CHESA-PEAKE CARRYING DYES AND MESSAGE FROM KAISER TO PRESIDENT

proclaimed the headline on the *Washington Post* front page when the *Deutschland*—which the newspaper called "the world's first and greatest undersea boat"—completed its voyage.

Before arriving in Baltimore, the *Deutschland* sailed into the Virginia capes under the pall of darkness. The sub was accompanied through the Hampton Roads corridor by a tugboat that pointed its way up the Chesapeake. Commanding that tug, the *Timmins*, was none other than Captain Frederick Hinsch. Paul Hilken was in charge of the *Deutschland*'s goods and its gala reception in Baltimore.

Hidden in the cargo holds of the U-boat were fresh cultures of glanders and anthrax germs for the Chevy Chase germ factory, as well as new incendiary pencils for sabotage at munitions factories, Herrmann said later. The day before the *Deutschland* appeared off the Virginia Capes, Hilken and "Lewis"—a code name for Fred Herrmann—met with Hinsch in Newport News. An investigator observed later:

> It is significant that Hilken and Herrmann, who had taken part in the sabotage conference in Berlin in February 1916, should have been together with Hinsch, the sabotage master in this country, at Newport News awaiting the arrival of the *Deutschland*. This is further and significant evidence of the intermingling of sabotage and commercial submarine activities.

Herrmann said later that the germ sabotage was still going on in Newport News "until almost the day of the arrival or a few days before the arrival of the *Deutschland*." At that time, Eddie Felton, the foreman who paid dockhands to jab horses and mules, "was down in Newport News and those places around there, distributing germs."

Later that year, Hilken and Hinsch would receive medals from both Germany and Austro-Hungary for their work in arranging the *Deutschland*'s docking, trade, and reception in America. The medals included the Order of the Red Eagle and the Order of Franz Josef. "They were about the last decorations that [Austrian Emperor] Franz Josef conferred" before his death, Hilken recalled later.

Showing remarkable PR savvy, König—a popular figure for evading the blockade—talked with eager newspapermen and issued a press statement: "We trust that the old friendly relationship with the United States, going back to the days of Washington, when it was Prussia who was the first to help America in its fight for freedom from British rule, will awake afresh in your beautiful and powerful country." The chief stoker in his crew was moved to write a poem about the *Deutschland*'s voyage, beginning:

> *That's a celebration we all hold dear,*
> *A German U-boat in Baltimore!*

When the U.S. government allowed the *Deutschland* to dock at U.S. ports and unload and load cargo in the summer of 1916, the Allies protested. They demanded that "any belligerent submarine entering a neutral port should be detained there," even if a sub were designated as a merchant vessel, because no one could check its neutrality or cargo on the high seas. The State Department quickly rejected that demand. It also rejected a German request that the U-boat be escorted by U.S. Navy ships once it reached American waters off the coast and in Chesapeake Bay. The U.S. government remained neutral.

Trying to squeeze every ounce of publicity it could out of the *Deutschland*'s arrival, a high-level committee of German Americans worked relentlessly to gin up media coverage. In one publicity stunt, the group proposed publishing "the world's largest book"—the size of a grand piano—to commemorate the U-boat's sixteen-day voyage across the embargoed Atlantic. "When this work is completed and placed in the Royal Library in Berlin, it will be the first monument ever put there by the American people," wrote a former editor of the *New York Staats-Zeitung* in a fundraising letter.

That letter was issued on behalf of the American Deutschland Committee, whose members included numerous heavy-hitting U.S. business and political leaders. The editor described the *Deutschland*'s achievement as "the dream of ages," and a separate flyer for the piano-sized-book campaign boasted that the "undersea voyage of the *Deutschland* is the wonder of the age." The flyer was illustrated by a drawing of the "greatest book ever made," which would be "bound in solid silver with solid gold clasps and corners tooled by the best artists in the jeweler's world." And it claimed that "the press of all America burst forth in praise of the daring undertaking," while news of the U-boat voyage "swept over the world, emphasizing the achievement of the German people." That was a wild exaggeration, but many American newspapers had indeed covered the *Deutschland*'s maiden voyage.

One of the captain's admirers was H. L. Mencken, who met König at a *Volksfest* in Baltimore a few days after the *Deutschland* arrived. He visited the captain in Connecticut, shortly before the submarine departed on its perilous voyage back to Germany. After the war, they kept in touch, with Mencken visiting the captain in Bremen and the two exchanging cards and letters well into the 1930s. Mencken called König "a tough mariner, but a very quiet and unassuming man."

A decade after the war's end, Mencken revealed in a memoir that Paul Hilken had tried to convince him to ride the *Deutschland* back to Germany in the summer of 1916—an offer that Hilken had not bothered to clear with the U-boat's captain. Confiding that the *New York Tribune* had offered to pay $50,000 for one of its writers to ride the submarine, Hilken told Mencken that "he was against it because of the *Tribune*'s violent support of England." Instead, Hilken invited Mencken. "If I would consent to make the trip back to Bremen," Mencken wrote, "I would have the exclusive right free of charge, and would be free to sell my reports to the highest bidder."

Mencken refused Hilken's 1916 offer because "there seemed to be something fishy about this ... Indeed, I'd have refused if there had *not* been anything fishy, for I knew that a large British fleet was waiting for the *Deutschland*, outside the Chesapeake capes, and the chances of its getting through seemed very slim."

The *Deutschland* did make it up to its next port, New London, Connecticut, but Mencken claimed later that the sub was able to escape the British fleet "only because he got some unexpected help from friendly American naval officers, many of whom disliked the British." He contended that the sympathetic Americans had recommended a seldom-used course along the Maryland coast that helped the U-boat elude British warships.

A private shipping company, the Bremen-based Deutsche Ozean Rheederei, operated the *Deutschland*, which had been built along with its sister sub, the *Bremen*, to carry one thousand tons of cargo. Launched with great fanfare from a Flensburg shipyard on March 28, 1916, the *Deutschland* made two highly publicized voyages to U.S. ports, carrying mostly dyestuffs to America and returning to Germany with rubber, nickel, tin, and other strategic supplies that were badly needed for war production.

The propaganda promise of the initial voyage to Baltimore in June 1916 was not sustained. The *Bremen* was lost at sea, and the image of the *Deutschland* was tarnished when it rammed a tugboat near New London, dooming the plan for the "greatest book."

Less than three weeks after the *Deutschland*'s arrival in Baltimore, a new wave of highly public sabotage would begin to transform America's neutral view of ethnic Germans, eventually replacing it with the forbidding new concept of German Americans as "the enemy within."

THE FIRST MAJOR JOLT to public opinion came from a series of nighttime explosions that struck the New Jersey side of New York Harbor, concussions that some writers compared to the awful onslaughts of the war's Western Front.

The worst of those blasts sent shrapnel flying so far that it struck the Statue of Liberty, ricocheting off her green copper skin and splashing into the dark waters below. The Great Lady was so shaken that a hundred of her rivets popped loose.

In the darkness, one tremendous eruption followed another, as if someone were firing artillery rounds from a gunship. Thousands of windows in lower Manhattan and Jersey City shattered from the blast pressure, sending sharp missiles onto the empty streets and sidewalks as far away as Fifth Avenue. Shock waves rumbled through the darkness for ninety miles, causing the Brooklyn Bridge to sway and rattling late-night riders in the train tubes under the Hudson River.

After the initial confusion, the pattern of the fires that broke out soon made it clear that the blast's epicenter was a railroad yard called Black Tom, where warehouses, buildings, and barges full of munitions were exploding with a fury that lit up the night sky for hours. The harbor was bedlam that early morning of July 30, 1916, as rescue and fire-fighting ships encountered a series of explosions, continuing until dawn, which consumed two million pounds of explosives and killed seven people. The next day, smoke wafted skyward from a three-hundred-foot-wide crater that yawned where the rail yard and thirteen warehouses had exploded and burned. Losses included eighty-five rail cars and a hundred barges loaded with ammunition.

The explosions at Black Tom—at the time, the most important point in America for the transfer of munitions to Allied transport ships—were listed by police as an accident at first, but investigators soon grew suspicious about foreign sabotage. They also alerted federal law enforcement to the gravity of the threat from sabotage—a threat that would lead the following spring to draconian new laws against espionage and sedition. In the end, Black Tom became the best-known act of German-financed sabotage in America.

Anton Dilger was in Germany when Black Tom blew, but his circle of saboteurs was central to the planning and financing of the munitions attack. Dilger's main collaborators in germ sabotage—Hinsch, Hilken, and Herrmann—each played a role, as did another shadowy German agent, Kurt Jahnke, a master spy who would become Dilger's nemesis.

Before this dramatic success, most of the German sabotage focused on ships carrying the munitions. But that effort—like the horse sabotage—had not been achieving the desired results by 1916, leading German planners to shift the targets to large munitions plants and the transport yards where munitions were warehoused and then shipped.

Planning for the Black Tom sabotage had begun months earlier, with the mission code-named "Jersey." The saboteurs paid "inside men" at the LeHigh Valley Railroad Company—the main rail operator at Black Tom—to report on the movement of munitions, the design of the compound, and the best ways for a saboteur to get in. Meanwhile, Jahnke and fellow saboteur Lothar Witzke arrived from San Francisco, and a young Hungarian immigrant, Michael Kristoff, was recruited to help.

The incendiary devices to be used in the blast and various other sabotage operations had been delivered in two waves, beginning with the false-bottom trunk that Herrmann had brought back from Berlin and followed by whatever fire-starters were brought on the *Deutschland*. It is also possible that the new devices brought by Carl Dilger, who apparently knew nothing about the plan, might have been available shortly before the Black Tom sabotage.

The night before the blast, some of the saboteurs had gathered at the townhouse on West 15th Street operated by a former opera singer, Martha Held, who arranged for attractive young women to spend time with visiting Germans and their guests. That evening, one of the escorts, Mena Edwards, saw a group of foreign-sounding men sitting around the dining-room table, which was covered by blueprints, maps, and photographs showing scenes of the New York waterfront.

While the exact details of the sabotage were never clarified, investigators said during the 1930s that the most likely scenario involved Jahnke and Witzke rowing a small boat full of explosives, incendiary devices, and time bombs to a secluded area of the Black Tom terminal. (At one point, Witzke reported, rough waves struck the boat and nearly capsized it.) Just before midnight, the two men met up with Kristoff, who had walked into the depot from a vulnerable entrance on the land side. The saboteurs set fires in a few gunpowder-filled boxcars and affixed incendiary devices as well as a time bomb to an explosive-laden barge just off the pier. A watchman told investigators he had put out one of the small boxcar fires and then caught sight of a two-man rowboat heading out into the harbor.

Two nights after the explosion, Madame Held threw a big party at her townhouse. A large crowd of guests arrived, including "some captains" from interned German ships as well as several German reservists.

The Black Tom explosion was the prime subject of talk, and "there was a great deal of drinking and hilarity," Mena Edwards said later. When that party closed down at 1:00 a.m., about twenty of the revelers took taxis to the Bismarck Café, where they "drank further toasts and sang German songs."

Hinsch was likely one of the guests at Held's townhouse that evening. He never admitted his Black Tom planning role to American investigators, but the portly captain boasted about that role later to fellow German saboteurs, claiming credit for orchestrating the sabotage. A year after the explosion, Hinsch even enlisted the testimony and backing of Anton Dilger in an effort to back up his braggadocio in a message sent to Berlin.

The day after the blasts, Hinsch showed up unannounced at the New York office of Norddeutsche Lloyd and asked for $2,000 from the local manager, whose office windows had been cracked by the shock waves. When that manager refused, "Hinsch was indignant and left him and told him what he thought of him," recalled Hilken. Then Hinsch called Hilken in Baltimore to plead for the money "immediately." The Baltimore paymaster sent Hinsch the cash from his own strong box. "He seemed much elated over the Black Tom explosion," Hilken recalled later. "I asked him whether he had anything to do with it and he said, 'You had better not ask any questions.'"

Chapter 10

GATEWAY TO THE WEST

I don't believe Wilson will go to war unless Germany literally kicks him into it.
—Former President THEODORE ROOSEVELT, February 1917

WITH THE BLACK TOM DESTRUCTION casting suspicion on America's enemies within, the presence of a secret germ lab and a basement assembly line for incendiary devices in the middle of the nation's capital suddenly seemed like a bad idea. Even though Tony's Lab had been kept secret for nine months, the Chevy Chase cottage was much too close to Justice Department investigators who would soon be hunting for saboteurs.

Moreover, the unexpected return in late July of Carl Dilger—who Captain Hinsch and Paul Hilken had tried unsuccessfully to strand in Germany—further complicated an already dangerous situation. Neither of the sabotage leaders trusted the talkative, hard-drinking Carl, especially now that police would be paying informants to report any suspicious comments.

And then there was the matter of the explosive "pencils," some of which had been taken to New York for sabotage jobs. Ever since Fred Herrmann had moved into the cottage that spring, the cellar lab had been producing small rod-shaped incendiary devices as well as anthrax and glanders germs. Hinsch himself had met the newly-arrived Herrmann at the Hansa Haus in Baltimore, driven him to the Chevy Chase house, introduced him to Em and Carl, and proudly shown him the basement laboratory.

A few months earlier, Carl had been indispensable, as the only person Anton had shown how to operate the incubator and culture the bacteria in the lab. But the crafty Hinsch had instructed Herrmann "to stay there with Carl and learn how to breed those things [germs], and always keep 24 to 36 bottles [of germ cultures] on hand, that he would pick them up once or twice a week as he needed them." It was the first step in Hinsch's plan to ease Carl out of the picture without alienating his brother Anton, who had been working in Germany since January.

Now that the saboteurs had scored their first major coup at Black Tom, they could ill afford to have a man they didn't trust being a caretaker of the Chevy Chase house. So Carl—at odds with both Hilken and Hinsch over money, and making it clear that his role in sabotage would end if the United States ever declared war—was instructed to help shut down Tony's Lab a few weeks after the Black Tom blast. "Hilken told me that the incendiary and germ work was going to be stopped and he wanted to collect some money that my brother [Anton] had given me," Carl recalled. "I had previously had a row with Hilken about money matters. I had about three or four thousand dollars of the money left, and after some argument with Hilken I turned the money over to him."

Having decided to jettison Carl and abandon the house in Chevy Chase, Hilken and Hinsch had to break the news to Em Dilger that she was being evicted. The latter task was easy because Em, who missed her brother Anton and had become increasingly suspicious about what was going on in her basement, quickly left the house and moved in with her sister Jo's family in Washington. Until her dying day in 1947, Em would claim that she didn't know what Anton and Carl had been doing in the basement lab, even though Anton's disingenuous explanation about medical experiments must have seemed suspicious after he moved out and his brewer brother was able to continue the same project. And it is difficult to believe that the sharp-witted Em did not put two and two together when Fred Hermann started carrying chemicals into the cellar and brewing the foul-smelling ingredients of the incendiary devices.

With Em and Carl out of the way, and Anton still working in Germany, the task fell to Herrmann—who knew virtually nothing about laboratories or bacteria—to load all of Anton's equipment and glassware into boxes and move them out of the cottage. At about the same time Hinsch told Carl that the germ work was finished, he asked Herrmann to carefully pack "the [germ] incubator and things we had down there" and put them into storage. Once Carl was out of the way, they planned to rebuild the germ laboratory somewhere else—much farther away from federal investigators in the nation's capital.

Meanwhile, Herrmann had found a new recruit who could be trusted to help him with the sabotage work and keep quiet about it. The new assistant, a young immigrant named Raoul Gerdts, was living at a boarding house on West 79th Street in New York. Friendless and foreign, Gerdts and his mother had emigrated a few months earlier from South America and were living hand-to-mouth at "Mrs. Kelly's boarding house." Gerdts, who spoke German and Spanish but hardly any English, was desperate for work, and Herrmann had promised to pay him well.

Shortly after he was recruited as Herrmann's assistant, Gerdts accompanied his new boss to a modest cottage in Roselle, New Jersey, about forty miles southwest of New York. He followed Herrmann up the stairs of the typical immigrant home, with the sounds of German conversation echoing down the wallpapered hallways and the aroma of sauerkraut and baked pork emanating from the kitchen.

Closing the bedroom door behind them, Herrmann retrieved a battered brown suitcase from the closet, placed it on the bed, and opened the latches. Inside, Gerdts recalled later, was the cotton-lined wooden box, carefully packed with "small glass tubes which contained a liquid. I was told that these tubes contained germs of all kinds." Gerdts had no idea that the yellowish contents of those tubes—bacterial cultures—also could have infected and possibly killed him.

That summer of 1916, while Hinsch had busied himself with the *Deutschland* project and the planning for the Black Tom sabotage, Herrmann and Gerdts had taken over the distribution of germ cultures to dockhands at East Coast ports, from New York City to Savannah, Georgia. Aside from the jabbing technique, the saboteurs now told the dockhands to snap on rubber gloves and try "rubbing the [germs] on the mouth of one of the animals" so that "eventually the germs would be communicated to the mass of animals."

Once the Chevy Chase germ cultures had been depleted, they would need a new laboratory to propagate more. With Hinsch, Herrmann discussed where best to move the laboratory. "I made a trip all through the west first and came back and reported to him," said Herrmann. "Hinsch gave me the names of the cities and more or less where the stockyards were. I remember him distinctly describing Memphis to me and he thought it best for me to open up [a germ lab] in Memphis."

But Memphis was not the final choice. Herrmann ended up in another Mississippi River city that had an even larger horse market and was closer to the Missouri mules: St. Louis.

THE DUSTY, NOISY, AND STINKING stockyards of Middle America were the lifeblood of the British Remount Service's horse-buying operations. Those sprawling yards in East St. Louis, Chicago, Memphis, and Kansas City were the places where horse trading was done before the animals were shipped to the East Coast for their perilous voyages to the European battlefields. That made the Midwestern stockyards prime targets for sabotage. As early as the spring of 1915, German agents had planned to blow up a cattle train from the Chicago yards and had scouted other yards in the Midwest. Herrmann's assignment in the fall of 1916 was to scout those stockyards as prime targets for germ sabotage, especially after port security on the East Coast was tightened.

Journalist Basil Clarke reported in 1917 that saboteurs were trying to poison or infect horses as they were being bought by the British Army in the Midwest and shipped to Europe.

> German agents tried every conceivable means to destroy British war-horses before they were shipped. In several cases disease germs were poured into depot [bins] or water supplies; in another case, small steel German agents' spikes, each of them barbed at the sides like the end of a fish hook, were mixed with oats intended for horse food. These, if swallowed by a horse, were calculated to perforate the stomach and bowels—a most barbarous thing to do to any horse.

Based on his interviews with British remount officials, Clarke added: "No outrage that was calculated to kill a horse or to give him disease that would spread to other horses—in fact, no outrage of any kind—was too bad for these German agents to attempt, and the watch maintained to prevent this sort of thing had to be most strict."

At that time, the world's largest horse and mule market was the National City Stockyards, situated on the edge of East St. Louis, Illinois—just across the Mississippi River from the thriving commercial and transportation center of St. Louis. In 1916, that stockyard sprawling expanse of pens, corrals, and wooden shacks encompassed 650 acres, enough to process tens of thousands of horses, mules, cattle, hogs, and sheep a day. Hundreds of buyers lined up for the auctions. In the distance were the giant slaughterhouses of the Armour, Swift, and Hunter meat companies, which at their peak employed some 10,000 workers.

Long lines of immigrants, many of whom spoke little English, sought work in the National City yards and packing houses. In an effort to keep wages low and to avoid a unified labor force, business owners also brought many African American workers from poor southern states to work in the hellish environment of the slaughterhouses. The goal was to use ethnic and racial tensions to help keep the disparate workforce from organizing, but those tensions would break out of control in July 1917 when the worst race riot in twentieth-century American history erupted nearby in East St. Louis.

From 1914 to 1919, the National City Stockyards handled the sale of 1.4 million horses and mules—more than twice the number of equines that passed through its biggest competitors in Kansas City and Chicago. The war years, particularly 1915–17, saw the peak of horse and mule sales in the United States.

Shortly after the Black Tom explosions, in early August 1916, Herrmann and Hinsch talked at length about the future of their germ sabotage during a party at the Astor Hotel in New York. "We had arranged and agreed upon taking this germ affair out to St. Louis and establishing it out there," Herrmann recalled. A month later, Herrmann made his first trip.

Like Baltimore, St. Louis was a city with a large and influential German American community—a basis of support that Herrmann and his accomplice could rely on if they got into a fix. With the growth of traffic on the Mississippi and Missouri rivers, the city had been the nation's second largest at the turn of the nineteenth century. Although in 1904 it had hosted a successful World's Fair and the Olympics, St. Louis lost out to Chicago as the Midwest's most important rail center, but it remained the Gateway to the West, a center of trade and transport between the western and eastern United States.

Fred Herrmann spent a week in St. Louis in early September 1916, scouting horse and mule operations at the stockyards, meeting with local German American contacts (including a relative of Hinsch), and looking for a place to rent that would be appropriate for a germ-propagation laboratory, the Midwest successor to Tony's Lab.

He then returned to Baltimore and New York to confer with Hinsch and Hilken about the best way to set up the new lab. That mission had been relatively simple for Anton Dilger, who had studied germ cultures and knew the machinery and the methods for working in a microbiology laboratory. But Herrmann, a high school graduate, had no training other than what he had picked up under Carl the brewer's tutelage at the basement lab that spring.

A few weeks later, Herrmann returned to St. Louis—this time with fresh starter cultures of anthrax and glanders germs, and most likely with some incubation equipment. He also brought along another saboteur, code-named "Wolfgang," whom he had met in New Jersey in the summer of 1916. Wolfgang in turn recruited "some fellows down around Gillespie, Perth Amboy and in Jersey" to help with sabotage. His identity remains uncertain, but it is clear that Wolfgang was a German American from New Jersey and that he had been helping with the bio-sabotage at East Coast ports as a middleman, "assisting us," Herrmann said, "in distributing these germs through [stevedores] to the horses and mules that the Allies had bought."

There is no doubt that Wolfgang knew a great deal about Herrmann's sabotage operations. In a secret message that Herrmann sent after he fled the country in 1917, he worried about "Wolfgang and that Hoboken bunch. If cornered they might get us in Dutch with authorities." (Norddeutsche Lloyd had a major office in Hoboken that had been a hub for sabotage.)

Anthrax and glanders were no strangers to the vast Midwest stockyards, although naturally-occuring outbreaks of both diseases were waning among livestock by the time of the Great War. During the nineteenth century, infected cattle had spread anthrax along the cattle trails of the Midwest and the West. When a cow died, the anthrax bacteria inside the animal formed into spores that could survive for decades. Animals that later breathed in spore-laden dust or chewed grass where spores had landed would come down with anthrax.

But strict control measures had made natural cases of anthrax and glanders relatively uncommon by 1916. Herrmann and Wolfgang wanted to cause outbreaks of both diseases at the stockyards, but neither man was an expert in growing germ cultures. Herrmann helped set up the germ lab in St. Louis and then left Wolfgang to mind the store.

WHILE HERRMANN TRAVELED to dusty livestock markets in the Midwest and Southwest that fall, the U.S. Cavalry was competing with British and French military buyers for fresh supplies of horses and mules. Severe disease outbreaks among horses being shipped to Texas from the Midwest were suddenly complicating the buyers' mission.

At that time, most of the U.S. Cavalry units were either with the punitive expedition against Pancho Villa in Mexico or stationed at various bases or encampments near the border. It was the first major engagement that received horses from the new Army remount depots, including the Front Royal depot, which included Dilger Field.

The Mexican expedition subjected units of the U.S. 7th and 10th Cavalry, led by General Pershing, to grueling endurance tests. Significantly, there were horse shortages—not only because of the harsh conditions in Mexico but also because of severe disease outbreaks among horses and mules. The emergence of the mysterious horse infections dealt serious blows to the U.S. Army's horse supplies. In the expedition's first two days, about seventy of the animals died or "dropped out" of the ranks; three weeks later, General Pershing asked for 804 horses and 146 mule replacements. The Army was hard-pressed to provide them.

"We were caught without the reserve animals which many had foreseen for some years would be needed," wrote Captain F. L. Case of the U.S. 3rd Cavalry in an article in the October 1916 issue of the *Journal of the U.S. Cavalry Association*. "The problem was much complicated by the existence of a very severe infection, especially virulent in the Mississippi Valley"—what he called an "exceedingly persistent and very infectious" disease that he speculated was "septic influenza" or pneumonia.

Case said army veterinarians had told him that the infection was "a variety of disease of rather recent origin" that had also struck the American horses being shipped to the British and French armies. "European governments have lost very seriously from it, in some extreme cases 90 percent, in a shipload."

At Fort Sam Houston in Texas—the closest major U.S. Army base to Pershing's expedition—about half of the animals were sick at any one time, according to Case. Six mules died during a single rail shipment from the East St. Louis stockyards, and many of the horses that were shipped from Front Royal and a new auxiliary depot in El Paso were also infected. Case asserted that "our small reserve [of remounts] has been wiped out, and that very malignant types of disease threaten all the mounts and mule transportation of the army unless stringent precautions are taken."

A copy of Case's disturbing article about horse disease outbreaks was later found among Herrmann's notebooks and other papers. His sketchy notes from the summer and fall of 1916 show clearly that he was scouting horse stockyards, companies, and shipping depots in the Midwest and Southwest, with an emphasis on Texas, which borders Mexico.

The saboteur also spent time at stockyards at Dallas, Fort Worth, and Houston—jotting down the names of two firms, Bowser Horse & Mule in Houston and H & M Stables in San Antonio. He also visited the ports of New Orleans and Galveston as well as the Midwestern stockyards in Memphis, Tennessee, and Paducah, Kentucky.

The most important company listed in Herrmann's book was western Missouri's giant Guyton & Harrington—the largest single provider of mules and horses to the British Army. He also visited the Burnett horse company, which had offices in both East St. Louis and Fort Worth, Texas. During a train trip through southwestern Missouri, Herrmann made note of features along the tracks that might make good sabotage targets.

He seems not to have spent much time at his germ lab in St. Louis, for he also traveled back and forth to the East Coast several times. "After I established [the germ factory] and had it running in St. Louis, I made four or five trips to Baltimore, to New York, and saw Hilken and Hinsch at these times, leaving the [St. Louis] plant with Wolfgang," Herrmann told investigators.

If it weren't for a cold snap that fall—and probably the limited competence of the two saboteurs at propagating germs—St. Louis might have ended up as the second main hub of the German biological warfare effort to stop the supply of American horses and mules. But the two men apparently shut down their germ operation in November, when the cold killed the cultures. According to Herrmann, the "plant" in St. Louis operated "until the day before Thanksgiving.... It was getting too cold out there to breed the cultures or use them. That is why I gave it up." He wasted no time in getting rid of the equipment and the dead cultures and heading back East, taking a train that night with Wolfgang and arriving in Baltimore on Thanksgiving. The next day, pausing only to ask Hilken for $300, Herrmann headed back to New York City.

THE ST. LOUIS GERM FACTORY had been a bust, and Herrmann felt he needed to redeem himself with the Germans. He figured—rightly, it turned out—that he could do better with fires than with germs. It was time to use a few more of the incendiary pencils he had carried home from Berlin in the secret compartment of his trunk.

The previous summer he and Hinsch had discussed potential targets in the munitions industry, and Herrmann had chosen the Canadian Car & Foundry ammunition plant in Kingsland, New Jersey—an area he knew well. The plant's fourteen hundred workers were producing 3 million pounds of shells, cases, shrapnel, and gunpowder per month for shipment to the Russian Army. The massive factory, which also repackaged munitions from more than one hundred other factories around the country for shipment to Europe, encompassed thirty-seven frame buildings on several acres of land.

On paper, Kingsland seemed to be a vulnerable target. But Herr-mann found out that the plant complex was surrounded by a six-foot-high fence and patrolled day and night by a force of two hundred armed guards. Every worker was searched when he or she entered the plant, and matches and lighters were confiscated because the alcohol vats in the shell-cleaning shacks were extremely flammable. After the Black Tom debacle in July, the security at Kingsland had been tightened even further.

Clearly, an attack on Kingsland would have to be an inside job, and Captain Hinsch's sources soon found a mole to do it. A young Ukranian immigrant named Theodore Wozniak was working at the plant's Build-ing 30, where workers used gasoline-soaked cloths to clean metal artillery shells. No friend of Russia, Wozniak agreed to help the German saboteurs—for a price.

When Herrmann met Wozniak near New York's McAlpin Hotel in December, they agreed on a plan to set a fire in Building 30. After the failure of the St. Louis germ plot, Herrmann was excited by the prospect, even though he admitted later that he had doubts about Woz-niak, who seemed as volatile as the gasoline he would set afire. Herr-mann "thought he was slightly out of his mind."

In the mid-afternoon of January 11, 1917, a fire started near Woz-niak's bench in Building 30 of the Kingsland plant. Within minutes, ammunition shells began to explode, setting off a chain reaction that lasted for four hours and sounded like a cannonade during a great battle. About a million three-inch explosive shells—fortunately, nearly all of them without detonators—were shot hundreds of feet into the air, rain-ing down on nearby residential neighborhoods and tearing holes in roofs and walls. As dusk fell, one resident compared the scene to the "repeated opening of a furnace door in a darkened cellar."

Police began the investigation with the assumption that it had been an accidental fire, the *New York Times* at first reporting "no hint of a plot" and attributing the fire to a spark that fell into a tub of alcohol. But it did not take long for arson experts to suspect sabotage in Building 30. Interviews and forensic analysis made it clear that the initial fire had broken out near Wozniak's workbench. By that time, the Ukranian saboteur was nowhere to be found, but it was clear that the Germans worried about what he would say if interrogated by police.

A week after the Kingsland explosions, Hilken's assistant—jokingly calling Hilken the "Hindenburg of Roland Park"—mentioned a note from Herrmann, then staying at the McAlpin Hotel in New York, asking him "to advise his brother that he is in urgent need of another set of *glasses*." The "glasses" Herrmann requested were not spectacles but rather glass tubes—incendiary devices—that he and others had carried from Berlin the previous year. Hilken then sent a coded message to Herrmann suggesting that he should phone the Astor Hotel the following Tuesday "regarding an appointment" with the "brother."

At a party that month on the roof of the Astor Hotel in New York, a mistress of Hilken met Herrmann, who was then calling himself "Lewis." When she asked Hilken what the thin blonde fellow did, he replied: "He is the best spy I have." At a luncheon later with prominent German Americans in New York, she overheard Hilken joking about a newspaper article that described a munitions factory explosion—perhaps Kingsland.

"Wasn't it wonderful?" Hilken laughed. "He is marvelous."

THE LAST GREAT U.S. cavalry campaign was still thundering across northern Mexico in January 1917 when Germany made two crucial mistakes that would alienate Washington and, eventually, cause the United States to enter the Great War.

On January 25, President Wilson ordered Pershing to withdraw the last American forces from Mexico and ride back across the border. Pancho Villa remained at large, but Wilson—at the request of Mexico's President Carranza—had decided to withdraw the troops after eleven futile months. By the end of the first week of February, all the Americans and their horses were out of Mexico.

The withdrawal did not mean that U.S.-Mexican relations were stable. Ever since the *Lusitania* sinking in 1915, U.S. relations with Berlin had been strained. But that strain reached the breaking point when the British intercepted a secret message later dubbed the "Zimmerman Telegram," after its author, German Foreign Minister Arthur Zimmerman. The cable from Berlin ordered German U-boats to resume unrestricted warfare against Allied vessels, starting in February 1917. Even more disturbingly, it disclosed a German proposal for an alliance with Japan and Mexico that would allow the Mexicans to "reconquer its lost territory in Texas, New Mexico, and Arizona" with the help of "generous financial support" from Berlin. That alliance would be pursued if the United States declared war, but in the meantime Zimmerman wrote, "we will endeavor ... to keep the United States neutral."

The cable had been sent on January 16 to German Ambassador Johann-Heinrich von Bernstorff in Washington, with instructions to transmit the message to the German consul in Mexico City. That mode of transmission proved to be a terrible mistake—British Naval Intelligence intercepted and decoded the message. The original plan had been to send the message aboard the *Deutschland*, which had been scheduled to depart for Baltimore on January 15. But that voyage was cancelled at the last minute; the "commercial" sub soon would be converted to a warship.

The British did not immediately tell the White House about the Zimmerman Telegram, holding it to be revealed at the right moment.

On the last day of January, Germany's ambassador in Washington officially informed the U.S. government that it would resume unrestricted submarine warfare, starting the following day. "Unrestricted" warfare meant that U.S. and other neutral cargo and passenger ships were once again subject to possible attack by German U-boats. Two days later, the United States broke off diplomatic relations with Germany: Ambassador Bernstorff was sent back to Berlin and U.S. Ambassador Gerard began packing to return to the United States.

About three weeks afterward, the British presented the decoded Zimmerman Telegram to the U.S. ambassador in London; a few days later the text was leaked to the press, with the *New York Times* reporting in its March 1 editions under the headline:

GERMANY SEEKS ALLIANCE AGAINST U.S.

Asks Japan and Mexico to Join Her; Full Text of Her Proposal Made Public.

The combination of the unrestricted submarine warfare, Germany's secret efforts to create a diversionary war with Mexico, and the contin-

Medical student Anton Dilger relaxes during a visit home to Greenfield Farm in 1905. *Carl Keyser Archive (CKA).*

Anton's father, Hubert Dilger, was known as "Leatherbreeches" as a captain in the Union Army during the Civil War. Photo circa 1864. *Library of Congress.*

A portrait of the Dilger family at Greenfield in the early 1890s shows the white-bearded Leatherbreeches and his wife, Elise, in the back row; Elise's father, Dr. Tiedemann, in the middle row; and young Anton (laughing), at far lower right. *CKA.*

(*Above*) Young Anton Dilger (far right) watches his older brother Edward care for a new colt at Greenfield. Photo circa 1893. *CKA.*

(*Left*) A teenage Anton Dilger poses with his nephew Carl-Erik Koehler (a future German cavalry general), circa 1900. *CKA.*

Anton Dilger's surrogate family in Germany: his sister Eda, nephew Carl-Erik, and brother-in-law Martin Koehler. *CKA.*

Leatherbreeches walks in the Greenfield garden with his son Anton during the medical student's visit home in 1903. *CKA.*

Anton Dilger's official portrait as a new M.D. in Heidelberg, circa 1911. *CKA.*

Soldiers set up camp at the new U.S. Army Remount Depot in Front Royal, which purchased about a third of the Dilger farm's acreage. Photo circa 1914. *CKA.*

Anton's older brother Carl, shown here in a 1916 passport photo, helped out in the Chevy Chase lab but quit the sabotage gang after the United States declared war on Germany in 1917. *National Archives and Records Administration (NARA).*

Em Dilger kept house in Chevy Chase for her brothers, but claimed not to know what Anton and Carl were doing in the basement laboratory. *CKA.*

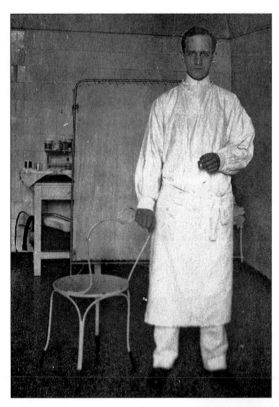

Cigarette in hand, Dilger strikes a pose in his surgical outfit, probably at the Heidelberg surgical clinic. *CKA.*

The war surgeon Dilger wears a Red Cross band as he poses next to an ambulance, possibly in Karlsruhe in 1915. *CKA.*

Submarine Capt. Paul König *(center)* poses with Dilger's friend and fellow saboteur Paul Hilken *(right)* after the U-boat *Deutschland* docked in Baltimore in 1916. *NARA.*

(Above left) Fred Herrmann, shown here in a passport photo, tried unsuccessfully to set up a new germ sabotage laboratory in St. Louis in 1916. *NARA.*

(Above) Soldiers load American war horses onto a train car for shipment to the Great War battlefields, circa 1917. *NARA.*

(Left) A liberty bonds poster from 1918 shows German aircraft strafing the Statue of Liberty. *NARA.*

THAT LIBERTY SHALL NOT PERISH FROM THE EARTH
BUY LIBERTY BONDS
FOURTH   LIBERTY   LOAN

Dilger is captured in a contemplative moment during his final visit to the United States in 1917. *CKA.*

The last known family photo of Anton Dilger shows him next to his Winton auto during his final visit to Greenfield in July 1917. *CKA.*

ued German sabotage and espionage in the United States—not to mention the intense pressure from the Allies and their American proponents—led President Wilson to decide in favor of war.

Wilson was a thin-lipped professor, not a soldier or a warmonger. As a student of the Civil War with a Virginia heritage, the president had probably read about the Chancellorsville exploits of Hubert Dilger. While he would not have been aware of the exploits of Anton Dilger, Wilson had followed keenly the reports of German American sabotage. By 1915, Wilson had already denounced the "creatures of passion, disloyalty and anarchy" who served the Kaiser as spies and saboteurs in America.

Former President Theodore Roosevelt had taken the rhetoric several steps further in 1916, denouncing as unpatriotic those Irish Americans and German Americans who called for U.S. neutrality in the Great War. Insisting that patriots had to be one hundred percent American, not "hyphenated-Americans," Roosevelt charged: "The German-Americans and [those]who call themselves such and who have agitated as such during the past year have shown that they are not Americans at all, but Germans in America. Their action has been hostile to the honor and interest of this country."

Blasts or fires at U.S. factories engaged in munitions or related production between 1915 and the spring of 1917—from the obvious sabotage of Black Tom and Kingsland to the more mysterious explosions or blazes of unknown origin at forty-two other plants—had caused well over $1 billion in damage (measured in 2005 dollars). And a week after Congress declared war, a mysterious fire destroyed a Hercules Powder Company plant in Pennsylvania, killing more than a hundred workers.

The streets were slick and shiny with rain as Wilson's limousine arrived at the light-splashed Capitol the evening of April 2, 1917. There was a sense of foreboding in Washington as members of Congress packed into the chamber of the House of Representatives and newspapermen and VIP guests filled the galleries. The president, greeted by tumultuous applause, spoke eloquently for thirty-six minutes, interrupted often by applause. In calling for a declaration of war "to make the world safe for democracy," Wilson not only denounced the Zimmerman

Telegram and Germany's Mexican intrigues, he also lashed out at German espionage and sabotage within the United States.

Blaming the Kaiser's "Prussian autocracy," Wilson said: "From the very outset of the present war it has filled our unsuspecting communities and even our offices of government with spies and set criminal intrigues everywhere afoot against our national unity of counsel, our peace within and without our industries and our commerce. Indeed it is now evident that its spies were here even before the war began."

The president said investigations related to the first wave of German sabotage showed "that the intrigues which have more than once come perilously near to disturbing the peace and dislocating the industries of the country have been carried on at the instigation, with the support, and even under the personal direction of official agents of the Imperial Government accredited to the Government of the United States."

While Wilson said the United States had repeatedly tried to "put the most generous interpretation possible" on the acts of German espionage and sabotage, he said "they have played their part in serving to convince us at last that that Government entertains no real friendship for us and means to act against our peace and security at its convenience. That it means to stir up enemies against us at our very doors the intercepted [Zimmerman] note to the German Minister at Mexico City is eloquent evidence."

Well aware that he was walking a political tightrope with so many ethnic Germans in the United States, Wilson took pains to draw a distinction between the German people and the Kaiser's militarism. He claimed that the United States remained

> sincere friends of the German people, and shall desire nothing so much as the early reestablishment of intimate relations of mutual advantage between us ... We have borne with their present government through all these bitter months because of that friendship—exercising a patience and forbearance which would otherwise have been impossible.
>
> We shall, happily, still have an opportunity to prove that friendship in our daily attitude and actions towards the millions of men and women of German birth and native sympathy, who

live amongst us and share our life, and we shall be proud to prove it towards all who are in fact loyal to their neighbors and to the Government in the hour of test. They are, most of them, as true and loyal Americans as if they had never known any other fealty or allegiance. They will be prompt to stand with us in rebuking and restraining the few who may be of a different mind and purpose.

But in a threat that would soon become embodied in the Espionage Act and the Sedition Act, Wilson warned: "If there should be disloyalty, it will be dealt with with a firm hand of stern repression; but, if it lifts its head at all, it will lift it only here and there and without countenance except from a lawless and malignant few." The House chamber exploded with cheers as the president finished, and members of Congress and gallery visitors stood and waved small American flags.

That moment represented the beginning of the end of the Great War, as well as the official beginning of the witch hunt for German spies, saboteurs, and sympathizers. Anton Dilger and his circle of saboteurs were certainly among what Wilson termed the "lawless and malignant few." But, for the most part, it was the innocent German Americans who suffered far more from Wilson's threats than did the guilty ones.

As soon as Washington declared war on April 6, the few American citizens who had remained in wartime Germany began scrambling to leave. Many of them had departed two months earlier, when diplomatic relations between the two countries had been severed and Ambassador Gerard had returned home.

By mid-April 1917, police began questioning holders of U.S. passports who were still living in Germany. Some of those Americans were placed under surveillance; others were ordered to stay in their homes or to report daily to local police. All were encouraged to leave—via Switzerland, Holland, or another neutral country—as soon as possible.

Even though Anton Dilger was still a U.S. citizen on paper, he stayed in Germany a full six weeks after war was declared and did not arrive back in New York until three months after Wilson's war message.

He had applied for German citizenship, possibly that spring, and one of his German uncles wrote later that Dilger had embraced a "newly adopted Fatherland," implying that citizenship had been granted to him.

Whatever his official status, Dilger was a German intelligence agent in 1917 and had likely been training in Berlin that spring for his next mission. That training would have involved studying Spanish, learning ciphers, using the most recent secret-ink formulas, and meeting with his handlers in the General Staff's Political Section.

Shortly before leaving Berlin, Dilger used the stationary of Berlin's Königshof Hotel to write an unusually long and frank letter to his sister Eda in Mannheim. It reads like a farewell from a man who suspected he might never return to Germany.

Dilger gave few hints about the reasons for his departure, but he made it clear in the letter that he had been given an assignment that came from a high level in Berlin. "I think this time I will be away longer than the last time," he wrote, probably referring to his last trip to America, the mission to Washington in 1915 and early 1916 to assemble Tony's Lab and start producing germ cultures. "Our higher authorities are this morning in great turmoil so that for the time being I cannot say anything about my orders."

That turmoil likely had to do with both the war and the internal political problems in Germany. On the day that Dilger wrote the letter, May 12, General Pershing was named commander of the new American Expeditionary Force, which would start arriving in Europe that summer. Pershing predicted that there would be a million U.S. troops aligned against the Germans within a year; if victory proved elusive, America was prepared to pour as many as three million soldiers into France to defeat the German Army.

That year German forces had launched five "spring offensives" along various sectors of the Western Front, probing for Allied weak points but encountering stiff resistance each time. Casualties on both sides were high. At the Chemin des Dames sector alone, the French had suffered 187,000 casualties; the Germans, 163,000. Morale among French soldiers was declining, but the prospect of American reserves offered some hope, and British troops made several advances in May.

In Berlin, the General Staff—led by Hindenburg and the mercurial General Erich Ludendorff—had been granted sweeping powers, with the military and industry manipulating the weakening Kaiser. The Chancellor, Theobald von Bethmann-Hollweg—described by an American diplomat as "a very tall, pleasant, Abraham Lincoln sort of a man"— had sought to maintain political coherence but found his influence declining as the war took precedence. The emergence of the Third Supreme Command the previous year had created what had become, in effect, a military dictatorship. Hindenburg, convinced that Britain would abuse any peace settlement, wanted to build a "Fortress Germany" that would be capable of fighting for another three years against the Allies.

A few days before the United States formally declared war, Chancellor Bethmann-Hollweg asserted that "Germany never had the slightest intention of attacking the United States" and that the submarine warfare had been a direct and logical consequence of Britain's "illegal and indefensible policy of blockade," which U.S. officials also had criticized. He also accused Britain of seeking the "annihilation" of imperial Germany. He added: "If the American Nation considers this a cause for which to declare war against the German Nation with which it has lived in peace for more than 100 years, if this action warrants an increase of bloodshed, we shall not have to bear the responsibility for it."

Behind the scenes, Bethmann-Hollweg had advocated a negotiated settlement to the war, which the High Command—confident of an eventual breakthrough—had rejected. The Chancellor contended that American entry into the war would ensure an eventual Allied victory, and he opposed unrestricted submarine warfare because he feared it would draw the United States into the fray. The General Staff gambled that it could seriously weaken British forces before their American allies arrived with reinforcements.

By May 1917—at the time Dilger wrote his letter—the High Command had scored a complete victory over Germany's civilian government, but the spring offensives on the Western Front had failed to fatally weaken the Allies. With civil unrest worsening within Germany, Bethmann-Hollweg promised electoral reforms on April 7, the day after the U.S. Congress declared war. Meanwhile, the opposition Social

Democrats, led by Philipp Scheidemann and Friedrich Ebert—who became chancellors after the war—had reluctantly supported a new round of war funding but were pressing in 1917 for a compromise peace. The Chancellor's promised electoral reforms temporarily mollified the left wing but alienated the military and conservatives, who soon moved to force him out.

"I hope to God that [Bethmann-Hollweg] will drop an energetic word to anyone in the Reichstag who will listen to stop the agitators who threaten to hold out with bitter anger," Dilger wrote to Eda. "All parties would like to know the government's stand on Scheidemann's peace proposal. I cannot judge if that is right, but cannot deny that the government is behaving all too passively at the moment."

"But perhaps it is good to say too little as to say too much," Dilger continued. "Because of our brilliant military positions everywhere one must wait patiently for all other developments." Convinced that the Germans eventually would conquer Italy, he wrote: "We will do well with the Italians in the not too distant future—just another chicken to pluck."

In the spring of 1917, German generals still believed that they could win the Great War before U.S. troops arrived en masse. But worsening conditions within Germany belied that bravado. During the winter of 1916–17, coal was in such demand in Berlin that some elephants from the Hagenbeck Circus and Animal Show were enlisted at one point to pull coal carts from the rail cars to distribution points around the city. In the Bavarian capital of Munich, a coal shortage forced the occasional closure of theatres, museums, and motion-picture theaters.

The same month that the United States declared war, a Berlin strike was called to protest problems with distributing rationed food. Rationing was imposed for many food items, including the "war bread" that was made out of potato and rye flour. On Monday mornings, Germans were given cards with perforated segments to be used for rationed foodstuffs, which eventually included beef, potatoes, sugar, butter, milk, and soap.

So many working-age men had been sent to the front by 1917 that German women were doing a great deal of manual labor, including helping to build Berlin's subway system. Women wielded pickaxes in rail yards, drove postal carts to deliver mail, and took jobs as "motor-men" on tram cars.

For horses and other essential animals, a shortage of fodder developed in the winter and early spring. Even before the war began, Germany had imported fodder. Some of the needed oats were bought or confiscated from farmers in the Ukraine or other conquered territories, but by 1917 the Germans were mixing sawdust into the rations of the German Army's horses. Many of them died of starvation during the cold months.

With the United States now in the war and its government actively hunting for German spies and saboteurs, the Political Section had a new mission for Dilger. This time, his focus would be on Mexico. In his letter to Eda, Dilger seemed to be burdened by the new assignment, rather than looking forward to it.

> This restless living is not pleasant. For two or three years I thought it was great fun. Now one thinks seriously and critically and has a so much greater feeling of responsibility that everything is looked upon from a more serious viewpoint.
>
> If only I can say after this effort ends, that I have done something special for Germany, it will have been the crowning achievement of my life. It is so noble in war to set aside all personal ambition for the greater general good.

AS AMERICA PREPARED for war and Dilger delved deeper into the underworld of espionage, Hollywood suddenly took an interest in German spies. Most of the silent feature-film plots were completely unrealistic, but a few would have resonated with ethnic Germans like Dilger and Herrmann who had decided to betray their native land.

Espionage movies featuring traitorous German Americans became popular. In *The Hun Within*, pioneering director D. W. Griffith told the story of a German American who becomes involved with German agents plotting sabotage against the United States. His father, a proud American tormented by conflicting loyalties, must decide between supporting his adopted homeland and betraying his traitorous son. Starring Erich von Stroheim as an evil German agent, *The Hun Within* might have amused Dilger and Herrmann, had they not already fled the country.

Another film, *The Spy*, was released by Fox Films, at about the time that Anton Dilger visited America for the final time in the summer of 1917. Sadly for U.S. counterintelligence, the movie was not well founded in reality. The plot centered on an American secret agent, Mark Quaintance, assigned to travel undercover to Berlin to find and secure a top-secret list of German spies in the United States.

Soon after he sets sail for Europe aboard a luxury liner, Quaintance meets a glamorous German woman, Greta Glaum. When they fall in love, he is unaware that she is a German spy, assigned to prevent him from getting his hands on the list. Once in Germany, the smitten Glaum decides to forsake the Kaiser and help the handsome American find the spy list. When he is arrested, it is up to Glaum to deliver the list to the U.S. ambassador. In the end, both Quaintance and Glaum are tortured and executed. But Quaintance had accomplished his mission: the network of German agents is exposed.

The Spy became a cause célèbre after its release. Former U.S. Ambassador Gerard—after fleeing Berlin to spread his anti-Kaiser message in America—fought to have *The Spy* shown widely in 1917. He claimed improbably that a German American had succeeded in blocking its release in Chicago theaters, but that Fox Films convinced a judge to issue an injunction "preventing anyone from interfering with the exhibition of the film."

The next year, a propaganda film based on Gerard's own anti-Kaiser story, *My Four Years in Germany*, found an enthusiastic public. Gerard himself attended the premiere at New York's Knickerbocker Theater, where the packed crowd "found much to applaud, considerable to hiss, and not a little to cheer," enthused the *New York Times*. The film depicted helpless Russian and English war prisoners being shot by firing squads and wantonly exposed to fellow inmates who suffered from typhoid. While much of the prison footage was billed as captured German newsreels, the most shocking scenes, including those depicting the inmates' exposure to typhoid, were filmed at a studio in New Jersey.

That summer the U.S. government itself began churning out anti-German propaganda, further adding to the suspicion of Germans as spies and sympathizers. *The Spy* fit nicely into the mix. The war freed moviemakers to turn Germans into complete villains. Among the most emotive titles were *The Claws of the Hun*, *The Prussian Cur*, and *Wolves of Kultur*.

In *Stolen Orders*, a group of evil German agents entangle a conflicted German American and his perfectly innocent daughter in a web of wartime intrigue. The film mixed fictional action with actual footage from the war and newsreel clips of President Woodrow Wilson giving his famous speech warning of "enemies within." Another drama that year, *Inside the Lines*, told the story of a British army captain who tracks down a German spy to thwart an evil plot to blow up Gibraltar and the British ships in its harbor.

By 1918, nearly a quarter of all U.S.-produced feature films (more than 200 out of the 845 total) would at least touch on some aspect of the war, ranging from home-front espionage dramas to battlefront heroism to wartime melodrama and undisguised propaganda screeds against Germany and the Kaiser. There were even war-related comedies, such as *Johanna Enlists*, which features megastar Mary Pickford playing a pretty farm girl who tantalizes soldiers who camp on her parents' property.

The Eagle's Eye took an unusual approach, telling the story of an American investigator and a government agent teaming up to expose a ring of German spies. The film claimed to present the true story of "the imperial German government's spies, plots and propaganda in the United States," as well as a nefarious plot to invade Canada.

The film's German characters were named for real spies and diplomats who had been expelled or had left the United States two years earlier. Actors with suitable scowls played the major German figures in America: the conniving German ambassador, Bernstorff; the two military attachés accused of overseeing sabotage, army attaché Franz von Papen and naval attaché Karl Boy-Ed; as well as the "Dark Invader" saboteur, Franz von Rintelen, who ended up in jail.

The germ sabotage gang escaped portrayal in a film, but some of Anton Dilger's life was worthy of Hollywood-style intrigue. One memorable moment would even require the old visual gag of one brother being mistaken for another. Anton Dilger had traveled by train from Berlin to Zurich in June 1917, almost certainly crossing the border using a German passport or other travel document using his false name Delmar. But he could not use that document to get to the United States, and his U.S. passport had expired. With the U.S. Embassy in Berlin closed, he needed to convince an American consular official in Europe to certify his American citizenship so he could obtain an emergency U.S. passport.

When Anton Dilger checked into his brother's hotel in Zurich, the clerk at the Hotel Eden zu Lac might well have done a double-take. For Anton—a dead ringer for the clerk's long-term American guest Louis Dilger—had registered under the surprising name Delmar with a German passport.

Hotel clerks in Switzerland were often paid informants for spies from one country or another. The interesting coincidence of the look-alike Dilger guests—one American and the other German—was a juicy enough tidbit for Allied agents. Louis's daughter remarked later that Anton Dilger had been guilty of "crazy recklessness" for registering with a German passport at his American brother's hotel.

After exchanging family greetings and small talk—which included the question of how to settle a tailor bill that Louis had once charged in Germany—Anton got down to business. He asked Louis for a favor: To verify Anton's identity as a U.S. citizen so that an emergency passport could be issued to him for a planned trip to New York. That request put Louis in an awkward position, for he must have known that his brother worked for German military intelligence. Later, he claimed to be unaware that Anton Dilger was a spy and possibly a German citizen.

Louis Dilger was in a position to help his brother because he had once been the U.S. Deputy Consul General in Hamburg. When the Hamburg consulate was closed in 1915, Louis had been posted to Aix-la-Chappelle (Aachen). At that time, he met and fell in love with Fanny Sauerbeck, who had been attracted to his look-alike brother Anton when she met him in Mannheim but liked Louis even more. Although born in England, Fanny was the daughter of two German parents. Her extremely wealthy grandfather had founded Badische Anilin Soda Fabrik (BASF), one of Germany's powerful dyestuff and chemical companies. After World War I broke out, she and her family were obliged to move to neutral Zurich, where they spent the war years. Her brother William, however, opted to join the British Army and was sent to the Western Front to fight the Germans. Louis Dilger, granted a leave of absence from the State Department, married Fanny in Zurich late in 1916 and tried to return with his new wife to his consular post in Germany. But the Germans refused to issue her a visa in late January 1917, and a week later the United States broke off diplomatic relations with Germany— meaning that all U.S. diplomats left the country.

That break had stranded Louis and his wife in Zurich, where they hoped for an early end to the war. One of his worst nightmares came true, however, when the United States declared war on Germany, jeopardizing his consular career. Two months later, Anton Dilger was knocking on his door.

Louis could not refuse Anton. On June 6, 1917, he vouched for his brother's U.S. citizenship. On the form, Anton Dilger swore that he planned to travel to the U.S. "for the purpose of residence." The U.S. Consulate then asked him to sign the "Oath of Allegiance" that was part of the emergency passport application:

> I do solemnly swear that I will support and defend the Constitution of the United States against all enemies, foreign and domestic; that I will bear true faith and allegiance to the same; and that I take this obligation freely, without any mental reservations or purpose of evasion; so help me God.

In contrast to the signature on his previous passport application of January 1916, Dilger's signature under the oath appears scratchy and hesitant. Louis himself signed the document as a witness certifying that Anton Dilger was "a native-born citizen of the United States." That signature that would haunt Louis for the rest of his life.

At the top of the passport application was hand-written: "Good for Two Months." That was all the time Anton Dilger needed to accomplish his missions in America and make his way to Mexico.

CARL DILGER was in potentially even deeper trouble than Louis. With the United States now at war with his brother's employer, the former germ propagator was suddenly desperate to escape any connection to sabotage.

If federal investigators did their job well, they would find enough to put Carl on a list of possible enemy sympathizers: he had socialized with German saboteurs, met in Berlin with General Staff officers, helped operate the germ laboratory in Washington, and had carried incendiary tubes into the United States.

Carl Dilger wanted out of the mess. He claimed later that he had told his brother Anton, Hinsch, and Hilken all along that he would drop all sabotage if the United States declared war on Germany. Once war was declared, Carl could have been charged with high crimes as a U.S. citizen engaging in sabotage for an enemy nation. Years afterwards, he testified:

> I had several conversations with Captain Hinsch about what would happen in case the United States got into the war. I told him that in that event I was going to quit, and I did quit before the United States entered the war, and had nothing to do with any work after that for Germany.

Shortly after Congress declared war on Germany, Carl said, "I went back to Montana in about April 1917, where I bought a ranch and I have lived there ever since." But that statement, if true, does not explain why Carl was in Norway two months after the war declaration. Family records include a mysterious postcard, postmarked in Bergen, Norway, on June 15, 1917—a week after Anton had filed his emergency passport application in Zurich and less than three weeks before he would depart Europe for America.

In the Norway postcard to his sister Jo in Washington, Carl Dilger scrawled an oddly sentimental message that gave no clue to what he was doing in Europe or how he had paid for the voyage. He wrote to his sister and her children that "my heart is with you. Tomorrow is our dear Mother's birthday. Give my love to all kiss each dear one with much love & many hearty kisses ever your Fat."

Years later, Jo's son speculated that Carl might have met his brother in Norway to explain his decision to "stop working for Germany," in light of the U.S. declaration of war. "The break was traumatic for both brothers," the nephew wrote, suggesting that the two brothers parted in tears because they might not meet again.

Anton Dilger was resolute. He had abandoned America in favor of Germany. Until that time, one could argue that his germ propagating did not break any specific federal laws, and that the sabotage against horses merely violated laws against the destruction of property.

But once Anton undertook his next mission for the General Staff in Berlin, he would be officially classified as a traitor and subject to the penalties of harsh new U.S. wartime espionage and sedition laws. He left Switzerland for France on June 21 and sailed from Bordeaux five days later aboard the steamer *Espagna*.

On board that ship, the German spy carried an emergency U.S. passport that would get him into New York but would cost his brother Louis dearly—the diplomat's career would be sacrificed as a result of his decision to assist Anton.

But later that summer Louis would suffer a more immediate loss: his brother-in-law Willie—born in London of German parents—was killed by a German bullet while he fought for the British in the third Ypres offensive.

Chapter 11

SPY HUNTING

There is not a state in the Union that is not infested with German spies...
—JUDGE GEORGE C. WEBB, Kentucky, 1918

THE AMERICAN PASSENGERS aboard the *Espagna* cheered as the ship approached the Statue of Liberty and steamed toward New York's teeming wharves on July 4, 1917. Hundreds of flags flew proudly on buildings ashore, and the distant sounds of patriotic songs echoed from parades on the streets of Manhattan.

America was openly at war with imperial Germany. Gunboats were anchored in the city's harbor and, from the ship's deck, Anton Dilger could see the uniforms of soldiers and sailors on shore. For the first time, he felt apprehensive about returning to his native land, even though his papers were in order and he had no reason to fear arrest.

On his previous return home, Dilger had arrived as a mere saboteur. On this trip, he was entering U.S. territory as a traitor. Dilger's new mission—to bribe or goad Mexico into invading the United States—had put him in another category entirely.

Three months after declaring war, America was finally getting around to waging it. That same day the American flag flew proudly in Europe as a regiment of fresh-faced doughboys led by General Pershing paraded through Paris for the first time. They promised much-needed relief for the French and British soldiers who had fought for three years along the merciless Western Front.

Elements of the 1st Division of Pershing's American Expeditionary Force (AEF) had arrived in Europe a few weeks earlier but waited for the Fourth of July to show the U.S. flag in Europe. The AEF did not take an active role at the front until October, when the 1st Division entered the trenches at Nancy, France. Within a year, a million Americans would be at the Front.

German Americans no longer had the luxury of dual loyalty, of living in one country while supporting the other. Now that America was at war, they had to choose. The brothers Anton and Carl Dilger took opposite paths.

In a letter sent in May to his sister Eda, Anton wrote: "I know that all my work and trouble are an infinitesimal and quite modest part of the effort of millions to protect our ... German values." By that time, he seems to have lost touch with America, except for visiting relatives.

Fireworks lit the Manhattan skyline that evening, bathing the Statue of Liberty in red, white, and blue. Patriotism was in the air, making life uncomfortable for many German Americans. In the three months since war was declared, ethnic Germans had been threatened, forced to take loyalty oaths or kiss American flags, forbidden from speaking German in public, and shunned by people who had once been friendly.

A wave of anti-German hysteria was swelling—a trend that would worsen once American soldiers began to die on the Western Front. Just two weeks before the Independence Day celebrations, former President William Howard Taft had called German militarism "a cancer which would absorb the wholesome life of the world unless it is cut out." President Wilson described the fight against Germany as "a people's war, a war for freedom and justice and self-government." Others in Washington dredged up images from the Crusades to urge young men to serve in what Secretary of War Newton Baker termed a "high and holy mission" to defeat Germany. Another cabinet member described the war against the church-going Kaiser as being a battle of "the world of Christ" against the world of force. One of the government's propaganda publications called the war "a crusade not merely to re-win the tomb of Christ, but to bring back to earth the rule of right, the peace, goodwill to men and the gentleness he taught."

Engaging in their own crusading missions, anti-German vigilante groups combed the country for spies and saboteurs, toppled German statues, lynched one German American, and tarred and feathered others for offenses ranging from refusing to buy Liberty Bonds to failing to renounce the Kaiser. H. L. Mencken, who had suspended his newspaper column and declined to write about the war, complained that the Germania Club in Baltimore was so "harassed by spy hunters" that it closed down. His own newspaper, the *Evening Sun*, often referred to Germans as "Huns" and its patriotic editorials were a factor in driving Baltimore's German-language newspaper, the *Deutsche Correspondent*, out of business.

"A violent spy-hunt was in progress, and one day I suggested casually that it was bound to bear heavily upon many German Americans who were completely innocent," Mencken recalled later. When he complained to the editor, Mencken was told that "they deserved it for being Germans."

Dilger was one of the relatively few German Americans who could have been legitimate targets for harassment and arrest. In the smoke-and-mirror world of espionage and sabotage, however, the majority of innocent ethnic Germans would pay for the crimes of a malignant few. Nearly all of the real German agents managed to escape the country or to avoid arrest in 1917.

When he arrived in New York harbor that Fourth of July aboard the *Espagna*, Dilger's bags contained secret coded messages from Berlin to German agents and diplomats in America and Mexico. Even so, he was not worried by the customs search, for the messages to the German envoy in Mexico were not on paper but instead in his dirty laundry: the notes had been written on soiled shirts that, according to Hilken, "would be deciphered some way . . . by [chemical] solutions or heat after he reached Mexico." Also, an American investigator found evidence that Dilger "carried with him a newly-developed chemical ink to be used in secret communication."

While he had declared on his passport application that he planned to stay in the U.S. as a loyal American—and would later profess the same to a federal agent in Washington—Dilger already knew when he landed in New York that he would be heading to Mexico within a month on a mission to stir up trouble for America.

Once he and his precious dirty shirts made it through customs unscathed, Dilger took a cab to the McAlpin Hotel, a frequent haunt of the "Baltimore group" of German saboteurs before they had fled. Feeling some heat related to the Kingsland investigation, Herrmann had left the country in February aboard a banana boat to Cuba. Hinsch, knowing he was under scrutiny, had headed directly to Mexico by rail soon after the U.S. government declared war and seized all of the interned German ships.

With a business to operate and German assets to distribute, Hilken had stayed in Baltimore, risking possible investigation but reasoning that he had been a paymaster rather than an active saboteur. Dilger was clearly a full-fledged German agent: Hilken and Herrmann confirmed it; Dilger told his sister that he was operating under new "orders"; and cables intercepted by British naval intelligence showed that "Delmar" later became the chief agent for the German Army's Political Section in Mexico City. In the summer of 1917, however, investigators in the U.S. and Britain were unaware that Dilger was the same person as Delmar.

Hilken told investigators later that the main purpose of Dilger's stop in the United States that summer was to deliver messages and put his affairs in order before heading to Mexico. Among the documents found later in Hilken's house was a mysterious note in Dilger's handwriting— on the back and around the edges of a Winton auto repair advertisement—apparently outlining how to handle Dilger's bank accounts in the event of his death or disappearance.

The doctor, who had never had a private medical practice and had worked mostly as a Red Cross surgeon, had somehow amassed large sums of cash in those accounts. He granted power of attorney to his brother-in-law and benefactor, Martin Koehler. Under Koehler's name he wrote "Schw. Kreditanstalt"—a Swiss bank in Zurich—and the sum of 338,000 Swiss francs (more than $1 million in 2005 dollars). In a separate listing of his personal U.S. assets, Dilger wrote four sums under the name of his brother-in-law in Washington, totalling $28,400 (about $434,000 in 2005 dollars). Dilger also listed a name and address in Bern as well as the name of a business in Stockholm, Gylling & Company. Under that is scrawled what appears to be a formula and instructions for using "invisible ink" for coded messages:

1 powder 20 cc. #20
1 inch hot water equavin
white [paper] without gloss
aqua ammonia and water
both sides dry

In the first two weeks after Dilger's arrival, he and Hilken traveled up and down the East Coast between New York and Baltimore on missions that were never fully explained. By July 9, the two saboteurs were together in Baltimore for dinner with Paul's father and business partner Henry Hilken, a pillar of Baltimore's German-American community. When questioned later about the dinner, the elder Hilken denied knowing anything about his son's work as a sabotage paymaster or Dilger's role as a German agent. Next, the two saboteurs left for Philadelphia and New York, where they lunched at the McAlpin Hotel's rooftop restaurant. Afterward, Hilken went to his vacation place near Atlantic City, presumably with Dilger.

A few days before departing with Dilger on a road trip to Kentucky, Hilken was given a second immunization against an unidentified disease—an injection likely administered by Dilger, who had immunized himself earlier. Those shots would make them less susceptible to infection by disease germs to which they might be exposed.

In a diary entry from July 18, Hilken took note of "another antitoxin treatment." He added: "Dr. D. with me."

IT WAS BAD ENOUGH to be beaten, stripped, wrapped in an American flag, and then pushed by a mob down the town's main street, his bare feet bleeding from sharp rocks.

For German-born Robert Prager, however, that humiliation in the coal-mining town of Collinsville, Illinois, was only the prelude to the most violent incident of anti-German hysteria that raged across America from mid-1917 until the war's end.

A few hours after the flag-wrapping, another group of drunken townsfolk dragged the hapless Prager from a holding room in City Hall, marched him to a tall tree outside of town, tightened a noose around his neck, and strung him up. On the first try, they forgot to tie his hands, allowing him to hold onto the noose and avoid a broken neck. Prager was then duly lowered to the ground, allowed to pray, and then hanged again—fatally, this time—to the cheers of two hundred onlookers in the early morning of April 5, 1918.

Other than the fact that he had been born in Germany thirty-one years earlier, Prager's main offense seems to have been applying to join a union and work in the coal mines. He had lived in the United States for more than a dozen years before the lynching and had been patriotic enough to apply for U.S. citizenship, as well as to try to enlist in the Navy when America declared war. Even so, the miners got the false impression that he was a German spy. A dozen members of the mob were brought to trial for murder; all were acquitted.

The Illinois lynching may have been the most violent, but it was hardly an isolated incident. In 1917, German shepherds in America suddenly became "police dogs." Restaurants renamed hamburgers "liberty steaks" on their menus and served "liberty cabbage" that tasted exactly like sauerkraut. The sausage-shaped Dachshund became the Liberty dog. Statues of Goethe, Schiller, and "Germania" were toppled from public buildings and crushed. The teaching of German was forbidden in many school systems; some religious groups stopped using German in church services and German-language theaters bolted their doors shut. A popular song, "Don't Bite the Hand That's Feeding You," even suggested that disloyal immigrants should return home to Europe:

> *If you don't like your Uncle Sammy,*
> *Then go back home o'er the sea,*
> *To the land from where you came . . .*
> *Don't bite the hand that's feeding you!*

Across the country, U.S. patriots kissed flags, bought war bonds, rolled bandages, accepted ration cards, volunteered for military service, worked in munitions factories, and wrote letters to the boys at the Front in France. Vigilantism swept across the country, with thousands of Americans denouncing their immigrant neighbors and anyone else suspected of disloyalty.

In Florida, a vigilante group flogged a local man with a Teutonic accent who was hesitant to buy war bonds. In California, a group calling itself the Knights of Liberty strung up a German American tailor from a tree—but let him down before his neck broke. Another California man who had defended the Kaiser was tarred and feathered before being chained to a cannon. In Oklahoma, yet another ethnic German was whipped fifty times after being tarred and feathered.

"We had our own personal German" to taunt in Salinas, California, wrote novelist John Steinbeck in *East of Eden*. That was the town's tailor, Mr. Fenchel, who bore the brunt of the anti-German sentiment. A mob tore down his fence and burned the front of his house. The narrator described the taunting as "one of those memories of shame that still makes me break out into a sweat and tighten up around the throat.... The nation slid imperceptibly toward war, frightened and at the same time attracted. People had not felt the shaking emotion of war in nearly sixty years."

The most insidious wartime act of Wilson's White House was to form the Committee for Public Information (CPI), an all-American propaganda machine that churned out hate material against the Kaiser and Germany. German soldiers were often depicted as apes, pigs, and monsters; 75,000 volunteer speakers, dubbed the Four-Minute Men, were dispatched to give short talks that incited public fear and hatred of Germans. Every trick of the new media was employed in an unparalleled propaganda effort led by George Creel, the former newspaper muckraker who was Wilson's choice to head the committee.

Creel and his staff worked at a furious pace. Not only were outrageous posters and pamphlets churned out by hack writers, but Creel's minions used the latest and most potent media tools—motion pictures and sound recordings for Victrolas—to stir up public outrage against

Germans and German spies in America. The CPI vetted most of the written publications about the war and issued pamphlets such as "The German Whisper," "German War Practices," and "Conquest and Kultur." Psychologists and marketing experts were hired to help devise new approaches to propaganda so each of the nineteen CPI departments could focus on a different area. One of the Creel panel's experts posed the rhetorical question: "Will it be any wonder if, after the war, the people of the world, when they recognize any human being as a German, will shrink aside so that they may not touch him as he passes, or stoop for stones to drive him from their path?"

Creel's counterpart in Britain was Charles Masterman, director of the War Propaganda Bureau, which produced 1,160 pamphlets and books during the war. Among the authors who contributed to the propaganda effort were Rudyard Kipling, Arthur Conan Doyle, and G. K. Chesterton. After touring Royal Army camps at the invitation of the propaganda bureau, Kipling wrote patriotic books about the British army and navy. When the army refused, for health reasons, to enlist his only son, John, Kipling pulled strings to get the boy into the Irish Guards. Six weeks later, the seventeen-year-old was killed at the Battle of Loos. Kipling wrote: "However the world pretends to divide itself, there are only two divisions in the world today—human beings and Germans."

Following the British example, the Creel committee enlisted the help of well-known scholars and columnists such as John Dewey and Walter Lippmann to spread the patriotic word. Among its most popular speakers was former Ambassador James W. Gerard, who claimed that the Germans planned to use Mexico as a base for launching a hemispherewide revolt against U.S. hegemony. In one speech, Gerard advised townsfolk to look for "paid German propaganda" in local newspapers and, if they found it, "take the editor and tie him up and send him back" to Germany.

Some of the most vicious insinuations about the German war effort were not officially sanctioned, but came to have a life of their own. One widely repeated piece of disinformation was the "corpse factory" story, which made the grisly claim that Germans were boiling down soldiers' corpses for fat.

The "corpse factory" myth, invented in 1917, survived the war before being exposed as a lie. In reality, the rendering vats in those "factories" were used to boil down the remains of dead horses—not humans.

ANTON DILGER'S RETURN to America hurled him into the national wave of Germanophobia. Inevitably, allegations quickly surfaced—possibly originating with Front Royal neighbors or townsfolk—that Dilger had returned as a German spy.

The Bureau of Investigation sent U.S. federal agent George W. Lillard to track down and interrogate the German doctor. It was a strange choice: Lillard had spent his boyhood in Front Royal and, although he did not know Anton well—since Anton was living in Germany by then—he considered himself a friend of the Dilger family. Understandably, Lillard did not prove to be the most probing of investigators.

In those days, the understaffed Bureau was looking into hundreds of reports of possible German agents in America. Just before the U.S. declared war in early April, the agency had compiled an index of 1,500 suspicious persons. Nearly 100 of those were to be arrested as soon as war was declared; another 140 were required to post bail; and another 574 "strongly suspected" German spies or saboteurs were to be fully investigated.

In mid-1917, the Bureau and the federal Secret Service were in charge of domestic security investigations, joined later that year by the War Department's new Military Intelligence Section. Sensing a lack of eyes and ears in the country, the Bureau's chief, Bruce Bielaski, and Attorney General Thomas Gregory endorsed a proposal by three Chicago businessmen to establish a citizens auxiliary called the American Protective League (APL) to provide tips that might help the Bureau find German agents.

One such tip apparently identified Anton Dilger. Assigned to investigate the allegation, Agent Lillard first approached Dilger's sister Jo, an old acquaintance who promised to contact her brother and arrange for him to meet with Lillard at her home in Washington.

The interview was awkward for both men. Dilger, carrying the secret messages and the new ink formula in his baggage, was preparing to flee the country for his new assignment in Mexico. For his part, Lillard was hesitant to aggressively interrogate the brother of an old friend. Years before, Lillard had "gotten to know" the Dilger family in Front Royal. He knew that Hubert Dilger had been a decorated war hero and a pillar of the Front Royal community. He had even met Leatherbreeches and also recalled meeting Anton Dilger: "While I have not known Dr. Dilger intimately, I have seen him on several occasions," he explained in a report that reads more like a testimonial than an interrogation: "I have personally known the Dilgers for about fifteen years, and have always known them to be law-abiding citizens, upright and honest, and above board in everything they did or said."

From the start of his report to the Bureau in Washington, Lillard took the view that Anton Dilger had been singled out for allegations because of anti-German hysteria and the fact that there were relatively few ethnic Germans residing in the region. "The Dilger family is one of the very few [German American] families who live in the vicinity of Front Royal, and the return of Dr. Dilger at this time from Germany has naturally aroused some suspicion in that vicinity."

Polite to a fault, Lillard asked the cultured and personable Anton Dilger to discuss why he, as an American, had spent so many years in Germany, and what his intentions were in returning to the United States. Recounting his history to Lillard, Dilger was smart enough to embellish his medical connections to the Red Cross and the U.S. Medical Corps officers, which he had cultivated during the Balkan wars— even giving Lillard the impression that he worked with the Medical Corps, when in reality he worked for the Bulgarian royal family and Red Cross. Dilger said the purpose of his trip back to Germany in January 1916 was "to do hospital relief work [at] base hospitals 3 and 5 of the Red Cross" in Karlsruhe.

Dilger also told Lillard that the Spanish ambassador—who had represented U.S. interests in Berlin after Washington cut off diplomatic relations—had told him that "the President did not want any American citizens to remain in Germany" after February. He claimed that in response, like any other American patriot, he "immediately began to make preparations to leave Germany." He said he had left in April, a month earlier than his actual departure.

Interweaving complete lies, half-truths, and a few facts, Dilger aimed to convince Lillard that he was a loyal American who planned to stay in the United States. Lillard was quite willing to be convinced: "Dr. Dilger states that it is his intention not to return to Germany, but that he expects to remain here in this country. He has not decided just what he will do as he has not been licensed to practice medicine here."

Lillard continued that Dilger "expects to either go with his brother Carl Dilger in his ranch in Rosebud County, Montana, or go to Front Royal and make an attempt to operate a manganese mine, which is on their farm." The vision of the sophisticated doctor working a Montana ranch or a Virginia manganese mine would have been laughable to anyone who knew Anton. But Lillard did not know any better and duly reported the untruths. He also said Dilger "expressed a willingness to keep in touch with this Department if it so desires." However, Lillard did not burden the doctor by requiring him to check in. "I did not request him to keep in touch with this Bureau, because it is very easy to learn of his whereabouts at any time through his sister." Within a week of that interview, Jo would have no idea where her brother was.

There seems to have been little, if any, follow-up by the bureau in the months after Lillard's report. It was not until a year afterward that federal officials began to connect the doctor from Front Royal with the German spy in Mexico.

What eventually would bring Dilger to the attention of the federal government was not suspicion of germ sabotage—which police should have known about from various sources, but apparently did not—but rather an investigation of German assets in the United States. Hilken, worried that American officials would seize those assets, had been rushing to spend the proceeds from selling cargo carried by the *Deutschland* the previous year. Some of that money ended up in accounts linked to Dilger and other German agents.

At about the same time that Lillard interviewed Dilger, an industrious young law-school graduate named J. Edgar Hoover was starting his $990-a-year job as a clerk at the U.S. Department of Justice—the Bureau of Investigation's parent agency. It was not long before Hoover was assigned to the department's War Emergency Division, specializing in "enemy-within" investigations of German saboteurs and, later, communists and anarchists. The focused workaholic quickly earned a favorable reputation in high circles.

After he became the director of the Federal Bureau of Investigation a decade later, one of Hoover's tasks—not a pleasant one, considering that the bureau had let Dilger slip through its fingers in 1917—was to locate and forward copies of Lillard's report and other bureau memos about Dilger to investigators at the Mixed Claims Commission who were collecting evidence of German sabotage in prewar America. Only at that time did the government finally discover that Anton Dilger had been a saboteur in Chevy Chase.

THE CHORUS OF CICADAS at Greenfield Farm reminded Anton Dilger of his boyhood, but he did not spend his final night at the family homestead in the company of his brothers and sisters, now further scattered and divided by the formalities of war. Instead, he passed those hours mostly with Paul Hilken, the paymaster of the German saboteurs.

It was a "pleasant evening at the Dilger farm," according to Hilken in his diary. The two men had driven over the dusty roads from Baltimore and Washington to Greenfield in one long day. They greeted Anton's older brother Butz, who still operated the farm, and Anton gave Hilken a tour of Greenfield and the surrounding countryside. Both men took on a rakish look when they strapped on their driving goggles to keep out the dust.

They were driving a Winton, a stylish auto that was known for its reliability on long-distance trips, which was exactly what they had planned for the following day. A Winton advertisement in 1912 boasted that the car had "the world's lowest repair expense record." It was a convertible with a fold-down top, an upright windshield, running boards, and spoked wheels. Two days before they drove to Front Royal, Hilken had loaned Dilger $2,050 to buy the used Winton, and Dilger had signed a promissory note to repay that sum.

One of the last known photos of Dilger shows him posing with the car, perhaps shortly before he and Hilken left the farm. Dilger looks thin, drawn, and older—wearing an overcoat in the middle of the summer. Another late photo, probably taken during his final day at Green-field, shows him sitting in an armchair, looking somber and reflective as he holds a cigarette in his right hand.

Just before he left, Dilger gave Butz a handshake and a hug and then took one last look around. There, across the driveway, were the house and barn his father had built and the vegetable garden where his mother had picked tomatoes. In the distance were the low rock walls that he and his brothers had jumped on horseback. He asked Hilken to take the wheel for the drive down the dusty Greenfield road. Dilger leaned out the window and waved to Butz—as always, a fixture of Greenfield—who waved back. It was the last time the brothers would see one another, and the final view that Dilger would have of the farm where he had been born.

A thunderstorm struck later that day, pummeling the Winton with rain and high winds as the two saboteurs headed across the Appalachians toward Kentucky. They were forced to stop the car under a bridge and set up the canvas roof to keep out the pouring rain. Lightning crashed into the high trees on the foothills around them. That day, they got as far as Staunton, ninety miles southwest of Front Royal. The next day they headed westward through the forested mountain valleys toward the Bluegrass State. They encountered storms and floods along the route through the rolling hills to Covington, a major rail-freight center across the Ohio River from Cincinnati.

Before the war began, Cincinnati had been one of the nation's centers of German culture. Well over half the city's population was ethnic German, but that had not stopped the city council—voting shortly after the United States declared war—from changing every German street name in the city. Librarians removed most German-language books from the shelves, and a third of Cincinnati's German newspapers folded.

Hilken's diary gives no details about his and Dilger's business in Covington, but it seems likely that their mission had to do with horses or rail transport. As a rail-freight transfer center, the city was one of the points through which Midwestern stockyards transported horses and mules to Newport News.

Dilger and Hilken arrived in Covington on July 23 and spent the better part of the next two days in the area between there and Lexington—

the site of numerous horse farms, including August Belmont II's Nursery Stud Farm, just east of U.S. Highway 25. Three months earlier, Man o' War—a chestnut Thoroughbred that would become the century's greatest racehorse—had been foaled on that farm, and Belmont had joined the Army as a major, expressly charged with the task of procuring horses for the war.

Belmont had inherited a love of horses from his father, a Prussian immigrant who had amassed a fortune as a railroad financier and become the most powerful man in American horse racing from the Civil War's end until his death in 1890. The younger Belmont bought one of America's best racing stables, helped found the Jockey Club, and chaired the New York State Racing Commission. He was also a leading exponent of improving the stock of war horses for the U.S. Army.

When the war broke out, the sixty-five-year-old Belmont had volunteered for the infantry but, being too old, was given the rank of major and asked to apply his horse sense to army procurement. The multimillionaire son of the "King of Fifth Avenue," the husband of the Queen of the Met, and the breeder of Man o' War donned his uniform and headed to Spain in 1917 to buy mules for the American Expeditionary Force in France.

One of the Lexington gentry whom Belmont would have known was Leslie Combs, a retired diplomat who was the son of a famous general of the same name who had served in the War of 1812. During the Civil War, the elder Combs wrote a scathing letter accusing German American soldiers under General Carl Schurz of being a "gang of freedom shriekers" who had showed cowardice at Chancellorsville, the battle in which Hubert Dilger had distinguished himself and earned the Medal of Honor. The younger Combs, however, developed a more positive opinion of Germans, at least until America joined the Great War.

On the surface, Anton Dilger's purpose in meeting Combs was to send greetings from the Kentuckian's daughter in Germany; in reality, Anton was trying to determine whether the former diplomat—who had served as the U.S. minister in Honduras, Guatemala, and Peru—might be enlisted to help the German cause in the Americas. Soon after arriving in New York that month, Dilger mailed a letter to Combs asking to deliver a message from his daughter, who had married a German army officer. Two days before their arrival, Dilger sent Combs a telegram, and the former diplomat decided to meet them at the Phoenix Hotel when they arrived in Lexington.

"Immediately after Dilger came down [from his hotel room] he opened up a discussion of the war in such a way as to get [Combs] to express his attitude," a federal agent reported later. "Dr. Dilger seemed very anxious to draw him out as to his attitude, and ... indicated his sympathy with Germany." The three men drove to Combs's house for dinner, during which they discussed their experiences, including Dilger's story that "he was in Vienna taking a special course when the war broke out and immediately became connected with the German Red Cross." Dilger said Combs's daughter had sent to Dilger "a number of photographs and other messages" to carry to her family in Kentucky, but Combs told the agent that Dilger "had destroyed them before going through France, fearing that they would cause him trouble" with border police.

When the federal agent questioned Combs later about Dilger's visit, the retired diplomat conceded that he had spoken out and written several articles in support of Germany before the United States declared war and had received notes from the German ambassador "thanking him for his expressions on behalf of the German government." But Combs insisted in September 1918 that Dilger's visit was a complete surprise and that he never heard from him again. Combs professed to be astounded that Dilger would travel to Kentucky just to pass along a greeting from his daughter. The diplomat told the bureau agent that "he has often wondered why Dr. Dilger wanted to stop off in Lexington to see him when he had such indefinite and meager information" about Combs's daughter. "He could not believe that this was [Dilger's] purpose in stopping off."

It was likely not Dilger's only reason for visiting Kentucky. The Combs family had longtime associations with Kentucky's horse breeders; the diplomat's son would later go on to develop his Spendthrift Farm into one of Kentucky's most famous Thoroughbred horse breeding operations. Judging from Hilken's diary, which lists the name of a contact associated with breeding, one of Dilger's reasons for visiting Kentucky likely had something to do with horses. But the diary, as usual, offers few details. After the Covington stop, the two saboteurs split up—with Hilken heading east and Dilger, west.

No one knows for sure what, if anything, Dilger might have distributed with contacts in the region. But eight months after his still-unexplained mission to Kentucky, a train full of U.S. Army warhorses was struck by a virulent malady at Covington's rail yards. About 720 horses were stricken; 277 of them died at the yards.

The horses had been loaded onto the train at Camp Grant in Rockford, Illinois—west of Chicago—and were on their way to the port of Newport News for shipment to the French battlegrounds. The extent of the illness was highly unusual—the most deaths of any shipment of Army horses during the war—and puzzling to the handlers.

An army veterinary report later listed the Covington case as the "most striking" single incident of sudden equine deaths, which also involved the deaths of as many as 40 horses and the sickness of as many as 752 animals on other rail shipments. "In several shipments there occurred an unusual number of sudden deaths, both en route and subsequent to arrival at destination under circumstances which warranted full investigation," the report said.

When the scores of horse carcasses were dragged away for burial, rumors about a mass "horse poisoning" soon spread through Covington and the surrounding area of Kentucky. Responding to fears that the town's water reservoir had been poisoned, officials ordered tests of the water. Some local officials strongly suspected sabotage. Judge George C. Webb asked a Fayette County grand jury to investigate the possible link between the horse poisonings and saboteurs. On April 4, Webb told the grand jury that "he had reliable information that many emissaries had been sent into Kentucky to injure the horse industry," reported the *New York Times*. "He charged the jury to do its utmost to uncover any activities of German spies, and either indict them for treason or furnish the Federal Government with evidence to deal with them."

Webb was convinced that German saboteurs were behind the horse deaths. "Men of this ilk who sow seeds of dissention or work against the U.S. government and its people should be prosecuted, imprisoned and shot if necessary," the judge said. "There is not a state in the Union that is not infested with German spies, and they do not hesitate at anything to spread

German propaganda, which is the most villainous, barbarous, and extensive menace that this country has to cope with." According to the *New York Times*, "the statement, which follows the recent poisoning of a large number of Government-owned horses at Covington, was greeted with cheers."

Tests of Covington's water supply found no poison. The *Kentucky Times-Star* reported on March 16, 1918 that officials had dismissed as "groundless" the fear that the local reservoir was under threat. Even so, to help reassure local residents, guards were posted along Covington's water supply route. The newspaper's headline took pains to reassure the reading public:

NO DANGER FROM COVINGTON WATER BUT RESERVOIRS MAY BE GUARDED

Groundless Alarm Felt Following Poisoning Of Army Horses.

As of mid-March, the newspaper said, it was "not established that the horses were poisoned by the water they drank." The Army's veterinary inspector, Major Cotton, was sent to Covington to get to the bottom of the horse deaths.

Although Cotton found "no evidence of poison of any kind," nor could he adequately explain the deaths of 277 animals, a list of "Enemy Outrages against the United States" compiled by a U.S. Army official later that year included, along with the Black Tom fire and the Kingsland explosion, the Kentucky "horse-poisoning."

IT WAS A CROSS-COUNTRY JOURNEY through a bizarre landscape of anti-German hysteria—a trail of riots, fires, and poisonings—by a German American who had helped to incite that hysteria. Either by car or by train or a combination of the two, Anton Dilger made his way from Kentucky to Mexico in the summer of 1917, probably with a stop in St. Louis for yet another shadowy mission.

Along that route, Dilger would have driven his Winton through streets lined with smoke-blackened buildings and shattered windows in East St. Louis, which just two weeks earlier had been the scene of the worst race riot in American history. Boiling into the streets and neighborhoods, the rioting lasted for nearly a week, with most of the arsons, beatings, and drive-by shootings targeting the African American community. Hundreds of blacks and nine whites were killed in the riots; hundreds of homes and businesses were burned down or damaged; and more than six thousand residents fled the city.

In an angry speech the week after the riots, civil rights and black nationalist crusader Marcus Garvey blamed the city's ethnic German mayor and denounced "the alien German, the Italian, and other Europeans who came here but yesterday" for attacking Africans who had been Americans for much longer. "The mob and entire white populace of East St. Louis had a Roman holiday. They feasted on the blood of the Negro, encouraged as they were by the German-American Mayor."

One of those "Europeans who came here but yesterday" was Theodore Wozniak, the Ukrainian immigrant who had been implicated in the Kingsland fire, which had started next to his workbench. He had fled New York—probably using sabotage cash paid to him through Herrmann—and hidden from the police in various places. Later, Wozniak would give conflicting stories about his hiding places—working in a lumber camp, traveling in the Midwest—but the postmarks on his letters indicate that he was in St. Louis in early August 1917.

Years later, an investigator who had tracked Wozniak's 1917 movements suggested that Dilger had gone to St. Louis to find the Ukrainian immigrant and spirit him out of the country. "Dilger drove on to St. Louis in his car," wrote the investigator, Mixed Claims Commission counsel H. H. Martin. He speculated that Dilger then "made contact with Wozniak and arranged [to] get Wozniak down to Mexico." Martin also pointed out that it was possible that "Hinsch before he left for Mexico made arrangements with Dilger to see that Wozniak was gotten out of the country."

Dilger's odyssey continued unhindered throughout his journey to the border. On his route westward, he likely passed through Kansas City, another site of an "outrage" that later would be blamed on a disaffected German American: a severe fire at the Kansas City stockyards, where Allied army buyers purchased thousands of cattle and horses for the war. The sprawling yards in the Kansas River bottomlands were a key link between western livestock producers and eastern markets—handling as many as a million animals a year.

On the morning of October 16, 1917, a fire of suspicious origin broke out in the stockyards, spreading quickly and causing massive destruction. The blaze badly damaged the yard's loading and receiving facilities as well as one-eighth of the buildings and pens, killing several thousand animals inside.

Sabotage was considered a possibility from the start. A headline in that afternoon's *Kansas City Star* said investigators were searching for "war plot evidence." Police quickly made arrests. The first suspect—described in the next day's headlines as a "German" and later identified as L. S. Kromeich—had been fired from the stockyards a few weeks before for labor agitation.

A lumber company's full-page advertisement in that same issue of the *Star* featured a sinister drawing of the Kaiser's "mailed fist"—part of a knight's armor—and accused him of trying to make Europe and the United States "mere provinces of Germany." The provocative ad warned that the Kaiser "has spies in every country of the globe, and he has them everywhere in America—not only men of German blood, but hirelings of other nations."

The search for such hirelings continued in Kansas City. Two days after the blaze, the *Star* reported that "it is now firmly believed the fire is a result of pro-German activities at the stock yards." Police soon arrested six other men, mostly former employees of the stockyards. While officers claimed that they had gathered evidence of "seditious remarks," they were unable to prove that the fire was German-inspired sabotage.

By then, Anton Dilger was south of the border, trying to stir up trouble in Mexico.

part three

Mexico and Spain

Chapter 12

SOUTH OF THE BORDER

In the bull ring, the death of the horse tends to be comic while that of the bull is tragic.
—ERNEST HEMINGWAY, *Death in the Afternoon*, 1932

AN OUTLAW IN HIS NATIVE COUNTRY, young Fred Herrmann found himself stranded in Mexico in the spring of 1917. Down to his last few dollars, he rented a room at Mexico City's seedy Hotel Juarez while he tried, unsuccessfully at first, to convince the German legation that he had been a legitimate agent for the General Staff in Berlin.

Herrmann was the first of the germ saboteurs to make it to Mexico, so there was no one to vouch for his credentials. "I was in distress, practically marooned in Mexico," recalled the New Jersey native, who had grown accustomed to living well with cash from German sabotage funds. He had traveled first-class on transatlantic voyages at Berlin's expense and had run up tabs in cities from New York to Copenhagen and Havana. Now he was stranded and poor.

In the sweltering room, Herrmann cut a fresh lemon and squeezed its juice into a small glass. Taking a copy of the January 1917 issue of *Blue Book* magazine, the young American opened it to a novella called *The Yukon Trail*, a "virile story of Alaska" by William Raine. Opening to page 695, Herrmann turned the magazine on its side, dipped a pen into the lemon juice, and started writing perpendicular to the printing. As the longhand message dried, the lemon-juice writing disappeared. The invisible words could be made visible later with one swipe of a hot iron.

Herrmann's message to Paul Hilken was scattered with four-digit code numbers, each of which stood for a name or a sabotage event. Deciphered, his coded message complained that the top German diplomat in Mexico, Heinrich von Eckhardt, refused to believe that he was a legitimate agent, despite the young American's work on the Kingsland explosion and Tony's Lab. Herrmann wrote:

> Have seen Eckhardt. He is suspicious of me. Can't convince him I come from Marguerre and Nadolny. Have told him all reference Hinsch and I, *Deutschland*, Jersey City Terminal [Black Tom], Kingsland, Savannah, and Tony's Lab. He doubts me on account of my bum German. Confirm to him through your channels all OK and my mission here. I have not funds. Eckhardt claims he is short of money. Send by bearer U.S. 25000 ... Tell Hinsch to come here. I expect to go north but he can locate me through Eckhardt. I don't trust Carl Ahrendt, Michael Kristoff, Wolfgang and that Hoboken bunch. If cornered they might get us in Dutch with authorities. See that Hinsch brings with him all who might implicate us. Tell him Siegel is with me. Where is Carl Dilger? He worries me. Remember past experience. Has Hinsch seen Wozniak? Tell him to fix that up ... What do you do now with America in the war? Are you coming here or going to South America. Advise you drop everything and leave the States....

Herrmann then took a pen and began pricking tiny holes in the magazine—holes that covered specific letters on particular pages. The numbers in the message (with the first number always discarded and the other three numbers reversed) referred to page numbers, and the pin holes on that page would highlight letters that would spell something. It was a standard, relatively primitive technique for German code-making.

Once the message had dried, Herrmann gave the coded magazine to his sidekick, Raoul Gerdts—whose Colombian passport was still valid for U.S. entry—with instructions to deliver it to Hilken in either Baltimore or New York and to explain how to use a hot iron to make the lemon "ink" appear. When Gerdts delivered the magazine, Hilken took it to the basement of his house and deciphered the code. He sent Herrmann $1,000 though Gerdts but reserved the rest of the money to send to Mexico with Hinsch in May.

That seemed to be the end of the *Blue Book* message. But when the yellowed magazine was rediscovered more than a decade later, the Herrmann code provided a key for American investigators to break the Black Tom case and establish a connection between the General Staff's Political Section and prewar sabotage in the United States. Herrmann's appeal from the Hotel Juarez in 1917 ended up making headlines across America in 1929.

In the meantime, Gerdts returned to Mexico and delivered Hilken's $1,000 to Herrmann. The young American immediately started planning an operation he had first discussed the previous year in Berlin: setting fire to the petroleum tanks in Tampico, where drill rigs were pumping crude oil, mainly for export to the United States. When Herrmann offered to pay Gerdts to set the fires, he refused, and Herrmann told him to "Go to the devil," declining to pay Gerdts' fare back home. Instead of going to the devil, Gerdts went to the Americans. He returned to Columbia, and at the end of July 1917—just a few days after Dilger had been interviewed by a Bureau of Investigation agent in Washington, D.C.—met with an American vice consul in Colombia to confess full details about Herrmann's sabotage, including the germs and incendiary devices. But no one in Washington appeared to investigate the allegations until a decade later.

Herrmann's *Blue Book* message was an appeal for help. "I had told Eckhardt who I was, told him about all those [sabotage] activities ... and he did not seem to believe me. I wanted Paul [Hilken] to know just what I had told Eckhardt, so he would do something to establish me with Eckhardt," Hermann recalled. "I was simply stuck down there and I wanted Paul to know my predicament, and I was telling him just what my difficulty was."

Eckhardt had, indeed, distrusted Herrmann from the start—even suspecting that he and Gerdts were "English spies" who had been planted in Mexico with a half-baked sabotage plan designed to embarrass Germany.

He described Herrmann to Berlin as "blond, slender, [speaks] German with an American accent" and said that the German envoy in Havana had suspected the two men to be British spies. In Berlin, the General Staff's Political Section confirmed Herrmann's overall story but gave Eckhardt the flexibility he needed to cancel the mission and distance himself from the young American.

"The firing of Tampico [oil fields] would be valuable from a military point of view, but the General Staff leaves it to you to decide," the message said. "Please do not sanction anything which would endanger our relations with Mexico or if the question arises, give Herrmann any open support."

Reasoning that sabotage linked to Germany would anger President Carranza, Eckhardt ordered Herrmann to stop planning a Tampico operation. He also called Herrmann back from Sonora Province and cancelled his second mission: an effort to seize and arm an interned German ship that would be used to raid U.S. freighters. That plan, the German diplomat decided, would risk an immediate U.S. incursion into Mexico.

Herrmann had been trailed closely by American agents ever since he had left the United States the previous February. As soon as he started to feel the heat from his role in the January fire at the Kingsland munitions plant (he blamed a former girlfriend in New Jersey for telling police about his Kingsland connection), Herrmann and his fellow saboteur Gerdts booked cabin 48 on the *Pastores*, a United Fruit Line steamship. Disembarking in Havana, they were followed around the clock by an American agent who chronicled their every move in cables to the Bureau of Investigation in Washington.

Later, suspicions arose that Herrmann had been sent to Cuba to scout a way to assassinate Ambassador Gerard, who had stopped briefly in Cuba on his way back to the United States from Berlin during the time that Herrmann was in Havana. But when American investigators asked him later about the assassination rumor, Herrmann dismissed the idea with a flip comment: "Do you think I'm crazy?"

Herrmann and Gerdts enjoyed their two weeks in Havana, staying at the Hotel la Union, dining at rooftop restaurants, drinking heavily at the Black Cat bar, paying for women at a "fancy house," and riding jitneys through the Old Town. He also met with the German consul in Havana, who proved to be suspicious. Finally, Herrmann used a $20 gold piece to buy a Mexican visa for his passport. He and Gerdts then boarded a ship in mid-April that took them to Vera Cruz, Mexico.

He had seemed self-assured in the United States, but Herrmann—who spoke very little if any Spanish when he arrived—was adrift in Mexico. He was quickly identified by American intelligence and—along with Hinsch and Jahnke, the German Admiralty's chief agent in Mexico—was often closely watched or followed.

The greatest success by American secret services in Mexico came against Jahnke's naval intelligence operation. One of the U.S. Army's spies, a German-speaking Pole named Paul Altendorf, managed to join Jahnke's sabotage group, as did a British agent, William Gleaves. When Jahnke sent his most trusted agent, Lothar Witzke, on a sabotage mission to the United States, Altendorf tipped off the Army. Soldiers nabbed Witzke shortly after he crossed the U.S. border.

Under interrogation, Witzke revealed some crucial details about German intelligence operations in Mexico. Despite the saboteur's willingness to talk, a U.S. military court in Texas sentenced Witzke to death for his role in the Black Tom explosion. (That sentence would be reduced after the war.)

Jahnke's naval intelligence operations were seriously damaged by the betrayal and Witzke's disclosures. But one important German agent in Mexico that Witzke did not help identify was Anton Dilger.

THE SUN BEAT DOWN MERCILESSLY as Dilger walked out of the National Palace that summer and across the cobblestones of the Zócalo, the grand plaza of Mexico City. Pausing near the cathedral, he pulled out a handkerchief and mopped his brow. He had spent the past hour in his first meeting with Mexico's president, the gray-bearded Venustiano Carranza, and now had work to do.

Dilger looked up at the cathedral, with its two baroque towers dominating the square. Its stones had once been part of Tenochtitlán, the ancient Aztec city that had occupied the site four centuries earlier when the conquistador Hernán Cortéz had ridden his black stallion El Morzillo to meet the emperor Montezuma. The Aztecs had feared the horse more than the soldier, for they had never seen such an animal before.

Horses were everywhere in the city by 1917, hauling carts and wagons through the crowded streets. In the middle of the Zócalo, a mariachi band was playing local music and a few drunken fools were dancing around the musicians. Across the square were the grand hotels where wealthy businessmen and foreigners drank mescal and met their clients and mistresses. Anton Dilger, wearing a dark coat and formal tie, which he had deemed appropriate for a meeting with the president, was unbearably hot. He loosened the tie, took off his coat, and looked around for a taxi to the German legation.

That day's presidential interview represented a breakthrough for Dilger, who had arrived in Mexico City a few weeks earlier, in mid-August 1917, after crossing the border using his nearly expired emergency U.S. passport, as the General Staff's chief "confidential agent"—responsible for army intelligence—in the capital. He lived and worked in Mexico under the name Dr. Albert Delmar and signed all messages and cables as "Delmar." When he first arrived, he spoke little Spanish, and probably brought an interpreter with him for important interviews. In Mexico, Dilger had entered a new realm of neutrality and—as a result of the failed U.S. military expedition into northern Mexico that had ended just seven months earlier—outright hostility to Americans.

The U.S. State Department had first become aware of a mysterious "Delmar" in July, when the British shared an intercepted cable from Berlin asking the German legation in Mexico City "to give full confidence and support" to Delmar. A month later, a firm based in Mexico City sent an inscrutable message to Spain—also intercepted by the British—that requested instructions on Delmar's proposal for a six-month "renewal." This may have been a code giving Dilger access to a military espionage fund. Highly suspicious, State Department officials in Washington made a request of its Mexico City embassy that summer: "Please report fully regarding Delmar, his activities and present whereabouts."

As soon as he arrived in the sweltering heat of Mexico City, Dilger had gone to the German legation to introduce himself to the diplomats and to get his bearings. Then he reunited with the other saboteurs who had fled the United States, Hinsch and Herrmann. Mexico had become the haven for the former Baltimore-based agents who had escaped the country after the war declaration.

Captain Hinsch had left Baltimore in May, shortly after the U.S. government seized interned German ships—including his former cargo ship, the *Neckar*—to outfit them to carry troops or horses or other war cargo. Hinsch bought a train ticket from the East Coast to San Francisco but "left the train at El Paso," Hilken said, and crossed the border into Mexico. Carrying $23,000 from Hilken for sabotage operations, Hinsch took a train through Chihuahua to Mexico City. Federal investigators reported that Hinsch "escaped into Mexico after orders had been given for [his] internment about May 25, 1917." At the time the U.S. presidential warrant was issued for Hinsch's arrest, the portly German captain was already sipping tequilas in the town of Tecuba.

By the time Dilger arrived, the always-boastful Hinsch was sharing a house near Orizaba Plaza in Mexico City with a woman he described as his wife. Herrmann, who had been on a mission in Sonora Province, came down to meet Dilger and other German saboteurs at Hinsch's house that summer. The men shared sabotage stories and talked of new missions south of the border. "I frequently heard Herrmann or Hinsch on later occasions talking about fires in ships and in factories in the United States; about disease germs, incendiary pencils, the submarine affair [the *Deutschland*] and the placing of chemicals in crystal form in wheat," said another German who knew them.

After his brief visit with Hinsch, Dilger found a house not far from Hinsch's in Mexico City's fashionable Colonia Roma, a pleasant district of sidewalk cafés and bistros. His place was on a quiet block lined with flowering trees, where most of the homes were two-story brick and stone buildings designed in the Spanish style, with secluded garden areas, twelve-foot-high ceilings, spacious wooden staircases, and shutters that could be closed from the inside. Dilger lived just a few blocks from the Hippodrome race track, and on days when his windows were open, he could hear the crowd's roars and the thunder of hooves on the turf.

That long summer, the heat rose in waves from Mexico City's streets, and the parks were parched for scarce rain. When he had first arrived in Mexico, Dilger had carried in his luggage—along with shirts inscribed with messages from Berlin for Eckhardt—a new German secret ink formula. The ink could be made visible by painting the paper or cloth with a molybdenum solution, letting it dry, and then exposing it to sulfuric acid.

Most significantly, and a strong indicator of his clout in Mexico, Dilger was also bringing bank drafts or cash amounting to $95,000 (about $1.4 million in 2005 dollars) to support Mexican-based espionage and sabotage operations on the continent. Dilger's main mission from Berlin was "to assist in the interests of Germany in promoting an invasion of [the United States] from Mexico," Hilken said later.

One of Dilger's first tasks was to pay off and silence Wozniak, the Hinsch recruit whom U.S. authorities wanted to question about his role in setting fire to the Kingsland munitions plant. Earlier that summer, it appears likely that Dilger—in one of his final missions in America—had helped arrange to transport Wozniak across the border into Mexico. When Wozniak arrived, he began to press for another payment from the Germans.

During the weeks when Wozniak was in Mexico, a witness saw Dilger mollify an agitated man—probably Wozniak—by opening up a safe in his house in Mexico City and handing the foreign-looking fellow a thick wad of cash. "It was in the evening and Dilger opened the safe and gave him money," the witness said. "This [man] seemed nervous and suspicious and went away quickly when he received his money. I never saw him again."

Dilger took over as the General Staff's chief confidential agent from Vincent Kraaft, a former officer in the German colonial army in Africa. After the United States declared war and began tracking down and arresting German agents inside its borders, the Mexico City station had become the most important locus for coordinating German espionage, sabotage, and propaganda campaigns in North America. German agents used Mexico as a base, one witness said, for "various plans for causing trouble in the United States." Gaining access to the United States "was always easy," said that witness, claiming that German agents—mainly carrying false passports—traveled back and forth across the border almost at will.

"Dilger was an energetic man and had wide authority to raise money to finance the work that he was doing," recalled Frederick W. Hadler, a reserve officer in the German Army who worked for Dilger in Mexico and would later be interrogated by both American and German investigators about his dealings with him. His impression was that Germany's "secret service activities increased" under Dilger's supervision. While there was no longer a germ factory in the United States, biological sabotage continued there as well as in Argentina and possibly elsewhere in Latin America, likely with input from Dilger.

Dilger's staff of spies and saboteurs included Hinsch, Herrmann, and "Dr. Gehrmann," an agent who would die under mysterious circumstances later, after his cover was blown in Spain. A German named Heinrich Bode, who operated under the pseudonym Roberto Wilson, also worked with Dilger in Mexico and Spain. Yet another German saboteur, Julio Rico, would be arrested later in the United States for poisoning mules, but he apparently managed to escape punishment.

Before his arrival in Mexico City, Dilger had been asked in Berlin to help settle "the rows in [Mexico] between various German secret service organizations." In that particular task, the surgeon-turned-spy would fail miserably. There were tensions within his own staff, and Dilger soon found that his fiercest competition came from an unexpected source: the German Admiralty's confidential agent, a naturalized U.S. citizen named Kurt Jahnke.

At the same time, the well-oiled British, American, and French espionage networks throughout Mexico kept tabs on the movements of most of the German agents. Five separate U.S. intelligence services—representing the army and navy, as well as the State, Treasury, and Justice departments—deployed agents in Mexico. Those American agents successfully traced and followed all of the General Staff's espionage agents except for the elusive "Delmar." They knew the name but still had no idea who he was.

SOON AFTER HE SET UP SHOP in Mexico City, Dilger became embroiled in two complex and ultimately futile efforts: trying to broker a foreign-aid agreement with Berlin that aimed to convert neutral Mexico into a German ally, and arming and preparing elements of the Mexican army in Sonora Province to invade the United States.

In Mexico, ritual was part of the fabric of society and government. One did not bluntly approach a Mexican official and hammer out an immediate agreement. Negotiations were complex and long-lasting, and they followed traditional patterns. Sometimes a negotiator would work for many months on a possible agreement, only to have it slip away at the last minute.

Having remained neutral so far in the Great War, Mexico's government in 1917 was seeking financial help from all sides; President Carranza became adept at playing the Germans and the Allies against one another. As soon as the Germans thought Carranza was in their pocket, he would do something to ingratiate himself to Washington. Six months after the Zimmerman Telegram, Mexico's leadership had reached out to avoid confrontation with the United States.

Germany's first military goal in Mexico was to keep the Americans worried enough about their southern neighbor that they would continue to station large numbers of troops at the border—troops that otherwise would likely be sent to Europe to fight Germans. Ideally, as proposed in the Zimmerman Telegram, German agents would provide the Mexican army and government with the arms and financial incentives they needed to mount a diversionary invasion—sending troops into Texas, Arizona, and New Mexico.

President Carranza, a bespectacled and intelligent man who was the son of a cattle farmer, had made a strong protest against Pershing's incursion across the border in 1916, but stopped short of direct conflict. He complained that the Americans had blocked Mexican imports of munitions and he warned that "there are strong American interests and strong Mexican interests laboring to secure a conflict between the two countries." He did not mention German interests and pressures, which were also considerable.

As president, Carranza faced severe domestic financial problems and, on the political front, was forced to confront a threatening array of factions—some of them armed—that opposed his government. Those ranged from the separate bands led by militant populists Pancho Villa and Emiliano Zapata to the conservative Catholics and wealthy landowners who had preferred the old regime. Despite those challenges, Carranza was able to achieve advances in decentralizing power, making the judiciary independent, and reforming the land ownership system. He also oversaw the convention that wrote Mexico's new constitution, under which Carranza won a legitimate election as president in March 1917.

Some Americans, including Ambassador Gerard, were convinced that the Germans were plotting struggle throughout the Western Hemisphere against U.S. dominance:

> South of the Rio Grande the Germans are working against us, doing their best to prejudice the Mexicans against the United States, playing upon old hatreds and creating new ones and, in the meantime, by their purchase of properties and of mines creating a situation that will constitute for us in the future a most difficult and dangerous problem.

Gerard recalled a dinner with the Kaiser in Berlin, during which one diplomat remarked that Americans moved entire houses by jacking them onto trailers and hauling them down paved roads. The Kaiser, ever suspicious of U.S. intentions toward Mexico, quipped: "I am sure that the Americans are moving their houses. They are moving them down towards the Mexican border."

At the time that Dilger arrived in Mexico, Carranza had already become irritated by German officials who promised financial and military assistance but seldom delivered on those pledges. In particular, Carranza was unhappy with Eckhardt's months of making vague promises without concrete results.

One welcome message Dilger brought was that the High Command had agreed in principle to loan Carranza's government 100 million pesos. But the German money, despite Eckhardt's warning to Berlin that the Americans were planning a similar payoff, did not arrive that summer. "In order to save the situation, Eckhardt and Delmar, who still had received no answer from Berlin, decided to make new promises to Carranza," wrote one historian. These included a letter from Dilger that held out "... the prospect of weapons, German military instructors, and so forth in the event of war" with the United States.

Dilger's fresh set of military promises that summer gave Carranza the impression that Berlin's High Command was in a better position to deliver on its aid promises than was the German Foreign Office. That was what led to Dilger's meeting with Carranza in the National Palace barely a month after his arrival. When the president began to negotiate personally with Dilger, he asked for "plans, and the like for as factory for Mauser rifles, 7 mm, with a daily output of 200 rifles ... as well as technical personnel and finally specialists for airplane construction." In October, after Washington failed to provide significant aid to Mexico, Carranza contacted Dilger again and requested "10,000 rifles immediately, 15 machine guns, [and] 4 million rounds of ammunition." That fall, the Mexican president also asked Dilger to transmit to Berlin his request for "a loan of 50 million pesos for the founding of a state bank," to match the sum expected to be raised within Mexico. The president also wanted another 20 million pesos "for pressing current needs." Wrote historian Friedich Katz:

> [Dilger] regarded this loan as essential for preserving Mexico's neutrality, but also as a means of transforming the country into a military and political semi-colony of Germany. He expressed this bluntly in the negotiations with the Mexican finance minister. As a condition for such a loan, [Dilger] specifically demanded that the government give assurances that the country will under no circumstances go to war against us, that money will be used for specified purposes and under German control, commercial advantages in the postwar period, and military supplies only from us.

Dilger told the High Command that Mexican leaders had promised to accept those conditions "unconditionally."

By then, Dilger was playing a complex game—to some extent, making an end run around the chief of the diplomatic delegation, Eckhardt—that depended to a great extent on his own influence with the High Command. At one point, Dilger sent his subordinate Gehrmann to Madrid to forward a secret, urgent message to Berlin. The gist of the message was that Eckhardt had lost the Mexican president's trust and that Germany had to find the money for a major loan to the Mexican government.

A German military attaché and intelligence expert in Madrid— Major Arnold Kalle, who reportedly had an affair with the German informant Mata Hari—supported the request to mollify Mexico with a loan. Ideally, he wanted military and financial aid to Mexico to help provoke a war with the United States. But at the very least, keeping Mexico's military strong would mean "Mexican troops on [the] American border [which] limit American troop transports to Europe."

But Germany's Foreign Office was slow to act, suggesting that Eckhardt keep promising the Mexicans that German aid would come eventually, perhaps once the war ended in Europe. Dilger and others in Mexico City were left hanging because they had implied that aid was immediately possible. At one point, the Foreign Office sought to raise the money by selling the huge stores of German-owned wool in Buenos Aires to a bank in a neutral country and then use the wool as security for a loan from a New York bank. But the planned transaction fell through, and money was not forthcoming.

Dilger told Carranza in November that the so-called "Argentine transaction" might provide the money needed for the Mexico loan. "In the interval," Dilger reported to the General Staff's Political Section, "I have started sabotage in the United States with the assistance of ... Hinsch who is representing me for the time being." He asked for more money for sabotage and espionage.

On December 6, the General Staff—beleaguered with requests for assistance directly related to the war—reported that "financial assistance through [Argentina] is impossible." The Political Section also informed Dilger, through an intermediary, that "fresh funds for espionage are unnecessary" and that he would have to settle for the $300,000 that Hilken was wiring to the German legation in Mexico. With the devaluation of Mexico's currency during the war, that represented a huge sum, apparently used by Dilger in trying to influence the Mexicans and prepare the army in Sonora for possible raids into the United States. One secret cable said: "Please ask Delmar whether the remittance of $300,000 by Hilken to the Minister of Mexico [Eckhardt] has taken place."

Hilken was sending as much cash as he could to the saboteurs because he knew that the U.S. government was seeking through its Alien Property Custodian to seize German assets in the United States, "We had a great deal of money," he said, "from profits made on the German dyestuffs and other cargo brought on the *Deutschland*." The saboteurs were paid "under orders from Germany," Hilken said, with the funds funneled to Dilger by courier or through a bank account: "I simply paid Dilger a larger sum to take to Mexico so the funds would not be seized by the Alien Property Custodian."

Despite that large sum of money, Dilger felt that he was not getting his message through to Berlin, so he decided to make a personal appeal for an aid package. In the middle of December 1917 he traveled to Madrid, probably on a Spanish steamer and then by train, to make his case. Communications with Berlin were more secure from Madrid, the Germans believed—unaware that British intelligence was intercepting and deciphering all of the Berlin-Madrid cable traffic. Besides, there was a possibility that Dilger could board a U-boat on the Spanish coast and make it to a German port and then to Berlin.

From Madrid, Dilger warned the Political Section that Carranza's government could fall for lack of funds—an event that could lead to the return to power of the former president, Porfirio Díaz, with Allied backing. If that happened, Dilger cautioned, "we will be finished once and for all" in Latin America. "The general consensus is that a break with Mexico must be followed by breaks with Argentina and Chile."

Dilger's warning went all the way up the chain of command to the General Staff's chief, General Erich Ludendorff, as well as to the Chancellor's office in Berlin. The Staff added a note to Dilger's communiqué endorsing the concept of a Mexico loan: "A tying up of American troops on the southern border of the United States is also of importance for the High Command. General Ludendorff would thus be grateful if such a development were expedited by us."

AT FIRST GLANCE, Kurt Jahnke did not appear to be the sort of man who could be a master spy and saboteur. Whereas Dilger was urbane and suave, Jahnke was provincial and poorly educated. Dilger was darkly handsome; Jahnke was sallow and pock-marked, with a memorably vulgar gold front tooth. And while Dilger spoke a refined, highly educated German, Jahnke "spoke German like a barber."

But Jahnke possessed the devious alertness, single-minded determination, and raw intelligence that a foreign agent needed to survive in hostile environments. He was a consummate survivor who proved to be much tougher in the end than Dilger.

The two agents—Dilger, American-born but a loyal German, and Jahnke, German-born but a naturalized American—arrived in Mexico City that summer from opposite ends of America. While Dilger represented army intelligence, Jahnke worked for the Admiralty—two different, at times rival, branches of the German military intelligence structure. Both men were well connected, and each sought to outmaneuver the other.

As an espionage agent, Jahnke was at least Dilger's match; as a manipulator and survivor within the bureaucracy, he had few peers. "He was probably the most intelligent of all the German agents" in Mexico, wrote one historian of German intrigue there. "Not only was he an extremely able saboteur, but he was also a man whose specialty it was to infiltrate popular organizations and use them for his own purposes. He thus set up sabotage networks in the United States with the help of Irish lodges and trade unions opposed to the war."

In San Francisco, Jahnke's cover had been as a private detective. A "rough dresser" with dirty blonde hair and a German accent, Jahnke would roam the port city's waterfront taverns to pick up gossip about ships and munitions. As a former U.S. Marine, he had sources in the American military, and he liked to talk up soldiers in the bars. Starting with ship sabotage and munitions explosions on the West Coast, Jahnke and his partner—Lothar Witzke, a tall, blonde former German naval academy cadet—had played roles in several major sabotage operations, including the Black Tom explosion.

Having been honorably discharged from the Marines in 1910, Jahnke had fled California in May 1917 after he found himself "shadowed and hunted by members of the American Secret Service" who had him on a list of German sabotage suspects. He ended up in Mexico City, where he made contact with members of the German legation and told them that a legendary Admiralty agent on the East Coast—Charles Wunnenberg, known as "Charles the Dynamiter"—had enlisted Jahnke as a saboteur and assured him of similar work in Mexico in the event that the United States declared war. Jahnke had to carve out his own intelligence role in Mexico but received instructions late in 1917 to "operate principally against ships with [sabotage] undertakings."

Another instruction for Jahnke was to "try and send an agent from Mexico to USA." For that purpose, Jahnke recruited his former sabotage sidekick, Witzke, who had fled San Francisco for Monterey. Jahnke said later that he was asked to lead "a service of agents" for naval intelligence, including sabotage operations against American munitions plants and efforts to incite "strikes and mutinies" in the U.S. military. At one point, he also advocated "submarine attacks on the American coast with a possible base in Mexico." After the war, an American counterespionage official in Berlin described Jahnke as "exceedingly intelligent [and] exquisitely alert."

After a few weeks in Mexico City, Dilger had identified Jahnke as his chief rival in espionage and sabotage matters—especially after Jahnke boasted to Eckhardt that he, and not Hinsch, had organized the Black Tom sabotage attack in New Jersey. "Hinsch then became very indignant and shouted that he himself has brought about the Black Tom explosion," reported fellow German agent Hadler. "On one occasion Jahnke came to the house ... and Hinsch accused him of making false claims and there was a terrific dispute" with both Dilger and Herrmann present. "Finally, Hinsch, Herrmann and Dilger determined to make a report to the General Staff" that established their claim to several major sabotage operations in the United States. It was a dangerous, vainglorious move that eventually would backfire for them. Dilger had the report typed by an assistant and then showed it to Eckhardt, who was required to initial all outgoing messages from confidential agents.

Hadler said he and Herrmann "went to the roof of the house ... a photograph [of the message] was taken and the negative of the report in reduced size was secreted in the cover of a book. The [book] was given to me to take to Vera Cruz, where I delivered it to Captain Meyer, agent for the Hamburg-America Line," who arranged for the book to be sent by ship to Spain. "On previous occasions I had taken messages for Dilger to Captain Meyer for transmission abroad. Meyer had means of secreting these messages on board Spanish steamships running to Coruna and Vigo."

The internal struggle among German espionage agents in Mexico City continued for months. In a message sent to his German superiors in early 1918, Jahnke criticized Hinsch as having "absolutely no organization; it is out of the question placing my services at his disposal; and besides, Hinsch has no experience, is incapable and tactless and works with characteristic pettiness and personal spite." In the same message to his Admiralty superiors, Jahnke claimed that Dilger "neither knows anything of my activities nor is he in a position to judge."

Shortly after he arrived in Madrid at Christmastime 1917, Dilger began planting hints at the General Staff that Jahnke could not be trusted. "From a conversation [Dilger] has received the impression" that Jahnke "is not entirely reliable," according to a cable sent to Berlin on December 27. Dilger said he preferred to send messages through Hinsch because "he is a German and also because he enjoys the confidence of the Minister [Eckhardt]. I have also given [Hinsch] the new method of ciphering." Sending secure letters from Madrid to Mexico City was a slow process because they were given to a special messenger who took a steamer that left Spain only once a month.

At another point, Dilger—in a message that seems hypocritical in light of his own background—told the General Staff that "Jahnke is doubtless an able agent, but on account of his double nationality, his American train of thought, his lack of organizing talent and his lively imagination, is unsuitable to work in Hinsch's place."

A newly arrived German naval attaché in Madrid, Werner Steffan, said later that he had "received rather unfavorable information about Jahnke from Dr. Delmar ... who in the meantime had arrived at Madrid from Mexico. Apart from that, Delmar's statements showed quite clearly that Jahnke had been unknown to the Admiralty staff up to the time." Steffan said he had "strongly mistrusted Jahnke's statement that he had received instructions from a confidential agent of the Admiralty Staff in the U.S."

At first, officials in Berlin seemed sympathetic to Dilger's complaints about Jahnke. A week after his message, the General Staff sent a secret cable to Dilger saying: "The Admiralty has withdrawn the commission to Jahnke for sabotage undertakings and contemplates appointing Hinsch [in]stead ... The Admiralty agree that Hinsch shall remain under your [Dilger's] orders and shall be occupied in naval business in January. His activities, however, must be under your control in agreement with the Embassy." That preliminary decision was a bureaucratic victory for Dilger, but Jahnke soon heard about the backbiting and took advantage of Dilger's absence from Mexico to cultivate Eckhardt and to launch a countercampaign to discredit his rivals.

After the war, Jahnke said that in 1917–18 he was angry that Dilger and Hinsch had "attempted to assume direction of the agents' organization which I had established, and to crowd me out or, at least, put me in a subordinate position." In an ominous note, Jahnke added that he had enlisted the support of "German central authorities" to help him "bring about the elimination of these men." He added: "For this purpose I wrote letters which I sent to the Naval Attaché in Madrid with the request that he pass them on to the Admiralty."

Those accusatory letters, sent early in 1918, while Dilger was in Spain, spurred a series of secret cables between Madrid and Berlin, seeking to resolve what had become a feud between Jahnke and Dilger, who was allied with Hinsch. The dissention among German intelligence agents and the incompetence of others opened the door for the Allied secret services to uncover the German espionage and sabotage and to identify the agents.

While Jahnke could claim to be more of a sabotage expert than either Hinsch or Dilger, Dilger was uniquely expert in germ sabotage. Despite the setbacks in the United States, that effort continued, targeting Argentina, another substantial horse supplier to the Allies.

WHEN THE GERMAN NAVAL ATTACHÉ in Madrid, Captain von Krohn, decided to send his French mistress, Marthe Regnier, on a luxury liner to Argentina, he asked her as a favor to take along a trunk with a secret compartment in its lid. Hidden in that space were vials containing cultures of anthrax and glanders bacteria.

Regnier filled the trunk with her clothing and travel items and had it loaded with her other baggage when she boarded the Spanish liner *Reine Victoria Eugenia*. As the ship headed toward Buenos Aires, she enjoyed fine food, wine, and dancing—having absolutely no idea that the British had dispatched a warship to stop her liner and find the trunk.

That tidbit of information had come to the attention of Admiral Reginald "Blinker" Hall, Britain's legendary director of naval intelligence during the Great War. He had assembled a small band of code breakers, housed in room 40 in the British Admiralty's Old Building in London. "Room 40," as it became known, would prove to have a profound effect on the outcome of the war.

If it had not been for Room 40's code breaking—as well as Hall's careful use of the intelligence gleaned from the German messages—the United States might not have declared war in 1917, the German U-boats might have had far more devastating results, and the decisive sea battle at Jutland might not have been fought. For it was Room 40 that deciphered the Zimmerman Telegram and more than twenty thousand other secret German cables and radio transmissions during the war.

Nearly four dozen of those intercepted messages dealt with Germany's germ sabotage campaign, providing proof that the effort was coordinated by the General Staff in Berlin as well as invaluable details about how the secret germ sabotage was carried out. Hall himself took a keen interest in the German biological campaign, but Room 40's disclosures mainly covered the sabotage in Europe and South America, with few disclosures related to the early germ factory in Chevy Chase.

When he found out about the secret compartment of Regnier's trunk, Hall contacted the Admiralty to request that a British ship, the *Newcastle*, be dispatched immediately to intercept the Spanish liner and search for the germ vials. "Hall knew exactly what was happening and even the lid of the particular trunk in which the germs were concealed," wrote British intelligence historian Patrick Beesly. But the *Newcastle* "missed her in a fog and Marthe Regnier was able to hand over her lethal consignment safely."

That agent who received the vials, code-named "Arnold," was Dr. Herrman Wuppermann, who, like Dilger, worked for the General Staff's Political Section. Beesly called him "Germany's most dangerous agent in South America." There is no reason to believe that Wuppermann was a medical doctor like Dilger, but a cable in June 1916 indicates that he was dispatched from Berlin to Madrid (possibly carrying cultures) to "organize the production of E and B." That same month, a German submarine may have delivered new germ cultures to Spain. After Wuppermann arrived in Madrid, the German ambassador there cabled to notify Berlin that the cultures (perhaps those brought by the U-boat) were still alive. The following month, Wuppermann took a steamer to Havana and then to Buenos Aires, where he became the local agent for Norddeutsche Lloyd and started a sabotage operation. He began corresponding with Paul Hilken that summer, asking to meet him either in Cuba or in Panama to discuss sabotage and business issues.

In a letter to Hilken from Buenos Aires in the fall of 1916, Wuppermann—writing as "J. A. Arnold"—said a terrible drought in Argentina had caused shortages of wheat and corn. "The animals are also in rotten condition, many of them are dying from thirst and hunger," he added. In 1917, however, Wuppermann reported frequent departures of mule remount transports from Buenos Aires on ships bound for Mesopotamia, where pack animals were an essential part of the British Army's campaign against the Turks.

By February 1918, when Dilger was in Madrid, Wuppermann was reporting that his work with anthrax and glanders cultures had gone well. He claimed to have achieved "very satisfactory" results by infecting as many as 5,400 mules and horses being shipped out of Buenos Aires, mainly intended for British forces in Mesopotamia. According to information intercepted by Room 40, Wuppermann "managed to infect 200 mules which were being shipped on board the SS *Phidias*, and they all died," reported Beesly. "A second shipment was similarly lost."

As a protest against the mule sabotage, the chief British diplomat in Buenos Aires took a sample sugar cube to the president of Argentina, Hipólito Irigoyen, and dropped the cube in a cup of water, dissolving the sugar to reveal the glass ampoule that had been inside. The British diplomat demanded that the Argentinians stop the German operation, but the president refused, arguing that they "could not prove that the mules had been infected on Argentine soil rather than at sea."

The germ-laced sugar cubes—similar to the ones deployed earlier in Finland—were now the germ sabotage weapon of choice for German agents.

British intelligence suspected that the deadly cubes were produced in Berlin and then sent overland to the Austrian port of Pola on the Adriatic Sea, then transferred along with other secret cargo to German U-boats, which delivered them to the Spanish port of Cartegena. When a major delivery by the submarine U–35 was scheduled for February 1918, it may have been more than coincidence that Anton Dilger delayed his departure from Spain until after the shipment arrived. Cables indicate that Dilger, while in Spain, was still trying to coordinate distribution of germ cultures to agents in the field.

On January 20, a cable announced to Berlin that Dilger "cannot travel for the next five weeks" from Spain but should instead send Gehrmann to Mexico. Germ sabotage was still on the agenda then, for another cable from the military attaché in Madrid that same week asked the General Staff for permission to allow Gehrmann to carry E and B cultures with him. Two days later, the General Staff affirmed the request. Having intercepted and decoded that cable, a British message warned that Gehrmann "had concealed about his person or baggage one or more phials containing germ culture for the purpose of poisoning cattle or human beings." But, for reasons related to his blown cover, Gehrmann never left Spain.

On February 14, 1918—while Dilger was in Spain—a U-boat secretly landed two German agents and a dozen wooden cases off the Spanish coast near Cartegena. Alerted by British naval intelligence, local police seized the cases, which contained germ-tainted sugar cubes. Police sent the confiscated cases by train to Madrid, but Admiral Hall arranged for an agent to pick up and deliver a sample of the sugar cubes to London.

Later, Hall sent his personal assistant to show the deadly sugar cubes to the King of Spain, who reportedly became upset and called in the German ambassador to protest. The German naval attaché, Captain von Krohn, lost his post in Madrid.

Despite that setback, the Germans continued to try to use Spain as a base for germ sabotage. Over the previous two years, the German Embassy in Madrid had been involved in coordinating a germ sabotage campaign that seems to have targeted horses and mules in Spain and the French Pyrenees. The earliest intercepted cables from that Spanish campaign are from the fall of 1915, the same time that Dilger was operating his Chevy Chase germ factory.

That October, a cable from Nadolny of the General Staff had informed the military attaché in Madrid that "shipments of [germ] agents are discontinued until further notice because the [Spanish] export of horses to France has ceased." However, later that year and early in 1916, intercepted German cables indicated that shipments of germ cultures from Berlin via neutral Zurich to Spain had been resumed. At least once, a shipment was seized, spurring Nadolny to advise that the germ cultures be described as "medicine for horses."

The British naval spymaster Hall had been fascinated by the General Staff's germ warfare effort since the earliest references appeared in intercepted cables in 1915. Room 40 had decoded an especially intriguing secret cable in June 1916 in which the German embassy in Madrid had suggested using cholera in an effort to disrupt communications at the Spain-Portugal frontier. "I suggest contaminating at the frontier, with cholera bacilli, rivers flowing through Portugal," read the cable, likely written by the naval attaché von Krohn. "It is necessary to have two glass phials of pure culture, which [we suggest you] send when safe opportunity occurs." The following day, Berlin rejected the cholera proposal, most probably because it would have targeted humans and because such disease outbreaks might get out of control.

It was Hall who took an interest also in various references to the German agent Delmar, which became more frequent as soon as Dilger arrived in Mexico. At the time, of course, Hall and other British officials did not realize who Delmar was.

"Delmar had plans for running arms to Mexico ... and for the supply of equipment for a wireless station, which was essential" for secret German communications with Mexico, wrote Beesly. From Spain, Dilger helped arrange for a new wireless transmitter in Mexico that could receive messages from the main German communications center.

Because of technical problems, the transmitter was ineffective until late in the war.

From places as far away as Spain and Argentina, Dilger and other agents were still trying to find ways to impede Allied horse purchases in the Americas. While no direct messages between Dilger and Wuppermann have survived, documents indicate that both had connections to another German agent, Julio Rico, who was arrested in the United States early in 1918 "in connection with the poisoning of mules."

After the war, American investigator Amos Peaslee asked Admiral Hall if anyone had studied whether the German disease cultures might have been "responsible for the terrible epidemic of disease which occurred among the soldiers in America and on shipboard in the spring of 1918"—an apparent reference to the first outbreaks of Spanish Flu. Hall responded that no one had studied the possible correlation. The admiral added: "It did occur to me at the time that there might be a connection between the disease in animals and disease in men."

THE CIPHERED TELEGRAM READ:

> On January 16th the Iron Cross of the Second Class ... was conferred upon you by the All Highest. Hearty congratulations from here.

It was marked "For Delmar"—from Captain Marguerre of the General Staff's Political Section, which directed Dilger's sabotage. The "All Highest" was the Kaiser, who in theory conferred all such medals.

The reasons for awarding the medal to Dilger were not spelled out in the terse "most secret" cable sent on January 19, 1918, but the Iron Cross clearly recognized his sabotage and espionage work. Perhaps not coincidentally, the cable announcing the award arrived in Madrid during the same week that Dilger complained about being "exceedingly depressed and embittered" by Berlin's handling of his requests for aid to Mexico.

Like his father before him, Dilger had finally received a significant military medal. The award represented a somewhat hollow victory for

Dilger, however, for he felt that the General Staff was trying to mollify him at the same time that it kept delaying his urgent request for the Mexican aid.

Apart from the recognition implicit in the medal, the Great War's final year had begun inauspiciously for Dilger. It would be a year of disappointment, illness, frustration, and betrayal. Family members heard through the grapevine, possibly through Eda and Martin Koehler, that Dilger was ill. He received treatment at a hospital in Madrid—probably the German Hospital—for what family members later described as a blood clot in his lung. There was also the possibility that the doctor was suffering from depression brought on from the stress of his five difficult months in Mexico and his feud with Jahnke.

One of Dilger's cables mentioned specifically that an intelligence agent had tracked him to a hospital, but gave no details of his illness. In March, his cover address was in the Calle Felipe section of Madrid, on Polonia Martin Street. But he may have spent much of that month in the hospital.

By mid-March, Dilger already knew that at least one layer of his cover in Spain had been blown. "Although I am staying here under the name of Albert Donde, the Allied espionage agent has succeeded in tracing me to the hospital here and identifying me as Delmar," Dilger reported to Berlin on March 15.

"There has obviously been an indiscretion on the part of the Mexican Finance Minister or the Mexican Foreign Ministry," Dilger asserted. In fact, it seems that the Allied spy—most likely a French military intelligence agent—got his information on the Donde-Delmar link from a Mexican diplomat in Madrid.

Connecting Donde to Delmar was an important link, which compromised Dilger and enormously complicated his planned travel back to Mexico. Even so, the doctor had managed to preserve his other layer of cover: still, no one knew who Delmar was. The false name that he and Hilken had cooked up by combining abbreviations for Delaware and Maryland remained a mask for Anton Dilger.

But as a result of an indiscretion by friends, that mask also started to slip that spring. The first clue for the code breakers—who had blithely filed away the Iron Cross cable under "Delmar"—was an innocent-sounding birthday cable from the General Staff in Berlin, marked as being "for Delmar." The cable, sent by Marguerre on February 13, Dilger's birthday, read: "Hearty congratulations on your birthday and good wishes for your recovery." Significantly, it also extended greetings from the Koehler and Giessler families.

By linking the mysterious Delmar to the birth date of Anton Dilger, that cable should have provided a significant clue for investigators who were working feverishly at the time to identify Delmar. The blatant mention of the Koehlers and Giesslers also would have provided potentially valuable family information to track down Delmar's roots. But it would be several more months before Allied investigators made the connection.

At about the same time Dilger's espionage cover was being peeled back, his enemies in Mexico City were trying to discredit him and Hinsch, as well as—by implication—their associate Gehrmann. In March, the naval attaché in Madrid cabled Berlin about Jahnke's accusations against Dilger: "A messenger from Mexico has handed in a long report from Jahnke to the Admiralty staff, which represents Delmar and Captain Hinsch as actually criminal and claims for himself sole direction. He demands telegraphic instructions to this effect."

Further complicating matters, German diplomat Eckhardt—by this point firmly aligned with Jahnke—then sent a secret message to Berlin asking permission to fire Dilger's group of agents. Eckhardt complained that

> cooperation between Jahnke and Hinsch is in consequence of their mutual distrust impossible. Jahnke's work must not be interrupted and he is therefore receiving financial support through me.
>
> In consequence of very grave discoveries I request permission to dismiss Delmar, Hinsch and [Herrmann?] from my intelligence service, approval to be indicated by telegraphing the word *Dismiss*.

That loaded word was not telegraphed, but Berlin soon decided to rescind a previous decision to subordinate Jahnke to Dilger. Instead, the two rivals would be coequals, one as the chief naval confidential agent and the other as the chief army agent. But only one of them was in Mexico City; Dilger was stuck in Madrid.

At the same time, Dilger's subordinate Gehrmann was suddenly reported to be "compromised" in Spain and unable to return as planned to Mexico. His cover also had been blown, and the General Staff went through the motions of finding a place for him at a civilian agency to get him out of the way.

In the end, the effort to place Gehrmann proved to be unnecessary, for the young agent was suddenly reported dead. The apparent cause of death was the first wave of the Spanish Flu pandemic, but there was suspicion that the troublesome agent might have been killed. It was the second wave of killings in Madrid that Dilger would come to fear.

Chapter 13

SPANISH FLU

Come now, Graylie, she said, taking his bridle, we must outrun
Death and the Devil.
—KATHERINE ANNE PORTER, *Pale Horse, Pale Rider*, 1939

I T SEEMED A PERFECT PLACE TO HIDE: a town in the middle of
nowhere, a province far from the capital, a quiet spot to relax and
watch the sea swallow the sun at dusk.

The fishing town of Redondela was hidden away in Spain's rugged
northwest province of Galicia, much closer to Portugal than to Madrid.
Sir Francis Drake had once raided the Galician coast for treasure, and
Napoleon had conquered its territory. But the province, like all of Spain,
had remained peacefully neutral during the Great War.

In the summer of 1918, Anton Dilger found no peace in that neutrality. He had been compromised by intercepted cables, betrayed by a
Mexican consul, and denigrated by a fellow German spy. He felt hunted
and, indeed, he was.

On the coast, he would watch the Atlantic's blue waves churn into
inky black in the growing darkness. Somewhere out there, under the
sea's mysterious swells, the U-boats were still hunting transports that
brought fresh American troops to fight. But the number of subs had
dwindled, and a million U.S. troops had already arrived in Europe. It
was now too late for the U-boats to change the course of the war.

Even in placid Redondela there were French informants and German operatives. The French soon began shadowing a man known locally as "the German physician"—tall, with a "long face" and black mustache "trimmed in the American fashion." A spy who had been dispatched to follow him described a man who walked "very slowly and with some trouble." Always wearing an overcoat, the German doctor "frequently stops and turns around to see if he is followed."

He was, indeed, being followed. The Americans, British, and French were all searching for him. While the British had traced his movements through intercepted German cables, the French seemed to have an edge in human intelligence about Dilger. Their agents learned from the Mexican consul in Madrid that Delmar was sending cables to Mexico from Galicia. And French agents also traced him to Barcelona, where he stayed in the Sarria district. The man suspected to be Delmar "often goes to Barcelona; and is frequently seen at the 'Sport' café where he meets German agents," a French informant reported in August 1918. He added that Delmar "lives with a woman," but no other cables or letters from Spain identify the woman or specify whether she was a mistress or a fellow spy.

Why would German intelligence agents send cables from the out-of-the-way town of Redondela? It was not far from Galicia's main port, Vigo, the closest major Spanish port to the north of Portugal. And there were reasons for German spies to keep an eye on ships steaming in and out of Portugal's ports: ever since the Portuguese had seized all German ships anchored in its ports early in 1916, German U-boats had targeted Portuguese vessels, sinking eighty of those ships by the war's end. The submarine captains had their periscopes, of course, but they also needed eyes in northern Spain to spot ship movements off the coast and to collect gossip at the sailors' bars in Vigo.

The Portuguese were at war against the Germans, sending soldiers to the Western Front as well as to African colonies. In the spring of 1918, Portugal's expeditionary force had suffered near annihilation at the hands of attacking German forces at the Battle of Estaires, losing more than a third of its soldiers. Spain, on the other hand, had remained stubbornly neutral—in part, because King Alfonso XIII was related by marriage to both the British King and the German Kaiser.

In keeping Spain neutral, the king had inadvertently transformed his capital into one of the world's most incestuous nests of spies, a place where countries on all sides of the war could maintain embassies and deploy confidential agents. German agents, French agents, British agents, American agents, Spanish agents, and Portuguese agents—all haunted the Madrid night spots and diplomatic functions. They closely watched one another, intercepting coded messages and trying to determine which code names referred to which agents.

The French agents sent detailed reports of Delmar's movements in both Redondela and Barcelona. Spotting him in a cabaret near Barcelona's Mediterranean shore, French informants reported that Delmar

> very frequently met in the last few days [a source named] Giannoni at the night cabaret Bobino. The place, which was recently opened, has become the actual headquarters of the Germans and officers of the German service. The presence among them, a short while ago, of a German who is tall, well dressed, [fair complexioned] and who was treated with great deference by those who approached him was noticed.

The French agent speculated that "Delmar may have gone ... to Barcelona direct and immediately after sending his telegram" from Redondela to a high-ranking Mexican diplomat, Manuel Barreiro y Vallejo, who had until recently been a special envoy in Berlin. The agent said he was not absolutely positive that "the man traced at Barcelona is Delmar, but I will have the closest possible watch kept on him."

German spies were also keeping track of one another, as Dilger knew from his feud with Jahnke in Mexico. By 1917–18, the budget for German espionage was $6 million a *month*, about $100 million in current dollars. In the eighteenth century, Prussia's Frederick the Great had once boasted that for every cook in his armies he had a hundred spies. Bismarck had prepared for Prussia's invasion of France in 1870 by paying an estimated thirty thousand spies to infiltrate every French agency. And now, as the Great War pitted the world's best spies against one another, the Kaiser had built a formidable array of military intelligence and secret service agents.

One of the books Dilger kept in Spain was *My Four Years in Germany*, written by James Gerard, the former U.S. ambassador in Berlin. Offering a harsh indictment of the Kaiser's regime, Gerard contended in his books that espionage so dominated German bureaucracy—as well as foreign affairs—that everyone lived in fear of "the spies of his rivals." "Spy spies on spy—autocracy produces bureaucracy where men rise and fall not by the votes of their fellow citizens but by back stairs intrigue."

The particular copy of the book in Dilger's personal library was an inside joke. Its front cover contained a secret pouch, in which film negatives or documents could be hidden. On the book's opening page, Roberto Wilson had inscribed a message in Spanish: "To my dear friend on his birthday, hoping that this book will change his Germanophile outlook."

Wilson was the false name used by Heinrich Bode, a trilingual spy with California connections who would be singled out for mention in a section of Gerard's next book, *Face to Face with Kaiserism*, which describes the worse side of German espionage. Gerard had been surprised when a uniformed German soldier named Bode showed up at the U.S. Embassy in Berlin in 1915 and claimed to have worked for Gerard's father-in-law before the war. Speaking perfect English, Bode "said that he was fighting on the Eastern front and that he had a temporary leave of absence," Gerard recounted in the book. "I gave him some money and later we sent him packages of food and tobacco to the front, but never received any acknowledgment."

About eighteen months later, in February 1917—when Gerard stopped in Spain on his way back to the United States after Washington broke off diplomatic relations with Germany—one of Gerard's assistants encountered Bode, fashionably dressed in a business suit, on a street in Madrid handing out calling cards identifying him as a mining engineer from Los Angeles. Asked how he had gone from being a German soldier in Russia to a mining engineer in Spain, Bode told "a most extraordinary fairy story, saying that he had been captured by the Russians on the East front and sent to Siberia, that from Siberia he had escaped to China and from there he had gradually worked his way back to America and thence to Spain."

The Americans didn't believe him. Gerard wrote that "it is far more likely [Bode] had landed from a German submarine on the coast of Spain and that he was posing as an American mining engineer—for a particular purpose." Gerard told high-level Spaniards that Bode was a German spy and intended "to visit the mining districts of Spain" posing as an American. "Bode must have suspected that I had given information about him," Gerard wrote, adding that he soon "received several post-cards of a threatening character, evidently from him."

Bode was one of many German spies operating in Spain. He had connections to the General Staff's Political Section and had been dispatched to China in the fall of 1915 on a mysterious mission. On his way back from China, he had visited his sister in Los Angeles and stopped in New York and then Havana to meet with fellow German operatives. Shortly after he arrived in Spain late in 1916, Bode began operating under the false name Roberto Wilson, joining an array of other agents who dealt with contraband landed in the country by German U-boats.

During Gerard's short stay in Madrid, the Spanish premier told him that police had found "a quantity of high explosives, marked by a little buoy, in one of the secluded bays of the coast. And that day a German had been arrested who had mysteriously appeared at a Spanish port dressed as a workman." The simple "workman" had traveled in a first-class rail compartment from Madrid, booked a room in the best hotel, and bought an expensive new suit.

"Undoubtedly the high explosives as well as the mysterious German had been landed from a German submarine," Gerard wrote. "Whether the explosive was [a munitions] depot for submarines or was [intended] to help overturn the Spanish government was hard to guess, but [the prime minister] was worried over the activity of the German agents in Spain."

German agents in the United States used to send messages by mail to a special post box in Cuba, from which they were sent aboard Spanish ships to the Spanish coast, where U-boats then picked up the messages and delivered them to Germany. "At all times since the war the Germans have had a submarine post running direct from Germany to Spain," Gerard revealed. An espionage novelist's description of Berlin during the Cold War might have applied just as well to Madrid during the Great War: "What a garrison of spies! What a cabinet full of useless, liquid secrets, what a playground for every alchemist, miracle worker and rat piper that ever took up the cloak."Anton Dilger soon discovered that there was nowhere safe for him to hide. It was in Madrid, after all, where the most exotic and notorious German spy, code-named H21, had made her crucial mistake the previous year. Her German lover in Spain, Major Arnold Kalle, was the same man who would later deal with Dilger.

It was Kalle whose machinations had helped put an end to the two-faced activities of the spy who called herself Mata Hari.

A FRENCH FIRING SQUAD had finally ended the career of Mata Hari, an adventurous Dutch woman with a German espionage code and an Indonesian stage name.

The most famous spy of the Great War, Margaretha Geertruida Zelle possessed an endless passion for seduction and an uncanny ability to reinvent herself. She was a consummate actress, a woman who used her persona as an exotic dancer—Mata Hari, the Eye of Dawn—to gain entry to the drawing rooms and bedrooms that became her stages for espionage.

At the dawn of her adult life, Zelle had been a mother and housewife, living in Indonesia. After a vengeful servant poisoned her two children, Zelle moved into the demimonde of prewar Paris. At first she performed on circus horses and posed as a nude model. Then, in 1905, she transformed herself into Mata Hari, a Javanese princess who performed ritual dances she had learned in Far Eastern temples.

Mostly male audiences in Paris, Berlin, and other European capitals were transfixed by her exotic dances, which were elaborate strip shows ending with her gilded gowns lying on the stage floor and the nearly nude dancer standing alone in the spotlight.

Having learned how to seduce audiences, Zelle soon discovered the secrets of attracting and seducing powerful men. After the war broke out, she became a courtesan and, by most accounts, a spy or—at the very least—an informant. As a citizen of neutral Holland, she was free to cross European borders, and she spent the war years traversing France, Holland, Germany, and Spain gathering lovers and information.

She was tall and captivating—a perfect *femme du monde* who moved easily with her fame into the upper echelons of society. She began to arouse suspicion shortly after the war began. When British interrogators asked whether she was a German spy, Zelle claimed to be an informant for the French. After she was questioned by counterintelligence officials in London, British officials warned their French counterparts in June 1916 that Zelle might be a German agent. She was put under surveillance while in Paris that summer and again early in 1917.

Whether it was at the suggestion of the French, or on her own initiative, Zelle traveled to Madrid in December 1916. She wasted no time in seducing the German military attaché, Major Kalle, while leading him to believe that he had seduced her. She then proceeded to play a dangerous game, providing tidbits of information to both sides—and inspiring suspicions in both the French and the German secret services.

Zelle began with some idle bedroom chatter, feeding Kalle tidbits of information that he recognized as recycled gossip. But she raised Kalle's suspicions by asking about sensitive German military plans. As a test of her suspected French connection, he mentioned a stale story that she might accept as a scoop: that he was trying to arrange a submarine to drop off German and Turkish officers in Morocco's French zone.

Believing she possessed a saleable item of intrigue, Zelle mentioned Kalle's story to a French agent, whose staff already knew about it. When she began to quiz him again at their next rendezvous, Kalle told her he knew she had passed along the submarine story to the French. He knew this, he claimed, because the Germans had "the key to their radio cipher"—which was false. He was testing her to see if she would also pass along that lie to French intelligence.

When Zelle returned to Paris, she tried to meet with a French military intelligence agent, Captain Georges Ladoux, who at first avoided her and then refused to pay her, saying that her information from Kalle had been worthless. Needing money, she appealed to Kalle to send funds via the Dutch ambassador in Paris. Kalle—who by then knew that she could not be trusted—sent a message to the German espionage chief at Amsterdam to send a small sum of money to "agent H21." The coded message was picked up by the Eiffel Tower radio station and the code name was traced to the infamous Dutch courtesan.

Arrested in Paris in mid-February 1917, Zelle was charged with espionage, identified as German agent H21 based on "information from a secret and very reliable source." Military prosecutors alleged that she had offered to serve French intelligence in 1916 with the intention of sharing everything she learned with German intelligence and that she had given such military and diplomatic intelligence to Kalle in Madrid.

A week later, the police department in Paris forwarded 114 surveillance reports on Mata Hari. The reports offered evidence that she was a spy who used well-known techniques to escape surveillance, such as waiting until only one taxi was available before she took it, or shouting an address to the taxi driver and then whispering that he should drive elsewhere. She used such techniques twenty-two times during the days in which she was followed, and she was twice observed talking to suspicious men who took notes while she spoke.

That evidence was circumstantial, so in April the French counterintelligence service was asked by prosecutors to produce fourteen decrypted telegrams—exchanged between the German military attaché in Madrid, Kalle, and the German General Staff in Berlin—that implicated Mata Hari as agent H21. Those cables revealed to outsiders that code breakers at France's Section de Chiffre already had cracked the ciphers used by the German military attaché in Madrid. Zelle denied being H21 and suggested that Kalle had gotten the information from someone else who was the true agent H21. Later, however, the accused courtesan made the mistake of changing her story and conceding that she had fed harmless information from the newspapers to Kalle and that she had received a fee from him. But she claimed that what she had told the officer had been of no importance and could not have done any damage and that she had done so only to get important information from him which she immediately gave to the French.

Found guilty of espionage, she was executed by a French firing squad on October 15, 1917. "During the whole of my life I have been a spontaneous being," Zelle told the French prosecutor during their last discussion. "I never went with small steps. I have great aims, and I go straight for them."

The Germans clearly knew that the French had broken the code that Kalle was using to discuss information from agent H21—information that he knew was of little value. In the deadly game of espionage, Kalle had cleverly set up his former lover to be exposed as a double agent—and callously got her out of the way.

Two months after Zelle's death, Kalle met for the first time with German agent Anton Dilger. Over the next ten months, Kalle would handle nearly all of Dilger's communications with Berlin—the Jahnke feud, the concerns about blown covers, and Dilger's outright refusal of orders that he return to Mexico.

And it was Kalle who would report Dilger's death to the General Staff—one year, to the week, after Mata Hari's execution in Paris.

WHEN ANTON DILGER first arrived in Madrid at the end of 1917, the General Staff still believed that the German Army could break through and win the war before American troops arrived in large enough numbers to make a difference on the battlefields.

There was still reason for optimism in Berlin. In March 1918, Russia's provisional regime signed the harsh Treaty of Brest-Litovsk, ceding territory to Berlin. And, with that, the two-front war had suddenly become a one-front war. Russia's withdrawal allowed the Kaiser's strategists to transfer soldiers to the west in a last-ditch effort to capture Paris.

In a sense, that spring the war hinged on how quickly the Germans could transfer and deploy those Eastern units to France—achieving numerical superiority on the Western Front for the first time since 1914—and how rapidly fresh American troops would arrive in France to reinforce the tired British and French units.

The Germans launched their spring offensive—the *Kaiserschlacht*—in late March before massive numbers of Americans arrived at the Western Front. Prepared to sacrifice as many as a million men to win the war, General Ludendorff ordered German units to strike with everything they had. Meanwhile, German U-boats redoubled their deadly hunt for troop-transport ships filled with U.S. soldiers.

Ludendorff's plan was ambitious but risky. A series of attacks would try to divert the Allied reserves slowly southward, isolating British forces in the northern part of the Front, and then the main assault would erupt in Flanders. That strategy aimed to knock the British out of the war and force a French surrender before American troops reinforced them. The first German attack, launched on March 21, pushed the British back, and by the end of April some German units seemed to be on the verge of a breakthrough, within forty miles of Paris. Suddenly desperate, the long-bickering Allies agreed to a unified command under the French marshal Ferdinand Foch. American divisions began arriving at the Front in May, and the Allies fought back with new confidence. By July the U.S.-bolstered Allied forces had broken through and swept the weakened Germans forces back toward the pre–1914 frontiers.

When they saw that American soldiers were pouring onto the European battlefields, the Germans realized that their U-boat campaign had failed. The submarines were not sinking nearly enough troop and cargo transports to slow the deployment of fresh troops on the Western Front. The British Admiralty's introduction of convoys in the spring of 1918 to discourage U-boat attacks proved to be the key to averting losses to torpedo attack. In June 1918 alone, 36 U.S. Navy transports carried 115,000 American troops while 70 British vessels took another 140,000 to the French ports. From May through September of that year, British and U.S. transports carried more than 1.3 million U.S. soldiers to Europe.

The German Admiralty, which had once boasted that its submarines could stop a significant number of American troops from reaching Europe, capitulated. To be sure, German U-boats sank several U.S. Navy and merchant vessels off the French coast that year—including the troop transports *President Lincoln* on May 31, killing twenty-six, and the *Covington* on July 1, killing six. But those sinkings represented only a small fraction of the total transport ships, and most of the soldiers aboard the vessels were rescued at sea.

Something drastic was needed to stop or slow that American influx to Europe. One possible option was the long-discussed Mexican invasion of the United States. In the early summer of 1918, Dilger was one of the most outspoken proponents of decisive German action to spur such an invasion. He made a last-ditch effort that July to convince the General Staff that his Mexico strategy was still viable.

"The fact that American troops, in spite of considerable disturbance by submarine warfare, are reaching France in ever increasing numbers, causes me to suggest (after discussion with the Military Attaché) that we should abandon our policy of inactivity in Mexico, sacrifice that country and drive it into war with the USA," Dilger wrote in a secret message to the Political Section on July 8, 1918. "I believe that I can achieve this by inducing General Calles, who is in command of the state of Sonora, to invade the USA. If you agree, I should try to get through to Mexico in spite of all difficulties."

Dilger, with help from Hinsch, Herrmann, and other German agents in Mexico, had been trying for months to cultivate and provide arms to General Plutarco Elias Calles, the governor of Sonora Province, which borders Arizona and New Mexico. A former teacher and journalist, Calles had fought with distinction in the revolution and become a nationally known political figure who would later become Mexico's president.

Calles was highly sympathetic to Germany, at one point extending tax breaks to German firms in Mexico that U.S. officials had blacklisted and were trying to drive out of business. In Sonora, widespread resentment against Pershing's Punitive Expedition of 1916–17 lingered and minor border incidents continued for years afterward. In 1918, Calles wanted his soldiers to have proper weaponry to be able to either launch an invasion or repel a possible attack from forces led by counterrevolutionary Mexicans who had taken refuge in America.

The same month that Dilger had written the cable suggesting that he could induce Mexico to invade the United States, he took part in several high-level meetings in Barcelona with German bankers and the Mexican diplomat Barreiro, who had been a high-level negotiatior in Berlin that spring. The main topic of the discussions was how best to transfer a large sum of German money to the Mexican government.

In Barcelona, an informant told the U.S. military attaché in Spain that Delmar had "arrived mysteriously in this town" that summer—possibly having "disembarked from the submarine which lately landed a wounded German officer here." The informant described Delmar as "a very important personage," a German who spoke little Spanish but perfect English and French:

> He is said to have been the guest at a private dinner given by the King of Bulgaria and his wife. Here [Barcelona], as also on the

journey which he made to Mexico, he is only known by the name
of Dr. Delmar ... probably Albert Delmar, whose real name is
Dillkan [*sic*], who is alleged to be going to Mexico as a representative of the Political Section of the German General Staff.

The name Dillkan was close enough to Dilger to hint that the Americans were closing in on Delmar's true identity.

The informant told the American attaché that Delmar had attended
six or seven meetings with Barreiro and bankers at the private home of
the head of the Spanish office of one of Germany's largest financial institutions, Deutsche Bank. On July 17, the American spy reported:

The result of these long and important conferences has been the
confiding to Manuel Barreiro of a mission to Mexico of the
greatest gravity. The object of his mission is to take to President
Carranza three documents which he is to destroy rather than let
them fall into American hands, for which reason he has learnt
them by heart.

These documents are relative to the taking up again of the old
project to provoke a rising in Mexico against the United States of
America. A sum amounting to Three Hundred Millions (whether
pesos, marks or pesetas unknown) is to be placed at the disposal of
Mexico. Barreiro, as a reward for executing the mission, is to
receive 100,000 pesetas [about $1 million in 2006 dollars].

But Barreiro—who had planned to take a steamship from Spain to
Cuba, and then on to Mexico—soon discovered that his travel plans
were blocked. U.S. officials warned Cuba's senior diplomat in Spain that
Barreiro was "a very dangerous man," and should be refused a visa to
Cuba. The Americans also telegraphed major Spanish ports, asking that
Barreiro or any other Mexican be prevented from boarding ships to
Spain or Cuba without first being interrogated. Stranded, Barreiro
wrote on July 20 from the Hotel Inglés in Madrid:

So that you may now realize how really and positively we are
blockaded here in Spain, I'll tell you that the gentlemen at the

Cuban consulate have not allowed me to get on board the steamer bound for my country "because I was not *persona grata* for the Americans." As a result, I am not leaving, and I am going to Barcelona.

Dilger also found himself stranded and frustrated in Spain. The American informant reported that Dilger had written a note to the Deutsche Bank official in Barcelona, saying "[Dilger] is sorry he cannot go to Mexico as it would give him great pleasure to 'do the Americans in.'" Less than a week after he made his offer to the General Staff to return to Mexico to "drive it into war with the USA," Dilger already was confronting serious logistical problems—not only in leaving Spain, but in locating the munitions sorely needed by Mexico's army if it were going to assemble a credible force to threaten the United States. He complained in a cable to Berlin in mid-July that Mexico's armed forces had only "108 field cannons and 36 mountain cannons," which would hardly sustain a legitimate invasion force. Dilger demanded: "Are additional arms shipments impossible[?]"

In Washington, the War Department's military intelligence section was taking both Delmar and the invasion threat very seriously. On June 17, the War Department sent a "for arrest" bulletin to all major ports, from Spain to Singapore, asking officials to be on the lookout for Dr. Albert Delmar, and attaching a physical description of him.

On July 20, the chief of U.S. military intelligence asked the State Department for a full report on Delmar, who was described as a former surgeon who had become an agent for the German General Staff and held the rank of colonel in the German Army. Ten days later, military intelligence officers in Madrid reported to Washington: "Dr. Delmar very important person, located in Madrid. Associated with Manuel Barreiro who was refused visa for Mexico. Barreiro to take large sum to Mexico to cause trouble undoubtedly."

The American military's concerns about the Mexican invasion threat seemed to peak at about the same time that the German military was losing interest. In Berlin, the General Staff's Political Section sent copies of Dilger's recent messages to the Foreign Office in Berlin for comment, which did not take long. The diplomats there quickly rejected out of hand the idea of sponsoring a Mexican invasion. For one, they questioned—probably at the suggestion of Eckhardt—whether the American-born doctor could wield as much clout as he claimed.

"First of all it appears questionable whether our agent has enough influence to push Mexico into a war with the United States which would from the outset necessarily seem hopeless to the Mexican government," said the Foreign Office, in a message probably written by the former German minister to Mexico, Paul von Hintze.

The Foreign Office argued that a Mexican invasion would be against Germany's long-term interests because it might lead to a U.S. counter-invasion and likely occupation of the country. "In a belligerent conflict between Mexico and America, we would have to provide arms sooner or later. The blame for the conflict, and for its outcome, would in any case be attributed to us. As a result not only our previous friendship with Mexico would collapse, but we would be giving America itself a reason for occupying Mexico, and with it, one of our important future sources of raw materials."

While the Foreign Office deferred to the General Staff on the German military advantages that would result from a war between Mexico and the United States, the diplomats contended that "from both the political and economic standpoint … a war between Mexico and America appears to be against our interests." Another reason to be cautious about any German backing for a direct attack against America was that in the summer of 1918 many German diplomats and civilian government officials, seeing that a military victory was out of reach, were pushing for negotiations with the United States and others to settle the Great War. As President Wilson's representatives would likely be involved in such talks, any German-sanctioned action against U.S. territory would hurt the chances for a diplomatic settlement.

When Dilger worked in Mexico in the summer and fall of 1917, he had talked with Calles as well as with President Carranza about the possibility of invading the United States with the help of secret military and financial assistance from Germany. All this time, the Mexican Secret Service had been sending its own agents to the border and clandestinely into the United States, where expatriate Mexicans were still discussing a possible counterrevolution. In addition to gathering intelligence, Mexico's spies engaged in surveillance, espionage, counterespionage, and propaganda.

One U.S. army intelligence agent had reported that as many as 900 Germans and 45,000 Mexicans were preparing for a possible attack across the border in 1917–18. The numbers are questionable, but historians believe "there is no doubt that German agents were preparing an attack on the U.S. from Sonora." Even so, circumstances had changed dramatically since Dilger departed for Spain.

Once the United States began conscripting soldiers and vastly expanding its armed forces, the German calculations shifted, leading to a reassessment of the potential military impact resulting from a Mexican incursion. After all, despite numerous border skirmishes since the end of Pershing's expedition, no major U.S. troop buildup at the border had resulted. The skirmishes had been largely ignored. Also, by the summer of 1918, the military, political, and diplomatic situations had altered with the German losses on the Western Front.

By mid-August, it was clear to Berlin that the Great War would have to be settled by negotiation. Germany's spring and early summer offensive had fizzled by late July, when the Germans—having failed to score a key breakthrough in the Second Battle of the Marne—retreated back to the Hindenburg Line and waited for the inevitable Allied attack. By then, some German units were beginning to lose their will to fight.

The increasingly depressed Ludendorff bemoaned the "Black Day of the German Army" on August 8 when trusted front-line German units fled the onslaught by a Canadian and Australian force. Backed by six hundred tanks, that Allied juggernaut blasted through the Hindenburg Line at Amiens, driving the Germans back eight miles as a prelude to the series of Allied offensives that would end the war within two months.

Weighing all of those factors, the Political Section wired Dilger in Madrid on August 25 to order him to stop working toward an invasion. The cable explained that because "Mexico would be unable to put up a very long resistance in case of war with America and no relief worth mentioning would be afforded to our Western Front, the plan proposed cannot be proceeded with." Accepting the cautious arguments of the Foreign Office, the Political Section added that "the defeat of Mexico by America would be very prejudicial to our investments in Mexico and our economic position during the transition period" after the Great War's end.

Having taken away Dilger's option to incite a war, his masters in Berlin encouraged him in the same telegram to help create the illusion of a continuing Mexican threat. While a Mexican invasion was to be avoided, the General Staff cabled, "it would be desirable that America should be constantly threatened by the situation in Mexico. Please report whether you can work in this direction."

Stranded in Spain, with his espionage cover blown and foreign agents stalking him, Anton Dilger had been ordered, in effect, to create a mirage in Mexico.

IN WARTIME LONDON, Edward Bell probably knew more military secrets than any other American. He was the liaison between the U.S. Embassy and British intelligence services. In that role, he was often the first to learn about British intercepts and pass them along to Washington.

One of Bell's most important contacts was the British Admiralty's intelligence chief, "Blinker" Hall. When Hall's men intercepted and decoded a secret German message that seemed relevant to the Americans, Hall would sometimes ask the Harvard-educated Bell to come to Room 40 in the Admiralty building and read the secret cables.

Bell was the first American to see the Zimmerman Telegram early in 1917, and it was Bell who was asked to find out what Hall knew about the identity of the German spy Delmar.

Suddenly, in late September and early October 1918, the State Department in Washington became intensely interested in Delmar. A deputy undersecretary in the department, Leland Harrison, sent Bell a frantic cable in mid-October demanding "a full report giving all the information in Hall's possession regarding Delmar."

The goal, it seems, was to arrest, charge, and try Dilger for treason. The grounds had nothing to do with his Chevy Chase germ sabotage, which had been disbanded before the United States declared war, but rather his efforts to spark a Mexican invasion. Wrote Harrison to Bell in London: "believe I have definitely established his identity and want to indict him for treason when the time comes." He added:

"Looks like a big case with many interesting leads. When completed will advise you fully."

Beginning to confirm that Delmar was Dilger had been a complex process that involved piecing together clues provided by Room 40's deciphered German cables, analyzing information from informants in Barcelona and Madrid, and a completely separate investigation by the U.S. Alien Property Custodian involving Hilken and seized German assets in America. That inquiry focused on Hilken's hoard of money from selling goods brought the previous summer by the *Deutschland* as well as cargo that had been scheduled to be shipped aboard its sister U-boat, the *Bremen*.

Fearing that the U.S. government would seize those assets, Hilken had diverted large sums of cash to finance German spies and sabotage, including Dilger's work in Mexico. In the spring of 1918, the Alien Property Custodian's office had ordered Hilken to show up at its office on 42nd Street in New York to answer questions about the German assets his firm held. "They examined me for days at a time," Hilken recalled later. "I know they went into my relations with Dilger, and I think also ... my payments to Hinsch ... They wanted to get on to the location of the German properties and German funds," he said, and they got his name after examining and searching the apartment of John Hammer, who represented the Krupps arms manufacturer. They also sent an agent to examine Hilken's files in Baltimore.

Later, a State Department official said that the connection between Delmar and Dilger had been nailed down "through [a] lead obtained in the investigation of disposition made of cargo which had been destined for the *Bremen* and never shipped." The investigators also tracked down a financial agent in New York who could help "establish the fact that Albert D. Delmar was identical with Doctor Anton Dilger."

By September, the investigators realized that Delmar was Dilger and should be tracked down. A high-ranking official of the Alien Property Custodian's office in New York asked that an agent be sent to Washington to "expedite this inquiry" into Dilger's travels and activities.

That month, federal agent Don S. Rathburn paid a visit to the house detective at the McAlpin Hotel in New York—a known haunt of German saboteurs. Rathburn wanted to know if "A. C. Dilger" had stayed there after his return to the United States in 1917. Ten days later, the same agent sent a cable to the head of the Bureau of Investigation "requesting certain information regarding passports issued to A. C. Delmar or Dilger." Once the Americans read through the intercepted German cables from February, they would also learn—from the birthday message from the General Staff—that Delmar and Dilger shared the same birth date.

While those investigations were continuing, the damaging spy-versus-spy controversy in Mexico City was temporarily resolved, mostly to the benefit of Dilger's rival, Jahnke. While on paper Dilger remained the General Staff's "sole confidential agent" in Mexico, in reality the diplomat Eckhardt had been given veto power over Dilger's plans.

It is unclear whether Dilger made it back to Mexico in the course of 1918. The cables from Berlin to Madrid, usually passed along by other channels to Mexico City, at times imply that Delmar was in Mexico by sometime in April. One witness reported that Dilger and Hinsch were seen together in Mexico City in late March. Also, it is difficult to believe that the General Staff would have named Dilger as its "sole confidential agent" in Mexico if he had no opportunity to return there.

A cable sent on April 9 from Berlin requested that the military attaché in Madrid ask Dilger "whether the [...] which he took with him proved satisfactory. Please communicate the results of any experience he had had with them." That may have been a coded reference to a new shipment of germ cultures or German weapons for Mexico.

The last reported sighting of Dilger in Mexico City came in mid-July 1918, but he was also spotted by an American informant in Barcelona at about the same time. In retrospect, the Barcelona sighting is more believable. He was engaged in a frenzy of activity that month related to his proposal to provide substantial German funds to support a Mexican invasion of the United States. But once Dilger and the Mexican emissary found themselves stranded in Spain, their options were severely limited. And after Dilger received the General Staff's cable on August 25 putting an end to the idea of a Mexican invasion, he appears to have dropped out of sight for awhile. There were no intercepted cables mentioning him until mid-October.

It must have been an extremely frustrating time for Dilger, who had worked on the Mexican invasion plan for more than a year. One report indicated that Dilger was hoping to receive permission to take a U-boat from Spain to Germany so that he could argue his case before the German General Staff. But submarines were getting scarce and were overextended as the war neared its end. Dilger never took the U-boat trip from Spain.

In Dilger's final intercepted message from Madrid, he seemed resigned to the fact that the war was lost. Acknowledging Berlin's cable from late August, he refused to follow the General Staff's suggestion that he return to Mexico and make that nation appear to pose a continual threat to the U.S. border.

"After thoroughly weighing all possibilities I do not think I am able to act in the desired manner. It is also my opinion that my return to Mexico is no longer desirable," Dilger wrote on October 10. "My mission raised hopes of financial and military assistance on Germany's part in the mind of the [Mexican] President, but these have not been fulfilled. I can therefore no longer count on [the backing] of his adherents."

Dilger's last message also denounced Jahnke, whom he accused of "intriguing against myself and Captain Hinsch to such a degree that he will also probably make the activities of the latter impossible, which is deeply to be regretted in the interest of our cause." He suggested that the General Staff again try to blunt Jahnke's influence by interceding with Jahnke's employer, the Admiralty. But that appeal came too late. Jahnke had the trust of the embassy and by then the government.

In the end, Dilger's refusal to return to Mexico in October 1918 sealed his final isolation. A traitor in the United States and a renegade in Germany, Dilger had trapped himself in a room with no exits.

THE "SPANISH LADY" had arrived in Madrid too late for the carnival.

In the festive season, everyone slept late. Masked balls began in the late afternoon and lasted all night. The rich, exhausted from long nights of dancing, struggled to wake at noon. Until the hour before dawn, the city's loud streets remained crowded with vendors, tired partygoers, and criminals who preyed on the revelers who passed out on the sidewalks.

In February 1918, however, the carnival represented the calm before the storm. In spite of the Great War and the pressures placed on Spain from all sides, the king tried to maintain the festive atmosphere during the holidays. But there was one disaster that King Alfonso XIII could not keep his people from. A feared and uninvited guest, the Spanish Lady—one of the many names for the Spanish Flu—showed up in Madrid four months after the carnival's end. The king, having done all he could to protect his kingdom from war, found he was powerless against the worst pandemic since the Black Death.

The influenza virus struck Europe hard in the summer of 1918. At the Western Front, feverish soldiers with hacking coughs suffered in the trenches. In cities around the world, streetcars shut down because so many workers were sick. Kings and queens fell ill, as did paupers. Hospitals and clinics were filled with the dying.

No one knows exactly how that virus originated, evolved, and spread across the globe. It may well have started at a crowded army base in America's Great Plains where soldiers were in contact with an animal reservoir for the flu virus, such as pigs, chickens, or horses. On March 11, 1918, more than one hundred soldiers at Fort Riley in Kansas complained of sore throats, fevers, and headaches at the base hospital. Before the week's end, there were five hundred cases of the flulike illness. The first reports of the severe influenza in Europe came in early April 1918, shortly after a transport full of American troops disembarked at the port of Brest, France. The flu struck Paris that same month and spread rapidly among exhausted British, French, and German soldiers at the Western Front.

By the end of May, the Spanish Flu "appeared with great violence," infecting tens of thousands of soldiers, including more than 36,000 British First Army troops who were hospitalized that month. Most of the British Grand Fleet remained in port for twelve days because more than 10,000 sailors were sick. At British General Headquarters, 700 officers fell ill; in London, King George V himself was among the sick.

During the same months, flu had broken out among warhorses near the Front. Equine influenza was common but had become more prevalent because of the transportation across the Atlantic of hundreds of thousands of horses in crowded ships. Some scientists now believe that horses might have carried the 1918–19 flu virus, much like chickens and wild birds are reservoirs for today's avian flu viruses. If so, the unprecedented horse transport between the Americas and Europe may have helped spread the pandemic.

The flu struck harshly in the United States as well. On September 7, one soldier at an army training camp near Boston complained of a high fever. The next day a dozen more became sick, and within two weeks, more than 12,000 cases of the flu had been reported in a camp of 45,000 soldiers. Nearly 800 of those Boston soldiers died from the outbreak.

By late September, the flu had spread elsewhere on the East Coast. Doctors in Philadelphia ordered churches, schools, and theaters closed after 635 flu cases were reported in a single day. In the end, more U.S. troops died of the flu (about 57,000 soldiers and sailors) than in combat with the Germans.

The flu struck soldiers and civilians on both sides of the Western Front with no respect to the colors of their flags. It caused havoc in the German trenches, reducing the number of healthy soldiers in some divisions to a few dozen. General Ludendorff complained: "It was a grievous business, having to listen every morning to the Chiefs of Staff's recital of the number of influenza cases, and their complaints about the weakness of their troops." He later blamed the failure of Germany's July offensive partly on the low morale of the influenza-weakened troops. Kaiser Wilhelm came down with the disease, as did 160,000 Berliners and probably a million other German soldiers and civilians.

It was dubbed the Spanish Flu, or Spanish Lady, not because the pandemic struck hardest in Spain, but because it was fully reported in the Spanish press. Wartime censorship had suppressed news about the pandemic in France, Germany, and Britain. In the late spring of 1918, the Spanish wire service *Agencia Fabra* reported to the Reuters agency in London that "an unusual form of disease of epidemic character has appeared in Madrid." But the Spanish report added quickly that "the epidemic is of a mild nature, no deaths having been reported." By late summer, several million Spaniards suffered from the disease, which grew more virulent as the weather became colder. When King Alfonso XIII himself came down with a serious case, the Spanish press ran banner headlines, and foreign news agencies spread the reports around the globe, giving the false impression that the pandemic had started or was most virulent in Spain. By the time the pandemic ended in 1919, an estimated 8 million Spaniards had been affected.

As the flu spread across the globe, many public gatherings were prohibited. In New York City, people were threatened with $500 fines for spitting, coughing, or sneezing in public. Some people wore gauze masks, often soaked in camphor, whenever they ventured outdoors. In Philadelphia's shipyards, so many men were sick that work came to a virtual standstill. From August 1918 until the following July, 20 million Americans became sick and more than 500,000 died as a result of the pandemic. In October 1918, the flu reached its peak, killing about 195,000 Americans. Ernest Hemingway, an ambulance driver in the Great War, described death from influenza: "in this you drown in mucus, choking, and how you know the patient's dead is: at the end he turns to be a little child again." Influenza cases were reported on nearly every continent during the summer of 1918, from China to Costa Rica.

In Spain itself, the flu's nickname was the "Naples Soldier." Americans called it the "three-day fever." The French came down with "*la grippe*." The Germans called it "*Blitzkatarrh*" or "Flanders Fever." The Italians dubbed it "sand fly fever." In Britain, the flu was at first called "P.U.O." (Pyrexia of Unknown Origin) and later the "Spanish Lady." Doctors were powerless to stop the pandemic. Remedies included quinine tablets, castor oil, digitalis, morphine, enemas, and aspirin. Some flu victims tried hot baths, others cold baths, others swallowed iron tonics or dosed themselves with pine-tar medicines. Some remedies relieved the symptoms, but none stopped the virus.

The Great War killed 9 million soldiers and civilians, but the Spanish Flu of 1918–19 killed as many as 50 million people worldwide, proving that the germ was mightier than the sword. It was the most devastating epidemic since the Black Death of the Middle Ages. Nearly a billion people—half the world's population—were affected in some way by the pandemic. It came at a time when nineteen nations were at war, and the disruption, stress, and privation of war certainly aided the flu's transmission.

As the disease spread uncontrollably, so did the rumors about its origin. Some claimed that the plague was a curse from God. Others suspected that it was generated by the massive war movements of troops and animals. Still others blamed German agents for spreading influenza germs as a desperate effort to win the war.

A Mississippi newspaper, prodded by a local U.S. Public Health Service official, alleged that "the Hun resorts to unwanted murder of innocent noncombatants. ... He has been tempted to spread sickness and death through germs, and has done so in authenticated cases." One Public Health Service laboratory was asked to investigate a German brand of aspirin as a possible agent of germ sabotage. In Alabama, a traveling salesman named H. M. Thomas was arrested in October 1918 on suspicion of being a German agent who intentionally spread flu. The unfortunate salesman was soon released from jail, but his disfigured corpse—its throat cut and wrists slit—was found several days later in a hotel room. Coroners ruled it a suicide.

Some American health officials making the flu allegations against German agents had high enough rank to be taken seriously. "It would be quite easy for one of these German agents to turn loose Spanish influenza germs in a theater or some other place where large numbers of persons are assembled," asserted Lieutenant Colonel Philip Doane, who headed the health section of a U.S. government agency that was building up the nation's Merchant Marine fleet.

Speaking in Washington, D.C., in late September 1918, Doane hinted darkly that Berlin—the home of many of the world's leading microbiologists—had launched a germ-warfare campaign using "agents ... from submarines." Referring to unfounded rumors that the Kaiser's sabotage agents had spread tuberculosis and cholera germs in France, he said: "The Germans have started epidemics in Europe, and there is no reason why they should be particularly gentle with America."

As the Great War neared its end and the Great Flu reached its peak, someone finally expressed what a few had suspected—but no one could prove. The allegation was demonstrably false, for no one then knew what caused the flu. German scientists believed incorrectly it was caused by a bacterium, known as Pfeiffer's bacillus or *Bacillus influenzae*, when in reality the flu was caused by a virus. One of the German biosaboteurs, Fred Herrmann, mentioned a decade later that the germ saboteurs had cultivated "a virus." But Herrmann, unlike Dilger, did not know a virus from a vole, and used the term to refer to bacteria.

If anyone knew the secrets of German germ warfare in America, it was Dr. Anton Dilger. At the time of Doane's incendiary speech, the germ-warfare pioneer was in Madrid, possibly himself suffering from the flu that the American colonel had blamed on Berlin.

The sick man's face, once darkly handsome, was now wan and wasted. He saw its reflection in the taxi window as it sped him through disease-ravaged Madrid, passing houses draped with funeral black, and Red Cross ambulances laden with the dying. When the cab arrived at the crowded German Hospital, the man paid his fare, climbed the stairs, and limped down a hallway lined with cots for flu victims. Laboring for every breath, he called weakly for a doctor.

It was the young century's darkest month. October 1918, at a time when the Great War was shuddering toward its bloody end and the Great Pandemic was killing millions. Eight million Spaniards, including the King, had been stricken. So many people in Madrid had the flu that most public events were called off and the city's trams had stopped running.

In the hospital, exhausted nurses mopped their new patient's brow and tried to calm him. Delirious with fever, his expression marred by a nervous tic, he spoke a mixture of German, English, and Spanish. Memories seemed to mingle with nightmares. On October 17, the man who called himself Alberto Donde was pronounced dead, at age thirty-four, from pneumonia, a complication of influenza.

The official scenario is that the man who had signed the hospital register as "Donde" was Anton Dilger, who died from complications of the Spanish Flu at 10:30 a.m. at the German Sanatorium on Francisco Silvela Street in Madrid's fashionable Salamanca district. There was no funeral service; he was buried in a local civil cemetery. His German relatives were notified of his death; the American siblings found out later.

Aside from being ironic—a germ saboteur felled by an infectious disease—the official story sounds plausible on the surface. The Spanish Lady had infected a third of Madrid's population that fall, and it became deadlier as the months progressed. Dilger had been reported sick in the same hospital earlier that year, suffering from a lung problem. He had been under great stress and probably was susceptible to the flu.

But the official story has inconsistencies that Dilger's fellow saboteurs and some members of his family could never quite reconcile. For one, Dilger was a physician who would have recognized the flu's initial symptoms and known exactly where to go for the best treatment. The sudden death also seemed odd because a family friend had visited Dilger in Madrid shortly before his death and found the young doctor to be in good health. Some family members wondered why a bloodied shirt was pointedly included in Dilger's personal effects rather than being discarded. Further, it appeared to be more that just a coincidence that Dilger's former subordinate Gehrmann was reported to have died from the same cause—the Spanish Flu—shortly after his cover was blown: the Allies had discovered Gehrmann's identity just as they later exposed Dilger's—making them useless as German agents, and possibly dangerous if disaffected.

"Once Donde was identified as Delmar, his usefulness to *Sektion Politik* ... diminished greatly and he became fair game for assassination by Allied agents," wrote one of Dilger's nephews later. "Delmar's risk of catching the Spanish flu (which had killed Dr. Gehrmann after he was compromised) increased."

Aside from the fact that Dilger's cover was blown and he was about to be indicted in America for treason, there were at least three other motives for German agents to want him to disappear. First, he knew all the details of the German biosabotage campaign, which the General Staff feared might be exposed after the war's end. Second, a week before his death he rejected a demand by the General Staff that he return to Mexico. And third, his bitter rival, Kurt Jahnke, had made "actually criminal" allegations against Dilger—most likely involving the abuse of official funds—and said he wanted to "eliminate" him "with the support of the German central authorities."

Two of Dilger's closest confidants in sabotage, his brother Carl and fellow agent Fred Herrmann, both testified under oath years later that he had been murdered in Madrid, possibly by German operatives. Citing the "rather mysterious disappearance of Anton Dilger," Herrmann said that he believed Dilger had been killed by German agents, who "poisoned him in Madrid because he knew too much." Years later, Louis Dilger's son Fred referred in a letter to Anton Dilger's "murder in Spain."

Certainly, the handling of Dilger's reported death and the disposal of his remains were both highly suspicious—the rushed arrangements supervised in secret by German representatives. In Madrid, the patient went to a German hospital, treated by German doctors and nurses, and falsely identified as German-born in documents from the German Embassy that were used to obtain his death certificate.

The German military attaché, Kalle, seemed to be under pressure to handle the matter quickly—as if there were reasons to dispose of the body before Spanish or American authorities could investigate thoroughly. Major Kalle, who had been involved the previous year in sending the cable that may have led to Mata Hari's arrest in Paris, took charge of Donde's affairs as soon as he got to the German hospital.

When Donde was pronounced dead, doctors first notified the German Embassy rather than relatives or friends of the deceased. Almost immediately after his death, the corpse was sent to a local funeral home, which dispatched "a day laborer" who had never met Donde to obtain the death certificate from a municipal court. A mere five hours after his death, the deputy municipal judge issued death certificate 1141. Informed that the deceased had filed no will, the judge ordered the body buried without ceremony at the Civil Cemetery, where thousands of flu victims had been interred.

There were numerous discrepancies in the judge's order and in the burial itself. Most notably, no listing for Alberto Donde could be found on the cemetery's registry subsequent to this alleged burial. On the death certificate, the victim's name, age, birthplace, and occupation were all incorrect:

In the city of Madrid at 15 o'clock on the 17th day of October, 1918, before [the Deputy Municipal Judge] appeared Don Gabriel Zamora y Lopez ... with a statement that Don Alberto Donde, born in Berlin, Germany, 35 years of age, single and a physician by occupation, died at the sanatorium, Francisco Silvela St., No. 5, at 10:30 of this day, from pneumonia, of which he gave notice under due authority.

In view of that declaration and of the medical certificates presented, the Judge ordered the entry be made with the following particulars: The names and other conditions of the deceased parents are not known; he left no Will; and that the body is to be buried in the Civil Cemetery of this city.

When he cabled the news to Berlin, Kalle made it clear that German military intelligence had expedited matters by paying for the medical treatment, arranging for the death certificate, and covering burial costs. His message to the General Staff, labeled "most secret" and sent after the body had already been disposed of, was brief and direct: "Delmar died yesterday. The expenses for his hospital treatment and burial are being borne by the Political Section."

Within hours, Delmar's apartment had been searched, sanitized of any secret documents, and emptied. While Germans were claiming the belongings, reports of the man's death were reaching Washington, London, Paris, and Mexico City. Once the British code-breakers in Room 40 had deciphered the cable reporting Delmar's death, Allied intelligence agencies wanted to confirm the death to make sure it was not a ruse to divert them from Dilger's real trail.

IN LONDON, Bell had just started gathering the information requested by the State Department about Delmar when Hall's Room 40 told him about the freshly intercepted German cable stating that Delmar had died in Madrid. Bell immediately sent a secret cable to Harrison, his State Department contact, who had said he was searching for "evidence to indict [Dilger] for treason."

If Donde was, indeed, Anton Dilger, it was too late to indict him for anything. "Delmar has just died so you will not be able to hang [him]." Bell wrote. He added in his telegram: "Who do you think he was?"

In Washington, Harrison was extremely disappointed. "Very sorry to hear that he is lost to us," he cabled to Bell. "Would there be any possibility of examining or obtaining possession of his effects? Presume there is no question as to the fact of his death."

But there was a question, one that has never been resolved, even after months of investigation by the American military attaché. Clearly, someone of interest to German military intelligence had died at the hospital in Madrid. But exactly who died, and of what cause, remained in question. Was the victim Dr. Delmar or perhaps someone else who was given his false papers, thus allowing Dilger himself to evade again the Allied agents who were tailing him?

As soon as they learned of the death in Madrid, American officials sought to claim jurisdiction over the man they were convinced was a U.S. citizen. The State Department pressed its diplomats in Madrid to verify the dead man's identity and to demand that Spain's Foreign Ministry give Americans control of the body and personal effects: Washington asserted that the death certificate information had been intentionally falsified—identifying the victim as a German-born doctor—"with express purpose in view of allowing German Consul to assume control over belongings of Donde."

The U.S. Embassy argued that it was entitled "to assume charge of [Dilger's] personal effects," but the German consulate refused to cooperate, sticking to the story that the dead man had been a German citizen. The Americans would have to prove that Donde was Dilger, giving German operatives time to sanitize the dead man's papers. Even so, the Secretary of State ordered his Madrid ambassador "to make every endeavor to locate some person in Spain" who could confirm Dilger's identity.

Later, historian Friedrich Katz—the most prominent expert on German machinations in Mexico during World War I—would question the Americans' motive in trying to claim Dilger's possessions. Was Washington trying to make his death a propaganda coup? Or were federal investigators still skeptical that Dilger had indeed died in Madrid? "It was hardly a question of Dilger's belongings. If there were any secret or compromising documents to be found, the German authorities had every occasion to remove them. The Americans were probably interested in an unequivocal, official identification of Delmar, which could have been exploited for propaganda purposes."

The Americans never got that confirmation of Dilger's death before they gave up in December 1919, more than a year afterward. Two months after his reported death, in December 1918, a memo from the U.S. War Department's chief of staff still listed Dr. Delmar as "apparently traveling abroad." A month later, in January 1919, a memo from the same office warned that Delmar "expects to go to Mexico from Spain shortly." The same document describes Delmar as a former surgeon "with rank of Colonel, German Army," who was "employed by [the] German General Staff as a secret agent for political work, principally in North America."

The hunt for firm proof of Dilger's death continued until the end of that year. As late as September 1919, the U.S. ambassador in Spain said that "substantiation" of the Dilger death was "improbable" and an undersecretary of state responded: "I have my doubts about obtaining the desired objective but I think it is worth taking a chance" and allocating more money to allow the U.S. military attaché to complete his investigation. His goal was to obtain an affidavit from someone who knew Anton Dilger that he was, indeed, the same man as Donde. The attaché showed an old passport photo of Anton Dilger to dozens of people at the hospital and elsewhere—nurses, doctors, cooks, and friends of Dilger in Madrid—and yet could not prove that the man Donde was in reality Dilger.

The final cable from Lieutenant Colonel Thomas F. Van Hatta Jr.—a cavalryman with the military attaché's office—reads like a private detective's report to a wealthy client:

> This office has located Gabriel Samora y Lopez who signed the death certificate of Alberto Donde. This man is an employee of a funeral company in Madrid. He has never seen Donde and was merely furnished with the fact of Donde's death by the German hospital in Madrid and swore to the certificate to supply the forms required by law.
>
> The cook at the hospital, a German, had been shown the photograph of Anton Dilger, from which the name had been removed, by an agent, stated that it resembled Donde but that he

could not state it was the same man. The concierge of the hospital stated that the photograph strongly resembled Donde, but
that Donde had a small moustache.

The American cavalryman then visited with "an intimate friend of
Donde"—von Drygalski, who directed the local branch of the Norddeutsche Lloyd shipping company. "According to von Drygalski, very
few people knew Donde, whose papers were turned over to the Consul
of Germany." He said Dilger's photo "was very like Donde" but declined
to make a positive identification. Another friend of Donde's, Dr. Stech-
lin of the German hospital, "returned to Germany about a month ago,"
as did "a nurse named Frieda who took care of Donde."

In mid-December 1919, Van Hatta concluded that "it is not believed
possible to obtain the affidavit desired," one linking Donde to Dilger. "As
far as can be ascertained, these are the only people acquainted with Donde
and [they] know him as a German and under the name of Donde." He
concluded that "this office has gone as far as it can in the case."

In Washington, the War Department did not want to give up on the
case of a Virginian who had sought to spark a Mexican invasion of his
native country. The military intelligence chief asked the Justice Department to track down Dilger's relatives and friends to determine "whether
the identity of Dr. Delmar and Anton Dilger can be established." Two
years after the Justice Department sent an agent who let Anton Dilger
get away, the federal investigators dispatched another one.

This federal agent, F. C. Baggarly, drove from Washington to Front
Royal and talked with townsfolk and the sheriff who knew the Dilger
family. A family friend talked with Dilger's brother Butz at Greenfield
Farm and later reported that Butz was convinced of his younger
brother's death. The family friend "explained that he always regarded all
the Dilgers as high toned and honorable gentlemen and he believed that
they were in every respect loyal to this country; that they had resided in
that community for a long number of years and were highly regarded by
everyone who knew them," the report said.

Agent Baggarly also interviewed the Warren County Sheriff, who
had heard "from a reliable source that Dr. Anton Dilger was now dead;
that he had died in Spain ... In accordance with the facts as disclosed by

the files, it seems quite evident that Dr. Antone [*sic*] C. Dilger, Dr. Albert Delmar alias Dr. Dilger or Dilga are one in the same person and that this man departed this life in Madrid on about October 17, 1918."

But the Bureau of Investigation agents were getting further and further from the direct evidence. The hearsay of folks in Virginia was all the new information they could find, and all it really told them was that no one knew for certain the fate of Dr. Anton Dilger.

While German relatives seemed to be convinced that Anton had perished from the Spanish Flu, some American family members were not fully convinced. "I guess we can never be sure of what happened to Uncle Anton," suggested his nephew Carl Keyser. "The best we can do is to consider all the possibilities and then place your bets." Louis Dilger's daughter wrote in May 1987: "I don't know why, but I can't feel wholly convinced about Uncle A's death. I mean the circumstances thereof...." Carl Dilger's daughter said that her father had always believed that his brother Anton was killed by the Germans in Madrid to silence him. "Nobody really knew what became of Uncle Anton," she said. "The feeling was that he was killed. He didn't really die of the flu." Two other authors—Michael Sayers and Albert E. Kahn—made a similar suggestion in their 1942 book *Sabotage! The Secret War Against America.*

The first writer to speculate on Dilger's fate, Henry Landau, wrote in his 1937 book *The Enemy Within* that: "It was whispered that [Dilger] knew too much. It was a deadly poison that removed him—at least so it was later intimated by a former German agent."

A half century later, Keyser—who had known Em Dilger well in his childhood—wrote that Landau's suggestion "jibes with the story Aunt Em [Dilger] told me, namely that [Anton] realized that he had betrayed his country and was planning to return home and was killed by German agents because he knew too much." Em Dilger had been as close to Anton as anyone, but she professed to be as much in the dark as every other family member.

A month after Donde's reported death, the French ambassador in Washington sent a curious letter to the secretary of state about the demise of "the German spy," who had been under close French surveillance. Suspected of preparing to travel to Mexico in a last-ditch effort to incite an invasion of America, Dilger "seems to have started for a different journey, the one from which no one returns," according to the Frenchman, who concluded that "Spanish influenza did not, on that occasion, observe neutrality."

If the French ambassador was implying that the Spanish Flu had been used as a ruse to disguise an assassination, Anton's brother Carl Dilger had the opposite theory: that the flu had been used as a weapon rather than a ruse. In 1930, he alleged that German agents had somehow deployed the influenza microbe to kill his brother, the germ saboteur.

Carl Dilger "told me ... that he was certain his brother Anton died as the result of being inoculated with influenza germs by some of his German associates because of the disputes he had gotten into with German officials in Mexico," wrote H. H. Martin. The American investigator added: "If this is so, it would, of course, be a rather just retribution. The incident would furnish a very good basis for a Greek tragedy."

Chapter 14

THE FOURTH HORSEMAN

[We] thought it was a dirty trick, working with germs. We never knew it would be allowed in any sort of open or closed warfare.
—FRED HERRMANN, saboteur with Anton Dilger, 1933

HUBERT DILGER'S MEDAL OF HONOR was lost in America, melted in the fire that destroyed Greenfield mansion. But his son's Iron Cross survived for many years in Germany. Anton Dilger had sacrificed his medical career, his loyalty to his native country, and apparently his life for the black cross of iron that his sister Eda Koehler kept in her dresser drawer.

At the end of 1918, the Great War had left swaths of Europe in desolate ruins. Eda among them, the defeated and exhausted Germans faced the reality of what had been an almost inconceivable loss. Nearly two million of their soldiers had perished in the Great War. The Spanish Flu had struck with biblical force. His empire disintegrating, the Kaiser had abdicated in November and, briefly, the possibility of a socialist revolution was in the air.

"Eda never overcame [Anton's] loss," her daughter-in-law recalled, "nor did [his nephew] Carl-Erik," who later named his son after Anton. Eda's sister Elizabeth Lamey, whose son Peter had been among the first German soldiers to die in the war, was "devastated" when she learned of Anton's death in Madrid. "One cannot believe that Anton is no longer among us—he so often had supported me in bitter times with advice and deeds, he helped calm me down when he talked about my Peter, and I have so many other proofs of his love for us," she wrote to her sister. "He was the best friend of my girls, not only an uncle but also a friend in the true sense of the word."

Among his relatives in Germany, Anton Dilger was regarded as a hero. Some had known that he was involved in secret missions, if not exactly what those were. His brother-in-law Hubert Lamey, a colonel in the German Army, described Dilger as being "as precious as if he had been a dearly beloved son," a hero who had "gone to his eternal reward" for his service to the fatherland.

"I certainly hope that his associates and the special mission of which he was part did not fail to look after him," Lamey wrote to the Koehlers in late October 1918. "I knew about Anton's business in a foreign country and the goal of his commission and endeavors. The many dangers associated with it led me to fear that fate might catch up with him. . . . His sacrifices for his newly adopted German Fatherland caused his death. He died as so many died on the field of honor, as a hero and a son of Germany."

A patriot to his German relatives, Anton Dilger had proved to be a manipulative traitor in America. In the Kaiser's service, he had ruined one brother's diplomatic career, dragged another brother into the germ plot, exposed a sister to possible recrimination, and tarnished the family's reputation. He had become the antithesis of the father he had idolized, the dark side of the once-bright German legacy in America.

"I have a feeling Uncle A[nton] will be haunting me to the end of my days," wrote Louis Dilger's daughter in the 1980s, recounting Anton's shameless manipulation of her father's goodwill and the family's subsequent harassment by federal agents. "Whatever [his] motives were, he certainly messed up his and our life thoroughly." She described Anton's actions as "irresponsible" and said her family "suffered so much from the results. My parents' life was ruined."

An American nephew, Carl Keyser, complained that spies like Anton Dilger become so wrapped up in their missions and false identities that they sometimes abused those closest to them. Noting that Anton had signed documents swearing to uphold the U.S. Constitution, Keyser wrote:

It is something that to anyone excepting a secret agent would seem both incomprehensible and reprehensible. However, it is to be expected in the spy business, which is a dirty one where anything goes in pursuit of the goal.... They end up suspicious of everyone and trust no one excepting themselves, take advantage of friends, and even of relatives, all for the sake of the goal, whatever that may be.

He was convinced that Louis and Em "were innocents taken advantage of and used by their brother." Carl had "barely escaped getting into serious trouble" when the existence of the germ factory was finally publicly revealed in 1929. Carl Dilger was never prosecuted for his connection to the sabotage, but he was subpoenaed to testify to a commission investigating sabotage claims. Also, he became the subject of harassment and suspicion when his role in the Chevy Chase operation was revealed and, later, rehashed in the popular press.

After Anton Dilger's death, the gap between the family's German and American sides would widen gradually into a chasm over the next two decades, as Germany descended into economic chaos and then embraced a Nazi regime. In the late 1930s, Anton's German nephew Carl-Erik Koehler, a cavalryman who had served with distinction in the Great War and risen steadily in the postwar ranks, was rejected when he applied for the position of German military attaché in Washington. He was told that the Americans would "not accept a nephew of Dr. Anton Dilger." The proceedings of the Mixed Claims Commission related to World War I German sabotage in America were still ongoing at the time, and it seemed out of the question that a saboteur's nephew would become one of Germany's official representatives in Washington. His wife recalled later that Koehler "was furious and sad" about the rejection.

In World War II, several grandsons of the old soldier Hubert Dilger served on opposite sides, in the American and German military. Koehler and another of the American war hero's German grandsons became generals in the German Army. Another German grandson lost an arm during the siege of Stalingrad. Yet another was imprisoned by the Russians until the 1950s. Meanwhile, one of the American grandsons served as an officer in the U.S. Navy and another, Louis Dilger's son Fred, in the intelligence branch of a U.S. Army airborne division. When the war ended, he was transferred to a mobile intelligence and interrogation team in Berlin, where he lived in the seized private home of the former Gestapo (secret police) director, Heinrich Himmler. Later, he became a civilian consultant to the Allies in postwar Berlin.

Carl-Erik Koehler, the blue-eyed boy who had once posed for photos while sitting on Anton's lap, eventually became a key officer of the General Staff, the commander of a division in the Soviet Union, and one of the highest-ranking cavalry officers in the German Army. For a time, he was the military commander of German-occupied northern Norway; and later he led one of the last German armored units to defend Berlin from the surging Red Army. When the war ended, General Koehler was captured, then interned and interrogated for months at a prisoner of war camp for high-ranking German officers in Belgium.

Only after the devastation of World War II did the relations between the family's American and German sides begin to thaw. Months after the war's end, Fred Dilger intervened to get General Koehler transferred to a more comfortable camp and to send food and other supplies to his family. When he was finally released in 1948, Koehler had dropped to a skeletal 103 pounds. His family's house in Mannheim—the home where he and Anton Dilger had spent their boyhoods together—had been bombed to rubble in 1943 by an Allied air attack, one of the many bombings that destroyed vast tracts of Germany's cities. By then, the former Nazi General was receiving care packages from his American relatives as his destitute family struggled in postwar Germany.

Koehler was bitter about the American, British, French, and Russian occupiers of Germany. But even after two world wars, after witnessing battlefield slaughter and the fiery Götterdämmerung of postwar Germany, he still recalled with incredible fondness his only visit to Greenfield Farm in Virginia.

"Do you remember the wonderful times that we had with Grandfather [Dilger] in Greenfield just 43 years ago?" Koehler wrote to his uncle Louis Dilger in 1948. "At the urging of Grandpa Dilger, I filled my belly with grapes and water so that I was about to explode.... Then I shocked the entire family when I cut off the tail and mane of good old

Uncle Edward's favorite horse," the general reminisced. "Ah, those were the days when we didn't have a care in the world."

THE SAME WEEK THAT, delirious with fever, Anton Dilger reportedly lay in a hospital in Madrid, a young soldier—like Dilger, a German-speaking foreigner who had volunteered to serve the Kaiser's regime— was caught in a stinging British gas attack in Belgium.

After enduring several hours in a poisonous cloud of gas that wafted invisibly across the night battlefield, the soldier's eyes were seized with pain and he stumbled back toward the German medics. "A few hours later, my eyes had turned into glowing coals," he recalled later. "It had grown dark around me." For that soldier, the war had ended.

The man's eyes were bandaged and he was sent home to Germany for treatment. On the day before the patient called Alberto Donde was reported dead in Madrid, the injured soldier arrived by train at a nerve-disease hospital in Pasewalk for treatment of what one neuropsychiatrist termed "hysterical blindness" initiated by the gas attack. After a month of intensive treatments, the patient was released with his vision intact.

The soldier's name was Adolf Hitler, an Austrian who had become a German patriot. The last he saw of the Great War was a cloud of poison gas, and the trauma of that experience stayed with him into the next war, for which he, more than anyone else, would bear responsibility. Hitler, the twentieth-century figure who in retrospect would seem to have been the most likely to deploy chemical and biological weapons—a man whose death camps had killed millions of Jews, Gypsies, and political dissidents—always opposed the use of both types of warfare on the battlefields of World War II.

Less than a year after the First World War ended, the German chemist Fritz Haber—the leading figure in the development of Germany's poison gas weapons—was awarded the Nobel Prize for an earlier achievement in chemistry. In accepting the prize, Haber famously and falsely warned: "In no future war will the military be able to ignore poison gas. It is a higher form of killing." And yet poison gas, except in isolated instances—such as Italy's deployment during its war against Ethiopia in 1935–36 and Japan's use of gas against Chinese guerillas in

1937–42—has not been used again in a major war, mainly because one side feared the other would respond in kind or an accidental blowback might devastate the forces that deployed first.

In the case of biological warfare, similar fears limited future use of germ weapons, with the major exception being the Japanese military's deployments against Chinese soldiers and civilians during the 1930s and early '40s. The first germ-weapon arms race, primitive but prescient, began toward the end of the Great War, in the wake of the biological sabotage carried out by Anton Dilger and others. The French, who were aware of aspects of the German biosabotage, also deployed the glanders germ as a weapon against German horses during World War I, although the campaign was limited in its scope and results.

In mid-1917—possibly while Anton Dilger was in Switzerland on his way back to America—French agents operating out of Bern dropped tablets of glanders germs in the water and feed bins of horses being sent through neutral Switzerland on their way to the German Army lines. Archives also tell the story of a French prisoner of war—most likely a military intelligence agent—who was found carrying twenty-four cigarettes that contained small glass tubes filled with bacteria cultures, presumably for use against warhorses and perhaps other livestock. Those details were sent to the General Staff's Political Section, which directed Dilger's work and used the French evidence as an excuse to justify Germany's own biosabotage campaign.

The pattern was followed through much of the century: unverified reports spurred clandestine arms races in which one side developed offensive germ warfare because it wrongly thought the enemy was doing the same or because it vastly exaggerated the enemy's research program.

Shortly after the Great War's end, the French were dismayed by secret, and apparently false, accounts in 1919 that German scientists were continuing surreptitious research on more advanced biological weapons. In response, the French military asked the director of France's Naval Chemical Research Laboratory to study how deadly bacteria can be transmitted by air in a "microbial cloud," a pathogenic aerosol that would prove important to the later weaponization of anthrax.

During the 1920s, while its diplomats in Geneva were helping to negotiate the disarmament treaty that would ban chemical and biological weapons, the French were secretly developing biological weapons. At the opposite pole, the Germans had sent as a Geneva negotiator the diplomat who had overseen the early stages of the germ-sabotage program while on loan to the General Staff: Rudolf Nadolny. Although he later denied his role in supervising germ sabotage, Nadolny was implicated by witnesses—and in several secret cables sent out under his name—as directing germ sabotage in 1915 and much of 1916. He was also present at the meeting in Berlin with Dilger, Herrmann, and Hilken in February 1916 at which North American sabotage was discussed.

Nadolny, who had left the General Staff to return to the Foreign Office late in 1916, had held several key diplomatic posts before becoming head of Germany's delegation at the Geneva disarmament conference. The Weimar Republic in Berlin, handcuffed by severe restrictions placed on the German military machine after the war's end, argued strongly, if somewhat hypocritically, in favor of banning poison gas and germ weapons in warfare. "Germany is already disarmed," Nadolny told the Geneva conference in February 1932, a year before Hitler's rise to power. "And German disarmament must be considered indicative of the direction the disarmament of all other members of the League [of Nations] must follow." He backed a ban on germ warfare as well as a prohibition on preparing such biological weapons.

The previous year, Nadolny had given an affidavit to Mixed Claims Commission investigators, denying any knowledge of a germ sabotage campaign during World War I, and denying—despite the sworn testimony of three other witnesses who had attended—that he had ever met in Berlin with Dilger. Even so, U.S. news coverage of the commission's hearings had spread the news of Nadolny's role in the sabotage, and an outraged letter writer to the *New York Herald Tribune* pointed out the irony of the count's position in Geneva: "I was astonished—to put it mildly—to discover that the spokesman was no other than Count Nadolny, Germany's war-time director of sabotage ... [who was] responsible for the dissemination of disease germs in the United States."

Rather than facing punishment for his role in supervising germ sabotage, Nadolny's diplomatic career seemed to be enhanced as a result of his wartime assignment to the General Staff. In the mid-1930s, he became the German ambassador to the Soviet Union. After World War II ended, the former germ-warfare strategist was named to head the German Red Cross, which had become a nationalistic tool of Hitler's SS during the war. In his memoirs, published in 1953, he did not mention his role in Great War sabotage.

Nadolny's chief assistant in the General Staff's Political Section, Hans Marguerre, was more forthcoming in his testimony on German sabotage, conceding that he had met with Anton Dilger, Fred Herrmann, and Paul Hilken. He also admitted destroying many of the Political Section's secret documents when the war ended, which is why so little evidence remains about the germ sabotage in military records.

Little more was heard of Marguerre during the 1930s. But then, suddenly, his name appeared during World War II as attending a meeting of the secret German committee set up to discuss the threats and prospects of biological warfare.

SHORTLY AFTER THE END of World War II, at a time when General Carl-Erik Koehler was imprisoned in a prisoner-of-war camp and Fred Dilger was in Berlin, an Allied investigative team showed up at a temporary hospital in the small Bavarian town of Tutzing to detain for questioning a professor of bacteriology, Heinrich Kliewe.

After interrogating Kliewe in Munich, the team traveled to a monastery in the village of Niederviehbach in southeastern Bavaria, where they uncovered the scientist's secret files in a locked vault. The soldiers took the documents for analysis at the headquarters of the U.S. occupying forces in Heidelberg, the site of Anton Dilger's medical education.

Kliewe had been the German medical corps' chief advisor on bacteriological warfare and perhaps the most important figure in Germany's small program during the Second World War. His files provided a window for the Allied investigators from the top-secret ALSOS Mission—carried out by a team of experts assigned to evaluate Germany's development of weapons of mass destruction during the war—to assess the extent to which Nazi Germany had researched or developed biological warfare agents.

During the early years of World War II, Kliewe had suggested several times that the High Command pursue a biological weapons program in light of the fact that "our enemies Russia, France and England have continued to develop bacteriological weapons in violation of the Geneva Convention..." He claimed that the German sabotage campaign during World War I had been effective enough that an expansion had been planned in that war's final years. But the germ sabotage effort had ended, he wrote, when some of the German agents backed off or were arrested.

"Glanders bacilli were actually used with success in Romania and America by the methods outlined in the literature quoted," Kliewe wrote in 1941, in one of the few official German acknowledgments of Dilger's biosabotage campaign. "For example all horses on one transport from America to England had to be thrown overboard because the animals were diseased with glanders." The bacteriologist reported that the General Staff had planned to step up the germ sabotage against Allied horses at the war's end, but those plans were dashed after the Allies tracked down or drove away the saboteurs.

During the 1920s, Germany—its military research severely restricted by postwar peace agreements—avoided research into bacteriological weapons and argued for a ban. But the Japanese, who had been intrigued by the German biosabotage efforts and faced no such postwar restrictions, decided to aggressively pursue the development of new weapons.

Beginning in the 1880s, there had been numerous connections between German and Japanese bacteriology institutes, with several leading German scientists teaching in Japan and one prominent Japanese scientist working at Robert Koch's laboratory in Berlin. During the 1920s and '30s, Japan's development of bacteriological weapons had benefited from German scientific knowledge that was applied by Japanese medical doctors.

When the Japanese began to deploy biological weapons in China in the 1930s, Hitler ordered a group of medical officers—led by a military toxicologist—to stay in Japan to observe the effect. Both of the pathogens that had been used by Dilger, anthrax and glanders, were also developed as weapons by the Japanese in China—this time to be deployed against humans, not horses. Between 1933 and 1945, as many as a quarter million Chinese soldiers and civilians perished as a result of attacks or experiments using anthrax, glanders, or other biological weapons deployed by the Japanese Army's notorious germ-warfare groups, Unit 731 and Unit 164. Glanders had been wiped out as a horse disease in China by 1906, but new, often fatal, cases of glanders broke out among humans there in the early 1940s, most likely as an indirect result of the Japanese biological warfare program.

The Japanese Army sent a germ-warfare expert—Dr. Hojo Enryo, an assistant to the chief Japanese expert on biological weapons, Dr. Shiro Ishii—to Berlin in 1941 as the embassy's science attaché. Enryo delivered a lecture at the Berlin Military Academy of Medicine with the title "On Bacteriological Warfare" in the fall of 1941. He discussed the results of secret Japanese germ-warfare research in that talk, and he often visited the Koch Institute in Berlin to discuss advances in bacteriology.

When the German Army occupied France, Kliewe had been sent from Poland to inspect four French labs in the town of Bouchet that had been researching possible biological weapons. He wrote: "We learned for the first time how promising the enemy considered this field." Based on those and other arguments, Kliewe also advocated strongly for a German bacteriological warfare development program. Even after Hitler himself issued a directive in May 1942 expressly forbidding any further German research into offensive bacteriological warfare, discussions continued behind the scenes—mainly in response to reports of Allied programs—about the need to continue researching biological agents in case they were deployed by the enemy.

The "Blitzableiter group," which included Kliewe and Marguerre, was set up in 1943 under the Wehrmacht's Ordnance Bureau to discuss biological warfare. And a cancer institute in Posen, Silesia (now Poland), set up a small germ research program. Separately, some of the pseudo-scientific experiments at Nazi death camps—most notoriously, Dr. Josef Mengele's experiments with twins at Auschwitz—involved injections of disease germs.

But, in the end, the German military opted not to pursue an offensive biological warfare program during World War II.

WHEN AMERICAN INVESTIGATORS tracked down Fred Herrmann in Chile in 1929 to question him about German sabotage during the Great War, their focus was almost entirely on Black Tom and other munitions explosions. But other matters were weighing on Herrmann's conscience: he told the Americans that his single greatest concern was whether "anything had come out about the germ work" in Chevy Chase—whether the sabotage had become known and whether its perpetrators would be punished.

The anthrax and glanders sabotage in America had remained a secret for a dozen years while the munitions explosions had received all the attention. Herrmann said he was concerned that the germ sabotage "was of much more importance to Germany and [to] everyone than the sabotage work in reference to the destruction of munitions factories" at Kingsland, Black Tom, and other sites in America.

After the war, Herrmann had fled to Chile, where he found work in a bank. But when he heard about the postwar sabotage proceedings, he approached a diplomat at the German legation in Santiago in 1929 in an effort to negotiate a deal to keep silent about his own role. "I told him everything, told him about the horses, the germ affair...," he recounted later. When Herrmann mentioned his meeting with Nadolny of the General Staff in 1916, the German diplomat said Nadolny had risen to be the German Ambassador to Turkey "and by no means to bring him into this case, not even to mention his name to anyone."

Berlin did not want "the germ work [to be] disclosed," Herrmann said, "because we all knew that it was a much more serious affair than the destruction of the munitions plants. That was the way it appeared to me, to all of us ... [We] thought it was a dirty trick, working with germs. We never knew it would be allowed in any sort of open or closed warfare."

A German diplomat who talked to Herrmann in Chile later accused the American of "extreme braggadocio ... calculated to create a sentiment for his reappointment as [a German] agent." Apparently conflating Herrmann's germ work and the separate munitions sabotage projects, the diplomat recalled that Herrmann had claimed to have "organized the infection of munitions plants and piers with so-called influenza bacterias [sic] imported from Germany in small tubes. That through the infections with these bacterias [*sic*] many hundreds had died. That, in order to cause glandular [*sic*] disease."

Herrmann reported afterward that the Germans had offered him a position—a sinecure that would be understood to be a payoff for keeping quiet—but he declined it because he feared he would suffer the same fate as did Anton Dilger, who Herrmann believed had been assassinated. Worried about "the rather mysterious disappearance of Anton Dilger," Herrmann said, "...I thought that I better stay in Chile."

Instead of keeping quiet for the Germans, Herrmann was convinced—in a meeting brokered by his former paymaster, Hilken—to testify on behalf of the Americans who claimed damages from Germany's World War I sabotage actions. Attorneys for one of the American claimants tracked down Herrmann in Chile and convinced him to testify, offering him immunity from prosecution as well as payments for travel expenses.

The Mixed Claims Commission had been established in August 1922 by an executive agreement between Washington and Berlin to investigate and settle all disputes and determine the amounts to be paid claimants. The largest group, involving 153 claimants seeking $23 million in damages, related to the Black Tom and Kingsland explosions. The task of linking the German government to that sabotage was extremely difficult, especially with German officials initially resisting or stonewalling affidavits and the nation's representative claiming that the Black Tom explosion had been caused by "spontaneous combustion." With millions of dollars at stake, the companies that had lost the most in the Black Tom and Kingsland explosions hired a tenacious and well-connected lawyer, Amos J. Peaslee, to lead its investigation.

To prove their case, U.S. investigators needed clear evidence that saboteurs had worked directly on behalf of the imperial government, in most cases with the Political Section—the same group that had coordinated the germ-sabotage campaign. Herrmann's testimony, along with the coded, lemon-juice message he sent on a copy of *Blue Book* magazine from Mexico City in 1917, became crucial to the American case.

Peaslee's group was able to elicit the key testimony of Hilken and Herrmann—affidavits that, in turn, revealed the details of the germ sabotage based in Chevy Chase. The German side sought to discredit Herr-mann's testimony—especially his *Blue Book* message, which mentioned Black Tom, Kingsland, and Tony's Lab in conjunction with German guidance and support—and won the initial claims decision in 1930. But the persistent investigators, bankrolled by the companies determined to reach cash settlements, discovered enough new witnesses and evidence that the Americans eventually won the final settlement of damages in 1938.

None of the official claims related to the horse and mule sabotage. And in North America, at least, no one connected with the biological sabotage was ever punished. In fact, the details of the germ warfare did not become public until the Mixed Claims investigation—without which the germ sabotage might have remained a secret until this day.

In addition to Herrmann and Hilken, Carl Dilger was also called to testify. In a 1930 affidavit he admitted to playing a role in the germ sabo-tage. Although he was humiliated by the press coverage of his testimony, Carl Dilger was never prosecuted and spent the last years of his life on his cattle ranch in Montana. Later in the 1930s, at a time when U.S. government officials began worrying again about potential German agents, Carl was harassed by federal agents to the extent that his mail was screened and an occasional surveillance aircraft flew over his ranch.

One of the state's ranchers even blamed Carl for an outbreak of anthrax in the 1930s. Carl's daughter said that he "was upset" by such accusations and the published reports of his role in the biological sabo-tage, and that he was sorry his brother had convinced him to take part. "But he never seemed to feel anger towards his brother Anton." Carl Dilger, who had helped cultivate germs for use against horses, never lost his affection for the animals. A granddaughter commented that "Carl always loved horses. He rode them as a boy at Greenfield in the begin-ning and he rode them on his ranch in Montana in the end."

Carl Dilger's former Chevy Chase housemate Herrmann moved back to the United States after his Mixed Claims Commission testimony and lived for another quarter century, first in New Jersey and later in Richmond, Virginia, where he raised a family and died in peaceful obscurity in 1969.

The sabotage paymaster, Paul Hilken, also testified at length and was ostracized from his former social circle in Baltimore. H. L. Mencken, who had "high esteem" for Hilken's father, wrote that the old man even shunned his son after the sabotage revelations: "[Paul Hilken's] father never mentioned him in my presence after the war, and it was understood that he was not to be mentioned by anyone else where the old man could hear."

The other key member of the Baltimore-based germ-sabotage group, Captain Hinsch, returned to Germany after World War I and set up a stevedore company in his home city of Bremen. Some of the American dockhands whom he had paid to inject the horses were called to testify in 1930, but none of them were punished. The statute of limitations had passed, and the nature of any crime was unclear.

The only German spy associated with Anton Dilger who made a career in espionage was his fierce rival, Kurt Jahnke. Two weeks after Dilger's reported death in Madrid, Jahnke was specifically instructed in a "most secret" radio transmission from Germany that "every [sabotage] activity is to be suspended as soon as truce has been conceded." When the armistice was signed the following week, Jahnke accompanied Germany's senior diplomat, Heinrich von Eckhardt, to a farewell appearance at the German Club in Mexico City. The contrast between their responses to the news was stark: while Eckhardt's "emotions overcame him, and [he left] in tears," a witness described Jahnke as "entirely cool and collected." Within a few months, he was back in Germany.

A consummate espionage agent, Jahnke was not one to get emotional. A prominent historian of German intelligence, Reinhard Doerries, listed both Dilger and Jahnke among the "leading group of German agents in the United States" during World War I. In the end, Jahnke gained far more recognition than Dilger did for his sabotage and espionage, in part because he survived the war, gave testimony about his role in sabotage, and continued as an important German intelligence operative during World War II.

Returning to Germany after the Great War, he became an advisor to the military intelligence bureau, directing espionage agents in England and America. In 1923, he helped organize a covert infiltration of the French military occupation of Germany's Ruhr region. His saboteurs disrupted the railroads to prevent the French transport of coal and iron from the Ruhr. After the Nazis rose to power in 1933, Jahnke worked under the deputy chancellor, Rudolf Hess, on intelligence matters. And when World War II began, he was drafted into military intelligence to lead a battalion that penetrated the enemy's front lines to sabotage communications and disrupt operations.

Near the end of World War II, Jahnke was apprehended by the notorious Soviet counterintelligence group SMERSH, an acronym for a phrase that means "Death to Spies." SMERSH arrested "traitors, deserters, spies and criminal elements" as the revengeful Red Army swept into eastern Germany in the spring of 1945. Shortly before the war's end, Jahnke was interrogated and likely tortured in March and April.

As soon as SMERSH had finished with him, Jahnke was probably executed. At least, no one heard from him again. It seems fitting that the spy who had played a key role in Dilger's demise—in terms of his espionage career, if not outright assassination—himself fell victim to spy hunters.

ANTON DILGER WAS the only German agent directly involved in the sabotage campaign who studied medicine and laboratory techniques of microbiology. For that reason, he is regarded as one of the fathers of modern biological warfare—as opposed to other saboteurs, who were mostly clueless about the germs they deployed.

Before Germany's Great-War biosabotage, there had been many crude attempts to deploy germs in wartime. Bur no one involved in those efforts had the advantage of knowing what microbes caused disease, how to isolate those germs, and how to spread them to target victims. Dilger abused his medical knowledge in the service of sabotage, and the pathogens he cultured eventually would become important weapons in the arsenals of germ warfare.

How did Dilger justify the transformation from his pursuit of a medical mission to help humankind, aspiring to what he once called "the greater good" as a surgeon, to the nether world of sabotage and espionage—a mission that led him to cultivate the same germs he had once sought to destroy? Judging from the few surviving letters in which Dilger discussed his decision to work on behalf of imperial Germany, it appears that his motive was a zealous patriotism. He sacrificed everything—his surgical career, his health, his status as a U.S. citizen, his family's reputation in America—to support a Prussian autocracy that eventually abandoned him.

Beneath the surface, however, Dilger's betrayal of his native land and his Virginia family was likely a sign of a far deeper insecurity. He was the proud son of a soldier whose military prowess he could never hope to match and of a mother descended from a renowned German scientist whose achievements he could never rival. He embodied the at times conflicting family traditions of medicine and warfare: in essence, healing and killing.

Like many espionage agents, Dilger was a consummate liar, a man who did not blink at deceiving family members and using his cover as a Red Cross surgeon to open doors to dark sabotage. The espionage novelist John le Carré once described spies as "a squalid procession of vain fools, traitors ... people who play cowboys and Indians to brighten their rotten lives."

Dilger's own role-playing ranged from the wildly comic to the deadly serious. One side of him was charming, brilliant, effervescent—a practical joker who would switch shoes outside of hotel rooms and send humorous post cards. The other side was reckless, devious, and duplicitous—not only to strangers but also to those he loved. The "deep anxiety and seriousness" observed by one of Dilger's German relatives may have been symptomatic of mental turbulence, with the divisions in his national loyalties reflecting subtler divisions within his own personality.

Several members of the Dilger family had suffered from depression—most notably, Anton's brother Edward, who committed suicide so painfully and melodramatically. The patriarch, Hubert, was described as having mercurial mood swings. And some of the siblings, including Carl, had problems with alcohol abuse at one time or another. Judging from the family history and hints in letters, it seems possible that Anton Dilger suffered from bouts of depression. Certainly he had a mercurial personality—periods of ups and downs, likely exacerbated at times by extreme stress, such as the long hours of surgical work following the Karlsruhe bombing.

Two years before Dilger's birth, author Robert Louis Stevenson created a character, Dr. Jekyll, a benevolent physician, who swallows a potion that turns him into a murderous monster, Mr. Hyde. Reflecting on the experience of having been Mr. Hyde, the doctor observes that "all human beings, as we meet them, are commingled out of good and evil." Few who are aware of Anton Dilger's work as a war surgeon would consider him wholly evil. He never aimed to kill *people*; the victims were always horses. And yet the intensity of Dilger's German patriotism, combined with the strain of witnessing battle wounds as well as the massacre of innocents, seemed to warp the character of the physician who had once claimed to be "devoted to the relief of humanity's suffering."

The fact that Dilger targeted horses for destruction was telling, even though the dockhands did the dirty work. The Virginia farm boy who had once loved horses—and whose father had once been rescued in battle by a stallion—became a driven saboteur who devised ways to kill them. The doctor who had devoted himself to saving wounded soldiers ended up working just as diligently to infect helpless animals. He was a man in conflict with his own past, the fourth horseman of a family split irrevocably by the Great War.

In the final analysis, Anton Dilger's motives, targets, and methods are less significant than the precedent he set as the first physician in the modern era who abused his expertise—and, some would argue, sullied his medical oath—to cultivate and spread disease germs. Dilger's Chevy Chase laboratory was the first place in America devoted to propagating disease germs for sabotage or war. Whatever his intentions, his actions helped pry open the Pandora's box of twentieth-century germ warfare and, later, biological terrorism.

Anton Dilger broke the fourth seal, the seal of pestilence, in the name of patriotism. But the doctor who sought to spread disease among horses succumbed, the official story goes, to a far deadlier natural pandemic.

Chapter 15

"THEY HAD NO CHOICE"

Cast a cold eye on life, on death. Horseman, pass by!
—Epitaph, WILLIAM BUTLER YEATS, d. 1939

I N THE FINAL MONTHS OF WORLD WAR II, German prisoners of war helped build a stone wall and a viewing platform on a hilltop at the U.S. Army's horse-breeding depot in Virginia. Looking west from that vantage point, the German POWs admired the misty Blue Ridge Mountains—so much like the Black Forest of their fatherland. To the east, they saw the verdant hills of Greenfield, the farm where Anton Dilger had been born.

On that same hilltop, the German prisoners helped tend a row of simple gravestones, each carved with the name of an army horse. Today those stones remain, at times overgrown with weeds or wildflowers, as one of the few reminders of the millions of warhorses that perished during the twentieth century.

One of those lonely gravestones on the Front Royal hilltop was marked with the name Kidron, the favorite warhorse of General Pershing, who commanded the American troops in Europe. Pershing rode Kidron in the great victory parade that passed under the Arch de Triomphe in Paris to celebrate the Allied victory in the Great War. In those shining moments, Kidron—with the haughty look of an equine conqueror—proudly carried his American hero through the tumult.

When a British Army division first marched over a Rhine River bridge into Cologne in December 1918, its horses and mules joined the parade past a statue of the defeated Kaiser. "The horses were all fit and hard as nails, and the buckles of the harnesses were all burnished like silver," wrote a proud British captain. "The mules were as fit as the horses, and went on wagging their old ears as if they crossed the Rhine every day of the week." A local German said the unit "must have come fresh from England."

In reality, those robust horses were the exception rather than the rule. For Kidron and the Great War's other famous horses were little more than poignant symbols of a bygone era. By then, Pershing only rode Kidron in parades, never on the battlefield. The role of the horse cavalry had taken a fatal blow after cavalrymen and their steeds had ridden into trench-burrowed European battlefields demarcated by barbed wire and bristling with machine guns and rapid-fire cannons that massacred both men and horses.

Millions of horses died as a direct or indirect result of World War I, temporarily devastating the equine populations of large areas of Europe and North America. In the European part of Russia alone, the horse census declined by nearly 9 million between 1913 and 1922; the Germans and the French each lost well over a million horses, although some of that loss is attributable to factors other than the war itself. Before the war began, there were about 4.5 million horses in Germany; that equine population declined to 3.2 million by the war's end, and it took many years before the number of animals would again reach prewar levels.

No one knows exactly how many horses and mules were sickened or killed as a result of the German biosabotage campaign during the Great War. The number was probably in the thousands, if contemporary claims can be believed, but the sabotage campaign in North America clearly did not kill enough horses and mules to be a significant factor in the war. In the case of the American Expeditionary Forces, 2,721—about 1 percent of its horses—were destroyed in Europe after becoming infected with glanders, with most cases probably resulting from natural outbreaks rather than germ sabotage. Despite all the advances made in diagnosing and preventing the spread of the malady, a U.S. military veterinarian still called glanders "the most dreaded disease of animals in the Army."

In 1921, the U.S. Army's former chief of cavalry, General Willard A. Holbrook, dedicated a bronze tablet in Washington that had been donated by Red Star Animal Relief to honor the American horses that had died in the Great War.

Describing those animals as "indispensable to the successful prosecution of the war and to final victory as were shot and shell," Holbrook said the horses that were killed on the European battlefields "passed to the great beyond in silent agony, and while many of them now sleep on the gentle slopes made beautiful by the poppy's bloom, no white crosses, row on row, mark their last resting places."

WITH A FEW HUNDRED EXCEPTIONS, none of the three-quarters of a million North American horses and mules sent to the Great War ever returned home. The fortunate ones found homes on French, British, or Belgian farms, where they were overworked to make up for Europe's postwar shortage of animals. The least fortunate were slaughtered, skinned, and eaten. Their reward for years of military service—for enduring the gunfire, poison gas, and knee-deep mud—was to be served as a main course on French dinner tables or chopped into hash spooned out to German prisoners of war.

"A good market for horse flesh fit for human food was found among the civil inhabitants in the lines of communication area," according to the official British history of the veterinary service during the Great War. "At first, sale was restricted to horse butchers who lived near veterinary hospitals, but when the supply exceeded the local demand, contracts were made with approved firms of butchers in Paris."

The British Veterinary Service, which had made heroic efforts to prevent the spread of disease among horse and mule remounts en route to Europe, also expended great energy toward developing the best ways to dispose of horses that were no longer of any use to the army. Late in 1916, the Army Veterinary Corps issued a temporary commission to an official of one of London's horse-slaughtering firms to help dispose of unwanted animals.

Army Waste Products Ltd., a military trading company appointed by the Army Council, was charged with taking over the disposal of horse carcasses in an efficient manner. And when a meat shortage struck in England, officials set up a system to sell horsemeat in London and Liverpool. "The plan worked well, and it became possible to dispose of large numbers of otherwise worthless animals at prices which varied between 9 Pounds and 12 Pounds," said a postwar report.

Meanwhile, detailed regulations were issued on how best to flay a horse, how to cut up and store its meat, and how to boil its bones and hooves in rendering vessels. The tools recommended for such operations included steel blunt hooks, butchers' knives, axes, mallets, and shears.

Faced with a growing need to dispose of unwanted horses, British military ingenuity eventually developed what were called "horse carcass economizers"—slaughterhouse factories that were built near areas where injured, sick, or just plain old horses were gathered to be destroyed. One such rendering factory was built near Cologne, Germany.

The horse carcass economizer design included a "slaughtering and cutting-up floor," which housed four large vats: the bone tank, the feet tank, the heat tank, and the oil tank. In another area, a portable steam engine turned turbines that operated a "meat-chopping machine," a "centrifugal fat extractor," and a "fat melter and dryer." The adjacent boiler house, for rendering the remains, contained a Rodney portable boiler. The slaughtering floors were surrounded by "hide store" rooms, in which the horse or mule skins were stored for later processing.

No part of the animals was allowed to go to waste. "Each of the horse carcass economizer plants could deal with 30 carcasses a day," the report said. From September 1916 to March 1919, the British Army facilities in France shipped nearly forty thousand horse and mule hides to England. "The supply was an important addition to the resources of the country at a time when there was a great shortage of leather," the report concluded. The by-products from the horse carcass economizer plants—hides, hair, dried meat, grease, bones, and hooves—"were sold to merchants in England, Paris, and elsewhere." The average value of those by-products, per horse, was about £4.00. The once noble creatures had been reduced by industrialized processes to various useful products—nothing more.

The disposal of army animals was a sensitive political issue in Britain, with its active animal welfare movement. People were accustomed to horses dying in battle, but many were appalled by the butchering or destruction of animals that had served their country. More than 100,000 horses were repatriated to Britain and sold at auction.

But even though the War Office in London had promised to stop the practice, retired war horses continued to be sold to the Egyptians for hard labor quarries and local transport. Disgusted by the terrible conditions endured by the horses, the wife of a British officer exposed the scandal in the 1930s and established a charity and a horse hospital to help the beleaguered animals that had been sacrificed by the Army.

The American Expeditionary Force lost 63,369 horses and mules during the war itself, well over a third of the 182,000 animals in the entire force.

Only about two hundred of those horses, mostly the mounts of high-ranking cavalry officers such as General Pershing, made it home to the United States.

THE PUBLIC OUTCRY about the suffering of horses during the Great War spurred a worldwide animal welfare movement that sought to improve their deplorable conditions. That movement to protect helpless animals, building on the shoulders of the early efforts in the nineteenth century, has since grown into an influential and effective international campaign.

After tens of thousands of animals were killed on European battlefields during the war's first months, an international group met in Geneva to expand the Blue Cross animal relief organization, which provided horse ambulances and other assistance to wounded animals on the battlefields. Separately, the Royal Society for the Prevention of Cruelty to Animals (RSPCA) helped the British Army Veterinary Corps by building and equipping horse hospitals with private, voluntary contributions.

Originally founded in Britain under the aegis of Our Dumb Friends' League, the Blue Cross supplied drugs, veterinary requisites, and horse comforts. Animals in more than a thousand British units benefitted from extra supplies of horse rugs, chaff cutters, portable forges, and "humane killer" guns. "The Blue Cross had no regard for the nationality of a horse," wrote one journalist, noting that French, Belgian, and Italian horses were also cared for. In 1916, the American Humane Society, under an agreement with the War Department in Washington, established its Red Star animal relief operation, which sent medical supplies, bandages, and ambulances to the front lines to help vets treat injured horses.

Many of the soldiers who witnessed the slaughter of loyal animals on the battlefields wrote touching memoirs about their horses or mules. When soldiers had no choice other than to destroy a wounded horse in battle, they described such moments as they might recall the death of a fellow soldier, a trusted friend. When British Captain C. H. Trehane was forced to put down his trusted horse, Shaitan, the officer was in emotional turmoil:

> We got his girth undone and pulled the saddle away and slipped the bit out of his mouth. And he lay there on his side, a poor worn shadow of what he used to be. I rubbed the velvet muzzle gently with my knuckles, I pulled an ear that was cold and damp with sweat ... and said goodbye to him. There was nothing else for it. I brushed aside a wisp of forelock and put my revolver to his temple—and shot him.

Not all warhorse stories were brutal; there were also some happy endings. An artillery-gun team of black horses, the "Old Blacks," was returned to England after the war and honored with the task of transporting the coffin of the Unknown Soldier in a caisson to Westminster Abbey for burial. The horse team was retired in 1926, and its members lived the rest of their lives in green pastures. In another heartening story, four British officers pooled their money to buy and peacefully retire a celebrated warhorse named David that had served in the Boer War and, later, on the Western Front throughout the Great War.

In Washington, cavalry General Holbrook said he hoped the bronze tablet that he dedicated near the White House would "bear silent witness of the great debt we owe our equine friend and will inspire in the hearts of the present and future generations a determination to see that they receive the fair treatment and consideration which is their due."

On Armistice Day every year, the sacrifices of the men and women who perished in the Great War are honored throughout the United Kingdom. But the efforts of the hundreds of thousands of horses and mules that went to the Front and never returned were not officially commemorated in a memorial until eighty-five years after the war's end.

In November 2004, Princess Anne dedicated the Animals in War Memorial at the edge of Hyde Park in London. Warhorses and other animals are sculpted in bas-relief along a curved wall, and two life-size bronze mules carrying heavy military packs struggle up the steps toward a gap in the wall. The inscription: "They had no choice."

ONCE THE GREAT WAR had ended and the parades were over, the public forgot about the hundreds of thousands of American warhorses that had been sacrificed on the battlefields and in the slaughterhouses of Europe. They pined for a racehorse hero, not a warhorse hero.

Man o' War—named in honor of the War to End All Wars—gave Americans exactly what they wanted. The chestnut stallion won his first race by six lengths on June 6, 1919. When a spectator asked, "Who's he by?" the Thoroughbred's groom quipped: "He's by hisself, and there ain't nobody gonna get near him."

Only one horse ever got near him at the finish line. Winning twenty of its twenty-one races, Man o' War joined Babe Ruth as the first sports stars of the Roaring Twenties and in the process rejuvenated horse racing in America. Nicknamed "Red," he was so popular that souvenir hunters snatched hairs from his mane and tail.

While Man o' War was winning race after race across the country, Kidron—whose sire had been a French racehorse—was stuck in quarantine aboard a ship appropriately named the *Kentuckian*. A month before Pershing left France, the general had personally bought Kidron from the Army and arranged for the horse to be one of the two hundred—out of the 180,000 horses that served the American Expeditionary Force in Europe—to be sent home.

At a time when nearly every other surviving U.S. warhorse was being sold to French butchers or farmers, Kidron's own transport was handled at the highest levels—arranged by the Army's chief quartermaster and an ambitious colonel, George C. Marshall, who would later become a five-star general, secretary of state, and creator of the Marshall Plan to rebuild war-shattered Europe after World War II. An expert army veterinarian was sent on the *Kentuckian* with "personal charge and supervision over [Kidron]." Also, "special instructions [were] sent to Newport News with respect to General Pershing's horse."

Kidron's travels in the United States seem to shadow some sites of Anton Dilger's life and sabotage career. The horse spent five months in disease quarantine at a stable at Newport News, Virginia, where German-paid dockhands had infected horses and mules with glanders and anthrax in 1915 and 1916. Once that ordeal ended, Pershing stabled the horse in Chevy Chase, not far from Dilger's former germ factory. Later, Kidron was retired to the Front Royal Remount Depot near the Dilger farm.

Kidron and Man o' War had a link other than their prominence in the public eye: the millionaire August Belmont II, who had bred the racehorse in Kentucky and had helped acquire warhorses such as Kidron for the U.S. Army in Europe. Belmont also was a great backer of the Front Royal Remount Depot—Kidron's final home—having donated several of his great Thoroughbreds for warhorse breeding there.

The same year that the remount program was ended, 1947, Man o' War died at age thirty at the Kentucky farm where he had sired War Admiral and other great racehorses. He was embalmed and lay in state in a casket lined with his racing colors. Two thousand persons lined up for a last look at the great racehorse, some reaching into the coffin and patting him. Later, a sculptor created a magnificent bronze statue that stands in front of the Kentucky Horse Park in Lexington, just a few miles from the Belmont farm where the chestnut colt was born in 1917.

Man o' War's owner, Samuel D. Riddle, had once turned down a $1 million offer for the horse. "You go to France," he said, "and bring back the sepulcher of Napoleon from Les Invalides. Then you go to England

and buy the jewels from the crown. Then to India and buy the Taj Mahal. Then I'll put a price on Man o' War."

In contrast, Kidron had died with little fanfare on October 10, 1942, at the remount depot. Whereas Man o' War died naturally of heart failure, Kidron was destroyed before his hide—intended for preservation by the Smithsonian Institution—was ruined by age. But Kidron's carcass decomposed too quickly, and the Smithsonian's taxidermist was unable to display the famous warhorse. Kidron's skull and hide are part of the Museum of Natural History's research collection; the rest of the horse's remains are buried on the Virginia hill near Greenfield.

In southern Virginia, Robert E. Lee's great horse Traveler—who had carried the defeated general to the Confederate surrender at the Appomattox courthouse and later led Lee's funeral cortège—is buried a few yards from the general's crypt.

When Traveler died from lockjaw in 1872, two years after his master's death, his remains were laid to rest near the chapel of Washington and Lee University in Lexington. For decades afterward, mourners left gifts near his headstone, including small Confederate flags, pennies, and peppermints.

Traveler's bones were disinterred in 1907 and its skeleton was mounted and displayed at the university's museum. After more than sixty years on exhibit at the university that bears his master's name, the famous horse was reburied in May 1971 outside Lee Chapel. Even today, people leave gifts at Traveler's landscaped grave.

Less than a mile away, the remains of the warhorse Little Sorrel are interred near Stonewall Jackson's grave. For two decades after the general was mortally wounded while riding him at Chancellorsville, Little Sorrel traveled to county fairs and Confederate reunions throughout the South. Strangers often pulled at his hair for a souvenir, leaving the famous horse skittish. At the Virginia Military Institute (VMI) in Lexington, Little Sorrel was allowed to graze on the parade ground, where he reportedly would run up and down the line of cadets, snorting loudly, whenever they fired rifles or cannons.

At the advanced age of thirty-five, Little Sorrel was retired to the Confederate Soldiers Home in 1885. The following year he died from a broken back when the hoist used to lift him to his feet slipped. The sorrel bay's hide was stretched over a plaster-of-paris base, and his bones were preserved. The stuffed horse was on display in a museum at the soldiers home until 1949, when the remains were returned to VMI.

One hundred thirty-four years after Stonewall Jackson's death, VMI had Little Sorrel's bones cremated. In an elaborate ceremony that featured mounted cavalry, a fife and drum corps, a bagpiper, and ladies in Civil War–era dresses, the steed's remains were buried on the VMI parade ground, at the base of his master's statue, in 1997. The hide is still on display in the school's museum.

Through much of human history, horses shared the sufferings and dangers endured by cavalrymen and common soldiers. Countless battlefields were consecrated with the blood of those animals but precious few of the noble steeds or lowly pack horses are remembered. Except for those of the famous steeds like Traveler, Little Sorrel, and Kidron, there are no gravestones for warhorses.

What remains are the poignant memories, long after poppies have overgrown the battlefields once stained with the blood of men and horses, long after all signs of the "War to End All Wars" have vanished from the landscape, and long after the last echoes from great cavalry charges have thundered into the distant past.

EPILOGUE

The whole is a riddle, an enigma, an inexplicable mystery.
—DAVID HUME, 1775

T HREE MONTHS AFTER THE UNITED STATES declared war on Nazi
   Germany, the unpredictable Fred Herrmann—who had not talked
with Carl Dilger in two dozen years—mailed a book to his fellow germ
saboteur's address in Montana out of the blue.

The book, *Powder River: Let 'er Buck*, was about cowboys and buck-
ing broncos in Montana's Powder River valley. Enclosed in the package,
sent in March 1942 from New Jersey, was a letter from Herrmann, saying that he wanted to get reacquainted with Dilger "for old times sake."
Herrmann didn't know that Carl Dilger had died the year before.

The reason for the mailing was a mystery. Was Herrmann trying to
revive the old German espionage network now that the United States
had again declared war on Germany? Or, perhaps more likely, had Herrmann been asked by federal agents to smoke out Carl Dilger and find
out whether any part of the former sabotage network still existed and
whether his brother Anton had somehow survived the war?

The book package was returned by the local post office in Montana
and ended up at the Washington, D.C., house of Carl's late sister, Jo.
That's where his nephew Carl Keyser found the package. Keyser was an
ensign in the U.S. Navy and was sensitive to any hint of disloyalty in the
family, in part because of the harsh publicity during the 1930s and also
because his mother had named him after Carl and Anton Dilger.

Recalling from press accounts that Herrmann had once used a book
to send a crucial German code from Mexico, the suspicious Keyser took

the book and letter to the FBI, which was then on the alert for possible Nazi sabotage or fifth-column organization in America. Crime lab investigators discovered a pin between pages 224 and 225—reminding them that Herrmann had used pinprick markings in his 1917 code—but found no secret message on the book's pages. At about the time Herrmann mailed the mysterious book, U.S. agents in Switzerland warned Washington that German submarines were planning to transport small units of saboteurs to America with the mission of blowing up aircraft factories, bridges, and railroads. That secret mission, approved by Hitler as "Operation Pastorius," began in earnest when the U-202 submarine clandestinely landed eight German saboteurs on Long Island on June 13, 1942. Another saboteur landed in Florida the same month.

This time around, however, the German saboteurs did not encounter weak law enforcement and the strong ethnic support that had helped their forerunners three decades earlier. This final wave of German sabotage against America ended in failure weeks after it began. In late June 1942, Hoover's strengthened FBI—tipped off serendipitously by the confession of a German agent—tracked down and arrested all eight saboteurs. Within months, six of the Germans had been executed in Washington, D.C., and the others were in jail.

Although that was the last gasp of German sabotage in America, federal agents apparently still suspected as late as 1942 that Anton Dilger himself and some other Great War–era agents were still at large. About a year before Herrmann mailed the book to Carl Dilger, a man who identified himself as an FBI agent had approached yet another Dilger relative to ask about Anton. Federal investigators, it seemed, still had doubts about the story of his demise in Spain.

As she went about her job as a sales clerk at the Garfinkel's department store in Washington, D.C., Louis Dilger's daughter Emmy-Margaret was "tracked down and pestered." The harassment was not a total surprise. When a *Reader's Digest* article was published in 1940 detailing the World War I sabotage and mentioning Anton and Carl Dilger, "it was plain hell at Garfinkel's," she recalled. Her father had been hounded for years by agents who knew he had helped his brother Anton Dilger obtain an emergency U.S. passport in 1917 which allowed him to make his way to America for his clandestine missions.

In a letter written to her cousin Carl Keyser in 1983, Emmy-Margaret described the FBI agent's surprising curiosity about the whereabouts of a German spy reported dead more than two decades earlier in Madrid. "He pulled out a little notebook and said, 'I know all about your uncle.'" At first, she thought the hard-driving G-Man meant another of her Dilger uncles. But he soon made it clear that he meant the long-disappeared Anton: "He got real nasty and said, 'You know exactly what I mean.' He then opened the notebook and stuck it under my nose, saying 'Look at that.'"

"There was Uncle Anton's name with an address in Mexico. There was mention of a hotel, a street, and I believe the town *Juarez*," a Mexican city near the U.S. border—and also the name of the Mexico City hotel where Herrmann and other German agents had once stayed. After Emmy-Margaret had glanced at the Mexico address, the federal agent pressed her: "'What I want to know from *you*,' with that he stuck his finger in my chest, 'is when was your uncle at that address?'"

When she told the agent that she did not know, he answered, "Don't worry, I'll find out."

BUT THE FEDERAL AGENTS never did find out. And neither did anyone else—at least, to the extent that all doubts were dispelled. Had Anton Dilger, whose corpse was reportedly interred in a Madrid graveyard, somehow staged his death and reappeared in Mexico?

The nagging suspicion appears highly improbable. None of his siblings—either in the United States or in Germany—ever reported seeing him after 1918. If Dilger somehow survived the Spanish Flu, he covered his subsequent tracks masterfully.

And yet doubts lingered, for no investigator could ever find the hard evidence to confirm his death conclusively. And descendants of his siblings later reported hearing about another Dilger family in Mexico—including photos of a man who bore a resemblance to the Dilgers of Anton's generation.

In Mexico City's old quarter, a lovely blue-tiled building called *La Casa de los Azulejos* stands at a busy corner of Condesa Street, just off the grand square that surrounds the city's marble Palace of Fine Arts. The three-story *Casa*, once called the Blue Palace, had been built in the 1650s in the Spanish style called churrigueresque, with tiles produced by Dominican friars, brass banisters imported from China, and a grand staircase copied from the palaces of Seville.

In the 1930s, that blue-tiled building housed the Jockey Club, the nation's first soda fountain, and several offices—including the headquarters of a German-speaking businessman who one Mexican suspects may have been Anton Dilger.

There is no real proof, although it is clear that a man of approximately Dilger's age used the office in his position as consultant representing German companies that did business in Mexico. Surviving photos depict a man with a moustache who was stockier in the 1930s than Anton Dilger had been in the last known photos taken of him in 1917.

The businessman was mysterious about his family roots, telling his descendants a flagrantly improbable story about growing up in the remote Chiapas region, riding out of town on a donkey and eventually marrying well and becoming a wealthy consultant in Mexico City. The story explained why he had no relatives in Mexico but not how he came to be fluent in German and to represent large German companies.

For most of the 1930s, the businessman lived the high life in Mexico City's fashionable Los Lomas district, marrying a lovely Mexican woman and buying a Gatsby-like mansion near Chapultepec Palace, where Emperor Maximilian had once reigned. Surrounded by a stone wall, the mansion boasted a garden with palm trees, a pool and a ballroom where the man and his wife threw lavish parties on Friday nights.

Many of his guests spoke German, for his clients included some of the biggest German companies in Mexico. He was fabulously rich until the early years of World War II. Anxious to distance itself from Hitler's regime, Mexico began to choke its trade with Germany and, in doing so, ruined the consultant's business. As his fortunes declined during the war years, he had to sell all the furniture in his ballroom, and guests for the Friday-night dinner dances were asked to bring their own chairs.

Late in 1943, the once-rich businessman, who had lost nearly all of his Mexican fortune, died virtually penniless.

Could the Mexico City businessman have been Anton Dilger? At first glace, it seems possible, but recent family research makes it highly unlikely. The businessman's chronology does not parallel Dilger's travels during the Great War. And an old wedding portrait of the man, found recently, is dated three years before Dilger's first known trip to Mexico.

If the likelihood that Anton Dilger escaped to lead a long life in Mexico is remote, some doubts linger about whether Anton Dilger indeed died in Spain in 1918 from complications of influenza. Two decades after the Great War's end, relatives and fellow saboteurs continued to receive pointed questions from investigators about Anton's whereabouts—especially during the early years of World War II, when fears resurfaced of "the enemy within" and the possibility of a new wave of German sabotage.

At least one of the German agents who had worked with Anton Dilger in Mexico was later harassed when he gave an affidavit to the Mixed Claims Commission giving previously undisclosed details about their espionage work. That former agent, Frederick Hadler, had moved to California after the Great War and applied for American citizenship. In April 1938, investigators asked him to disclose new details of his work with Dilger and others in Mexico City.

It seems as if Hadler's disclosures touched a nerve in Nazi-era Berlin. About the time he submitted that affidavit, Hadler reported being followed and harassed in California by "Nazi detectives." He then took refuge with his children in Louisville, Kentucky, but the German investigators tracked him down there, too. Hadler's daughter then sent a frantic letter to U.S. investigators, expressing her fear that "our lives are in danger.... We are afraid to leave the house for fear of having it ransacked."

In September 1938, Hadler received a mysterious postcard from Berlin, signed "P. Neumann"—presumably a Spanish-speaking German who had known Hadler and Dilger in Mexico. Written in Spanish, the note said:

> Friend Hadler. I am here [in Berlin], called by the government to testify about the triangle, Delmar, Hinsch, Herrmann. I read about your declaration and answered only what I was asked; but

know more and would like you to write me.... There are still several dark points not cleared up.

On the front of the postcard, in the white margins around a photo of a Berlin neighborhood, was written in Spanish: "I shall be in Mexico at the beginning of November. I would like to see if we can do something!"

While there is no hard evidence to disprove that Anton Dilger died in Madrid in 1918, the possibility that he had faked his death in Spain has never been completely eliminated. Dilger had polished his spycraft by then, and—in the confusion of Madrid at the height of the influenza pandemic and the final month of the Great War—he might have been capable of hiding his escape trail by transferring his false name and identity papers to a pauper who died at that hospital. No one who knew Dilger ever identified his body in Spain, and such identification would have been complicated by steps he had taken, such as growing a moustache, to disguise his appearance.

Decades afterward, some in the family still expressed doubts about the circumstances of Anton Dilger's mysterious death. American officials never conclusively confirmed it. No one in Spain could be found to positively identify Donde as Dilger after the reported death despite more than a year of efforts by the U.S. military attaché's office in Madrid. The State Department, the War Department, and the Bureau of Investigation in Washington all wanted proof positive of Dilger's death and never received it. No gravestone bearing his name has ever been found.

Nine decades after Anton Casimir Dilger's reported demise, pressing questions linger about aspects of his life and his death. As the mysterious Berlin postcard noted: "There are still several dark points not cleared up."

NOTE ON SOURCES

Piecing together the elusive story of Anton Casimir Dilger was like reassembling shards of a mosaic that had been smashed and scattered for the better part of a century. Some pieces were in family letters and post cards; others were deep inside archival vaults or hidden in obscure medical journals and personal reminiscences. No one source reflected a complete image of Dilger; pieced together, they offer an intriguing portrait.

In the wake of the anthrax bioterrorism attacks in Washington, D.C., New York, and Florida in the fall of 2001, I began researching the history of the use of the anthrax bacterium as a weapon of war and sabotage. I ran across references to Dilger and the modern era's first germ-sabotage campaign, which had been based in a rented house in the Chevy Chase area of Washington, D.C., in 1915–16.

The primary reason why Dilger's story has remained obscure is that there are so many gaps in the records and precious little of his personal writings survive. Espionage, by its very nature, tends to be poorly documented. Complicating matters, many documents of the German Army General Staff's Political Section—which coordinated the germ-sabotage campaign—were intentionally destroyed when the Great War ended. Many of Dilger's own letters and documents also were lost or destroyed during World War II. Even so, enough evidence remained to tell his story.

The search for details about Dilger's life and the germ factory in Chevy Chase first led me to the extensive files of the Mixed Claims Commission at the National Archives. Discovering the address on an obscure document, I approached the home's present owners, who graciously gave me a tour. I also unearthed a number of previously undisclosed documents, including a lengthy article that Dilger wrote about war surgery; an eyewitness account of a bombing in Karlsruhe, where Dilger had claimed to be present; and a U.S. medical officer's account of Dilger's work during the Balkan Wars.

Some of the most valuable information came from surviving family members, including Dilger's closest surviving American relatives, especially a niece, a grandniece, a possible grandson, and a grandnephew who allowed me access to the family archives. I continued my research at the family's former home,

Greenfield Farm in Virginia, and then—drawn deeper into the story of espionage and biological sabotage—I pursued historical research at the Library of Congress, the National Library of Medicine, the U.S. Army veterinary archives at the Walter Reed Medical Center, the National Library of Agriculture, and the Smithsonian Institution. Probing the mystery of Dilger's reported death, I also explored the possibility that he might have been assassinated by German agents rather than dying from complications of the Spanish Flu in Madrid.

The Fourth Horseman was conceived and written as a biographical narrative, based as much as possible on primary or secondary sources and interviews; on occasion, when there were significant gaps in documentation, I extrapolated from documents, testimony, or recollections to add details that help achieve a narrative.

My main sources and references for each chapter are listed below. The best published sources for personal details about Anton Dilger and his family are *Leatherbreeches* and *Leatherbreeches' Legacy*, researched and written by the late Carl Anton Keyser. His archives are kept by the family. For the details of the World War I–era germ sabotage campaign in North America, the most comprehensive files are those of the Mixed Claims Commission, Record Group 76, at the National Archives and Records Administration in College Park, Maryland. (Many documents related to Dilger are found in Boxes 2, 3, 5, 8, 10.) Details of the germ sabotage are mentioned in various affidavits and testimonies of Fred Herrmann, Paul Hilken, and Carl Dilger along with affidavits from several stevedores who were involved in jabbing horses and mules. Several publications provided extensive coverage of the Mixed Claims Commission testimonies and revelations during the late 1920s and early 1930s, including the Baltimore and Washington newspapers.

For a wider look at the World War I–era German biological sabotage campaign, the most comprehensive source in English is Wheelis's chapter, "Biological Sabotage in World War I," in *Biological and Toxin Weapons: Research, Development, and Use from the Middle Ages to 1945*, edited by Erhard Geissler and John Ellis van Courtland Moon. From a German perspective, the most comprehensive treatment is in Geissler's book *Biologische Waffen—Nicht in Hitler's Arsenalen: Biologische und Toxin-Kampfmittel in Deutschland von 1915 bis 1945* and in his article "Anwendung von Seuchenmitteln gegen Menschen nicht erwünscht: Dokumente zum Einsatz biologischer Kampfmittel im Ersten Weltkrieg," which was published in the German military history journal *Militaergeschichtliche Mitteilungen* in 1997. Geissler presents the results of his exhaustive search through German archives, some of which are incomplete because of intentional or accidental destruction of documents in the wake of the two world wars.

For an overview of German sabotage in America during the Great War, with an emphasis on Black Tom and other munitions-related explosions, Witcover's *Sabotage at Black Tom* presents a more accurate treatment than Captain

Landau's earlier *The Enemy Within: The Inside Story of German Sabotage in America*, which was the first book to mention Anton Dilger and the germ sabotage campaign. From a German perspective, I would recommend articles and books by intelligence historian Reinhard Doerries, including his chapter "Deutsche Sabotage in den Vereinigten Staaten von Amerika im Ersten Weltkrieg." Doerries has conducted extensive archival studies on Dilger's nemesis and fellow German agent, Kurt Jahnke.

For an analysis of how Germany and other nations sought to influence Mexico during World War I, the best source is Katz's *The Secret War in Mexico*. For more on Admiral Hall's code-breaking coups, read Beesly's *Room 40*. Sources on horses in warfare and horse disease outbreaks include Singleton's "Britain's Military Use of Horses 1914–1918." An important primary source is the U.S. Army Veterinary Corps Archive, OHA 344, Box 1 ("Veterinary Corps History, 1916–1940). For a contemporary account of horses in the Great War, see Clarke, "The Story of the British War-Horse from Prairie to Battlefield."

Abbreviations

AD	Anton Dilger
L	*Leatherbreeches: Hero of Chancellorsville*
LL	*Leatherbreeches' Legacy*
CKA	Carl Keyser Archives
MCC	Mixed Claims Commission documents

Prologue

Eda Koehler's receipt of Anton Dilger's bloody shirt and other belongings is recounted in a letter written by her daughter-in-law in the CKA and is also mentioned in *LL*. A copy of the letter from AD's sister Elizabeth is also in the CKA. The biblical quotation preceeding the prologue is from the New Jerusalem Bible.

Chapter One: War Horses

Numerous books and articles describe Hubert Dilger's exploits at Chancellorsville and Gettysburg, including Catton's *Glory Road*, Schurz's *Reminiscences*, Commager's *The Blue and the Gray*, Keyser's *L*, and Lloyd Lewis's *Sherman: Fighting Prophet*. The story of the local boy bringing a horse to Dilger was first published in 1896 in Hamlin's *The Battle of Chancellorsville*. Dilger did not receive his Medal of Honor until 1893, the year before ten-year-old Anton moved to Germany with his sister. It was a memory that the young AD would have preserved.

Civil War literature includes many references to Robert E. Lee's horse Traveler and Stonewall Jackson's horse Little Sorrel. Most of the Dilger and Tiedemann family history and reminiscences are derived from *L*, *LL*, and the CKA. There are varying accounts of Stonewall Jackson's fatal wounding at Chancellorsville, but all agree that he was riding Little Sorrel at the time. Sources for the description of the role of horses and cavalry in the Civil War include Urwin's *The United States Cavalry*, Black's *Cavalry Raids of the Civil War*, Ellis' *Cavalry: The History of Mounted Warfare*, and Fordney's *Stoneman at Chancellorsville*. General Grant's "headquarters in the saddle" instruction to General Philip H. Sheridan during the Shenandoah Valley campaign is quoted in an article by John Wukovits in the March 2001 issue of *America's Civil War*.

A thorough description and analysis of the glanders outbreak among war horses can be found in Sharrer's "The Great Glanders Epizootic, 1861–1866." The glanders editorial, quoted by Sharrer, is from the September 1865 issue of *American Agriculturalist*. The description of Elise Dilger's family séances is derived from her essay on spiritualism, *LL*, and Schurz's autobiography. A good source of information on Schurz's career is *Carl Schurz: A Biography* by Hans L. Trefousse. Sources on Germans in America between the Civil War and World War I include Trommler and McVeigh's *America and the Germans*.

Chapter Two: Greenfield Farm

AD's poem about Greenfield (translation by the author) was written on the back of a photograph in the CKA. Details of AD's boyhood are based on *L*, *LL*, and various letters, postcards, and other documents in the CKA. Elise Dilger's séances with her aging father are described in her essay "Man Has a Spiritual and Terrestrial Body" in the CKA. More information about AD's famous ancestor Friedrich Tiedemann can be found in Stephen Jay Gould's 1999 article "The Great Physiologist of Heidelberg." AD's post cards are from the CKA, which also includes a letter to AD from a Tiedemann relative in Germany, answering some of AD's questions in 1911 about the famous professor.

Chapter Three: Tissues and Cyanide

Huxley's "The Tissue Culture King: A Parable of Modern Science" was published in the *Yale Review* in April 1926. AD's *Lebenslauf*, translated by the author, is part of his medical thesis, *Über Gewebskulturen in Vitro: Unter besonderer berücksichtigung der Gewebe Erwachsener Tiere* (Concerning Tissue Cultures in Vitro: With Special Consideration of the Tissues of Adult Animals), which is available at the National Library of Medicine. Hubert Dilger never attained the rank of general in the U.S. Army, but served as Adjutant General of Illinois from March 1869 to January 1873, and was at times called "general."

According to archivists at the Alan Mason Chesney Medical Archives of the Johns Hopkins Medical Institutions, AD was among the "physicians attending graduating courses during 1908–09." AD is listed in the university's records as an M.D. from the University of Heidelberg then residing in Front Royal, Virginia. He enrolled in the summer "Medicine" course rather than the other summer offerings: Anatomy, Surgery, Genito-Urinary Diseases, and Surgical Pathology. The AD post cards cited are from the CKA. Among the professors that AD met was Johns Hopkins's first professor of pharmacology, John Jacob Abel, according to a letter in the CKA. In Boston, the Harvard Medical School and Massachusetts General Hospital archivists say there is no record of AD studying or visiting there. However, the CKA includes a letter, dated October 24, 1909, addressed to "Dr. Anton Dilger" at Massachusetts General Hospital; he may have visited medical researchers there. On the early history of tissue culture research, the biography of Alexis Carrel on the Nobel Prize website provides useful background: http://nobelprize.org.

The postcard AD sent to his brother Edward is from the CKA. The description of Edward's suicide and of Hubert Dilger's will are derived from *L* and from a copy of the will in the CKA. "Dilger Field" is marked on a plat map of the old Front Royal Army Remount Depot provided to the author by the Nebraska State Historical Society, which had obtained the map when the Remount Depot closed. Sources for description of remount depots and the Army's war horse program include *War Horse* by Livingston and Roberts. Louis Dilger's letters and the local newspaper clippings from 1912 that mention the remount depot are in the CKA.

Sources for descriptions of the problems with horse disease and casualties during the Anglo-Boer War include Pakenham's *The Boer War*. Descriptions of changes in British remount and veterinary services in the wake of Boer War mistakes include Singleton's "Britain's Military Use of Horses 1914–1918." Sources of biographical information about General Pershing include the *Papers of John J. Pershing, 1860–1948* at the Library of Congress, Smith's *Until the Last Trumpet Sounds*, and Pershing's *My Experiences in the World War*.

Chapter Four: Disquiet on the Western Front

Sources for background on the role of Bulgaria's Queen Eleonore in medical care include Morgenthau's *Ambassador Morgenthau's Story* and in the text of Zwerdling's *Postcards of Nursing*. The queen's recruitment of AD is mentioned in Ford's "Some Medicomilitary Observations in the Late Balkan Wars." The most comprehensive description of AD and Arthur W. Meyer's work and movements in Bulgaria appear in their paper, "Kriegschirurgische Erfahrungen aus den beiden Balkankriegen" ("Battlefield Surgical Experiences from the Two Balkan Wars"), which appeared in the *Deutsche Zeitschrift für Chirurgie* (*German Journal of Surgery*) in 1914. While AD's letter to Count Ferdinand von Zeppelin has

been lost, the dirigible designer's response, dated January 28, 1914, is in the
CKA. The description of Peter Lamey's death is derived from *LL* and from family letters. Hugh Gibson's description of the aftermath of the Battle of Haelen is
from his memoir, *A Journal from Our Legation in Belgium*. For a summary of that
battle, see http://www.firstworldwar.com/battles/haelen.htm. Other sources on
the German cavalry at the beginning of the war include Herbert Wilson's *The
Great War*, vol. 1, *Opening Moves* and the essay "German Cavalry Units
1914–1918" by Gavin Hughes.

A good analysis of Fritz Haber's role in the development and deployment of
German chemical weapons is Charles's biography of the German chemist, *Master Mind*. I am indebted to Mario Marchisio of the Italian Army's veterinary
corps for sharing the results of his historical research into the effects of poison
gases on horses during the Great War; the statistics used are from one of his
presentations.

The discussion of how AD became a saboteur for Germany is mainly
derived from family letters and other documents in the CKA, as well as a Karlsruhe register that lists AD's various assignments. Otherwise, no official German
documents that survived the Great War refer to him until the British began
intercepting coded messages mentioning his pseudonym, Delmar, in 1917.

For H. L. Mencken's exchange of letters with Theodore Dreiser, see Riggio's *Dreiser-Mencken Letters*. The important record showing that AD was
ordered to America "in the service of the Imperial Prussian War Ministry" is
from the Generallandesarchiv Karlsruhe, in a Great War–era duty list of the
reserve hospital where AD once worked. The original German says that AD was
sent "im dienstlichen Auftrag der Abteilung A.Z. des königlich preussischen
Kriegsministeriums in Amerika."

Chapter Five: Deadly Cultures

The Edith Cavell quotation—inscribed on the pedestal of her statue in St.
Martin's Place in London—is from her statement to a chaplain the night before
her execution. The timing of AD's return to the United States has been vari-
ously reported as the spring, summer, or fall of 1915; the author found his
name listed as a passenger on the *Noordam*, arriving in New York on October 7,
1915. Unless AD had been to the United States earlier that year, that voyage
represented the beginning of his role in the germ sabotage campaign in North
America. The section on AD's return to the United States and his visits with
relatives in Washington, D.C., and Front Royal, Virginia, is extrapolated from
LL and family documents in the CKA. The "B" (*bos*) and "E" (*equus*) markings
indicating germ cultures are described in Herrmann's MCC testimony and
from the detailed description of seized vials at the German Legation in Romania that also appears in the MCC files. See Geissler for more details on the B
and E markings.

Chapter Six: "Absolute Security" in Chevy Chase

The author found the address of the Chevy Chase house in the MCC files and verified it by consulting the 1916 city directory of Washington, D.C. The description of the house is based on a tour given by its current owners in the summer of 2005. Parts of the house have been renovated, but the original design was consulted. Sources for Chevy Chase history include several unpublished documents in the local history file at the Chevy Chase branch of the Washington, D.C., Public Library, including "A Backward Glance, 1898–1933" by a local schoolteacher and an unsigned document titled, "Chevy Chase, part one." AD's listing as a physician was found by the author in the Washington, D.C., city directory from 1916. The description of the lab is derived mainly from Herrmann's MCC testimony.

The account of Walter Scheele's meeting with Captain Erich von Steinmetz is based on Scheele's March 1918 statement to the Bureau of Investigation and a lengthy memorandum from the bureau's chief, Bruce Bielaski, who traveled to Cuba to interview Scheele. (The memo, marked as "File #925," is in the MCC files, RG 76, Box 5, Exhibit 464). Other sources on German sabotage activities in the United States include numerous MCC files, *Sabotage at Black Tom* (Witcover), and *The Enemy Within* (Landau). The former Scotland Yard Special Branch informant who was sent to Chicago was Casimir Pilenas-Palmer, who submitted an MCC affidavit in September 1928 and is mentioned as an informant by Spence in "Englishmen in New York." The description of the hiring of dockhands to infect horses and mules at East Coast seaports is based mainly on the affidavits of three stevedores, Edward Felton, George Turner, and John Grant, in the MCC files (Exhibits 761, 772, and 773), along with testimony by Herrmann. Sources for description of the British horse depot at Newport News, Virginia, include Davis's chapter "Newport News in War Time." Sources consulted for the description of the mule and horse trade at the Guyton & Harrington firm include documents from the Missouri Mule History Project Records of the Western Historical Manuscript Collection in Columbia, Missouri, and mule history files at the Missouri Historical Society in St. Louis.

The medical description of a man who contracted glanders while working on horse-transport ships is from an article published in October 1916 (Potter, "Human Glanders"). AD's movements in late fall of 1915 and early 1916 are from MCC documents, *LL*, and letters in the CKA. Robert Patterson's letter of endorsement for AD, dated December 31, 1915, is in the MCC files. Patterson was U.S. Surgeon General from June 1931 until May 1935. Sources for the description of British horse-transport ships include the work of Singleton and Clarke. Details of a German U-boat sinking a horse-transport ship are from *U-Boat 202*. The figure of 6,600 horse deaths on Atlantic transports is from a British veterinary statistical summary.

Chapter Seven: Crossings

The main source on AD's meeting with Herrmann aboard the *Kristianafjord* and their subsequent movements in Denmark and Germany is Herrmann's MCC testimony. A letter from the Norwegian-American Line confirms that the two men were both on that voyage. Clarke's description of a British horse-transport vessel is from "The Story of the British War-Horse." The description of the stallion with glanders is presented not as a historical fact but rather as an example of how an infected horse would be dealt with aboard a British animal-transport ship during the war. Sources for the February 1916 meeting in Berlin involving Rudolph Nadolny include MCC testimony by Herrmann, Hilken, and Hans Marguerre. Details of AD's and Hilken's life in Berlin are extrapolated from Hilken's 1916 diary and Herrmann testimony, both in the MCC files. Ambassador Gerard's descriptions of Germany and Berlin are from his memoirs. Evidence of AD's relationship with Frieda Hempel is described in *LL* and in family letters in the CKA; the Hempel quotation is from her memoir, *My Golden Age of Singing*.

Chapter Eight: Bacilli in Berlin

H. G. Wells, who studied biology in London under T. H. Huxley, wrote *The Stolen Bacillus and Other Incidents* in 1895 and *The War of the Worlds* three years later. The reference to the German army manual is from Wheelis; an English translation of the manual is Morgan's *The War Book of the German General Staff*. The Nadolny quotation (translated by the author) is from his memoirs, *Mein Beitrag*, which do not mention sabotage. The destruction of Political Section and other sabotage-related German documents after World War I was described by Marguerre and is mentioned in Geissler as well as in a letter, dated November 9, 1935 (MCC files), from H. H. Martin to John J. McCloy, then one of the main attorneys for U.S. claimants. Summaries of the Nobel Prize–winning research of Emil von Behring, Robert Koch, and Paul Ehrlich can be found on the Nobel Prize website, www.nobelprize.org. The most recent biography of Koch in English is by Brock, *Robert Koch: A Life in Medicine and Bacteriology*. Koch's "dream about horses" remark is described at http://www.whonamedit.com/doctor.cfm/ 2987.html. A short biography of Fredrich Loeffler and a description of his scientific achievements can be found in "Pioneers in Medical Laboratory Science," at http://www.hoslink.com/pioneers.htm.

    Geissler conducted an exhaustive study of the possible sources of the *B. anthracis* and *B. mallei* bacterial cultures used in the German sabotage campaign and presented his findings in his book *Biologische Waffen—Nicht in Hitler's Arsenalen* as well as in his 1997 article "Anwendung von Seuchenmitteln gegen Menschen nicht erwünscht." He concluded that it is likely that the source of the glanders and anthrax germ cultures was the Military Veterinary Academy in

Berlin. Wheelis, in an email exchange with the author, did not challenge that conclusion.

Most of the documents that tell the story of the German biological sabotage effort in Romania are in the MCC files and State Department archives; see also discussions by Wheelis and Geissler. For the campaign in Norway, see Wheelis, Geissler, and "During World War I, Terrorists Schemed to Use Anthrax in the Cause of Finnish Independence" (Bisher). The front-page story about germ sabotage in Romania appeared in the September 22, 1916, issue of the *New York Times*.

On the question of whether AD was involved in preparing germ cultures or devising new techniques for deploying them while he was in Germany from late January 1916 until May 1917, see Wheelis' article. He confirmed in an email to the author in July 2006 that he still believes AD was involved in the biological program in Germany itself, but he has found no German documents that offer clear proof. Details of that period of AD's life are not well documented, other than the breakup with his fiancée, his service as a surgeon in Karlsruhe, the visit of his brother Carl, and AD's apparent assignment to the sanitation department in Berlin early in 1917. The story of Carl Dilger's trip to Germany is derived from the MCC testimony of Herrmann, Hilken, and Carl Dilger. Marguerre said later that he did not recall meeting Carl but confirmed that he had met with AD several times. AD's Karlsruhe service record is in the CKA; it was sent in October 1987 with an accompanying letter by Herr Raab of the Generallandesarchiv Karlsruhe.

Chapter Nine: "A Difficult Inner Struggle"

Karlsruhe municipal archivists confirm that the city was bombed on June 22, 1916, the day of the Corpus Christi feast, and that bombs struck the Hagenbeck Circus. Details of the bombing and aftermath are based on a June 23, 1916, article in a local newspaper, the *Badischen Presse*, and on the recollection of an eyewitness, Dr. Ludwig Arnsperger, who helped care for some of the wounded and said he believed that Anton Dilger was assisting a Dr. Roth as a surgeon at the military reserve hospital, Reservelazarett V. AD told friends (see Hilken's MCC testimony) and family (*LL*) that he had suffered a nervous breakdown after a Corpus Christi bombing, but some investigators later suspected that he used that story as a cover to mask his true reasons for leaving surgical practice and becoming a full-time espionage agent.

Details of AD's response to Herr Katz's angry letter are in the CKA. Some family members believed that AD became a German citizen before departing Berlin in 1917; it is clear from one document that he applied for citizenship (*LL*), but no record could be found that proves he received it. AD's threat to initiate a Court of Honor to settle the dispute with Katz is puzzling unless AD had military status, and there were rumors (as well as mentions in at least two U.S. Military

Intelligence documents) that he held the rank of colonel. But no German documents could be found that substantiate that rumor. AD was awarded the Iron Cross, second class, in 1918, but civilians occasionally received that award.

Sources for the account of Pancho Villa's raid include Katz's *The Life and Times of Pancho Villa*. Numerous books and articles detail Sir Roger Casement's relationship with German intelligence, including Dorries, *Prelude to the Easter Rising: Sir Roger Casement in Imperial Germany*. Arthur Zimmerman's comment about German Americans and Ambassador Gerard's "lamp-post" retort are reported in Tuchman's *The Zimmerman Telegram*. Katz and others have provided reports that Villa's forces had accepted support from the Germans and perhaps from other foreign powers.

The story of the *Deutschland* and its arrival in Baltimore is told in Captain König's book, *Voyage of the Deutschland*, which includes the German poem by the U-boat's chief stoker, Hans Dowidat (verse translated by the author.). The disputed report that the *Deutschland* carried germ cultures is from Herrmann's MCC testimony; not surprisingly, bacteria cultures do not show up on the cargo list. The Austrian medals to Captain Hinsch and Paul Hilken are mentioned in MCC testimony. The American Deutschland Committee's propaganda campaign, including brochures for the proposed "greatest book," is documented in the MCC files.

Mencken describes the *Deutschland* offer by Hilken in his memoir, *Thirty-five Years of Newspaper Work*. Evidence in the MCC files indicates that the U-boat collided with the tugboat. Sources for the chapter's section on Black Tom include numerous MCC files, Witcover, and Landau. Hilken's recollections about Hinsch's actions after the Black Tom blasts are from the former's MCC testimony. (Note: The author is unrelated to the two Germans with the same surname who had roles in the story: Captain Paul König of the *Deutschland* and Paul Koenig, a detective for the Hamburg-Amerika Line.)

Chapter Ten: Gateway to the West

Details related to the closing of Tony's Lab derive from Herrmann's and Carl Dilger's MCC testimony as well as *LL*. The description of the germ cultures in Herrmann's grandparents' house in New Jersey are from Gerdts's MCC testimony. Clarke's observations are from "The Story of the British War-Horse." Information about the National City Stockyards comes from the Missouri Historical Society and local newspaper clippings. The story of the failed germ-laboratory project in St. Louis is derived mainly from Herrmann's MCC testimony. The article by Captain F. L. Case about horse infections in the Southwest appeared in the October 1916 issue of *The Journal of the U.S. Cavalry Association*, which can be found in the MCC files. The list of stockyards and horse/mule companies is from Herrmann's notebook, also found in the MCC files. Sources on the Kingsland sabotage include Herrmann's testimony, other MCC files, and Witcover. Hilken's remark about Herrmann is from the MCC testimony of Martha Held.

Sources on the Zimmerman Telegram include Tuchman (*The Zimmerman Telegram*) and Witcover. See Zieger's *America's Great War* for a detailed account of Wilson's war declaration speech. AD's farewell letter in Berlin, dated May 12, 1917, is in the CKA. The plot summaries of anti-German Hollywood films are available online by title at the Internet Movie Database (IMDb), http://www.imdb.com. The anecdote about AD surprising his brother Louis in Switzerland is from *LL*, as is the background information on Louis's wife, Fanny Sauerbeck. A copy of the emergency passport application, signed by Louis and Anton, is in the MCC files. Carl Dilger's quotations are from his MCC affidavit. His post card to his sister is in the CKA.

Chapter Eleven: Spy Hunting

For descriptions of the initial American Expeditionary Force deployment in Europe, see Pershing's *My Experiences in the Great War* and Ziegler's *America's Great War*. Hilken's MCC testimony describes AD's return to the United States carrying coded messages and a new type of secret ink. Mencken's "spy hunt" quotation is from his memoir, *Thirty-five Years of Newspaper Work*. AD's document listing assets and an ink formula is from the MCC files. AD and Hilken's movements are from Hilken's 1917 diary (MCC files). Sources on the wave of anti-German hysteria following the U.S. declaration of war in 1917 include Kirschbaum's *The Eradication of German Culture in the United States: 1917–1918*. The popular song "Don't Bite the Hand That's Feeding You" was composed by Jimmie Morgan, with lyrics by Thomas Hoier, in 1915. Ambassador Gerard's claims about a German conspiracy in the Americas are mentioned in his two memoirs. A copy of J. Edgar Hoover's letter forwarding the FBI's Dilger/Delmar/Donde reports is in the MCC files, as is George Lillard's entire report on his interview with AD in Washington, The fact that Lillard knew the Dilger family in Front Royal is reported in *LL*.

The account of AD's last visit to Greenfield and his driving trip westward is derived from Hilken's 1917 notebook (MCC files), the Winton car-loan receipt (MCC files), *LL*, and family photos showing AD at Greenfield. The description of AD's meeting with Leslie Combs in Lexington is from a Bureau of Investigation memo by agent L. O. Thompson dated September 21, 1918, with the title, "In Re: Dr. Albert C. Dilger—under investigation, New York City."

The letter by General Combs accusing Schurz's troops of cowardice during the Civil War was published on November 3, 1863 in *The Louisville Journal*. An account of the Covington horse deaths can be found in the U.S. Army Veterinary Corps Archive ("Veterinary Corps History, 1916–1940"). The *New York Times* article about Judge Webb's comments is dated April 5, 1918. The "enemy outrages" list is in the MCC files. Information about Theodore Wozniak is in

MCC documents, as are H. H. Martin's speculative conclusions about AD's travel in July 1917. Information about the Kansas City stockyards fire is from news articles in the *Kansas City Star*, October 16–18, 1918.

Chapter Twelve: South of the Border

Sources for this chapter include MCC testimony and affidavits by Herrmann, Jahnke, Hilken, and Hadler. Dilger's activities in Mexico and Spain are known primarily from German cables intercepted and decoded by Room 40 of British Admiral Sir Reginald Hall. These are found in the MCC files as well as in Beesly's *Room 40* and Peaslee and Hall's *Three Wars with Germany*. The text of Herrmann's *"Blue Book"* message is the decoded version; the original consisted of coded four-digit numbers. Katz's *The Secret War in Mexico* describes Delmar/Dilger's negotiations with the Mexican government, which are also mentioned in the decrypted German cables. The "most intelligent" assessment of Jahnke is from Katz. The story of Captain Krohn and Admiral Hall's interest in the German biological sabotage campaign is told in *Room 40*. Most of the background information about Jahnke—including his Marine Corps service record—is from MCC files, along with Doerries' chapter "Deutsche Sabotage in den Vereinigten Staaten von Amerika im Ersten Weltkrieg." The Dilger-Jahnke dispute is described in intercepted cables and various MCC files. The exchange of letters between Peaslee and Hall in the 1920s about germ sabotage is from *Three Wars with Germany*.

Chapter Thirteen: Spanish Flu

The French intelligence surveillance report on the man identified as Delmar (AD) is in State Department archives (NARA Record Group 59), appended to a letter from the French ambassador to the U.S. secretary of state, dated November 16, 1918. For the purposes of the narrative, the author assumes that the French agents correctly identified Delmar/Dilger. The French reports say Delmar lived at times in "Sarria," which the author interprets as the Barcelona district of that name, rather than the Galician town of Sarria. *LL* mentions Dilger's copy of Gerard's book, as does a letter in the CKA. Copies of the decrypted cables and other documents on Heinrich Bode (a.k.a. Roberto Wilson) are in the MCC files. The report of Gehrmann's death from influenza is from *LL*. (Gehrmann's name is spelled with a single "n" in some references.) A debate continues to rage about whether Mata Hari (Margaretha Geertruida Zelle) was a German spy, a double agent, or simply an occasional informant. The circumstances of her arrest and trial (including Major Arnold Kalle's role) are discussed in numerous books and articles, including Schirmann's *Mata-Hari: Autopsie d'une machination*. The 1918 German offensive is documented in Middlebrook's *The Kaiser's Battle*. Statistics cited on U.S. military-transport losses are from the appendix of Vice Admiral Albert Gleaves's *A History of the Transport Services* and from lists of Allied ships sunk by U-boats. The messages of Edward Bell and State Department responses are in the MCC files. The account of the Mexican diplomat Manuel Barreiro y Vallejo's meetings with Delmar and bank officials is in Record Group 165, Records of the WFGS, Military Intelligence Division Correspondence, at NARA.

Two readable and informative accounts of the Spanish Flu epidemic are *The Great Influenza* (Barry) and *Flu: The Story of the Great Influenza of 1918 and the Search for the Virus that Caused It* (Kolata), both of which mention Lieutenant Colonel Philip Doane's unfounded suspicion that German agents had spread the flu. The incident of the traveling salesman who was accused of being a German agent who spread flu is cited by Barry. The U.S. surgeon general was also on the alert for possible German biological warfare; an August 22, 1918 memo from the surgeon general's office to the chief medical officer of the American Expeditionary Force in France noted "some anxiety" about reports by U.S. military intelligence that German troops were being vaccinated against cholera, typhoid, and smallpox. Expressing concern that "malicious attempts to spread [cholera] might at some time be made," the memo said that the Army Medical School was preparing cholera vaccine for possible use if the disease began to strike U.S. troops.

The question of whether war horses might have been a reservoir for the influenza virus is discussed in Oxford et al., "A Hypothesis: The Conjunction of Soldiers, Gas, Pigs, Ducks, Geese and Horses in Northern France . . ." which appeared in *Vaccine* in 2005. Also, in 2005 the author interviewed Jeffery Taubenberger, an expert on the molecular biology of the 1918–19 influenza virus, who did not rule out the possibility of an equine reservoir, even though it was clearly an avian flu virus.

Questions about the officially reported circumstances of AD's death are raised in various MCC, U.S. military intelligence, State Department, and CKA documents. The MCC files include copies of the Donde death certificate and the Madrid judge's order, as well as cables from the State Department and the U.S. Embassy in Madrid about the effort to confirm that Dilger died there. Landau's speculation that Dilger may have been poisoned appeared in *The Enemy Within* in 1937. Keyser, in *LL*, also mentioned the possibility of foul play in AD's death, but did not question whether he died in Madrid. Carl Dilger's suggestion to H. H. Martin that German agents may have killed AD by infecting him with the influenza virus is recorded in a note from Martin in the MCC files. Herrmann's suspicion that AD was poisoned "because he knew too much" is expressed in his MCC affidavit from October 11, 1933.

Chapter Fourteen: The Fourth Horseman

Dilger family quotations are from *LL* and from letters in the CKA. For an interesting but controversial analysis of how poison gas exposure and subsequent treatment affected Adolf Hitler, see *The Man Who Invented Hitler*, by David Lewis. A detailed discussion of French biological warfare research is in Lepick's "French Activities Related to Biological Warfare, 1919–45." Also see the early section of Guillemin's *Biological Weapons: From the Invention of State-Sponsored Programs to Contemporary Bioterrorism*.

Heinrich Kliewe's comments about the World War I–era biological sabotage are quoted in the ALSOS Mission archives in Record Group 165 at the National Archives and Records Administration. Kliewe's original article appeared in an internal German publication in July 1941. His assessment, based on sources he did not specify, represented one of the few official German acknowledgments of the World War I biological sabotage campaign. Significantly, he mentioned only glanders—and not anthrax—in the analysis. Military veterinary records cite thousands of cases of glanders—with most diagnosed horses being immediately destroyed—but only a handful of anthrax infections among war horses and mules. Even though aerosolized anthrax emerged as the germ weapon of choice later in the twentieth century, the methods that AD and other biosaboteurs used to deploy that pathogen apparently were ineffective. Anthrax did strike a few dozen U.S. soldiers during the Great War in cases that at first appeared to be highly suspicious. But medical experts discovered that the cutaneous anthrax infections on facial skin came from spores in Army-issue horse-hair shaving brushes. The problem was solved by replacing those with new shaving brushes made from the bristles of animals that do not carry the disease: badgers and boars. See "Anthrax in Man" in the 1917 annual report of the Surgeon General.

See *Sabotage at Black Tom* (Witcover) and *The Detonators* (Millman) for thorough discussions of the Mixed Claims Commission investigation, including details about how Herrmann was convinced to testify. Attorney Amos Peaslee's story is told in *Three Wars with Germany* (Peaslee and Hall). The final Mixed Claims Commission settlement awarded the United States $55 million (which included interest) in damages related to the Black Tom and Kingsland sabotage. For a description of the early history of German-Japanese cooperation, see Martin's lecture, "German-Japanese Collaboration in the Development of Bacteriological and Chemical Weapons and the War in China." For an overview of the Japanese biowarfare program, see Harris's *Factories of Death* and Barenblatt's *A Plague upon Humanity*. For a thoughtful evaluation of AD's role in the German biological sabotage campaign, see Wheelis. Geissler, citing the scanty German documentation on AD, questions his importance in the overall campaign. An American historian, Russ Van Wyk, was able to obtain transcripts of the SMERSH interrogation of Jahnke from Russian sources. In those transcripts, Jahnke took credit for numerous acts of sabotage in the United States during World War I, but Van Wyk told the author in 2005 that the notes on Jahnke's interrogation did not mention AD. After his years as a key figure in the Mixed Claims Commission case, Fred Herrmann relocated to Virginia after World

War II and died in Richmond in 1969, according to Virginia state records and newspaper obituaries.

Chapter Fifteen: "They Had No Choice"

About six hundred German and Italian POWs were housed at the Front Royal Remount Depot during the last years of World War II; many of them were given menial tasks there and at surrounding farms. A description of the POW camp can be found at http://nationalzoo.si.edu/ConservationAndScience/CRC/FrontRoyal.

Details about Pershing's horse Kidron, its transport to the United States after World War I, and its death at Front Royal are in the Library of Congress (*Papers of John J. Pershing, 1860–1948*). The letter from the Front Royal Remount Depot requesting permission to destroy Kidron was dated May 28, 1942; the horse died on October 12 of that year. Kidron's gravestone is no longer at the Front Royal site, but it was there during the last two years of World War II. Local historians say that the horse's remains (other than the skull and hide, which had been sent to the Smithsonian) are still there, but the gravestone was moved to the Army's Quartermaster Museum in the late 1950s or early 1960s.

In 1948, the remount depot at Front Royal became a U.S. Department of Agriculture cattle research center; in 1974 the property was bought by the Smithsonian's National Zoo to be developed as a Conservation and Research Center. The old "Dilger Field"—sold to the Army in 1911–12—is now part of the Center's Posey Hollow ecological monitoring station that is used for biodiversity studies.

Excerpts of the speech by General Holbrook can be found in Waller's "Horses and Mules and National Defense," published in 1958 by the Office of the Quartermaster General, which also lists the Holbrook speech on its website, http://www.qmfound.com/horse.htm. Books on the racehorse Man o' War range from the early biography *Man O' War* (Cooper and Treat) to the most recent treatment, Ours's *Man o' War: A Legend Like Lightning*. Those books and numerous articles tell the story of the horse's birth, career, and elaborate funeral.

Blenkinsop and Rainey's *History of the Great War Based on Official Documents: Veterinary Services* describes how the British Army disposed of many of its horses after the Great War. In chapter 31, "Disposal of Animals," the authors describe the horse carcass economizer. Sources on the animal welfare movement during the period include the historical section of the Royal Society for the Prevention of Cruelty to Animals website, http://www.rspca.org.uk; Moss' *Valiant Crusade: The History of the RSPCA*; and Clarke's "The Story of the British War-Horse." After the war, American Red Star Animal Relief became part of the American

Humane Association, which outlines the history of animal emergency services on its website, www.americanhumane.org.

Epilogue

Sources on the story of Herrmann mailing a book to Carl Dilger include *LL* and copies of pertinent FBI files on Carl Dilger. For a detailed description of the World War II sabotage raid, see Dobbs, *Saboteurs: The Nazi Raid on America*. The anecdote about the harassment of Emmy-Margaret Dilger is from one of her letters in the CKA. The Hadler post card and related documents are in the MCC files. The author flew to Mexico City in July 2005 to look into the possibility that AD might have staged his death in Madrid and lived incognito in Mexico after 1918, but found no direct evidence to confirm the theory.

BIBLIOGRAPHY

Alibek, Kenneth, and Stephen Handelman. *Biohazard: The Chilling True Story of the Largest Covert Biological Weapons Program in the World*. Delta, 2000.

Barenblatt, Daniel. *A Plague upon Humanity: The Secret Genocide of Axis Japan's Germ Warfare Operation*. HarperCollins, 2004.

Barry, John M. *The Great Influenza: The Epic Story of the Deadliest Plague in History*. Viking, 2004.

Beesly, Patrick. *Room 40: British Naval Intelligence 1914–1918*. Harcourt, Brace, Jovanovich, 1982.

Bisher, Jamie. "During World War I, Terrorists Schemed to Use Anthrax in the Cause of Finnish Independence." *Military History* 77 (August 2003).

Black, Robert W. *Cavalry Raids of the Civil War*. Stackpole Books, 2004.

Blenkinsop, L. J., and J. W. Rainey. *History of the Great War Based on Official Documents: Veterinary Services*. His Majesty's Stationery Office, 1925.

Brock, Thomas D. *Robert Koch: A Life in Medicine and Bacteriology*. American Society of Microbiology Press, 2000.

Bryden, John. *Deadly Allies: Canada's Secret War, 1937–1947*. McClelland and Stewart, 1990.

Case, F. L. "Remounts in Southern Department." *Journal of the U.S. Cavalry Association* 28 (October 1916): 235ff.

Catton, Bruce. *Glory Road*. Peter Smith, 1995.

Chapman-Huston, Desmond, and Owen Rutter. *General Sir John Cowans GCB GCMG: The Quartermaster General of the Great War*. Hutchinson, 1924.

Charles, Daniel. *Master Mind: The Rise and Fall of Fritz Haber, the Nobel Laureate Who Launched the Age of Chemical Warfare*. Ecco, 2005.

Clark, Christopher M. *Kaiser Wilhelm II*. Longman, 2000.

Clarke, Basil. "The Story of the British War-Horse from Prairie to Battlefield." In *The Great War—The Standard History of the All Europe Conflict*. Vol. 9. Ed. H. W. Wilson and J. A. Hammerton. Amalgamated Press, 1917.

Collard, Patrick. *The Development of Microbiology*. Cambridge University Press, 1976.

Commanger, Henry Steele. *The Blue and the Gray*. Gramercy, 2006.

Cooper, Jilly. *Animals in War*. Lyons Press, 2002.

Cooper, Page, and Roger L. Treat. *Man o' War*. Westholme, 2004.

Crane, Stephen. *The Red Badge of Courage and "The Veteran."* Modern Library, 2000.

Davis, Arthur Kyle, ed. "Newport News in War Time." In *Virginia Communities in War Time: Publications of the Virginia War History Commission*. Vol. 7. State of Virginia, 1927.

DeBarneville, Maurice F. "The Remount Service in the A.E.F." *The Cavalry Journal* 33 (April 1921).

Deichmann, Ute. *Biologen Unter Hitler: Porträt einer Wissenschaft im NS-Staat*. Fischer, 1995.

Dilger, Anton. *Über Gewebskulturen in Vitro: Unter Besonderer Berücksichtigung Der Gewebe Erwachsener Tiere* [Concerning Tissue Cultures in Vitro: With Special Consideration of the Tissues of Adult Animals]. Vogel, 1913.

Dilger, Anton, and Arthur W. Meyer. "Kriegschirurgische Erfahrungen aus den beiden Balkankriegen 1912/13 (bulgarisch-türkischem und bulgarisch-serbisch-griechischem Krieg)" [Battlefield Surgical Experiences from the Two Balkan Wars, 1912/13 (the Bulgarian-Turkish and the Bulgarian-Serbian-Greek War)]. *Deutsche Zeitschrift für Chirurgie* (German Journal of Surgery) 127 (1914): 225–378.

Dilger, Elise. "Man Has a Spiritual and Terrestrial Body," handwritten document in the Carl Keyser Archives.

Dilger and Tiedeman family letters and documents, collected by Carl Anton Keyser, used with permission.

Dobbs, Michael. *Saboteurs: The Nazi Raid on America*. Knopf, 2004.

Doerries, Reinhard R. "Deutsche Sabotage in den Vereinigten Staaten von Amerika im Ersten Weltkrieg: Die Jahre den amerikanischen Neutralität, 1914–1916." In *Macht und Moral: Beiträge zur Ideologie und Praxis amerikanischer Außenpolitik im 20 Jahrhundert*. Ed. Manfred Berg, Michaela Hönicke, Raimund Lammersdorf, and Anneke de Rudder. Münster, 1999.

———. *Prelude to the Easter Rising: Sir Roger Casement in Imperial Germany*. Cass, 2000.

Dossenbach, Monique, and Hans Dossenbach. *The Noble Horse*. Portland House, 1985.

Ellis, John. *Cavalry: The History of Mounted Warfare*. Pen and Sword, 2004.

Feuchtwanger, Edgar. *Bismarck*. Routledge, 2002.

Fish, Pierre A. "Morbidity and Mortality in Army Animals." In *Report of the Surgeon General*. U.S. Army, 1919.

Ford, Clyde S. *The Balkan Wars*. Press of the Army Service Schools, 1915.

———. "Some Medicomilitary Observations in the Late Balkan Wars." *The New York Journal of Medicine* 102 (1915): 52–58.

Fordney, Ben F. *Stoneman at Chancellorsville: The Coming of Age of the Union Cavalry*. White Mane Books, 1998.

Geison, Gerald L. *The Private Science of Louis Pasteur.* Princeton University Press, 1996.

Geissler, Erhard. "Anwendung von Seuchenmitteln gegen Menschen nicht erwünscht: Dokumente zum Einsatz biologischer Kampfmittel im Ersten Weltkrieg." *Militaergeschichtliche Mitteilungen* 56(2) (1997).

———. *Biologische Waffen—Nicht in Hitler's Arsenalen: Biologische und Toxin-Kampfmittel in Deutschland von 1915 bis 1945.* Horst Fischer, Ruhr-Universitaet Bochum, 1999.

———. *Anthrax und das Versagen der Geheimdienste.* Kai Homilius, 2003.

Geissler, Erhard, and John Ellis van Courtland Moon, eds. *Biological and Toxin Weapons: Research, Development and Use from the Middle Ages to 1945*, Stockholm International Peace Research Institute (SIPRI) / Oxford University Press, 1999.

Gerard, James W. *Face to Face with Kaiserism.* Doran, 1918.

———. *My Four Years in Germany.* Doran, 1917.

Gibson, Hugh. *A Journal from Our Legation in Belgium.* Doubleday, Page, 1917.

Gleaves, Albert. *A History of the Transport Services.* Doran, 1921.

Gould, Stephen Jay. "The Great Physiologist of Heidelberg." *Natural History* (July 1999).

Grams, Grant W. "Karl Respa and German Espionage in Canada During World War One." Journal of Military and Strategic Studies, Vol, 8, Issue 1, Fall 2005.

Gray, Edwyn. *Submarine Warriors.* Presidio Press, 1988.

Guillemin, Jeanne. *Biological Weapons: From the Invention of State-Sponsored Programs to Contemporary Bioterrorism.* Columbia University Press, 2005.

Hamlin, August Choate. *The Battle of Chancellorsville.* U.S. Medical Corps, 1896.

Harris, Sheldon H. *Factories of Death: Japanese Biological Warfare, 1932–1945, and the American Cover-up.* Rev. ed. Routledge, 2002.

Hempel, Frieda. *My Golden Age of Singing.* Amadeus Press, 1998.

Hugh-Jones, Martin. "M. Wickham Steed and German Biological Warfare Research." *Intelligence and National Security* 7 (1992): 379–402.

Jünger, Ernst. *Storm of Steel.* Penguin, 2004.

Katz, Friedrich. *The Life and Times of Pancho Villa.* Stanford University Press, 1998.

———. *The Secret War in Mexico: Europe, the United States, and the Mexican Revolution.* University of Chicago Press, 1981.

Keegan, John. *The First World War.* Vintage, 1998.

Keyser, Carl Anton. *Leatherbreeches: Hero of Chancellorsville.* Amherst Press, 1989.

———. *Leatherbreeches' Legacy.* Amherst Press, 1990.

Kirschbaum, Erik. *The Eradication of German Culture in the United States: 1917–1918.* Academic, 1986.

Kolata, Gina. *Flu: The Story of the Great Influenza of 1918 and the Search for the Virus that Caused It.* Simon and Schuster, 1999.

König, Paul. *Voyage of the Deutschland, the First Merchant Submarine.* Hearst's International Library, 1916.

Landau, Martin. *The Enemy Within: The Inside Story of German Sabotage in America.* Putnam's Sons, 1937.

Lee, John. *The Warlords: Hindenburg and Ludendorff.* Weidenfeld and Nicholson, 2003.

Lepick, Olivier. "French Activities Related to Biological Warfare, 1919–45." In Erhard Geissler and John Ellis van Courtland Moon, eds. *Biological and Toxin Weapons: Research, Development, and Use from the Middle Ages to 1945.* Stockholm International Peace Research Institute (SIPRI) / Oxford University Press, 1999.

Le Queux, William. *Spies of the Kaiser: Plotting the Downfall of England.* Cass, 1996.

Lewis, David. *The Man Who Invented Hitler: The Making of the Fuehrer.* Headline, 2003.

Lewis, Jon E., ed. *The Mammoth Book of Eyewitness World War I.* Carroll and Graff, 2003.

Lewis, Lloyd. *Sherman: Fighting Prophet.* University of Nebraska Press, 1993.

Livingston, Phil, and Ed Roberts. *War Horse: Mounting the Cavalry with America's Finest Horses.* Bright Sky Press, 2003.

Manchester, Harland. "The Black Tom Case." *Harper's Magazine* 180 (December 1939).

Mangold, Tom, and Jeff Goldberg. *Plague Wars: The Terrifying Reality of Biological Warfare.* St. Martin's Griffin, 1999.

Martin, Bernd. "German-Japanese Collaboration in the Development of Bacteriological and Chemical Weapons and the War in China." In Christian Spang and Rolf-Harald Wippich, eds. *German-Japanese Relations, 1895–1945: War and Diplomacy.* Routledge, 2006.

Marchisio, M., and W. Noreisch. "Chemical Warfare During World War One (1914–1918); Remarks Related to Horses Employed in the Main Armies." Conference presentation, 35th International Conference on the History of Veterinary Medicine, World Association for the History of Veterinary Medicine, Turin, Italy, September 2004.

Mencken, H. L. *Newspaper Days: 1899–1906.* Knopf, 1975.

———. *Thirty-five Years of Newspaper Work: A Memoir by H. L. Mencken.* Ed. Fred Hobson, Vincent Fitzpatrick, and Bradford Jacobs. Johns Hopkins University Press, 1994.

Middlebrook, Martin. *The Kaiser's Battle.* Penguin, 2000.

Miller, Judith, Stephen Engelberg, and William Broad. *Germs: Biological Weapons and America's Secret War.* Simon and Schuster, 2001.

Millman, Chad. *The Detonators: The Secret Plot to Destroy America and an Epic Hunt for Justice.* Little, Brown, 2006.

Missouri Mule History Project. *Records, 1980–1993* (C3954), in the Western Historical Manuscript Collection, Columbia, Missouri.

Missouri State Board of Agriculture. *Jack Stock and Mules in Missouri.* Extension Division, University of Missouri-Columbia, 1987 [1924].

Morgan, J. H. *The War Book of the German General Staff: Being "The Usages of War on Land" Issued by the Great General Staff of the German Army.* McBride, Nast, 1915.

Morgan, Jimmie (music) and Thomas Hoier (lyrics). "Don't Bite the Hand That's Feeding You" (popular song). Feist, 1915.

Morganthau, Henry. *Ambassador Morgenthau's Story.* Doubleday, 1918.

Mosier, John. *The Myth of the Great War: A New Military History of World War I.* HarperCollins, 2001.

Moss, Arthur W. *Valiant Crusade: The History of the RSPCA.* Cassell, 1961.

Nadolny, Rudolf. *Mein Beitrag: Erinnerungen eines Botschafters des Deutschen Reiches.* Limes, 1955.

Ours, Dorothy. *Man o' War: A Legend Like Lightning.* St. Martin's Press, 2006.

Oxford, J. S., et al. "A Hypothesis: The Conjunction of Soldiers, Gas, Pigs, Ducks, Geese and Horses in Northern France during the Great War Provided the Conditions for the Emergence of the 'Spanish' Influenza Pandemic of 1918–1919." *Vaccine* 23 (2005): 940–45.

Pakenham, Thomas. *The Boer War.* Abacus, 1979.

Peaslee, Amos, and W. Reginald Hall. *Three Wars with Germany.* Putnam's Sons, 1944.

Peat, Frank E., and Lee Orean Smith, eds. *Legion Airs: Songs of "Over There" and "Over Here."* Feist, 1932.

Pershing, John J. *My Experiences in the World War.* Military Classics Series, 1931.

———. *Papers of John J. Pershing, 1860–1948.* Archival Manuscript Material, Library of Congress, LC Control Number: mm 79035949.

Porter, Katherine Anne. *Pale Horse, Pale Rider: Three Short Novels.* Harcourt Brace Jovanovich, 1990.

Potter, Nathaniel B. "Human Glanders: A Report of Three Cases, One of Which was Unsuccessfully Treated with Large Doses of Autogenous Vaccines." Department of Public Charities, *The Bulletin* 1 (October 1916).

Quarstein, John V. *World War I on the Virginia Peninsula.* Arcadia, 1999.

Radziwill, Catherine. *The Firebrand of Bolshevism: True Story of the Bolsheviki and the Forces that Directed Them.* Small, Maynard and Co., 1919.

Rees, Simon. "The Forgotten Army," article on FirstWorldWar.com, 2004.

Regis, Ed. *The Biology of Doom: The History of America's Secret Germ Warfare Project.* Henry Holt and Co., 1999.

Riesenberger, Dieter. *Das Deutsche Rote Kreuz: Eine Geschichte 1864–1990.* Schoeningh, 2002.

Riggio, Thomas P., ed. *Dreiser-Mencken Letters: The Correspondence of Theodore Dreiser and H. L. Mencken, 1907–1945.* University of Pennsylvania Press, 1987.

Robins, George Dougall. "A Study of Chronic Glanders in Man with Report of a Case." *Studies from the Royal Victoria Hospital* 2 (May 1906).

Rouse, Parke. *Endless Harbor: The Story of Newport News.* Newport News Historical Committee, 1969.

St. Leger, Stratford. *Mounted Infantry at War.* Galago, 1986. (A facsimile of the 1903 edition.)

Sayers, Michael and Albert E. Kahn. *Sabotage! The Secret War Against America.* Harper and Brothers, 1942.

Scanlan, Lawrence. *Wild about Horses: Our Timeless Passion for the Horse.* Harper-Collins, 1998.

Schirmann, Lèon. *Mata-Hari. Autopsie d'une machination.* Italiques, 2001.

Schurz, Carl. *The Reminiscences of Carl Schurz,* McClure, 1907–1908.

Sharrer, G. Terry. "The Great Glanders Epizootic, 1861–1866: A Civil War Legacy." *Agricultural History* 69 (1), (Winter 1995).

Singleton, John. "Britain's Military Use of Horses 1914–1918." *Past and Present* 139 (May 1993).

Smart, Jeffrey K. "History of Chemical and Biological Warfare: An American Perspective." In *Textbook of Military Medicine: Medical Aspects of Chemical and Biological Warfare.* Office of the Surgeon General, U.S. Department of the Army, 1997.

Smith, Gene. *Until the Last Trumpet Sounds: The Life of General of the Armies John J. Pershing.* Wiley and Sons, 1998.

Spence, Richard. "Englishmen in New York: The SIS American Station, 1915–21." *Intelligence and National Security* 19 (Autumn 2004).

Spiegel, F. von. *U-Boat 202: The Personal Story of the Sea Wolf of the Atlantic.* Mews Books, 1976.

Steiner, Paul E. *Disease in the Civil War: Natural Biological Warfare in 1861–1865.* Charles C. Thomas Publisher, 1968.

Teachout, Terry. *The Skeptic: A Life of H. L. Mencken.* HarperCollins, 2002.

Totten, Christine M. *Roots in the Rhineland: America's German Heritage in Three Hundred Years of Immigration.* German Information Center, 1983.

Trefousse, Hans L. *Carl Schurz: A Biography.* Fordham University Press, 1998.

Trommler, Frank, and Joseph McVeigh, eds. *America and the Germans: An Assessment of a Three-Hundred-Year History.* University of Pennsylvania Press, 1985.

Tuchman, Barbara W. *The Proud Tower: A Portrait of the World Before the War, 1890–1914.* Bantam Books, 1980.

———. *The Zimmerman Telegram.* Ballantine Books, 1994.

UK War Office. *Statistics of the Military Effort of the British Empire During the Great War, 1914–1920.* War Office.

Unger, Hellmuth. *Robert Koch: Roman eines grossen Lebens.* Deutschen Arzteschaft, 1936.

Universitätsarchiv, Ruprecht-Karls-Universitaet Heidelberg, Studentenaktien und Promotionsaktien H-III 862/14, folio 98–102; and H-III 162/18, folio 30–32. This archive confirms Anton Dilger's medical degree at the University of Heidelberg.

Urwin, Gregory. *The United States Cavalry: An Illustrated History, 1776–1944.* Red River Books, 2003.

U.S. Army Veterinary Corps Archive, OHA 344, Box 1 ("Veterinary Corps History, 1916–1940) and Box 45 ("Remount Service"). Otis National Archives, National Museum of Health and Medicine, Armed Forces Institute of Pathology.

U.S. Department of Agriculture, Statistical Bulletin No. 5, "Horses, Mules and Motor Vehicles." Government Printing Office, 1925.

U.S. Government. *Army Veterinary Service,* Hearing of the Subcommittee of the Committee on Military Affairs, U.S. Senate. U.S. Government Printing Office, 1914.

U.S. Government. *Brewing and Liquor Interests and German and Bolshevik Propaganda: Report and Hearings of the Subcommittee of the Judiciary,* U.S. Senate, vol. 2. U.S. Government Printing Office, 1919, pp. 2676ff.

U.S. Government. "Anthrax in Man." In *Annual Report.* Surgeon General's Office, 1917.

U.S. National Archives and Records Administration (NARA). Record Group 76, Records of the Mixed Claims Commission; Record Group 165, Records of the WFGS, Military Intelligence Division Correspondence; Record Group 59, General Records of the Department of State.

Von Rintelen (von Kleist), Franz. *The Dark Invader: Wartime Reminiscences of a German Naval Intelligence Officer.* Frank Cass, 1997.

Vuksic, V., and Z. Grbasic. *Cavalry: The History of a Fighting Elite, 650 BC–AD 1914.* Trans. Srdjan Vujica. Cassell, 1993.

Waag, D. M., and D. DeShazer. "Glanders: New Insights into an Old Disease." In *Biological Weapons Defense: Infectious Diseases and Counterbioterrorism,* ed. L. E. Lindler, F. J. Lebeda, and G. W. Korch. Humana Press, 2004.

Waller, Anna L. *Horses and Mules and National Defense.* Office of the Quartermaster General, 1958.

Wells, H. G. "The Stolen Bacillus." In *The Stolen Bacillus and Other Incidents.* IndyPublish, 2001 [1895].

———. *The War of the Worlds.* Penguin Books, 2005 [1898].

Westwall, Ian. *World War I Day by Day.* MBI, 2000.

Wheelis, Mark. "Biological Sabotage in World War." In Erhard Geissler and John Ellis van Courtland Moon, eds. *Biological and Toxin Weapons: Research, Development, and Use from the Middle Ages to 1945.* Stockholm International Peace Research Institute (SIPRI) / Oxford University Press, 1999.

Williams, P. and D. Wallace. *Unit 731: Japan's Secret Biological Warfare in World War II.* Free Press, 1989.

Williamson, Gordon. *U-boats of the Kaiser's Navy.* Osprey, 2002.

Wilson, Herbert Wrigley, and J. A. Hammerton, eds. *The Great War*, vol. 1, *Opening Moves.* Trident Press, 1999.

Witcover, Jules. *Sabotage at Black Tom: Imperial Germany's Secret War in America, 1914–1917.* Algonquin Books, 1989.

Wukovits, John F. "John Mosby and George Custer Clash in the Shenandoah Valley." *America's Civil War* (March 2001).

Zieger, Robert H. *America's Great War: World War I and the American Experience.* Rowman and Littlefield, 2000.

Zwerdling, Michael. *Postcards of Nursing: A Worldwide Tribute.* Lippincott Williams and Wilkins, 2003.

ACKNOWLEDGMENTS

I am grateful for the cooperation, support and guidance from dozens of people who have helped in my research. I thank Mark Keyser for graciously allowing me access to, and granting permission for me to quote from, various Dilger family documents and files collected by his late father, Carl Anton Keyser, as well as allowing me to reproduce several photographs and to quote from portions of his father's two valuable books about the family's history: *Leatherbreeches: Hero of Chancellorsville* and *Leatherbreeches' Legacy*. I am also grateful to the owners of the German saboteurs' former rented home in Chevy Chase for their willingness to show me the house and to describe its layout when Anton Dilger lived and worked there in 1915–16. I also thank the current occupants of Greenfield Farm near Front Royal, Virginia, for allowing me to tour the farm, which includes several original buildings.

My PublicAffairs editor, Clive Priddle, provided invaluable advice on how to shape the book and to write a narrative. I also owe a debt of gratitude to my agent, Jeff Kellogg, who helped me conceptualize the book. On scientific questions, I thank Tim Read—an expert on the anthrax bacterium, *Bacillus anthracis*, at the Naval Medical Research Center's biological defense research directorate—for his early insights. Also, I thank William Nierman of The Institute for Genomic Research, who led the team that deciphered the genome sequence of the glanders microbe, *Burkholderia mallei*, for his help in understanding the pathogen. One of the few scientists who have contracted glanders, David DeShazer of the U.S. Army Research Institute of Infectious Diseases, also provided insights about the pathogen and the disease. I also thank Jeff Taubenberger, the scientist who led the molecular analysis of the

1918–19 influenza virus, for taking time to talk with me about the possibility that horses may have been a reservoir for the virus. And I am
indebted to Mario Marchisio of the Italian Army's veterinary corps for
sharing his conclusions on the impact of poison gas on horses and also to
Martin Furmanski for his early guidance about archival sources concerning the prevalence of horse diseases during the Great War.

On matters relating to the history of biological sabotage during
World War I, I am grateful to microbiology professor Mark Wheelis of
the University of California-Davis for his valuable comments and his
willingness to share certain historical documents with me. I also thank
German microbiologist and historian Erhard Geissler for providing
early guidance and advice. On issues related to German espionage and
sabotage in North America, I thank Reinhard Doerries for his e-mail
comments related to the relationship between Kurt Jahnke and Anton
Dilger. On the question of early Japanese and German BW research, I
am grateful to historian Bernd Martin of the University of Freiburg for
sharing information from his lecture on the topic. For their help in confirming details about the bombing of Karlsruhe in June 1916, I owe a
debt of gratitude to the city of Karlsruhe's municipal archivists.

I also thank helpful researchers and other staff members of numer-
ous libraries, archives, universities, and historical institutions, including:
the National Archives and Records Administration in College Park,
Maryland; the Library of Congress, the Otis Archives at the National
Museum of Health and Medicine in Washington, D.C., the Smithsonian
Institution (the current owner of the property that used to be the Front
Royal Remount Depot), the National Library of Medicine in Bethesda,
Maryland, the National Agricultural Library in Beltsville, Maryland, the
Enoch Pratt Free Library in Baltimore, the Alan Mason Chesney Med-
ical Archives of the Johns Hopkins Medical Institutions, Harvard Uni-
versity Medical School, the Missouri Historical Society in St. Louis, the
Kansas City Library, the Washington, D.C., Public Library and its
Chevy Chase branch, the Northern Kentucky Historical Society in Ft.
Thomas, Kentucky, the Missouri Mule History Project Records of the
Western Historical Manuscript Collection in Columbia, Missouri; the
Virginia War Museum in Newport News; and the Samuels Public
Library in Front Royal, Virginia.

Special thanks to Vincent Fitzpatrick, curator of the H. L. Mencken Collection at the Pratt Library, for his guidance on Mencken's work. Quotations from the writings of H. L. Mencken are used by permission of the Enoch Pratt Free Library, Baltimore, in accordance with the terms of Mencken's bequest to that institution. I also thank Tim O'Neil of the *St. Louis Post-Dispatch* for helping track down information on the Kansas City stockyards fire and on Fred Herrmann's itinerary in St. Louis and in the Southwest; Jeff Noonan for helping me find the lyrics to World War I–era songs about German Americans; Josie Shumake for conducting research for me in Madrid; and my daughter Laura, a library scientist who conducted research at the Boston Public Library. Genealogist Stephen Yautz also deserves thanks for helping me track down the fate of Fred Herrmann. Finally, I thank my wife, Mary Ellen, for her valuable critiques of the manuscript, and for her patience and forbearance during my three years of work on this project.

—R.K.

INDEX

PublicAffairs is a publishing house founded in 1997. It is a tribute to the standards, values, and flair of three persons who have served as mentors to countless reporters, writers, editors, and book people of all kinds, including me.

I.F. STONE, proprietor of *I. F. Stone's Weekly*, combined a commitment to the First Amendment with entrepreneurial zeal and reporting skill and became one of the great independent journalists in American history. At the age of eighty, Izzy published *The Trial of Socrates*, which was a national bestseller. He wrote the book after he taught himself ancient Greek.

BENJAMIN C. BRADLEE was for nearly thirty years the charismatic editorial leader of *The Washington Post*. It was Ben who gave the *Post* the range and courage to pursue such historic issues as Watergate. He supported his reporters with a tenacity that made them fearless and it is no accident that so many became authors of influential, best-selling books.

ROBERT L. BERNSTEIN, the chief executive of Random House for more than a quarter century, guided one of the nation's premier publishing houses. Bob was personally responsible for many books of political dissent and argument that challenged tyranny around the globe. He is also the founder and longtime chair of Human Rights Watch, one of the most respected human rights organizations in the world.

For fifty years, the banner of Public Affairs Press was carried by its owner Morris B. Schnapper, who published Gandhi, Nasser, Toynbee, Truman, and about 1,500 other authors. In 1983, Schnapper was described by *The Washington Post* as "a redoubtable gadfly." His legacy will endure in the books to come.

Peter Osnos, *Founder and Editor-at-Large*